When Tenants
Claimed the City

When Tenants Claimed the City

The Struggle for Citizenship in New York City Housing

ROBERTA GOLD

UNIVERSITY OF ILLINOIS PRESS

Urbana, Chicago, and Springfield

Library of Congress Cataloging-in-Publication Data
Gold, Roberta.
When tenants claimed the city : the struggle for
citizenship in New York city housing / Roberta Gold.
pages   cm
Includes bibliographical references and index.
ISBN 978-0-252-03818-1 (cloth : alk. paper)
ISBN (invalid) 978-0-252-09598-6 (ebook)
1. Minorities—Housing—New York (State)—
New York—History—20th century. 2. Housing—
New York (State)—New York—History—20th century.
3. Minorities—New York (State)—New York—
Social conditions. 4. Landlord and tenant—New York
(State)—New York—History—20th century.
I. Title.
HD7288.72.U52N473   2014
333.33'8—dc23   2013036280

In memory of my parents
Jack and Rhoda Gold

Contents

Acknowledgments

Marx's observation that we make history under circumstances we do not choose applies verily to junior scholars struggling with slim budgets and fat teaching loads. But in my case those pressures were eased by generous institutional support. I am grateful to the American Association of University Women, the History Department and the Harry Bridges Center for Labor Studies at the University of Washington, the Institute for Research on Women at Rutgers University, and the Tamiment Library at New York University for grants and fellowships that enabled me to complete this bit of history.

Engels' views are less illuminating here, as my family's organizing principle has not been the furtherance of economic interests. My parents always supported my academic pursuits, no matter how unremunerative (even if they were a bit slow to understand that "So, how's your dissertation going?" is not a great conversational gambit). Their encouragement for this project figured in the last talks I had with them.

My brother Matt and sister Stephanie score lower on the nudge-o-meter but just as high on the support scale. Their warmth and wit have kept me anchored on the uncertain seas of school and career. So have the abiding affection and holiday cooking of the Gerstmann, Chuman, Ogrin, Karp, and extended Gold branches of our family.

My family is further constituted by extraordinarily loyal and generous friends. Christina Nicolaidis, Monica Bubay, Laura Gottesman, Carl Hum, Ron Gutiérrez, Tad Toulis, Rob Hallock, Eric Schreiber, Leah Osman, Algernon Austin, Mike Mahon, and the Cracas family have stuck with me through thick and thin since our grade-school and college days, encouraging me to keep striving while preventing me from disappearing completely into the quicksand of solitary research and writing.

After college I landed in other communities that have sustained me day in and out. The brothers and sisters of Harlem EMS, especially my partner, Sam Benson, taught me more about solidarity than could many a labor-history book. Co-workers and friends at Riverbank State Park and New York Downtown Hospital have buoyed my spirits many times. Neighbors Sal Orochena, Alice Church Cheseborough, Deb Proos, Judy Thames, the Wilder family, Miriam Rivera, and others too numerous to name have provided much-needed doses of sanity at my doorstep. Indeed, my interest in work- and place-based fellowship, a theme of this study, owes in no small measure to these New York friends.

That interest would never have produced a book, however, without the guidance of wonderful teachers. At Wesleyan I was fortunate to study with Ann Wightman, who introduced me to the vocation of social history; John Finn, who provided a model of analytic rigor enlivened by mordant wit; Anne Greene, an incisive critic and extraordinary teacher of writing; and Jerry Watts, whose encouragement, wide-ranging intellect, and disdain for conventional wisdom sustained and challenged me over many years.

My time in Seattle was made worthwhile—which is saying a lot—by members of the UW History Department. Coll Thrush, Vera Sokolova, Ali Igmen, Kate Brown, Michael Reese, Robert Self, Ken Lang, Steve Marquardt, Nellie Blacker-Hanson, Susan Bragg, and Trevor Griffey taught me a great deal and did much to relieve the isolation that threatens to overtake doctoral students. Jen Seltz's relentless cynicism and caustic wit have remained tonics for the intellect and general outlook.

My UW professors are widely known as sterling scholars; it was a joy to find that they were also fine teachers who became good friends. To Susan Glenn I am grateful especially for pushing me to confront the complexities in social history rather than take the easy way out. Her warm encouragement made this less daunting than it might have been.

Jim Gregory believed in this project from the beginning, when I was an agnostic at best. His keen engagement with labor and political history informed my interpretations; his questions challenged me to rethink and sharpen arguments. And his generosity with time, counsel, support, and premium microbrew eased my way considerably. Finally, Jim's commitment to principled scholar-activism will remain a model for me long after this book is completed.

Suzanne Lebsock's presence in these pages is equally manifold. From astute suggestions on wording to probing questions on analysis to some well-deserved "duh-uh"s on forgettable passages, her editorial advice has been unerring. Her own work sets a benchmark for historical craftsmanship and reflective engagement with women's past. I am also grateful to Suzanne for serving as an offbeat Virgil, guiding me through various professional and personal infernos with an eye for the comedic dimensions of less-than-divine situations.

Research for this project would have been impossible without the expertise and dedication of a corps of archivists. I am obliged above all to Peter Filardo, Chela Scott-Weber, and the rest of the terrific staff at the Tamiment Library, and to program directors Marilyn Young, Zuzanna Kobrzynski, and the late Mike Nash. I am also thankful to Steven Fullwood, the late André Elizée, and their co-workers at the Schomburg Center for Research in Black Culture; Julio Hernández-Delgado and Manuel Rimarachin at El Centro de Estudios Puerto-riqueños; and Jenny Laurie and David Powell at Met Council. Charlotte Labbe and Christine Campbell at Fordham's Interlibrary Loan office deserve credit and thanks for processing endless requests for arcane materials. Many of the photographs were obtained through the generous help of Maggie Schreiner, Mario Mazzoni, Jim Torain, and Win Armstrong.

I owe an immense debt to the colleagues who took time from their own work to read and criticize the manuscript: Daniel Soyer, Jen Seltz, Emilye Crosby, Trevor Griffey, Steve Leberstein, Nancy Hewitt, Ellen Schrecker, and Danny Walkowitz. They steered me away from many errors—about which the less said, the better—and toward important insights. I am also grateful for the light managerial hand of Glenn Hendler, who allowed me to teach whatever I pleased as "American Studies" and thereby explore with students several themes of this book.

Laurie Matheson at the University of Illinois Press has been a model of patience and a source of reassurance and sound advice from our preliminary discussions through the final revisions. Illinois's reviewers and production staff contributed expert advice and support.

Finally, I owe a unique debt and responsibility to the people at the heart of this story: the veteran activists who spoke with me about their experiences in the tenant movement. They gave extensively of their time, reflection, critical analysis, and humor. Most generously of all, they trusted me with their stories. For all that, I sincerely thank Susan Brownmiller, Edwin "Tito" Delgado, Marge DuMond, Frances Goldin, Joe Hyler, Shirley Jenkins, Ruby Kitchen, Barbara Learnard, Kwame Leo Lillard, Lee Lorch, Claudia Mansbach, Thea Martínez, Michael McKee, Jack O'Dell, Frances Fox Piven, Florence Rice, Marie Runyon, Danny Schechter, Cleo Silvers, Jim Torain, and Jane Vélez; and the late Jane Benedict, Susan Cohen, Frieda Milgram, Yolanda Sánchez, Bess Stevenson, Walter Thabit, and Jane Wood. I hope I have done some justice to the history they made.

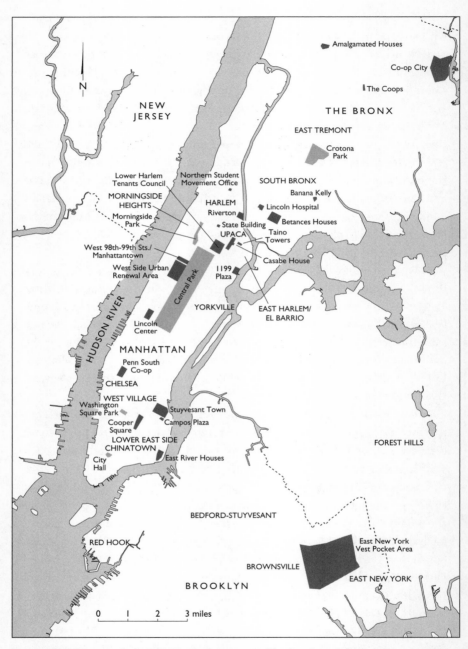

Tenant battlegrounds in New York. Activist neighborhoods and disputed development sites in the city's four most populous boroughs.

Introduction

One of the most-traveled roads in post–World War II America was the highway leading out of the city. Courted by realtors and dowered by Uncle Sam, millions of white- and blue-collar families moved out of their city apartments and bought single-family houses in the suburbs. Individually, they hauled furnishings and keepsakes; collectively, they shifted money and political power.

The transfer of those collective resources exacerbated long-standing disparities within American society. It created a prosperous, racially segregated suburban world that left the fiscally burdened cities and their growing populations of color to fend for themselves. It produced zoning patterns that separated residential from public space, reinforcing the notion of "separate spheres" for women and men. And it made the American dream of homeownership a reality for so many that it became the norm, the putative foundation of good citizenship. By thus widening the divides of class, race, and gender, the postwar suburban exodus redrew America's social map.

But not everyone took the road out. Against the backdrop of suburban expansion, New York City's tenant movement emerged as the leading voice for an alternative vision of residence and citizenship. For decades the city's tenants had rallied against evictions and rent hikes. Now they raised the stakes by challenging the postwar nation's newly dominant ideals of ownership, segregation, and domesticity. They insisted that renters as well as owners had rights to a stable home. They proposed that racially diverse urban communities had a right to remain in place—a right that outweighed owners' prerogative to hike rent, redevelop property, or exclude tenants of color. And they showed that women could participate fully in the political arenas where these issues were fought out. In all these ways New York tenants laid claim to what Marxists have called "the right to the city," a kind of democratic say over the uses of capital to shape the urban environment and the lives of its inhabitants.[1]

New York's leadership in this struggle owed not just to its size but to its remarkable rate of tenancy. Renters outnumbered owners in every borough in 1940; citywide, the rental rate surpassed 84 percent.[2] New York City, in fact, comprised more rental households than most states did households of any type.[3] Even compared to Chicago, San Francisco, and Los Angeles, New York was distinguished by a preponderance of tenancy.[4] Thus the city became the national capital of tenants' rights and a kind of laboratory for considering what American society might be like if homeownership did not prevail.

The tenant story brings out several understudied strands of postwar American history. One entails women's roles in the Old and New Lefts. Historians have now punctured the popular misconception that civil rights and other upheavals of the sixties and seventies "materialize[d] out of thin air" after two quietist decades.[5] In fact, recent scholarship shows, those movements were nourished by quite a few activists of Popular Front vintage who had courageously kept organizing through the early Cold War. Veteran socialists, Communists, peace advocates, and civil-rights organizers have begun to receive recognition for their steadfast labor behind the scenes.[6] Much of the early scholarship in this field, however, focused on men. That is changing, as new studies have brought to light networks of women who played vital roles within midcentury labor and black left movements.[7] This book adds to those studies. It reveals a cohort of leftist women who came of age during World War II and carried on for decades in defense of ordinary people's right to decent housing. These women, in turn, served as exemplars for younger activists who developed a feminist consciousness in the 1960s and after.

A second thread running through postwar tenant history is an ideological one concerning communities and rights. In popular memory the demand for "community control" in the urban setting is associated with racial polarization, most memorably during the Ocean Hill–Brownsville school crisis of 1968.[8] Certainly many black and white New Yorkers who demanded community control of schools, housing, and other resources during the 1960s did define community along racial lines. But a substantial number of New York tenants who fought to preserve their homes in heterogeneous neighborhoods developed a distinctive concept of "community rights" that was not racially drawn. Like the "beloved community" heralded by Martin Luther King Jr., the community of urban neighbors offered hope that traditional social fault lines could be bridged.[9]

Contrarian New Yorkers defended this notion through the 1960s and 1970s, when cities were widely portrayed as strife-ridden dystopias.

The ideological thread of urban community splices with material fibers rooted in the deindustrializing metropolitan economy. Heavy investment in suburbs sped disinvestment in urban structures and institutions, a process that caused significant hardship for the poor and middle-class people who, by necessity or choice, remained in the cities. In other words, suburban booster-ism and anti-urbanism found very concrete expression in the city's neglected schools, dwindling jobs, and decaying housing. Against these realities, tenant activists fought an uphill battle. But in New York they scored a few victories, particularly the enactment of antidiscrimination laws, rent regulations, and affordable-housing programs that provided a measure of security for thousands of poor and moderate-income residents.

Urban historians often justify their focus on a particular city by casting it as a microcosm of the nation, a manageable data set that represents the major features of American society. That is not possible here. New York is nobody's microcosm. While it has been an incubator for many cultural and political movements of national scope, its sheer size and diversity often make it as anomalous as it is representative in American life. So at times, New York's lessons derive less from typicality than from illumination—from the way the singular city sheds light on the features of other American places, much as a patient with a bizarre condition can help doctors understand the way things work in the normal population.

In its modern tenant history, New York is both representative *and* atypical at different times. During the Progressive and Depression Eras, tenant mobilizations in New York were larger in scale but not different in quality from those in other cities. And New York was just one of scores of industrial centers to which World War II brought federal rent control. But in the postwar period, New York's housing politics departed from the national pattern, as local leftists and other housing advocates preserved levels of tenant organization and protection that were obliterated elsewhere. These survivals contributed to the city's status as a relatively "open town" during the years of virulent McCarthyism and Jim Crow. They would also provide support when civil-rights-based housing activism surged again during the 1960s.

Thus New York's tenant history offers two kinds of insights. By showing what happened in a place where renters constituted a majority and claimed a say over housing and development policy after the war, it throws into sharper relief the gains and costs of the homeownership-based model of citizenship that prevailed nationally in that period (and that has increasingly taken hold in New York itself in recent years). It also invites us to consider how an atypical tenant politics fostered developments within feminism and the left.

Like New Yorkers themselves, the city's tenant history speaks in many registers. Sources for this book comprise traditional materials such as newspapers, court data, and organizational records, enlivened by the occasional poem and TV show. Best of all, the sources also include a remarkable number of long-lived activists, people who vary in many respects but share a fierce attachment to the city and a readiness to defend their place in it. "When we get into a fight," explains one, "we don't study for three months to figure out who our enemy is. That's not what New York is about. In San Francisco, you'll contemplate your navel for two years before you figure out [who is your enemy]. That doesn't happen here, thank goodness."[10]

The chapters that follow run chronologically. The first opens with the unprecedented housing crisis that faced New Yorkers at the end of the Second World War. Tenants responded energetically, mobilizing themselves in concert with leftist and liberal organizations rooted in the Progressive and Popular Front periods. Their first priority was to defend rent control.

Chapter Two traces contemporaneous struggles on three other fronts: public housing, slum clearance, and civil rights. Through the late forties, tenant positions on all these public-policy questions came under increasing fire from property holders and early Cold Warriors. But by organizing widely and using the courts and formal politics, tenants managed to hold the line on some of the gains they had made before and during the war.

Chapter Three takes up conflicting developments of the 1950s. Set against a national background of McCarthyite repression, suburban growth, conservative gender ideology, and class stratification, this account foregrounds two fronts of tenant activity: the construction of labor-union cooperatives and the fight against "urban renewal." The co-ops were successful for their upper-working-class beneficiaries. But struggles against urban renewal—a redevelopment policy that afflicted poorer working people and people of color most of all—usually went down in defeat. The city became more segregated and its lower working classes more marginalized.

The losing fight over redevelopment, however, brought certain gains. Tenants who mobilized to save their homes revitalized the local consciousness of tenants' rights. And because battles against the bulldozer were led by women, many of them Popular Front veterans, they sustained a kind of pragmatic feminism at a time when women were typically excluded from politics. In 1959 neighborhood organizers formed a new citywide tenant coalition to meet the challenges of the next decade.

Redevelopment schemes and ghetto disrepair continued to bear heavily on city tenants in the 1960s and became the main targets of new neighborhood-based protests. Chapter Four examines the rent strikes that erupted in Harlem and other ghettos in 1963. Invigorated by the burgeoning civil-rights movement and supported by New York's longtime tenant advocates, ghetto residents waged a dramatic campaign against negligent landlords and complacent officials. Their rent rebellion won modest material improvements and contributed to a growing movement for community power in the ghettos.

Community politics played out differently in racially mixed neighborhoods where tenants carried on struggles against redevelopment in the mid-1960s. Chapter Five examines two examples: Morningside Heights and Cooper Square. In both areas, tenants challenged the conventional ideology of property rights with a creative concept of community rights based on social bonds among diverse neighbors. Morningsiders lost most of their battles, but Cooper Square activists managed to foil a city-sponsored redevelopment proposal that would have razed their homes.

In the late sixties and early seventies, New York's persistent housing shortage and rich tenant history meant that tenants' rights would figure strongly in local manifestations of the nationwide radical upsurge. Chapter Six focuses on the work of young radicals in the Black Panthers, Young Lords, student left, and lower-profile neighborhood groups who sought to establish community say over housing. On their own the radical youth won improved city programs to prevent lead poisoning. In concert with older activists they launched dramatic squatter actions that preserved some of New York's scarce low-rent housing stock. Thus, under a banner—community control—often remembered as disastrous, New York's radicals developed constructive strategies to improve poor people's living conditions.

Further, the interaction between Old and New Left housing organizers amplified the feminist awakenings taking place in New York during this period. Young people who became active with Met Council on Housing, the umbrella group established by veteran leftists a decade earlier, found extraordinary female mentors among the organization's core leaders. The senior women led ably and unself-consciously and "showed you what could be done," as a young recruit put it. Their variety of feminism differed from what many women's liberation groups meant by the term, namely, a deliberate analysis of sexual exploitation. Understanding feminism to include the unspoken assumption of women's authority in the struggle for housing rights reminds us of the range of ways in which politically engaged women of this era ranked their concerns. Housing belonged to the broader universe of women's issues that included welfare, progressive health care, and racial equality.[11]

Chapters Seven and Eight trace outgrowths and aftermaths of the sixties tenant campaigns. City, state, and federal agencies responded to tenant pressure with new programs that promised community partnership in the construction and rehabilitation of housing. That ideal proved difficult to realize, due to internecine conflicts, officials' aversion toward power sharing, and fiscal meltdowns. But in a few cases, adept organizers, often with experience in the city's earlier tenant mobilizations, succeeded in bringing participatory democracy to project design. In other ways, tenants lost ground in the late sixties and early seventies as the ascending neoliberal political establishment dismantled rent control and slashed low-rent construction.

Overall, the 1970s brought tenants small yet significant achievements amid large-scale defeats. In the face of a continuing shortage of sound, affordable housing, a new generation of activists joined the city's older, female-led tenant councils. The young recruits could not stop the tide of neoliberal policy, but they did rebuild the tenant movement, help many families win improved conditions, and recoup some of the legislative losses. Further, a few government agencies launched legalized versions of the tenant takeover actions that young and middle-aged radicals had been staging in vacant buildings. These innovative programs institutionalized once-subversive tenant practices and provided security to some of the city's most vulnerable residents. Ironically, however, by turning tenants into owners, the new programs also chipped away at the constituency for the rights of tenants *per se*.

The tenants who fought for their homes in postwar New York left a complex legacy. It includes housing laws, rent regulations, and co-op programs that survive in weakened form to this day, making New York a place where working people and people of color still form a vital part of the city's social fabric. It also includes less tangible goods: a history of women's activism; an experience of multiracial and cross-class coalition; an expansive understanding of racial justice; a concept of citizenship based on human relationships rather than property ownership; and an urban vision that celebrates the intense forms of social interaction fostered by dense and diverse city neighborhoods. It offers reminders of roads not taken and, perhaps, of roads still open.

PART I

1

"A Time of Struggle"

Holding the Line in the 1940s

"Peace is sure hell," Marine Corps Captain Walter Mansfield told a reporter in 1945. The decorated war hero, just back from East Asia, explained that it was "far easier to locate a sniper in the jungles of China than to find an apartment in New York City."

At the end of World War II, New Yorkers faced their worst housing shortage ever. The housing supply, long inadequate for the city's population and containing many substandard tenements, had fallen even further behind as construction virtually ceased during the Great Depression and the war. Demand, meanwhile, was rising. Veterans came home and families that had doubled up during the lean years sought to disperse. Even the worst slum apartments found a market among African Americans who were moving north and discovering that *de facto* segregation confined them to a few crowded neighborhoods. By 1950, census figures would show that the city required an additional 430,000 dwelling units to properly house its population. As Captain Mansfield concluded, "finding a place to live in New York is more nerve-racking than anything the Japs or Nazis have to offer."[1]

But it was not only the market's pinch that made Mansfield's description telling. Like foreign theaters of war, New York's rental market was embattled terrain. On one side stood realtors and landlords, some small and some great, who collectively wielded considerable wealth and influence.[2] On the other stood tenants, whose strength lay in numbers. Indeed, New York was a city of tenants, its rate of rentership surpassing that of any other American place. Ninety-eight percent of Manhattan's dwellings were rentals in 1940.[3]

Disadvantaged by a nearly constant seller's market, New York's tenants—often led by women—had for decades fought to secure their place. As the postwar period dawned, they faced a watershed. New homes would be constructed now that the war was over; in fact, a new social and political economy would be built. Where and how people lived would play no small part in their ability to enjoy the fruits of this postwar society. The struggle over rental housing carried high stakes.

That struggle would be engaged fiercely by tenants, housing advocates, investors, and politicians, and its early rounds set some of the parameters for local housing politics over the next quarter century. In sum, the clashes of the late 1940s left tenants' position in New York both stronger and narrower than it had been during the war. Tenants had made some gains during the Depression and war years, as economic and military exigencies created openings for favorable new polices such as public housing and rent control. But those policies would be hard to defend after 1945. Even moderate renters' protections came under fire, while more ambitious social democratic measures were subject to battering assaults. Nascent McCarthyism, longstanding racism, and the clout of the housing, realty, and banking industries created formidable resistance to any constraint on the market.

By organizing widely and allying along the left-liberal spectrum, New York tenants managed not only to retain, but to institutionalize, the signal achievements of rent control and public housing. Coalition carried a price, however. Some elites sought moral authority over tenants in exchange for housing security. Loopholes were added to rent laws, enforcement of the building code was weakened, and efforts to loosen the ghetto market were quashed. Leftists within the tenant movement were increasingly marginalized. Finally, slum clearance, a left-liberal idea that *was* written into law, was institutionalized in a way that came back to haunt New York's working-class communities.

Tenant struggles affected not only New York's housing market, but also the city's larger political trajectory, during a time of profound national repression. The Cold War left its mark on virtually every area of American life, from the workplace to the cultural venue to the home. Central to its political economy and culture was mass consumption. Much more than a matter of private wants, postwar consumption was, as historian Lizabeth Cohen has argued, a public policy intimately bound with Cold War ideology. The new consumerism exerted deeply political effects on the Americans who took part, often making their daily lives more economically stratified and racially segregated than they had been in scarcer times. No form of consumption did this more powerfully than owning a home.[4]

But homeownership's gravitational pull toward disparity might be counteracted by a strong movement of home renters committed to racial equality and working class needs. This is what happened in New York. The city's tenant movement, of course, did not create its egalitarian impulses. Quite the opposite: from the early twentieth century through the Popular Front of the thirties and forties, New York's vibrant left schooled the local activists who organized tenants. But once launched, postwar tenant groups helped to *maintain* New York's left institutions and ideals into the postwar era, when such entities were virtually obliterated elsewhere. Notwithstanding the real losses of the late forties, New York's left survived better than any other, and tenant mobilization was one reason why.

The Sidewalks of New York

Both the politics and economics of postwar housing interwove with the city's variegated social geography. Gotham comprised five boroughs, once separate cities, towns, and unincorporated areas, which had consolidated as Greater New York in 1898. In the center lay the slim meridian of Manhattan, its scant acreage packed with the skyscrapers, tenements, monuments, and cultural and business headquarters that constituted "New York" in the public mind. Here people lived by compass points: "Uptown" and "downtown" signified north and south rather than social class, as in other cities. Blue-collar urban villages such as Harlem (uptown) and the Lower East Side (downtown) abutted well-heeled locales like the Upper East Side and Bohemian strongholds like Greenwich Village. Some areas had been razed and rebuilt several times in the cycle of "creative destruction" driven by real estate speculation and public works.[5]

Connected to Manhattan by dozens of bridges, tunnels, and ferries were the much larger "outer boroughs." The Bronx jutted down from the U.S. mainland to the north; Brooklyn and Queens lay across the East River, forming the western tip of Long Island; and Staten Island, an aloof step-sibling, kept to itself in New York Harbor. A good deal of outer-borough land had remained semi-rural through the nineteenth century while Manhattan was developed with a vengeance.

Each borough in turn contained neighborhoods, many evincing various stages of what sociologists called "ethnic succession." Harlem, for example, was by now established as the capital of Black America, yet retained traces of its earlier Jewish and other immigrant populations. Italian East Harlem was on its way to becoming El Barrio. The Lower East Side remained heavily Jewish, Eastern and Southern European, with growing numbers of Puerto Ricans and African Americans. Meanwhile the outer boroughs, where developments were newer and more spacious than Manhattan's tenement districts, became magnets for second-generationers who had climbed a rung on the economic ladder. Large swaths of Brooklyn and the Bronx were claimed by upwardly mobile Irish, Italians, and Jews. In some of those areas, Puerto Ricans and African Americans also started putting down roots. (Brooklyn's Bedford-Stuyvesant, integrated at midcentury, would eventually displace Harlem as the city's largest black neighborhood.) Similar dispersal occurred in Queens and Staten Island, though here development tended more toward detached one- and two-family houses than to multiple dwellings.[6]

Neighborhood is a slippery concept—scholars debate its definition, and people who believe themselves to be living in the same neighborhood may disagree on its boundaries, distinguishing characteristics, and interests—yet it is an indispensible one for housing history.[7] Tenants typically embraced collective identities based on vicinity. This was so even when they *also* understood their housing situations in the broader class terms of landlords versus renters. Often the social character of a neighborhood—its demographic contours, its cultural and political associations, the mundane meetings in its streets and shops—informed the sense of place that New Yorkers would defend when they fought for rights as tenants.

Grassroots Mobilization in the Prewar City

Postwar tenants inherited a rich legacy of ideals, institutions, and tactics developed by earlier activists. Housing was a leading concern for New York's turn-of-the-century radicals, and in 1904 the heavily Socialist Lower East Side was the scene of the city's first large-scale tenant mobilization: a series of rent strikes against steep hikes. The strikes, which won a temporary rollback, followed upon the heels of a kosher-meat boycott in the same neighborhood.[8] Both were organized by working-class immigrant housewives (although male leaders of the Socialist Party soon seized the reins) and both carried on a labor tradition of boycott forged in the Gilded Age. This tradition, Lawrence Glickman writes, held that in an interdependent, cash-based market economy, "consumers directly affected people through their purchasing decisions" and that seemingly private acts of consumption were therefore "inherently political, which is to say bound with the use of aggregate purchasing power to promote justice." Thus the conscientious consumer—often a woman—became the paradigmatic citizen.[9]

Yet the housewife-organizers of 1904 styled their mobilization after a predominantly male labor tradition: shop-floor conflict. "Tenant unions" was their term for the new neighborhood associations they established; the action itself was a "strike," and nonparticipants, "scabs." Such rhetoric was evocative on the Lower East Side, a center of organizing in the manufacturing industries.[10] Indeed, like conflicts in local sweatshops, the rent strike was both a class dispute and an intra-ethnic quarrel, inasmuch as most landlords, like most garment contractors, were Jewish and only slightly more prosperous than those they sweated.[11] The trade-union paradigm would continue to inform New York tenant mobilization over the next three decades, with tenants sometimes demanding collective bargaining with landlords as workers did with bosses.[12] The consciousness this paradigm reflected—that tenants constituted a class, and landlord–tenant relations a form of class exploitation—marked an exception to the pattern delineated by political scientist Ira Katznelson, in which class consciousness among American workers is "virtually nonexistent [in venues] outside the workplace" such as the "residence community."[13]

But the landlord's market persisted, secured by steady population growth in the years immediately following the rent strikes, and tightened further when defense workers flocked to the city during World War I. This led to a second round of rent hikes and rebellions in the nineteen teens. The largest strikes occurred in Harlem and the Jewish areas of Manhattan, Brooklyn, and the East and South Bronx where Socialists wielded strength. A few garnered mass participation; more than a few won rent rollbacks and repairs. These victories were achieved through the same kinds of discipline, solidarity, and physical courage that characterized interwar labor uprisings. Socialist Party affiliates such as women's consumer leagues lent crucial support to rent strikers; sometimes women foiled evictions simply by shaming the moving men into respecting their picket line. In other cases tenants endured beatings from police and private guards. Often neighbors took in evicted families while their cases went to court.[14]

The strikers' gains were fleeting, however, because tenant unions did not achieve the political clout needed to win meaningful legal protections. Commitment ebbed when crisis passed, a problem that would continue to plague tenant organizations more severely than labor unions. As well, the Red Scare drove Socialists from office, and moderate tenant councils sprang up to compete with strike-oriented unions. The strikes of the late teens did jolt state lawmakers into enacting some modest renters' protections, but these were made contingent on a miniscule vacancy rate and became void when new housing was built with "Roaring Twenties" capital.[15]

The Depression revived tenant militancy under different organizational structures. With the Communist Party (CP) overtaking Socialists on the left, it was the CP's Unemployed Councils that led rent strikes and eviction stoppages in Harlem, the Lower East Side, Brooklyn, and the Bronx in the early thirties. Cadre brazenly moved people and furniture back into apartments from which marshals had just put them out.[16] Court action and lobbying, meanwhile, were the preferred tactics of Harlem's Consolidated Tenants League, a group led by Garveyite professionals who offered legal representation in return for membership dues. At turns the Consolidated would compete or coalesce with uptown leftists in fighting the abysmal conditions forced upon African Americans by the segregated housing market.[17] And as in the past, many neighborhoods boasted consumer organizations that addressed tenant concerns along with the pricing of food. Although these pre–World War II mobilizations won few lasting gains, they further developed a tenant consciousness within the city's political culture.

Attempts to Loosen the Landlord's Grip

Leftists concerned themselves not only with the price and condition of existing rentals, but also with the problem of supply. In the nineteen-teens, Finnish dockhands in Brooklyn pioneered a new solution: the development of working-class cooperative apartment houses.[18] Jewish labor organizations quickly expanded on the idea, building more ambitious co-ops in the 1920s. The largest were the Communist "Coops," the social-democratic Amalgamated Clothing Workers' development, and the Yiddishist Sholem Aleichem Houses, all in the Bronx. These multistory dwellings, which together contained more than two thousand units, featured garden courtyards, moderate fees, and an associative life replete with literary events, art classes, and political activity.[19]

Large-scale construction of sound, affordable housing, however, was beyond the means of radical parties; it would require action by the state. And direct state provision was anathema not only to the housing industry but to paternalistic reformers who believed that the worthy poor would blush at such "charity."[20] Thus in the 1920s New York's legislature enacted compromise measures meant to stimulate private investment: tax exemptions for new construction, permission for insurance companies to invest in housing, and additional breaks for developers who limited their rents and dividends.[21] This last provision was won through hard lobbying by labor unions, and the Amalgamated Clothing Workers' co-op became its first beneficiary.[22] But even with the tax breaks, labor co-ops could not bring rents within reach of the poorer workers. Radicals remained eager for larger socialized construction programs.

Middle-class reformers' efforts to ameliorate New York's housing also dated back many years. As early as the mid-nineteenth century, charities such as the Association for Improving the Condition of the Poor attempted, not very successfully, to build "model tenements" that met humane standards but still turned a profit.[23] The Progressive Era ushered in a second generation of reforms that shifted the responsibility for housing improvement to the state. Chief among these was the Tenement House Act of 1901, a measure that raised the minimum standards for ventilation, plumbing, and fireproofing.[24] Henceforth New Yorkers would speak of "old-law" and "new-law tenements" to distinguish the airless nineteenth-century warrens (some of which still stand in lower Manhattan) from their more habitable cousins. The 1901 act was the fruition of more than a decade of research and lobbying by a coalition of philanthropists, journalists (notably Jacob Riis), civic-minded architects, and social workers based in the settlement houses.[25]

The settlement workers belonged to both the mixed-sex field of professional housing reform and the cohort of middle-class Progressive women whom historians have dubbed "municipal housekeepers." This latter group bridged the divide between separate spheres by taking woman's domestic authority as a rationale for her activism in the civic arena, especially the teeming turn-of-the-century urban spaces that needed cleaning up. In the end these women expanded both the state's jurisdiction and their own.[26] Settlements, where middle-class volunteers instructed, assisted, and lived among the poor, and where they developed skills in political advocacy, epitomized this sort of urban female activism.[27] New York became home to the country's very first settlement house in 1886; by the early twentieth century it boasted scores.[28] While settlement volunteers sometimes took a patronizing attitude toward their lower-class neighbors, they also advanced landmark legislation that benefited the needy and vulnerable. Consumer protection and housing improvement were prime areas of advocacy.[29] In 1919 the city's settlements launched an umbrella organization, the United Neighborhood Houses, to lobby for housing reform.[30]

Progressive housing advocacy advanced also through the Women's City Club of New York. This Upper East Side civic group, founded in 1915 to promote

woman suffrage, carried on afterward as a good-government advocacy organization with a particular concern for poor people's material needs. Its leadership
included Eleanor Roosevelt, Frances Perkins, and other luminaries. Club members did not move into the slums, as settlement workers did, but they made
common cause with the settlement movement on rent regulation and other
housing reforms.[31] During the Depression the club would also launch an innovative slum project: a detailed survey of poor women's own views on housing. Researchers learned that tenement housewives lamented their grim dwellings but
valued the social and familial networks their densely populated neighborhoods
sustained; that they kept their homes immaculate; and that they desired above
all privacy and ease of upkeep. Sample architectural plans drawn around those
goals completed the report.[32] The Women's City Club well illustrates historian
Estelle Freedman's insight that "separatism, or female institution building, did,
in fact survive as a reform strategy after [women gained the vote in] 1920."[33]

Progressive reforms, however, brought only marginal relief to tenants
subsisting in dismal slum apartments. Civic-minded developers continued to
experiment with model tenements, but these, too, failed to yield substantial
improvement and remained out of reach for the poorest renters.[34]

Thus, by the close of the 1920s, New York's radicals and reformers had accumulated much experience, some success, and no small amount of frustration
with the improvement of housing. The Great Depression opened new possibilities, particularly after the elections of 1932. Franklin Roosevelt's New Deal
incorporated a variety of economic philosophies, but its overarching principle
was stronger state intervention in the economy. Many erstwhile Progressives
became New Dealers, adding their support for regulation and public provision
to the emerging corpus of policy now known as "liberalism."[35]

This was not immediately apparent at the federal level, where early 1930s
housing programs were shaped by centrist New Dealers—those who believed
the state should act by encouraging private investment rather than by inter-
vening directly in the market. The main housing initiatives of Roosevelt's first
term were the Home Owners Loan Corporation (HOLC) Act of 1933 and the
National Housing Act of 1934. These established public agencies that extended
mortgages to owners hit by economic crisis and reduced the risk to housing
lenders. In a move with grave long-term effects, the HOLC also wrote racial
and anti-urban biases into federal policy by coding neighborhoods with black,
Jewish, integrated, or simply dense populations as bad risks.[36]

But locally New York's left-liberal alliance won two bolder programs: govern-
ment-owned, or public housing; and government demolition of substandard

housing, known as "slum clearance." This combination of razing and building, supporters believed, could finally make the tenement—with its dark rooms, barely ventilated toilets, and chronic overcrowding—a thing of the past. Both programs were central planks in the city's union and left party platforms from the early thirties on.[37] Both also won strong support from influential liberals.

The most crucial proponents were Fiorello La Guardia and Charles Abrams. La Guardia, a nominal Republican-Fusionist, had ridden into the mayor's office in 1933 on a wave of disgust with the Tammany Democratic machine, but then allied with New Dealers. Abrams was a Polish-Jewish immigrant (and descendant of the Vilna Gaon) who rose from working-class Williamsburg, Brooklyn, to become a lawyer and city planner, ultimately achieving a stature in the field of housing policy that equaled his forebear's fame in religion.[38] In the early 1930s these men began meeting with a coalition of reformers—settlement leaders, other Progressive veterans, socialists, architectural critics—who shared their interest in housing and were particularly taken with the example of public developments in Europe. Many of these reformers were women who would play crucial, albeit behind-the-scenes, roles in crafting local and national public-housing policy over the next decade.[39] In 1933 La Guardia asked Abrams to draft legislation authorizing a public housing agency. The bill passed in Albany and was signed by Governor Herbert Lehman in 1934.[40]

The result was the New York City Housing Authority (NYCHA), which completed the First Houses low-rent project on the Lower East Side the following year. First Houses was both the first government-built housing project in the country (save for a handful that lodged defense workers during World War I) and the first development created through public condemnation of slums.[41] As its name suggested, supporters hoped it would not be the last. Symbolizing a larger social endeavor and providing an example soon followed in other cities, First Houses enjoyed a gala dedication featuring speeches by La Guardia, Lehman, and Eleanor Roosevelt; music by the Police Band; and a parade of schoolchildren.[42] Although Congress would not fund public housing directly in the early thirties, the sympathetic President Roosevelt subsidized the construction of First Houses and other early NYCHA projects by assigning laborers via the federal public-works programs.

Depression politics also fueled new political alliances. In 1936 a German American writer, Heinz Norden, persuaded Harlem's Consolidated Tenants League and several middle-class tenant groups on the Lower East Side to join forces as the City-Wide Tenants Council (CWTC), a Popular Front federation of liberals and radicals, professionals and slum dwellers, who organized in blue-collar neighborhoods with the help of Communist cadre. Unlike the Unemployed Councils, however, City-Wide affiliates used the strike and the picket only after more moderate appeals had failed. And it worked in the political arena, lobbying for code enforcement and public housing. For a few years the City-Wide achieved a scope and stability unprecedented among tenant alliances. But the organization would decline precipitously after 1941, when Norden and other leaders went off to war, and the Communist left ratcheted down anticapitalist militancy in the name of anti-fascist unity.[43]

The year 1937 saw the formation of a more enduring advocacy group, the Citizens' Housing Council (later the Citizens' Housing and Planning Council or CHPC). This alliance of New Dealers with housing and financial expertise was led by Charles Abrams and would serve as a leading voice for expanded public housing and improved housing for African Americans.[44]

Relations among these 1930s activists were sometimes tense. Radicals bent on redistributing wealth and power coexisted uneasily with liberals embracing more modest aims. But on projects with broad appeal, diverse people and

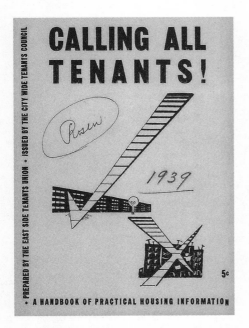
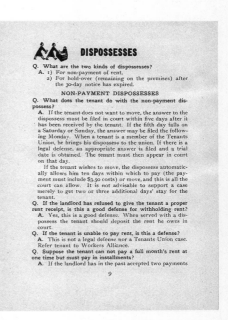

Figure 1. **A 1939 handbook by the East Side Tenants Council.** Cover drawing envisages replacement of tenements with modern housing. Inside pages explain tenants' legal rights. *Courtesy of Met Council on Housing.*

groups allied effectively, and liberal insiders like Abrams played a crucial role in realizing ideas, like public housing, that had been conceived on the left. The liberal-left coalition put forward a broad vision of public responsibility and tenant empowerment for New York.

The Postwar Terrain of Tenant Struggle

Much of the infrastructure of 1930s tenant politics would survive into the early postwar period. Tenant strength in those years rested not only on specialized structures such as building councils, but on the girders of New York's left-liberal politics: minor parties and labor unions. The Communist, American Labor, and Liberal Parties all appealed to the city's working-class immigrant electorate, and they gained strength in the formal political arena from proportional representation. This electoral system, set out in the 1936 city charter, apportioned City Council seats on the basis of boroughwide, not district, votes. Thus small parties could and did win council positions. The Communists, for example—who in their Popular Front heyday numbered nearly forty thousand in New York and could attract many more votes—elected two council members: Benjamin Davis, an African American from Manhattan, and Pete Cacchione, an Italian American representing Brooklyn.[45] They would be stalwarts for working-class causes like rent control.

Both the influence and the volatility of left politics can be seen in the career of the American Labor Party (ALP). This organization was founded in 1936 by anti-Communist leaders of New York's garment unions, who wanted to provide a means by which socialists could vote for Franklin Roosevelt without sullying their hands on a Democratic lever. But the party's base shifted as Communists and fellow travelers built power within its ranks. (The dismayed founders would decamp in 1944 to form an anti-Communist left rival, the Liberal Party.) The ALP ran several successful candidates who amplified tenants' voice within government. Best known were Mike Quill, president of the Transport Workers' Union, who won a council seat in 1937 and was reelected in 1945 with the highest vote count in the city; and Vito Marcantonio, a La Guardia protégé, fluent in Italian and Spanish, who represented East Harlem in Congress for fourteen years and served as national spokesman for the immigrant and minority poor. Both men sympathized openly with the Communist Party (Quill may have been a clandestine member) and both won office in part through Communist support. Yet both would eventually break with the Communists—Quill by supporting a subway-fare hike in exchange for a transit pay raise in 1948, and Marcantonio by opposing the CP's decision to jettison the ALP in the early fifties.[46]

Left parties spoke not only through electoral politics, but through media and neighborhood affiliates. The Communist *Daily Worker* kept rent strikes and protests prominent in the minds of its large readership. Local political clubs provided resources for tenants, especially after the demise of the City-Wide. On the Lower East Side, for example, the ALP clubhouse shared space with the neighborhood Tenant and Consumer Council.[47] East Harlem's ALP organized eviction blockades among the area's growing Puerto Rican population.[48] Residents might turn to such organizations in *ad hoc* fashion for help with a particular problem; they might also be drawn into lasting relationships with the tenant councils and political parties. Conversely, party members who learned organizing skills in the wards and the workplace could put them to use in tenant struggles.

Integrally tied to both the minor parties and the tenant cause was New York's labor movement. Party members were often union members, and in several locals, as well as in the city's Congress of Industrial Organizations (CIO) council, Communists held sway. Labor unions extended the power of the left beyond party rolls by fostering class consciousness and turning out votes that put pro-tenant candidates in office.

More broadly, Joshua Freeman argues, unions were the base for a "New York exceptionalism" that survived from the 1930s through the early Cold War. This political consciousness was characterized by a type of liberalism that included a good deal of social-democratic thinking—something that would become increasingly exceptional as Keynesian liberalism took over in Washington. And New York exceptionalism was expressed in very concrete institutions. Public colleges, hospitals, and other facilities raised social provision in Gotham to a level unknown in the rest of the country.[49] The New York City Housing Authority projects were perhaps the most distinctive elements of this social program. The city's public institutions maintained political support, and hence funding, largely through the labor vote.

Thus the tenant movement of the late thirties and early forties can be understood at several interlocking levels of organization. The basic units of association were local ones: building councils and neighborhood leagues, which thrived especially in highly politicized areas such as the Lower East Side and Harlem. This was the level that typically mobilized rent strikes and pickets, and that staffed "rent clinics" where knowledgeable volunteers helped individual tenants assert their legal rights. It was also the level at which women predominated.[50]

Through direct actions and legal advising, these local organizations perpetuated a measure of class-consciousness regarding the residential neighborhood. At the citywide level, the larger labor-left framework provided resources and lobbying muscle for tenant initiatives.

The movement's liberal wing included professionals like Charles Abrams, settlement volunteers, and Women's City Club activists who provided crucial links to the influence and funds of New York's upper crust. Mainline race organizations such as the National Association for the Advancement of Colored People and the Urban League also lobbied to alleviate the dismal conditions in the ghettos. Middle-class advocates rarely led tenant organizations themselves, but they made up the ranks of New York's "housers," as civic-minded specialists in housing became known. Housers' entrée with public officials helped to usher tenant proposals into government policy.

Tenants and their allies were up against the most powerful interest in the city. Real estate had been calling the tune at City Hall for more than a century. Speculators reaped the benefits of Manhattan's street grid, adopted in 1811, which broke land into regular parcels. The city's 1916 zoning policy was drawn largely to protect Manhattan's upscale neighborhoods from industrial uses that might lower property values. Even the creation of Central Park, which took some land off the market, boosted the values of nearby townhouses. Wealthy investors gained further during the Depression by snapping up the devalued properties of small owners who could not afford to ride out the storm. After the war, new rounds of speculative buying and building would be driven by surging industrial profits, which became surplus capital, ready to be sunk into the auspicious real estate market.[51]

Trench Warfare on Rent

As city tenants faced the housing crisis of 1945, their first major contest grew directly from the shift from wartime to postwar politics. In 1941, as war loomed, Roosevelt had made an unprecedented intervention into the housing market by creating an Office of Price Administration (OPA) with the power to freeze rents in cities with defense installations (lest workers be driven away by impossible housing costs). New York's tenant, consumer, and housing groups quickly prevailed on Mayor La Guardia to request an OPA freeze. The OPA refused, citing a "satisfactory" housing vacancy rate in New York.[52] But tenants kept up the pressure. Rent clinics, many staffed by women with CWTC and ALP backgrounds, rallied neighborhood residents. Liberal housers, labor leaders, and politicians such as Quill, Marcantonio, Davis, and Adam Clayton Powell Jr., called for rent relief. When the police shooting of a black soldier sparked a night of riot in Harlem, Powell declared that the anger had been fueled by "the unusual high rents and cost of living forced upon the Negroes" there.[53] On November 1, 1943, the OPA rolled New York's rents back to the levels of the previous spring.[54] The OPA freeze went far beyond New York State's sieve-like 1920s rent laws and constituted a major victory for city tenants.[55]

But that victory would remain secure for only two years. Nineteen forty-five brought peace and a flood of welcomes from the nation's pundits for the return of economic normalcy. Tenants could no longer justify rent controls on grounds of national security. Yet their need for rent regulation had only intensified with the postwar surge in housing demand.

Thus saving rent control became an urgent challenge. New York tenants fought for this goal on three fronts. In OPA courts they confronted individual landlords and demonstrated the continuing importance of strong tenant protections. In Washington and Albany they lobbied to preserve rent caps. In local politics they pressed city officials to join the state and federal campaigns to save rent and price control.

City tenants made the most of the special courts that the OPA created to adjudicate rent disputes. Some cases involved landlords' demands for under-the-table payments. In one extreme instance in 1946, a landlord with previous rent-gouging convictions was found guilty of extorting a "furniture fee" of $4,000 for a $112-per-month apartment; he received ten days in the workhouse.[56] That same year saw an unlawful eviction claim brought by a veteran who had lost a leg at Bataan. The OPA magistrate spent thirty minutes calling the landlady many things, including "a female Torquemada," before pronouncing sentence.[57]

The OPA strengthened tenants' hand in eviction cases especially. In the years directly preceding the 1943 federal edict, New York City courts issued eviction warrants at a rate of more than twenty thousand per year. In 1943 and 1944 that figure fell by half. This decrease did not reflect a change in the volume of disputes; the number of landlord–tenant cases that went to court, in fact, rose steadily from the early forties until 1947. In other words, landlords were trying as hard as ever to oust assertive tenants. What changed under the OPA was tenants' ability to push back.[58]

The OPA provided less leverage over landlords who neglected their buildings. Harlem was a center of disrepair, and both of the neighborhood's early postwar tenant leagues pursued redress for hazardous conditions. They used different tactics—the Consolidated furnished attorneys for dues-paying members, while the Communist-led United Harlem Tenants ran a rent clinic that schooled tenants in self-advocacy[59]—but neither they nor mainline race advocates such as the Urban League had much success at winning more than paltry fines.[60] By 1948 the Department of Buildings would be overwhelmed with a record 150,000 multiple-dwelling violations.[61] Nonetheless, individual tenants did win repair orders through the OPA courts, and their cases brought some public attention to the problem of landlord negligence.

The Making of Tenant Activists

For some tenants, the matter did not end when the judge's gavel fell. Rent clinics often served as the setting in which veterans organized newcomers into the movement. Frances Goldin started this way. She had grown up in Springfield Gardens, Queens, a place where neighbors kept their distance. "I hated where I lived. . . . We were one of nine Jewish families. The other eight Jewish families were shopkeepers. My father was a worker. So we were shunned by the non-Jews and shunned by the Jews, because my father worked with his hands." But life changed in 1944 when Goldin, then twenty, got married and moved to the Lower East Side. "And I felt like I had moved into heaven. It was totally integrated, it was working-class, people were very friendly." Living in a fourth-floor one-bedroom apartment, she and her husband had two children. "And I felt I was being overcharged. And so I went to the Lower East Side Tenant and Consumer Council . . . And I was articulate and bushytailed, and they asked if I could come back and help out. I never left the tenant movement since then."[62] Goldin became a leader in neighborhood and citywide tenant circles.

Her course had been charted by both personal experience and historical conjuncture. Goldin's father, an immigrant, a "freethinker," and "very much a union man," encouraged Frances to stick up for herself. Her years as a pariah in Queens primed her to sympathize with other outcasts. In another setting this history might preface the biography of a classic American "rugged individualist." In New York in the 1940s, it meant Goldin gravitated toward the Communist Party.

She met Communists at her job in the wartime shipping industry. "And they quickly converted me." At nineteen she joined the Party and enrolled at its Jefferson School, where she "became educated as to capitalism, what socialism was," and read Engels and Lenin. "And I was hot to trot. I was going to have socialism in my time. That was gonna happen. I was gonna help make it happen." It was through the Party that Frances met her husband, Morris and with him that she settled downtown. Suddenly she found herself in an environment where her ideals were widely shared.

"It was wonderful . . . to come from Queens, from that isolated, frigid community, to come to a vibrant community . . . of people coming from various parts of the world, who were involved in struggle, and who were landing on the Lower East Side and bringing their experience in organizing." Few places rivaled this corner of Manhattan in density of left-leaning people and networks. Immigration histories, rent protests, and the larger left flowed easily together. At the clinic Goldin translated for Yiddish-speaking tenants and met the local ALP organizers who shared the tenant council's office.[63] Interactions like these served to solidify local residents' political consciousness regarding housing.

Closely tied to the issue of rent was that of eviction. Nonpayment was the chief legal ground for eviction, and in many rental controversies an ouster was at stake. Sometimes tenants fighting eviction, like tenants challenging rents, found their way into a larger movement.

Bess Stevenson traveled that path. She had moved to New York as a teenager in 1939, hoping to make money to help her ailing mother back in North Carolina. Like many black women at the time, she took the only work she could get: domestic service. Then she married and set up housekeeping in a "kitchenette room" on 127th Street in Harlem. When her husband was drafted in 1941, Stevenson was left alone. "And then the landlord tried to get fresh. And I put him in his place." Soon after, Stevenson came home from work one day to find that "he had taken the mattress off my bed, and had taken the little two-eyed burner, that you cook on, out the kitchen. . . . I don't know why, other'n just to be nasty, because my rent always stayed six weeks [paid ahead]. I was afraid, I didn't know if I get sick and had nobody here, I wouldn't have nowhere to stay, so I always paid my rent up way ahead of time."[64]

Stevenson had been warned by her neighbor, a kindly maternal "Indian lady" who suspected that the landlord was up to no good. Now the older woman took Stevenson under wing. "She said, 'Don't cry, you're a big girl . . . I'm going to tell you what to do, and you do exactly like I tell you to do.' I said, 'Yes, ma'am.'" Following instructions, Stevenson went to the police precinct, filed a complaint, and returned home with the paper the officers had given her. "[The Indian lady] looked at it. She said, 'You going to court tomorrow.' Oh, Lord, now, court, I don't know what that is! I never been to a courthouse in my life. And I thought . . . she was gonna go with me, you know." But the next morning the neighbor said, "'No. I'm gon' tell you where to go, and you're going by yourself.'"

At the courthouse Stevenson had to wait her turn and made use of the time by listening to other cases and learning the routine. "By the time they got to me, I was well acquainted. And then they called, said, 'Stevenson versus Phillip!' . . . And the judge said, 'Are you Bessie Stevenson?' I said, 'Yes, Your Honor' ('cause from the others I had learned the rules). And the judge called, said, 'Mr. Phillip, did you go into Mrs. Stevenson's room on so-and-so date . . . ?' 'Yes.' And the judge said, 'Was her rent paid?' 'Yes.'" After a few more brisk questions, the judge told Phillip, "You are *guilty* of all charges."

Then he asked Stevenson for a list of missing items. "Well, frankly, I wasn't missing nothing but the mattress . . . and the stove. But I lied. . . . I was so mad at him—I [named] my husband's Christmas present . . . I was naming all the things. It came to five hundred dollars. And . . . in '41, that was *money*." The judge gave the landlord until noon to show up with the cash. "Oh, you don't know how I felt! Oh, I felt ten feet tall! I wanted to go run and tell her, so bad,

Figure 2. Bess Stevenson, circa 1970, leads protest against city's weakening of rent regulations. *Courtesy of Met Council on Housing.*

'I won, I won!' But I didn't. I sit there nice and quiet. And I won my first case without saying a word."[65]

Like Frances Goldin, Bess Stevenson went on to become a prominent tenant advocate. That a black woman with little formal schooling would represent others in court may have raised eyebrows, but in time courthouse regulars came to recognize Stevenson and her proficiency in landlord–tenant law. Decades later a young organizer who accompanied her through Housing Court was struck by the wave of "Good morning, Mrs. Stevensons" issuing from every clerk, janitor, and judge as she sailed down the corridor.[66]

In some ways Stevenson's initiation into tenant work differed from Goldin's. She started earlier, before the OPA rules took effect, so she cut her teeth on the older city-court system. She entered that system because of the landlord's opportunistic sexual advance, a form of exploitation to which black women were especially vulnerable. And her education came informally, through a sympathetic neighbor rather than an organization.

But in other respects the two women's stories were akin. Both young New Yorkers represented historic migrations—turn-of-the-century Ashkenazic Jewish influx in Goldin's case, the African American Great Migration in Stevenson's. And both were schooled in neighborhoods that were centers of tenant militancy in the early twentieth century. (It was no accident that the elderly Harlem lady knew what to do when the landlord put Stevenson out.)

Finally, both Stevenson and Goldin were women and may be seen as inheritors of a tradition of female urban activism. The women who crafted the 1901 tenement law, who led the downtown rent and meat protests, and who agitated for housing, labor, and consumer protections throughout the Progressive Era, made women's presence in civic and governmental chambers more and more commonplace. By the early 1940s, savvy women like Stevenson's older neighbor were part of the urban landscape.

Yet unlike women New Dealers, many of whom came of age in the settlement movement, Goldin and Stevenson did not see Progressive Era women's activism as part of their political genealogy. Neither, when interviewed, spoke at all of settlements, suffragists, or other such figures in the early history of women's rights.[67] Stevenson said the only organization she knew was the church; Goldin spoke of her father and the Communist Party as guiding lights. That these young women took their political bearings from more immediate sources is not surprising when we consider their formative experiences in blue-collar, racially marginalized households outside the urban center. Why would they identify with moneyed Manhattan WASPs of yore? (The 1904 Lower East Side rent strike must have struck a chord with Goldin, but she apparently learned about it only *after* she became politicized. Stevenson, for her part, described rent strikes as a tactic invented in the 1960s.) The relationship of these newly minted tenant activists to earlier ones illustrates what Susan Lynn has called the combination of "continuities and discontinuities in women's activism before and after World War II."[68] Lynn argues that among working-class women, CIO unions replaced older voluntary organizations as "the primary locus of . . . efforts to improve their conditions."[69] Like the unions with which they allied, tenant councils sought to build members' collective power rather than look to bourgeois benefactors.

And like labor unions, which mushroomed after the passage of the National Labor Relations Act in 1935, tenants gained leverage from a new, federally mandated legal structure, namely the OPA. Much as the National Labor Relations Board's certification of unions encouraged further union organizing, the OPA's recognition and enforcement of renters' rights emboldened many tenants to demand change.

From Federal to State Rent Control

But tenants' OPA rights depended on a quickly changing political arena. Or rather three arenas: federal, state, and city. This legal complexity reflected the unusual status of the original order—a federal wartime mandate affecting selected municipalities—and the idiosyncrasies of New York politics, which often pitted the city against upstate interests. With peace on the horizon in Europe and Asia, the housing industry girded for battle in Washington. As early as March 1945, industry representatives were maneuvering to have OPA rent controls eased.[70] In October, when the ink was still damp on soldiers' return orders, the industry called for a full repeal.[71]

This drive against the OPA was part of a massive effort, across major industries, to recast the American political economy. It was a successful effort. Business leaders and sympathetic economists sold a remarkably large portion of the American public on an ideology of patriotic mass consumption that historian Lizabeth Cohen has termed "Consumers' Republicanism." Under this credo, capital and citizens were to be partners in creating unprecedented levels of employment and material satisfaction for the "average American." Earlier economic paradigms, such as the consumer-protection consciousness of the Progressive Era and the valorization of consumer thrift during the Depression, had treated consumers as a class with a distinct interest. But Consumers' Republicanism erased the very idea of class antagonism from national policy. This was very much in keeping with Cold War politics, and indeed, Consumers'-Republican boosters posed purchaser satisfaction as the ultimate weapon against Communism.[72] Their "integrated ideal of economic abundance and democratic political freedom," writes Cohen, "became almost a national civil religion from the late 1940s into the 1970s."[73]

Two linchpins of Consumer-Republican ideology would matter critically for housing. The first was the belief that state regulation of the "free market" was bad for business, consumers, and society at large. Second, and related, was the conviction that owner-occupied single-family housing formed the bedrock of a sound economy. If postwar consumerism verged on a "national civil religion," its first commandment was, "Thou Shalt Own Thy Home." Buying a home was not only most families' largest act of consumption. It was also an act that stimulated further consumption—of appliances, furniture, and the cars and roads needed to get from home to anywhere else.[74] And each purchase benefited the citizenry at large by promoting full employment and good wages. Amid this faith in market-driven prosperity, any sort of price regulation would face tremendous ideological opposition.

Not surprisingly, then, developers' assault on OPA rent caps was but one front of a larger offensive against the OPA itself, an offensive that business interests waged in legislatures and public fora throughout the country during the last months of the war. Consumers, already organized through wartime rationing and price boards, fought back.[75] Nowhere were the protests more impassioned than in New York, where the landlord's market made rent caps indispensable to many family budgets. AFL and CIO locals, tenant and consumer councils, Communists, settlement-house leaders, the mayor, and Eleanor Roosevelt all rallied during the summer of 1946 to save the OPA. Mothers adorned toddlers with placards: "My Daddy Didn't Get a Raise"; "OPA is the American Way." Pickets shut down stores in Midtown, Harlem, Brooklyn, and the Bronx on "Buy Nothing Day" in July.[76] But ultimately a well-coordinated lobbying effort among retail, industrial, and agricultural sectors carried the day. Weak price caps were extended through early 1947, but that May the OPA closed up shop.[77]

Rent control, however, fared differently. Although at the federal level it simply went through more protracted death throes, in New York it won a second lease on life. Through 1946, when Congress was working to phase out other price controls, a tenant, consumer, and labor alliance succeeded in defending rent caps.[78] The next year Republicans gained control of Congress and realtors pressed their case again. Finally the lawmakers, heavily lobbied by both sides, enacted a compromise measure: a Housing and Rent Act that extended caps but permitted generous "turnover" and "hardship" increases and laid out a process of "decontrol" to return housing to the free market.[79]

Decontrol, however, was to be overseen by state boards; thus state and local politics became vital theaters of struggle. When New York's Republican governor, Thomas Dewey, named a slate of GOP realtors to the decontrol board, a coalition of tenant councils, ALP clubs, CIO unions, and liberal organizations such as the National Lawyers Guild mounted outraged protests that forced the new board to drop plans for immediate decontrol and to accede to a measure of municipal autonomy.[80] New York's City Council then appointed a rent commission to adjust increases, limit evictions, and regulate rents in residential hotels. Further lobbying battles ensued until 1950, when New York State enacted its own rent regulations in lieu of the now-threadbare federal system.[81]

The 1950 state law was a distinct compromise. It retained rent caps but placed them under the aegis of a state, rather than a city, board—a crucial detail given tenants' relative political weakness outside New York City. It approved rent increases to maintain a fixed rate of return on the landlord's investment. And it permitted landlords to negotiate—or, in the tight market, leverage—"voluntary" increases of 15 percent.[82] Compared with the 1943 OPA edict, the 1950 rent-control law was weak and full of holes. But seen against the background of national housing policy in 1950, it stood as a tenant victory. New Yorkers had written into the law of the prosperous postwar era a set of rules originally justified on grounds of wartime emergency alone. Nowhere else in America had tenants stood that much ground.

Conclusion

"It was a very good time," Frances Goldin recalled of the late 1940s. "It was a time of struggle and a lot of activities and a lot of rent strikes." The "good" here is not triumphs, but tenacious fights. Only through continuous organizing and protest did tenants maintain any protections at all.

The war over rent control was especially taxing. The policy had constantly to be defended, and the battle over renewing legislation became a biennial rite. Because the protections of rent control had become so integral to tenants' day-to-day survival, moreover, rent clinics and other forms of counseling and advocacy came to absorb much of the movement's energy. Historian Joel Schwartz has castigated New York's postwar tenant councils and ALP clubs for losing their stomach for confrontation, for devolving into filers of complaint forms within a compromised regulatory system rather than mobilizers of a mass movement.[83] His criticism provides an important reminder that prewar tenant visionaries had put forward a broad agenda for humane, socially fulfilling housing that included expansive *nonprofit* construction, both public and cooperative, as well as progressive design.

But for those who remembered the blows they had taken from police and landlords' thugs in the teens, twenties, and thirties, the option to wield the pen rather than the sword felt like progress. And the 1950 rent-control statute enabled many city residents to live on modest budgets. Given the rightward tilt of national politics after the war, the scaling back of the tenant platform comes as no surprise. What is remarkable is that New York's tenants held onto, and indeed institutionalized, as many rights as they did.

2

"The Right to Lease and Occupy a Home"

Equality and Public Provision in Housing Development

The rent-control statutes that tenants defended so tenaciously served to moderate prices that would otherwise be set higher by the law of supply and demand. But many tenants and housers understood rent control as a superficial fix. The underlying problem was scarcity of housing and a consequent landlord's market. Therefore from the Depression onward, city tenants and their allies also promoted programs to build new rental units and improve old ones.

These efforts extended "New York exceptionalism" in two important ways. One was expansion of public housing. As with rent control, so with public developments: Postwar politics set the stage for moderate forces to overtake radical impulses. Nonetheless, the city and state carried out substantial public construction during these years and thus augmented the unusual government support enjoyed by tenants in New York.

The second way in which development activists built on New York's distinctive political culture was by opening a new arena for the black struggle. Blacks faced many forms of discrimination in New York, but the city still counted as an "open town," a place where the color line was somewhat porous, and where "race men" and women, joined by white allies, challenged inequity. At a crucial moment in the mid-1940s when developers were gearing up for the postwar boom, New York's liberal and left organizations mounted a sustained attack on segregation. This campaign, which won landmark fair-housing legislation, drew power from the city's high rate of tenancy. Not only did a network of tenant organizations and housers lead the charge; on a grassroots level, rentership freed white residents from the equity-building concerns that drove segregationist passions elsewhere and thus created a mentality conducive to political support for fair-housing policy. Hence one New York peculiarity, overwhelming tenancy, contributed to another, racial liberalism. In the short term, however, the gains of the civil-rights housing struggle of the late forties and early fifties were more symbolic than practical.

Crossroads in Public Housing

Subsidized housing, like rent control, was a social-democratic policy in which New York became a postwar leader through the efforts of its liberal-left coalition. Public housing—that is, housing built and owned by the government— was pioneered by the New York City Housing Authority (NYCHA) in the thirties. It formed a milestone in state provision. But it raised thorny questions: Which people would live in the projects? How would managers supervise them? And what was the projects' ultimate purpose—to spare a lucky few from the harsh market, or to change substantially the market and the built environment? The advent of public housing posed an array of possible relationships among tenants, government, and private industry. Which possibilities would be realized was largely determined by a series of conflicts in the late 1940s.

NYCHA followed up on the success of First Houses with the Harlem River Houses, a development of 574 units designated for African Americans and completed in 1937. Like its predecessor, it was built by public-works laborers under the New Deal.[1] Larger projects soon went up in Lower Manhattan, Brooklyn, and Queens. Some were financed by the city and state; others received federal money, at first via public-works loans and later from a mortgage and subsidy program written by New York Senator Robert Wagner and enacted in 1937 after heavy lobbying by fellow housers from the city.[2] Built better than tenements, renting below market rates, NYCHA projects offered a significant improvement in housing for New York's poor.

Moderate-income tenants enjoyed a different type of subsidy through the state limited-dividend program enacted in 1926. This system of tax abatements spawned several privately owned, modestly priced developments in its first years, and was kept alive during the Depression with federal loans. Washington dollars flowing through Albany's limited-dividend board, for example, financed the completion of Knickerbocker Village on the Lower East Side in 1933. The garden apartment complex filled immediately with lower-middle-class tenants (later to include Ethel and Julius Rosenberg, who lived there from 1942 until their arrest in 1950).[3]

Public-housing proponents took hope from these early achievements but did not always agree about where they should lead. Leftists, social democrats, and liberals who favored strong state intervention saw the 1930s projects as a good start on an extensive public building program to remedy the nation's vast housing shortage. Still other liberals maintained faith in private enterprise and believed government's role should be merely adjunctive. And some housers, following in the moral-uplift tradition of model tenement and settlement-house reform, believed the projects must provide poor tenants not simply with housing, but with supervision by middle-class exemplars.[4]

The Housing Authority's first vice chairman, Mary Simkhovitch, was a settlement-house social worker, and the movement's supervisory principles could be seen in action as NYCHA selected tenants for First Houses. Nine thousand had applied for 120 units. Preference went to families with bank accounts and insurance policies—signs of thrift and stability.[5] Another noteworthy statistic in First Houses' tenant profile is that for "political clubs." It is zero. This suggests that managers deliberately barred applicants with political interests (or that savvy applicants kept mum). The Authority preferred benevolent and fraternal society members, who made up nearly half the chosen families.[6] Managers were directed to visit tenants in their homes—in part to collect rent, but also to keep an eye on the way tenants lived.[7]

But tenants developed different agendas and pushed them with a confidence emblematic of the times. The Depression had rendered so many families destitute that those who *could* pay rent were placed, paradoxically, in an advantageous position vis-à-vis conventional landlords, limited-dividend owners, and public-housing managers, all of whom needed rent revenue. This leverage emboldened both public and limited-dividend tenants to challenge managerial authority. On move-in day in 1934, Knickerbocker Village residents organized a rent strike to protest faulty construction. They won reimbursements, formed a lasting tenant association, and two years later joined forces with the militant City-Wide Tenants Council to demand collective bargaining over rent. The City-Wide also confronted public-housing officials. It demanded publication of NYCHA's selection system and criticized the preference for steady earners. It called for flexible payment schedules to accommodate tenants' financial exigencies. These protests yielded modest results—the Housing Authority made selection more transparent and ended some surveillance practices[8]—but they were significant for expressing a broad vision of the New Deal as a reordering of power and responsibility among poor people, government, and capital. Recipients of state benefits were full citizens who need not stand hat in hand. A federal housing administrator recalled that in the late thirties, "'Project people' was a term of pride."[9]

But the political and economic contexts that fostered tenants' assertiveness did not last. The United States' entry into World War II brought not only a turnabout in left politics, as support for the war displaced class agitation as the top priority, but also a federal budget regeared toward military spending and a suddenly taut housing market. Amid these pressures, New York's public tenant leaders lowered their sights. In 1942 they reconstituted the remnants of the City-Wide as a public-housing tenants' alliance, the United Tenants League (UTL). But the UTL focused on defending project residents whose incomes the war economy had lifted above official ceilings. Demands for democracy and a massive expansion of projects were set aside.[10]

As tenants and moderate housers clashed over the projects' social mission, architects engaged in a related debate that would stamp project construction for decades. First Houses' design was unique: Rather than raze the entire block, planners had elected to knock down every third building and renovate the remainder to admit light and air.[11] This was in part a bureaucratic dodge around Public Works Administration rules that allocated funds to rehabilitate, not build, housing.[12] But it also reflected an ethos of conservationism and visual engagement with the project's environs, a blue-collar district of attached medium-rise (four-to-six-story) structures. Both First and Harlem River Houses (the latter styled after the 1920s garden apartment) became "showpieces" for progressives.[13]

Then a minor coup within NYCHA handed control to architectural modernists. This school shared the progressives' concern with tenants' well-being but embraced a different prescription: fierce *dis*engagement from the environs—the presumptive reservoirs of social pathology. Modernist influence could be seen in the 1938 project in Williamsburg, Brooklyn, where detached buildings were set off at angles from the surrounding streets to emphasize the separation of project people from their neighbors. That separation would become vertical in the postwar years as detached geometric high-rises—"towers in the park"—came into favor.[14] Conceived as a buffer between the solid citizens within and the slums without, such architectural delineation would also neatly symbolize the stigmatization of project dwellers in a later era.

More than aesthetics were at stake: project planning was tangled with questions of pricing and politics, and some of the sharpest debate emerged not between supporters and critics of public housing, but among supporters with differing strategies. Modernist high-rises and mammoth developments offered economy of scale, something several public-housing proponents considered necessary for maintaining federal support. Indeed, as Washington pushed New York to cut costs, NYCHA's second director embraced design frugality with zeal. Tenants as a class arguably broke even here: more were housed in lesser quarters, where elimination of "luxuries" like closet doors made tidy living difficult.[15] Administrators could economize further by building on vacant land rather than condemning profitable tenements (and displacing their residents). But no sooner was land cost lopped off in this manner than two more hydra heads sprang up: If tenement districts were not razed, was the Housing Authority abandoning "slum clearance"? And did increasing the total supply of housing, rather than simply replacing bad housing, constitute a dangerous step toward state competition with the private market?[16] The cacophony on these issues and the muting of tenant voices allowed NYCHA leaders to exercise significant independence from federal dictates and to establish a business-like practice of public-housing administration in New York: condemnation of tenements, displacement of their residents, and ever-higher towers and larger "superblocks" in the new projects.[17]

As the war wound down, public-housing supporters saw a second chance to pursue the more expansive agenda of the thirties. Constant media attention to the looming shortage, particularly as it affected veterans, heightened many people's sense that far-reaching government intervention was both socially necessary and politically feasible. Indeed, the war itself—with its conscription, arms production, rationing, and rent control—had set new precedents for state involvement in citizens' daily lives. Charles Abrams, speaking for the Citizens' Housing and Planning Council, urged NYCHA to envision "a complete rehousing program for every low-income family in the City not provided for by private enterprise."[18] Roosevelt's 1944 State of the Union Address called for an "economic bill of rights" including "the right of every family to a decent home."[19] At both local and national levels, the AFL and CIO put their voting and lobbying strength behind public-housing and other social legislation.[20]

But such initiatives faced hard going in Washington. Even during the Progressive and Depression eras, realtors and other free-market believers had demonized public housing as an inherently un-American concept born of European socialism.[21] Now the rising ideology of the Consumers' Republic cast an even darker shadow over that program, much as it had done with rent control.

The Senate's postwar planning committee drafted a bill, the Wagner-Ellender-Taft Bill, to create a major federal public-housing program. It met with such vociferous opposition from industry that it was defeated for four legislative seasons.[22] Even in New York, a proposal for 50,000 units of low-rent housing, put forward by former federal housing administrator Nathan Straus (of the Macy's Straus family) and a coalition of civic and veterans' organizations, was denounced by the American Legion as "a Communist front."[23]

The immediate postwar years also heightened conflicts over the class character of existing public housing. NYCHA's preference for "the cream of the poor" had long been a sore point with the left, but now the converse problem arose: As the economy picked up, some project residents began to earn more than the poverty wages that had made them eligible in the first place. During the war, the UTL had defended these so-called "excess tenants" by arguing that their eviction would drive workers away from defense production. But in 1947, with the waiting list swelling to 200,000, NYCHA officials announced that thousands of excess tenants would have to go.[24] Tenant councils protested that the answer to waiting lists was more public housing.[25] This argument spoke to the immediate interest of council members, of course, but it also expressed the idea that public housing might constitute something more than a grudging short-term provision. In the end, evictions went forward. Limited-dividend tenants met with their own defeat when the state approved a 12 percent rent hike.[26]

In short, the forces that blocked federal public housing caused New York City to proceed cautiously—but not to abandon its mission. NYCHA's budget rules, architectural dictates, and excess-income evictions reflected administrators' belief that public housing was politically vulnerable and must be kept spare. New developments conformed to modernist principles, using cross-shaped towers or rectangular slabs situated far back from the neighboring streets.[27] Yet the program's utopian impulse survived through the late forties in NYCHA's attention to landscaping and play areas, and in the array of daycare, interfaith, and interracial educational programs that administrators and civic activists launched in the projects.[28]

Equally important, in public housing as in rent control, the trimming of ideological sails brought stability on the choppy waters of postwar politics. Gotham's public stock grew in size even if it shrank in quality after the war. Urged on by drastic shortage and the local left-liberal political base, New York City and State built twenty-two projects in the half-decade after the war. Advocates such as the CHPC and the Community Service Society (an old-line charitable alliance) joined tenants and labor leaders in supporting state funding for these low-rent developments.[29] New York's political will contrasted sharply with the partisanship and ideological opposition to social provision that made federal public housing a dead letter during these years.

That such resolve required careful maintenance can be seen in the contrasting saga of Los Angeles' public housing in the 1940s. L.A.'s and New York's paths ran parallel at first. In both cities a Popular Front coalition of left, labor, race, and liberal civic groups supported public housing as a social good and won favorable municipal legislation; in both, an alliance of real estate, banking, and anti-Communist interests decried the projects as socialistic; and in both, city agencies held critics at bay and built developments during the early forties. But while New York more or less stayed the course, Los Angeles made a U-turn. Fierce red-baiting drove L.A.'s liberal housing officials from office and caused erstwhile supporters on the City Council to switch sides. Public housing became the central issue in a 1953 mayoral race brimming with McCarthyite rhetoric. The victorious conservative canceled contracts for further public construction.[30] New York, meanwhile, continued to add to its public stock through the fifties and sixties.[31]

This divergence owed partly to longstanding differences in the cities' political landscapes. Organized labor in L.A. was crushed after the 1910 bombing of the *Los Angeles Times* building, while the anti-union newspaper itself rose from its ashes and remained an influential conservative voice. Tenants, for their part, did form a majority of households in Los Angeles in 1940; but their share of the total—59.5 percent—trailed behind New York tenants' by 25 points. Thus, while Los Angeles' public-housing coalition resembled New York's, its members started from a weaker position. Labor and tenant weakness was property owners' strength, as would be evident in the electoral slugfests of the fifties.

Still, Los Angeles historian Don Parson shows that the disadvantaged housers accomplished much in a few years. Further explanation for the cities' dissimilar long-term trajectories lies in the differing locations of public housing on their political maps. Parson cites the postwar left-liberal split that cracked apart the Popular Front coalition as the death knell for public housing in L.A.[32] That split occurred in New York, too, but here public housing did not land squarely on the left side of the chasm, notwithstanding its popularity with the city's left parties. In New York, liberalism had a wider span. And NYCHA's settlement roots and paternalist (or maternalist) tendencies, which so angered left-wing tenant advocates, draped the agency in a cloak of bourgeois respectability that would serve as armor against efforts to cast the whole enterprise as a Communist plot. NYCHA gained further protection from anti-Communists when it was added to the dominion of one of New York's most powerful red-baiters, city planner Robert Moses, discussed below.[33] By contrast, leading figures in Los Angeles' housing authority came from solidly left backgrounds and took pride in supporting tenant democracy.[34] That likely increased their vulnerability to McCarthyite attacks. Even design appears to have meant different things on different coasts. The very qualities that Parson identifies as leftist in L.A.'s projects—"large-scale rationalism, functionalism and 'creative destruction'" in the service of community and class equality—were matters of dispute among egalitarian housers in New York. Architectural historian Richard Plunz casts NYCHA's initial garden-apartment aesthetic as more genuinely progressive and engaged with existing working-class communities.[35]

Within its centrist guardrails, New York's low-rent public-housing stock grew to provide standard and affordable shelter for more 112,00 people by 1950.[36] (Today that figure has nearly quadrupled, cementing NYCHA's place as the largest public-housing system in the United States.)[37] In making city life materially bearable for so many, public housing represented a major achievement for New York's postwar tenants. There is no avoiding the irony that that victory was secured partly by tenant defeats on the fronts of design and democratic governance. Indeed, historian Nicholas Dagen Bloom argues that it was precisely NYCHA's diligent, top-down, middle-class-inflected management that made its projects eventually stand out from the dysfunctional national crowd as "public housing that worked."[38] Yet while administrators and managers are the heroes of Bloom's tale, their success is also evidence that New York's tenant–houser coalition flexed muscle enough to make quality public housing something that local politicians and bureaucrats cared to maintain. A similar combination of local interests and paradoxical outcome would characterize the unfolding story of federal housing policy.

The Seeds of "Negro Removal"

The Wagner-Ellender-Taft bill for federal housing died in the House in 1946, but it was resuscitated in the next session. It became the subject of intense public debate and congressional wrangling for three years, ultimately metamorphosing into the Housing Act of 1949, an omnibus law that arguably did more than any other piece of legislation to shape American life in the mid- to late twentieth century. Public housing was only part of the final statute. Of

greater consequence for American cities was the federal subsidy for redevelopment of blighted urban neighborhoods, a policy that came to be known as
"urban renewal." This program affected cities across the country, but it hit fast-
est and hardest in New York, where it demonstrated how adroitly a left-liberal
policy like slum clearance could be deployed for relatively conservative ends.
Under New York's urban-renewal program, federal money and local officials
dramatically redrew the city's map, razing and rebuilding neighborhoods, uprooting hundreds of thousands of people, intensifying racial segregation, and
galvanizing the tenant movement in the process.

The original bill was the offspring of strange bedfellows on the Senate housing subcommittee: Robert Wagner, the New York Democrat, houser, and labor
champion; Allen Ellender, a racially conservative New Dealer who had succeeded Huey Long in Louisiana; and Robert Taft, an Ohio Republican, business exponent, and longtime critic of the New Deal, who was now eyeing the
White House and needed some centrist appeal.[39] Wagner's lineage was clear in
the bill's public-housing allocation of $4 billion—far more than Congress had
directed to municipal-housing authorities under the 1937 law (which Wagner
had also sponsored).[40] President Truman, fellow New Dealers, liberal civic
groups, urban politicians, and organized labor strongly favored such a program
as a way not only to clear slums and house the poor, but also to create jobs to
offset a feared postwar depression.[41]

Taft's bloodline showed in the large concessions to real estate and finance
interests. Those sectors could rest assured of the "national policy to maintain
the predominance of private enterprise," the senators declared.[42] The committee put its program where its Cold War rhetoric was by yoking the public-
housing provision to a major expansion of the Federal Housing Administration
(FHA), the New Deal agency that insured private home mortgages. Federally
backed private construction would soon dwarf public housing and make the
United States a nation of home owners. Lizabeth Cohen portrays the FHA
program as a Consumers' Republican coup designed to "turn . . . a dire social
need for shelter into an economic boon" for private enterprise.[43] Under the
free market banner, the FHA would shield lenders from risk and guarantee
them profits. The agency also adopted the Home Owners Loan Corporation's
redlining rules, thus dealing people of color out of the suburban boom, even
as it helped working and middle-class whites to buy homes and build equity.[44]

The Wagner-Ellender-Taft bill (known as the WET and later the TEW bill)
well illustrates the ways in which New Deal liberalism had been recast over
a decade of political maneuvering. In response to the crises posed by the

"Roosevelt recession" of 1937 and the wartime imperative of defense production, liberal policy makers had shifted gradually—sometimes unwittingly— rightward in their economic thinking. In place of the "reform liberalism" of 1933, which envisioned active state planning and a restructuring of American capitalism, postwar politicians and advocates now served up a "compensatory liberalism" of Keynesian spending that accommodated the existing corporate landscape.[45] Accordingly, although the WET bill did contemplate an unprecedented government expenditure on housing, it would keep public housing marginal to the private market, where profit-making institutions were now to receive enormous state subsidies.

The breach between early and late New Deal visions was nowhere so critical as in the bill's provision for slum clearance, or "urban renewal," as it would be rebranded in the 1950s.[46] Prior to World War II, endorsements of slum clearance had been paired with calls for public housing. Housing advocates from the CP to the CIO to the CHPC presented these policies as twin planks: razed slums would be rebuilt with decent housing for the poor. NYCHA chairman Langdon Post—papering over the details of his agency's actual practice in tenant selection—had reinforced that assumption when he described First Houses as "the answer in brick and mortar to the question, is it possible to clear slums and rehouse the people who live there?"[47] New York's Depression-era coalition of tenant, labor, and other left and liberal organizations expressed faith in this pairing when they supported a 1938 state measure to eradicate blighted areas and build low-rent housing.[48] The idea that government would replace slums with better-quality, equally affordable housing was also plausible to black advocates. "[T]he Harlem community and political leaders all supported a greater government role in housing," writes historian Martha Biondi. "After all, the private sector was not building any housing for the poor or working class."[49]

But it was to that very private sector that the WET would now hand control of a large share of urban redevelopment. "To encourage private enterprise to participate more extensively in the . . . redevelopment of slum or other areas," the bill authorized federal funds for the purchase of land parcels to be turned over to private investors.[50] This provision was quite separate from the public-housing section and set few parameters on what the private developers could build; its implicit goal was "redevelopment of city slum areas for middle and upper income groups."[51] The poor would be pushed out so the more prosperous could move in.

For all the bill's outright largesse to private enterprise, it still sparked vocal opposition from conservatives. Realtors called it "the spearhead of the Communist front."[52] National veterans' groups opposed it despite the preferences it would grant servicemen. (New York veterans supported the bill.)[53] The burgeoning of conservatism in the late 1940s effectively moved the political goalposts, redefining a pro-business measure as left-wing. Early in 1946, the WET passed in the Senate, where some twenty Republicans followed Taft's example of bipartisanship.[54] But that fall, Republicans captured both houses, setting the stage for Joseph McCarthy and allies to keep subsequent versions bottled up in committee.[55]

By the time Democrats regained control of Congress in 1948, the TEW bill's public-housing provision had been pared down to 810,000 units over six years. (It would be minced to 35,000 per year under the Truman and Eisenhower administrations.)[56] Meanwhile, the slum-clearance section, Title I, retained its mission of "providing maximum opportunity for the redevelopment of project areas by private enterprise."[57] Government would condemn slum areas, pay for the land and its improvements, then sell it to developers at the estimated value of the undeveloped land alone. Truman promoted the Housing Act as part of his 1949 Fair Deal program; it became the only major part of that program to pass.[58]

That it did owed to the pork it dished out, but also to the plasticity of "slum clearance" as a concept. Historian Samuel Zipp has identified an "ethic of city rebuilding" shared by several stripes of urban advocate—from tenement reformers to public-housing proponents to modernist architects to ambitious private developers—starting in the early twentieth century. All wanted to modernize a nineteenth-century-built environment they believed harmful to its denizens. All understood "slum clearance" as modernization. To the attraction these ideals had held through the Depression and war years was now added a Cold War bonus: City rebuilding would demonstrate American progress and show up the Soviets. Absent public scrutiny of the details of implementation, this ethic rallied a good deal of support for the Housing Act.[59]

Amid the sausage making, liberal housers had inserted a requirement that a "local public agency" direct each city's Title I projects; this, they thought, would make slum clearance responsive to the citizenry.[60] But in practice the provision could work quite differently, handing well-positioned local players an unprecedented federal juggernaut with which to pursue their own ends. And the groundwork for that scenario was being laid in New York City during the very years when the federal Housing Act was taking shape. The man laying it was Robert Moses.

Rehearsal for Urban Renewal

Moses was a household name in New York well before World War II. He was the city's foremost public-works planner, a brilliant and polymathic law drafter, self-taught engineer, cultivated appreciator of arts, and pragmatic political operator. He had created New York's State and City Parks Departments from scratch; rewritten the civil-service code; and conceived and directed highway projects that changed the face of the region. But with his stunning intellect came an imperious temperament. By the mid-1930s he headed up no fewer than seven city and state agencies, including the wealthy Triborough Bridge Authority. This concentration of institutional power gave Moses remarkable freedom to pursue his own visions of public works without being accountable to the public. Reformers who discovered the planner's increasingly dishonest modus operandi found it nigh impossible to blow the whistle on a man who directed several agencies responsible for checking and balancing one another, who bullied and blackmailed mayors with ease, and whom the *New York Times* considered beyond reproach.

When Moses began to interest himself in the new public-works domain of housing in the late 1930s, an ill wind blew for New York's most vulnerable tenants. The man who would play a central role in orchestrating slum clearance and housing development was disdainful of working people, contemptuous toward blacks, and prone to red-baiting critics.[61] As postwar tenant leader Jane Benedict summed up Moses' dual legacy as planning wizard and political knave, "*Now* he's a saint. I assure you he was a son of a bitch when I knew him."[62]

But in his urban sensibility Moses was also a son of the patrician elite. He admired Baron Georges-Eugène Haussmann, the nineteenth-century planner who had remade medieval Paris into a dazzling confection of boulevards, opulent architecture, and shopping.[63] And he was strongly influenced by the Regional Plan Association (RPA) in New York. This alliance of bankers, railroad magnates, and real estate developers had obtained funding from major landholders—the Rockefellers, the Pratts—to create a regional master plan.[64] The city portion of the plan, completed in 1929, was drawn around goals of single-use zoning and class segregation. It bespoke an aesthetic of urban space 180 degrees opposite the mixed-use mosaic that characterized many of New York's neighborhoods. The preliminary survey took note of a cityscape in which "some of the poorest people live [near] patrician Fifth Avenue," and 400,000 factory workers toiled "in the very heart of this 'commercial' city. . . . Such a situation," the surveyor continued, "outrages one's sense of order. Everything seems misplaced. One yearns to rearrange things to put things where they belong."[65]

Robert Moses relished putting things and people in their place, and his embrace of the RPA vision would inform the way he did so as a public official. That way has become a matter of some debate. Contemporary urban scholars take issue with the megalomaniacal portrayal of Moses popularized by Robert Caro's 1974 biography, a portrayal that accords with Jane Benedict's memory. Caro's critics advance two claims: First, that Moses, far from being a uniquely malevolent and omnipotent figure, represented a widely shared liberal vision of the urban public good and achieved as much as he did precisely because his views enjoyed consensus. He "simply was swimming with the tide of history," writes Kenneth Jackson.[66]

It is certainly true that Moses had like-minded allies, as the RPA plan and the larger "ethic of city rebuilding" show. It is also true that zoning the lower half of Manhattan to favor high-yielding retail and financial concerns would merely accelerate already-operating dynamics of the commercial rental market—an unregulated sector—and hence that the RPA plan aligned with the logic of capital as much as with the fastidiousness of the planning gentry.[67] It is equally true, however, that Moses was an excellent swimmer, both literally (he competed in crawl for Yale) and figuratively. He could have fought the tide had he so desired.

But the argument over Moses' agency is driven largely by an underlying debate over the nature of his accomplishments: Were they good or bad for New York? The answer depends, of course, on who counts as "New York," and when. Midcentury working-class tenants, of central concern here, lost homes and neighborly ties by the hundreds of thousands on Moses' watch. Their loss was others' gain in middle-class housing, highways, and cultural icons, and the second thesis of the new Moses scholarship is that those gains were worth the price in the long term.[68] Such an interpretation—made more palatable, no doubt, by the passing of the generation that paid—skirts the question whether similar gains could have been realized at a more humane cost.

That question complicates the felicitous calculus, because from the start there were voices answering yes. Liberal consensus supported the general policy of state-assisted urban redevelopment more than the particular methods employed on New York's Title I projects. More than a few midcentury liberals opposed Moses' demolition schemes, only to be sidelined by more powerful liberals (not to mention conservatives). Rather than consensus, New York's slum-clearance projects would reveal the contradictions within postwar liberalism and the persistence of older liberal sensibilities in some quarters. The "tide of history" contained eddies and crosscurrents. Tenants were a principal force troubling the waters.

Moses' first attempts to commandeer funds under the 1937 U.S. Housing Act and the 1938 state slum-clearance amendment were thwarted by Mayor La Guardia, whose cunning matched Moses' and who took a strong personal interest in housing. But after the war began, the mayor, taken with Moses' pragmatic abilities, appointed him head of the City Planning Commission. From this position Moses and his minions assumed control of the design and siting of future city and state construction (while leaving the administration of public housing to NYCHA).[69] In 1946, scenting even bigger federal monies in the air, Moses prevailed upon La Guardia's successor, William O'Dwyer, to designate him "coordinator" of construction agreements between City Hall and state and federal agencies."[70] This would make Moses the gatekeeper of the postwar city's largest source of housing dollars: Title I.

During the mid- to late 1940s, as the WET bill floundered around Congress, Moses staged a dress rehearsal for Title I productions via a state-subsidized development called Stuyvesant Town. This project was sown on legal ground that had been spaded by the 1926 limited-dividend law and the 1938 slum-clearance amendment. But its seed was created in the early forties, in a deal struck between Moses and Frederick Ecker, chairman of the Metropolitan Life Insurance Company. Ecker wanted a new field of investment that could be squared with his corporation's business mission of promoting health—a goal nicely compatible with Moses' desire to draw private money into large-scale modernist housing redevelopment. Ecker, however, balked at the restrictions on public subsidy and developer sovereignty that existing state laws would impose. He and Moses hammered out terms they preferred, then teamed up with La Guardia's men to make them legal. They drafted a new law that would free state-subsidized limited-dividend developers from pesky rules on taxes, tenant selection, and provision of low-rent units.[71] Moses promoted this measure, the Hampton-Mitchell bill, as a forward-looking way to improve city housing.[72]

Sharp-eyed housers tried to sound the alarm and in so doing revealed the fissures that ran beneath the city rebuilding constituency's smooth surface: "[T]here is no provision for rehousing the tenants displaced from the slum buildings to be torn down," Charles Abrams wrote Governor Dewey. "[P]oor families will be driven from one slum to another, their rents spurting, while slum values skyrocket."[73] Similar objections were raised by the Women's City Club and the League of Women Voters.[74] These liberal groups still hewed to the Progressive mandate to protect the poor and the vulnerable. But Moses, using the brinksmanship that would become his favorite tactic, persuaded officials that slums would be cleared on Ecker's terms or not at all. Surrender to the "demagogues" and "radical housing boys" obsessed with "social objectives" would spell the end of modernization.[75] In April 1943 Dewey signed the Hampton-Mitchell bill.[76]

Two weeks later, La Guardia announced Stuyvesant Town, a complex of high towers comprising more than eight thousand middle-income units, to be built by Metropolitan Life on a "superblock" that would swallow eighteen former city blocks along the lower East River. Walled off from local streets, the project would be a "suburb in a city."[77] Among its suburban attributes would be a whites-only policy, which Ecker decreed in keeping with the conventional wisdom that blacks depressed property values, and which was now legal thanks to the Hampton-Mitchell law.[78] To make room for this middle-class enclave, the city would use its police power to buy and raze an historically working-class district inhabited by eleven thousand people.

Stuyvesant Town marked a turning point in housing history. As Biondi observes, it was "the first major publicly subsidized privately owned urban redevelopment housing project in the United States." As such it constituted "an unprecedented transfer of state resources to a private entity with few strings attached."[79] The tax exemption alone was worth $50 million.[80] The city also paid to clear the site and then simply gave it, and its throughstreets, to Metropolitan Life.

Stuyvesant Town provoked three types of objection. The first, voiced by site tenants facing eviction, was wholesale condemnation of the project. Most residents of what was known as the Gas House District wanted to stay put. Odors from gas tanks and inconveniences from outdated housing were outweighed, for them, by modest rents and social ties. "My husband died here and I want to die here," Mrs. Concetta Torabene told a reporter through tears. Miss Mary Kenney also expressed her grief in terms of kinship, referring to the children of the Italians in the neighboring apartment "as her own children." Men were "bitter about the prospect of losing small business shops" that they or their fathers had established.[81] Even residents who were dissatisfied with their current quarters said they "would accept inferior accommodations to remain in the district."[82]

But this notion never made it off the political starting block. The entire tenant infrastructure was already committed to slum clearance and unprepared to reckon with a challenge to that policy's first principle—"clearance"—put forward by tenants themselves. (Indeed, a few years earlier, the East Side Tenants Union had done its best to shush several hundred resentful families who were evicted to make way for a downtown NYCHA project.)[83]

The United Tenants League and the local assembly member did take up the second grievance, against the decoupling of slum clearance from provision of low-rent housing. But to no avail. La Guardia's early promise that the displaced would "be accommodated . . . in one of the city's low-cost [public] housing developments" evaporated under heat from Moses, who was determined that slum clearance not be hampered by such considerations.[84] The insurance company opened a "relocation bureau" to guide ousted families to private housing, but most of the apartments it listed were far away, unheated, or both.[85] Weeks after V-J Day, the last site residents were pushed into a gaping ravine in municipal housing policy. Seventy-five percent did not qualify for public housing (for which there was, in any case, a long waiting list). Yet most could not afford better quarters on the private market. So, as Abrams had prophesied, they moved into tenements on the East Side and elsewhere.[86] Rather than upgrade slum dwellers' housing, "slum clearance" had simply pushed them from one slum to the next.

The impotence of site tenants and their allies is unsurprising. They faced a new threat for which they had no programmatic rebuttal and little time to formulate one, at a moment when commitment to wartime unity made left organizations reluctant to hold La Guardia's feet to the fire. In any event, tenant slingshots would have been no match for the developers' publicity machine. La Guardia used his weekly radio broadcast to extol Stuyvesant Town; Metropolitan Life churned out glossy promotional materials that enthralled reporters and virtually ghostwrote their copy. As well, the Gas House district—unlike many areas that would soon be condemned under Title I—*was* in decline: Old-law tenements predominated, and half the population had been siphoned away in recent decades by newer housing in other neighborhoods. The HOLC had effectively barred new private investment by coding the area a D—very poor—lending risk.[87] Such data bolstered Moses' case for culling the district from the modernizing city. With these advantages and La Guardia's reluctant nod, Moses and Ecker successfully harnessed the power of Keynesian liberal discourse to the RPA vision: the erasure of blue-collar Manhattan.[88]

Tenant Rights as Civil Rights

Unlike site tenants, civil-rights advocates *had* been rallying troops and stockpiling arguments in the years before Stuyvesant Town was announced. Their struggle against the project's segregation policy grew into a vigorous and protracted fight. And that fight, along with local campaigns for fair employment and policing, made New York an epicenter of the larger African American civil-rights movement that was gaining steam after World War II.[89]

Skirmishes began immediately, when Abrams' planning group, the CHPC, presented a detailed critique of Stuyvesant Town's whites-only policy to the City Planning Commission. A dozen housing, labor, civic, and race organizations—from the UTL to the CIO to the NAACP—then urged the City Council and its upper legislative chamber, the Board of Estimate, to vote down "a company-owned walled town" from which "the owners would be free to exclude tenants . . . because of race, creed or color."[90] But Robert Moses commanded majorities in both chambers and won swift approval for the project. Next came a round of lawsuits brought by a Popular Front chorus of labor and tenant groups, the Anti-Nazi League, the CHPC, and the ACLU (American Civil Liberties Union).[91] The court ruled that Metropolitan Life could not be tried for its intention to discriminate before the project was built.[92] Civil-rights advocates made more headway in the City Council, where Stanley Isaacs, a liberal Republican and settlement-house leader, and Benjamin Davis, the black Communist, sponsored a bill barring tax exemptions for segregated developments. The law passed, but only after it was amended to exclude Stuyvesant Town.[93]

The major courtroom drama was thus deferred until the eve of occupancy in the summer of 1947. That was when three African American war veterans filed suit against Metropolitan Life and the city for violating their constitutional right to equal protection of the laws. Lead plaintiff Joseph Dorsey was an army captain and social worker who "exemplified the young, ambitious, returning African American soldiers whose refusal to accept second class status launched the civil rights movement."[94] He was represented jointly by the NAACP, the ACLU, and the American Jewish Congress (AJC).[95] These organizations played no part in grassroots tenant mobilization, but they figured centrally in the professional alliance for civil rights that was gaining traction in the 1940s as the nation's liberal establishment took up the cause of minority rights in lieu of broader economic restructuring.[96] Charles Abrams proposed the joint suit and would argue the case alongside the AJC's Will Maslow.[97]

The Dorsey team's hopes rested on a constitutional guaranty that had lain moribund for half a century, but that civil-rights advocates had recently started to revive. Equal-protection challenges to Jim Crow had been quashed in 1896 by the *Plessy v. Ferguson* decision upholding "separate but equal" treatment. In the 1930s and 1940s, however, NAACP attorneys brought a series of strategically chosen suits that nudged the Supreme Court down a path of change.[98] Dorsey sought to widen that path. Since the equal-protection clauses of both state and federal constitutions applied to government, not private, actors, an important part of the plaintiff's task was to argue that the massive state and city subsidies made Stuyvesant Town a public entity, bound by the rule of equality, the Hampton-Mitchell waiver notwithstanding.

The State Supreme Court rejected this reasoning and held that Stuyvesant Town was a private development unfettered by constitutional law.[99] Dorsey appealed. By now his legal roster sparkled with civil-rights luminaries—the NAACP's Thurgood Marshall, the CHPC's Abrams, AJC executive Shad Polier, and two other distinguished AJC lawyers—whose involvement indicates the seriousness with which the liberal legal establishment viewed the case. The legal team lost the state appeal and was denied a federal hearing, but in the process it articulated prescient views of housing and civil rights.

"The United States and New York Constitutions," Dorsey's attorneys declared, "forbid State action which . . . denies equal opportunity to housing on the ground of race."[100] Their brief advanced two far-reaching ideas: first, that "state action" included privately owned concerns like Stuyvesant Town that had received state subsidy; and second, that "equal opportunity to housing" was a protected right like voting and speech. An *amicus* brief submitted by a church group put it boldly: "The right to lease and occupy a home is a civil right."[101]

Equally important, an association of Stuyvesant Town tenants filed its own *amicus* brief for Dorsey. This action grew out of the leftist, grassroots wing of the antidiscrimination movement. Through the late 1940s, both Communist and anti-Stalinist left organizations had highlighted housing discrimination as an injustice that comrades were bound to fight. As it happened, several Communists and fellow travelers had moved into Stuyvesant Town. They provided the main organizing muscle for what grew into a sizable tenant mobilization, the Town and Village Tenants Committee to End Discrimination. Paul Ross, an ALP organizer and former city rent commissioner, represented the group in the Dorsey case.[102]

"Racial . . . segregation in Stuyvesant Town," Ross wrote, "deprives the present and future tenants of Stuyvesant Town of the right to live under conditions of American democracy as defined by State, Federal and local laws."[103] This statement stood at right angles to the increasingly racialized political economy of homeownership. Historians of postwar racial struggles have shown that segregationist white homeowners often rationalized what they called "neighborhood defense" through the seemingly raceless language of property values and rights. That is, whether or not segregation really was economically rational (studies showed that integration did not always lower home prices), many whites articulated their opposition to open housing as a matter of rational economic thinking rather than visceral race prejudice.[104] As one white resident of Pennsylvania's violence-wracked Levittown said of a black neighbor, "He's probably a nice guy, but every time I look at him I see a $2000 drop off the value of my house."[105]

Such self-justifying statements should be read skeptically, of course. But however much or little anti-integrationist feeling was really driven by economic calculi, the economic rationale was significant in that it offered a justification for racial exclusion by appealing to mainstream ideals of equity building and upward mobility for the common man. These were the ideals of the Consumers' Republic; of leading labor unions; of postwar liberalism itself. Indeed, these ideals *and* their racial corollaries were federal policy, through the FHA rules that coded integrated areas as poor lending risks. Consequently, these ideals had a kind of political-cultural standing to counter liberal open-housing arguments in a way that frank white supremacism did not.

Thus when Stuyvesant Town tenants cast the segregation policy as violative of the rights of *white* people, not just as injurious to blacks, they made an adroit move. Defining residential integration as something valuable for whites—one of the "conditions of American democracy"—rather than as a charitable obligation toward minorities, provided a way for integrationists to meet the rational economics argument on its own discursive turf. Against the image of the (implicitly white) common man, striving to enjoy American democracy by building home equity, Dorsey's supporters posed an image of white common men striving to experience American democracy by living in a heterogeneous community.

Did Stuyvesant Town's status as rental housing figure in the unfolding of this unusual housing politics? Studies of homeownership suggest that it did. Cohen identifies a paradox in the class and racial dynamics of the postwar housing market: although the Consumers' Republic promised economic equality, and did bring a new level of material comfort to millions, its housing sector also stratified and separated consumers. Burgeoning suburbs functioned as class and racial sorters, as new developments contained houses of similar plan and price, ensuring income homogeneity within each tract. Moreover, as the logic of property values took hold, not only did residents, realtors, and FHA redliners oppose racial integration of neighborhoods, but entire towns enacted zoning laws to bar developments for lower-income groups. In his analysis of urbanization and capitalism, geographer David Harvey writes that homeownership programs like the FHA's served to moderate working-class politics by "establish[ing] the workers' allegiance to the principle of private property. . . . A worker mortgaged up to the hilt is, for the most part, a pillar of social stability."[106] Cohen extends this line of thinking to show that home-ownership bound suburbanites—working- and middle-class alike—not just to property but to racial homogeneity and class stratification.

But Stuyvesant Town was rental housing, the occupants of which had little stake in its monetary valuation. Thus it carved out a niche within postwar consumer society. Tenants, of course, were still consumers of housing, but the form of their consumption—renting, not owning—placed them in a poten-tially adversarial relationship to landlords, a relationship better understood through the older tenant–union paradigm or the consumer-protection for-mulation of Progressive and New Deal politics. Free from considerations of equity, tenants were more likely than homeowners to follow a different liberal logic, the logic of racial inclusion. Eighteen hundred Stuyvesant Town tenants joined the Committee to End Discrimination. The group's survey found that two-thirds of project residents opposed the segregation policy.[107]

The clash between the two understandings of democratic rights sounded loudly in the 4–3 decision handed down by the appellate court in July 1949. The majority upheld the initial ruling, rejecting flatly Dorsey's claims that Stuyvesant Town was a public entity and housing a civil right. But the dissent-ing opinion by Justice Stanley Fuld denounced racial distinctions as "odious to a free people." (For jurists, this phrase held an ironic double meaning, for it was a quote from a 1941 Supreme Court decision that had, in fact, sanctioned racial discrimination against Japanese Americans.)[108] "The average citizen," continued Fuld, "aware of that truth but unschooled in legal niceties, will, I venture, find the decision which the court now makes extremely perplexing."[109]

Justice Fuld was right. Many New Yorkers were deeply troubled by Stuyvesant Town, and having lost in court they now turned to direct action. Jesse Kessler, a member of the project's antidiscrimination committee and an organizer for the left-wing retail workers' union, invited an African American couple to stay in his apartment while his family left town for the summer. Thus Hardine and Raphael Hendrix became the first black residents of Stuyvesant Town. Hardine was a war veteran, like Joseph Dorsey, and likely had met Kessler through his job at a warehouse.[110] The couple had been subsisting in a Harlem apartment so rat-infested that they sent their young son to stay with relatives.[111] Their circumstances showed why open housing mattered urgently to black New Yorkers. When Kessler returned, the couple moved to the apartment of Lee Lorch, a Stuyvesant Town tenant leader and mathematics professor who had recently been fired from City College on account of his political activism. Lorch invited the Hendrixes for the academic year while he took a teaching post in Pennsylvania and filed suit against City College. Other residents hosted eight more black houseguests for a weekend and stood ready to take in the Hendrixes.[112] A decade before the famous lunch-counter sit-ins in the south, these New Yorkers had orchestrated a similarly deliberate breach of the color line.

Metropolitan Life signaled that it would play hardball when it returned Jesse Kessler's September rent. Lorch, next in line for retaliation, stood firm: "Tenants here . . . will fight Jim Crow no matter what the Metropolitan tries to do."[113] The antidiscrimination committee continued to build tenant support for Lorch, Kessler, and the Hendrixes.[114] In the electoral arena, meanwhile, the ALP's Vito Marcantonio spotlighted Stuyvesant Town in his fall mayoral campaign, offering to drop out if the Tammany incumbent, O'Dwyer, canceled the development's tax exemption.[115] O'Dwyer declined.

Lorch and Ross were the tenant committee's public faces, but women were vital organizers within the project. Women were "crucial both in developing ideas and in implementing them," remembered Lorch. Several served as committee officers. And "[i]t was mostly women who went door-to-door or spoke with tenants on the grounds" about the segregation policy before the committee went public. The women's surveys "provided the knowledge base needed to develop effective strategies." This task took not only time but physical courage, as Stuyvesant Town dispatched security guards to put a stop to the polling. Lorch's wife, Grace, and the other women "resisted successfully the intimidation."[116] Raphael Hendrix, already an experienced organizer for the Domestic Workers Union, also became active on the committee once she moved in.[117] These gender arrangements followed the predominant pattern of the 1930s and 1940s, when women ran local tenant leagues and rent clinics while men headed the more prominent citywide organizations. The pattern would change in the 1950s.

Figure 3. **Leaflet by Town and Village Committee to End Discrimination in Stuyvesant Town.** Rafael Hendrix in center foreground. *Courtesy of Met Council on Housing.*

While residents kept up direct pressure on the company, other activists concentrated on the legislatures. In 1948 a coalition of liberal housing, civil-rights, and labor advocates who had been working on Stuyvesant Town formed the New York State Committee Against Discrimination in Housing (NYSCDH), a lobbying group dedicated to "fair housing practices and equality of housing opportunities, regardless of age, creed, color, national origin, etc."[118] Led by Ethical Culture Society chairman Algernon Black, the NYSCDH organized crucial support for two landmark laws.

The first, the Wicks-Austin bill of 1950, outlawed discrimination in future publicly subsidized housing projects in New York State. This statute would not affect existing developments but was written with an eye toward the Title I funds that would soon be flowing from Washington. NYSCDH members "were concerned with the tremendous potentials for good and ill in the new Housing Act" and hoped state legislation could fashion the federal program into "a tool for the overall democratization of housing."[119] The second law was a city measure sponsored by Stanley Isaacs and freshman councilmember Earl Brown (who in 1949 had ousted Communist Ben Davis with tripartisan backing from the Democratic, Liberal, and Republican organizations). The Brown-Isaacs law did finally outlaw racial discrimination in all tax-subsidized housing, Stuyvesant Town included. Like the Wicks-Austin law, it was the first of its kind in the country. The bill was tabled in 1950 while Mayor O'Dwyer sought "amicable negotiation" with Ecker, but the antidiscrimination coalition pushed it through the next year. Metropolitan Life fought it every step of the way.[120]

Losing in the legislatures, the company struck again on home turf. In 1950 Stuyvesant Town management sent eviction notices to thirty-five tenants who had agitated for change, starting with Ross, Lorch, and Daniel Davis, tenant committee co-chair and a prominent Reform rabbi.[121] Lorch had also just been fired from his second academic job. Pennsylvania State College wrote him that he was being let go because "his action in permitting a Negro family to live as guests in his New York apartment was 'extreme, illegal and immoral and damaging to the public relations of the college.'"[122] Ross observed that several college trustees were insurance agents.[123] Ecker appeared to have a long reach.

Metropolitan Life justified its actions in McCarthyite terms, pointing to the left-wing affiliations of tenant committee leaders like Ross and asserting "that the whole fight was communist-inspired."[124] This tactic, however, was not particularly effective. The civil-rights principals did exclude ALP and CP representatives from their litigation and lobbying coalition, but they embraced the noncommunist left, personified in the Liberal Party, with which both Abrams and Isaacs were affiliated. The far-left parties were, in any case, no asset in court or legislature by this time; their real contribution was direct action within the project. And although Abrams and the other lawyers considered the tenant committee an embarrassment, the two wings avoided an open breach, and liberals did ultimately speak up for the right of leftist tenants to remain in their homes.[125] Democrat Earl Brown picked up Ben Davis' torch on the council. As with public housing, a left-liberal split was present but not wholly determinative.

The Stuyvesant Town movement's practical gains were not only incremental in size and costly in hardship, but glacial in pace. Not until 1952 did the Hendrixes obtain a lease. Very few blacks followed.[126] The Brown-Isaacs law, while important symbolically, lacked an enforcement mechanism.

The company, meanwhile, kept evicting organizers until the NYSCDH and its civic and labor allies brokered a compromise that enabled about half the targeted tenants to remain. CIO representative Moe Iushevitz made the critical move at the bargaining table when he warned the insurance men, "[I]f you evict these people the pictures and the story will be front page news . . . in the far off villages of Russia and Siberia."[127] This use of anti-Communist rhetoric to leverage egalitarian policy concessions came straight from the Cold War civil-rights playbook that A. P. Randolph and Walter White had adopted a few years before.[128] Metropolitan Life agreed to a truce.[129]

But the company still pushed the most defiant residents, Lorch, Kessler, and Ross, to leave at a later date.[130] Lorch and his wife moved south, where he taught at black colleges and both continued to agitate for civil rights—Grace memorably stepping forward to defend high school student Elizabeth Eckford from a white mob during the Little Rock school crisis in 1957. For such transgressions Lee would be red-baited out of two more academic jobs until the family finally moved to Canada.[131]

Stuyvesant Town's significance extended far beyond the eighteen square blocks it covered, the eleven thousand people it displaced, and the potential black tenants it barred. It became a model for both developers and antidiscrimination activists. Within the grassroots tenant movement, the struggle against the insurance giant served as a touchstone of commitment to equality. Frances Goldin recalled a protest "with three thousand people [who] surrounded Stuyvesant Town" as a formative experience that contributed to her later insistence on integration in the Lower East Side's low-income cooperatives.

"Integration [was] as important as affordability."[132] As Goldin's involvement suggests, the struggle also galvanized a beleaguered left. People and groups across the city were drawn into the conflict through strategically placed leaders with dual affiliations. Paul Ross served as chairman of both the ALP—still vital through the late forties—and the New York Tenants' Councils, a successor organization to the left tenant coalition that had rallied for rent control in 1946–47.[133] Similarly, Jesse Kessler helped the project's antidiscrimination committee tap into the might of the retailer workers' union, Local 65, which turned out in force for the Hendrixes and their hosts. These political networks made Stuyvesant Town a familiar topic to far-flung tenants. The Communist Party, well represented both on the committee and in supportive labor unions, played a crucial role.[134]

Among professional reformers, Stuyvesant Town laid the groundwork for a national open-housing drive. It produced both the nation's first fair-housing legislation and the core leaders, such as Algernon Black, who would direct the National Committee Against Discrimination in Housing in future decades.

On the other side of the planning table, however, Stuyvesant Town became a model for urban redevelopment, one that would help make federal slum clearance an urban counterpart to the suburban mechanisms of class and racial segregation established by the FHA. The new state and city antidiscrimination laws would not touch federal agencies' racial practices. And New York's new laws said nothing about other crucial components of the Stuyvesant Town scheme, such as the giving of public money and streets to a private enterprise, the replacement of an entire working-class community with a middle-class citadel, and the eviction of thousands of poor people without provision of affordable alternative housing. Indeed, Stuyvesant Town site residents' failure to mount effective resistance on those fronts meant that opponents of future clearance projects would have to organize from scratch.

The laws were also silent about the power of elite business and political actors to decide upon such projects behind closed doors. And the man who had directed those players at Stuyvesant Town was now poised to bring his act to a much larger stage. In 1948 Robert Moses received a bit of news from an old Yale classmate, Robert Taft. It concerned details of the housing bill under consideration in Congress. Acting on Taft's tip, Moses advised Mayor O'Dwyer to create one more city bureau: the Committee on Slum Clearance, Robert Moses, chair.[135] When the 1949 federal Housing Act was finally signed into law, the "local public agency" it stipulated was already in place in New York.

Cleaning Up Ghetto Housing

Mass evictions fueled by postwar redevelopment projects would ravage racially mixed communities, prompting critics to dub urban renewal "Negro
removal." But most New Yorkers of color were not at risk for removal from
mixed neighborhoods, for the simple reason that they already lived in segregated neighborhoods. African Americans, Chinese Americans, and a growing
population of Puerto Ricans were largely confined to ghettoes like Harlem,
Chinatown, and El Barrio.[136] They were captive tenant markets.

Harlem tenants often paid 10 to 50 percent more for their apartments
than whites did for equivalent quarters elsewhere—a surcharge that was
particularly onerous since blacks were largely restricted to low-paying jobs.[137]
Ongoing migration from the South not only maintained demand for overpriced units but also eroded their quality. As new arrivals packed into old
buildings, landlords "accommodated" them by chopping regular apartments
into tiny sub-units. And these landlords could also get away with minimal
maintenance, because ghetto tenants had nowhere else to go. The Hendrix
family knew this well.

The campaign to ameliorate such conditions, through pressure on owners
and on city agencies responsible for enforcing the housing code, might have
constituted a second major front of assertive civil-rights activity in postwar
New York. It did not. The black tenant organizations rooted in Depression-era
militancy dwindled in the late forties. Ghetto improvement drives were spearheaded instead by social-uplift advocates who held garbage-strewing tenants
as culpable as landlords. These drives stood in contrast to the Stuyvesant Town
struggle, in which a politicized coalition took aim at a clear enemy.

Indeed, an omen of the relative weakness of postwar demands for code
enforcement could be found in the Stuyvesant Town coalition's precursor,
the City-Wide Citizens' Committee on Harlem (CWCCH). This biracial group
was founded in 1941 in response to a spate of sensationalized new stories on
Harlem street crime. African Americans resented such depictions, typically
purveyed by white journalists and officials who ignored what *The Amsterdam
News* called "the monster race prejudice." In the past, noted the Harlem paper, "nothing was done to correct the evils. The question is, 'What is going to
be done now?'"[138] The Citizens' Committee, headed by Ethical Culture leader
Algernon Black and Baptist minister Adam Clayton Powell Sr., resolved to
publicize racial injustices and lobby for reforms.[139]

Housing was high on the agenda. The group appointed a housing subcommittee, chaired by Charles Abrams and including Black, Stanley Isaacs, liberal developer James Felt, and representatives of NYCHA, the Urban League, and Harlem's Consolidated Tenants League.[140] This subcommittee's public housing advocacy yielded the appointment of black union organizer Frank Crosswaith to the Housing Authority board, along with a pledge for two public projects in Harlem.[141] Then it turned its attention to Stuyvesant Town, where it served as an early voice for racial integration, if not for rehousing the poor. (Felt would direct Metropolitan Life's ineffective relocation bureau for site tenants.)

At first the subcommittee members also looked to improve Harlem's existing housing. They learned that this was a herculean task. While Harlem's housing stock was newer than that in other slums, its safety had been severely compromised by "herding," as a committee report put it. "[Subdivided] dwellings . . . teem with . . . hazardous fire violations."[142] Disrepair and vermin were rampant.

The Citizens' Committee, however, did little to follow up on the study. Instead it put all of its limited resources into the mounting legal battles for fair housing. (Committee members Abrams and Black would play central parts in the courtroom and legislative struggles over Stuyvesant Town.) Although this was a rational decision for a shoestring operation, it also heralded a postwar pattern of civil rights politics in which ghetto safety would take second place to desegregation. The Citizens' Committee disbanded in 1947 for lack of funds; the next year, several members regrouped to form the NYSCDH, which led the successful fights for the Wicks-Austin and Brown-Isaacs fair housing laws.[143]

In the absence of sustained political pressure, city code enforcement was fitful at best. Inspectors would descend on a decrepit Harlem block with pens and ticket books in hand, issue a press release, and go back to business as usual. The Housing and Buildings Department's promise of stern action in 1946 gave way to a scandal involving bribes for falsified inspection certificates in 1947, followed by a heartbreaking rash of deadly fires in uptown apartments in 1948.[144] Meanwhile the courts, which many tenants used successfully to prevent wrongful eviction, had little power to ensure proper maintenance. As the Consolidated Tenants League president observed, Harlem landlords "would rather go to court and be fined $10 or $15 than to make repairs which might cost $500."[145] A 1948 Urban League study concluded, "conditions grow worse daily."[146]

With liberal reformers focused on Stuyvesant Town and grassroots mobilization on the wane, the most prominent postwar spokesman for Harlem's betterment was Glester Hinds, a Jamaican immigrant and postal worker who admired Marcus Garvey but believed "every Negro can't be militant."[147] Hinds' signature was the cooperative cleanup drive. These campaigns, sponsored annually by the YMCA and publicized by *The Amsterdam News*, called upon tenants, supers, landlords, officials, and even schoolchildren to work together in ridding Harlem's lots and courtyards of garbage.[148]

Unlike fair-housing demands, cleanup drives were compatible with the Tammany program. Hinds was on cordial terms with Buildings Commissioner Robert Wagner Jr. (the senator's son) and Deputy Commissioner J. Raymond Jones, the O'Dwyer administration's ranking African American. Jones averred a desire to balance his citywide responsibility with "the unofficial ways in which Harlem could be assisted." This boiled down to playground construction, minor adjustments to the inspection bureaucracy, and collaboration with Hinds. Like Hinds, Jones had observed that tenants were prone to throw trash in the wrong places "when they believe they are being taken advantage of by landlords." He saw the inculcation of better tenant habits as a critical answer to Harlem's sanitation problem. Leftists such as Benjamin Davis, Paul Ross, and the United Harlem Tenants and Consumers continued to insist that landlords and the city were ultimately responsible, but they did so from the sidelines.[149]

The civic drives spruced up a block here and there, but their overall effect was negligible. In 1950 the Citizens Housing and Planning Council found 250,000 open code violations on the buildings department's docket.[150] By that time O'Dwyer had won reelection, dismissing criticism of his administration's housing enforcement as a device of "the Commies."[151] (A year later he retired amid rumors of scandals in other agencies.)

Mayoral barbs were the least of leftists' problems. Davis lost his council seat after the major parties and the Catholic Church engineered the repeal of proportional representation in 1947.[152] The next year he and nine others were indicted under the Smith Act, an anti-Communist statute, and ultimately sent to federal prison.[153] The United Harlem Tenants and Consumers was listed as a subversive organization by the attorney general and disbanded.[154] The NAACP took pains to distance itself from the left in order to maintain legitimacy.[155]

Ghetto tenants' failure to win meaningful housing improvements, however, did not result simply from the suppression of the left, or from the competing priorities of the civil-rights establishment. Reforms met resistance in direct proportion to the cost of the remedies they proposed. And bricks, plumbing, and plaster cost much more than ink on a fair-housing bill. Tammany had no interest in forcing its landlord allies to spend money on such improvements and never took serious action against endemic corruption at the buildings department, where machine functionaries feathered their nests with bribes.[156] Absent the political muscle needed to overcome these entrenched interests, the housing studies conducted by the Urban League and the CHPC in the forties and fifties became themselves a weak form of activism, bearing witness to the conditions they could not change.

Public Housing and Race

Tenants of color pinned great hopes on public housing as a potential escape from the vermin and firetraps they faced on the private market. The CWCCH campaign for Harlem projects reflected this optimism, and civil-rights advocates went further by making NYCHA a venue for housing integration. Although New York's earliest projects were segregated, with First and Williamsburg Houses inhabited by whites and Harlem River by blacks, local housers and federal administrator Nathan Straus persuaded the Authority to adopt a policy of integration in 1939.[157] This front-office principle, however, hid some backroom disagreement. Civil-rights groups wanted a color-blind, need-based tenant selection policy, which would have led to a greater black presence in the projects; NYCHA thought it imperative that public tenants reflect the city's white supermajority if public housing were to retain political support. Once again the Authority steered a middle course. Blacks made up 12 percent of NYCHA tenants in the early forties, twice their share in the city census.[158] But NYCHA massaged each project's racial makeup to approximate that of the surrounding area.[159] Over time this mattered less and less, however, as many outer-borough projects were sited on the border between black and white districts and as white demand for public-housing slots declined.

If this system was not quite color-blind, it still stood for integration, no small thing at the time. NYCHA officials took pride in their "formula for removing tensions between Negro and white, and Catholic, Protestant and Jewish tenants." They forged ties with local civic, ethnic, and religious organizations and assigned social workers to the projects' cooperative educational centers, where "people of all kinds mingle in avocation. They repair furniture or shoes, dance and learn together, and talk and live as friends."[160] Such programming drew from New York's leftist and Progressive housing heritage: Both the Bronx labor co-ops and the settlements had long featured cultural clubs. Income homogeneity in the projects—later a point of great contention—may have served as an additional social glue. "When we come home," said one tenant, "we like to be among folks that have about as much as we do."[161]

These successes provided ammunition for liberals hoping to shape national housing policy. In 1950, NYCHA's chairman published a Sunday *Times* piece touting his agency's "progress in the serious problem of getting people of different races to live together in peace, with mutual respect and trust."[162] The next year psychologists at New York University completed a major study comparing relations within New York's integrated projects to those in Newark's segregated public housing. They found that the integrated tenants, regardless of politics, ethnicity, or religion, enjoyed far more social interaction and maintained friendlier views across racial lines than did segregated residents. Rejecting the saw that "stateways cannot change folkways," the authors concluded that under proper management, "as we break down the physical barriers between Negroes and whites in our projects, many of the social barriers will also disappear."[163] One of the salutary conditions cited by the project managers was able leadership by female tenant organizers. "Men may sometimes be the spokesmen" for project tenant associations, said one informant, "but the women run the show."[164]

City officials, however, took a firm line against confrontational blacks, particularly on the left, who claimed a say in policy. Even amid the Depression upheavals, when tenant leagues in New York's predominantly white projects were demanding collective bargaining, NYCHA had held a tight rein on a Harlem River Houses population fearful of being thrown back on the ghetto market.[165] Now the administration put down challenges raised by African Americans whose expectations had been heightened by the war for democracy. In late 1946 Mayor O'Dwyer brushed off a creative proposal from the left-leaning United Negro and Allied Veterans of America to provide relief for returning soldiers by rehabilitating 1,500 boarded-up apartments they had scouted in Harlem.[166] A few months later, NYCHA called the police against black tenants from a public-housing construction site who sat in to protest the Authority's retreat from a promise to billet them in the white neighborhood of Yorkville, after Yorkville landlords complained. Councilmember Davis' advocacy in both cases probably stoked official tempers. (He certainly irritated the mayor with a suggestion that the desperate veterans might "take things into their own hands.")[167] Black NYCHA director Frank Crosswaith, by contrast, proved useful to the administration, going so far as to back the Housing Authority's implausible claim that it had reneged on the Yorkville arrangement because putting eight black families in one building there would violate its integration policy.[168]

Assessing Progress in Private Housing

Public housing remained a significant achievement for tenants of all races, but it would be limited by the national commitment to "the predominance of private enterprise." Therefore the question for most black New Yorkers remained, how far would New York exceptionalism extend into the private housing market? This was precisely why Stuyvesant Town mattered as much as it did. So dire was African Americans' need for decent-quality private housing that when Metropolitan Life followed up on Stuyvesant Town with Riverton, a smaller parklike development built in Harlem and "limited . . . strictly to Negroes," twenty thousand families applied for leases, notwithstanding widespread anger at the separate-but-equal ploy and a short-lived effort by the NAACP to prevent the project's construction.[169]

How to understand the relationship between rental housing and black progress was one of the questions explored in a 1952 debate published in *Ebony*. Ted Poston, a black *New York Post* reporter, challenged Harlem expatriate Roi Ottley on the question which was the better place for African Americans: Chicago or New York. Ottley, famous for his Harlem reportage in the thirties and early forties, argued that his new midwestern home surpassed Gotham as a beacon of black progress. He cited figures on employment, wages, business ownership, and other indices of socioeconomic standing to show that Chicago's South Side outpaced Harlem in many ways.[170] One of Ottley's chief measures was housing: 21 percent of Chicago's blacks owned their homes, while just 5 percent of New York's did.[171] The South Side's lower prices and cluster of black-owned lending institutions accounted for this disparity.

Poston, however, had figures of his own. If Chicago's ghetto was moving past New York's, he argued, New York blacks were moving past the ghetto. Poston showed that African Americans were heading for the outer boroughs in droves; already Harlem housed less than half of New York's black population. Black New Yorkers had also made impressive gains in white-collar jobs, political offices, and education.[172]

But Poston's argument went further. In a way that economic figures could not fully capture, he wrote, New York sustained a democratic culture unequaled elsewhere. It was "the most cosmopolitan city in the country" and indeed "the least American of all the American cities."[173] (Poston clearly enjoyed this chance to flaunt New York exceptionalism, ribbing his friend Ottley about the "foreign-born" in New York "who come to our shores from such other countries as Mississippi, Georgia, Kentucky and even Illinois.")[174] Whatever problems New

York's blacks faced were "only a variant (sometimes more acute)" of the problems confronting the city's Jews, Irish, Germans, and Finns.[175] And whatever prejudice existed—Poston did not pretend there was none—found only limited expression because of New York's fair-employment and schooling laws (to which Illinois had no counterpart) and its *de facto* integration in many schools, workplaces, and other venues.

Thus for Poston the crucial question about housing in New York was not how many blacks owned homes, but how few pioneering black tenants in white neighborhoods—none—had suffered arson and assault at a time when white Chicagoans were burning and beating African Americans out of Cicero. In sum, he wrote, "more Negroes in New York live democratically with their non-Negro neighbors than in any city in America."[176] His vision of democracy was very much a tenant vision. It was rooted in neighborly relations rather than property relations. And it expressed faith that tenancy would continue to free New Yorkers from the crude calculations of value that drove white resistance in other cities.

Conclusion

Poston's upbeat analysis underscores the sense of possibility that still obtained among liberal New Yorkers through the late 1940s, despite the many disappointments of that decade. To such observers, Gotham's housing movement seemed to have made great strides. In some ways it had. Most remarkable was the Stuyvesant town mobilization: a biracial campaign against residential segregation—the kind many whites found hardest to give up—that drew sustained support from thousands and led to landmark legislation. New York's multiracial tenant movement had also spurred public-housing construction. NYCHA's growth in the latter forties, together with the rent-control statute of 1950, created an urban rental market in which radical ideals were largely unfulfilled but liberal measures achieved unprecedented institutional security.

Those measures carved out an exceptional space amid national housing politics. Lodged in an intensely capitalist setting, New York's regulated rental market and large public-housing stock harbored a population of millions who were not invested in property values the way "average Americans"—read homeowners—were. The security that New York policies granted to tenants helps explain how the city's left-liberal political culture was reproduced at a time when the left was devastated nationally.

Both rent control and public housing were "universal" benefits—that is, programs that aided tenants across lines of race (most public tenants before the 1950s were white) and, in the case of rent control, lines of class as well. On "particular" issues of interest chiefly to minorities, the picture was bleaker. Black rentals in Stuyvesant Town, Riverton, and NYCHA projects made up a tiny fraction of the housing needed by African Americans, who would number 740,000 in New York by 1950.[177] And it would be decades before the Wicks-Austin and Brown-Isaacs laws were enforced with any teeth. Thus hundreds of thousands of tenants of color were confined to the ghetto, with its high rents and minimal maintenance. Here Poston's picture was a bit misleading, for the outer-borough areas to which Harlemites were emigrating were not necessarily integrated in a stable fashion; many would become ghettoes in their own right, their buildings subject to severe neglect, as blacks and Latinos moved in and whites moved out. Changing these conditions would require far more political muscle than the civil-rights movement could flex. The ghetto market was lucrative and landlords lobbied to keep it that way.

Further, new programs were developing in ways that boded ill for both people of color and vulnerable whites. Following the Stuyvesant Town model, urban redevelopment was about to unleash a torrent of evictions upon African Americans, Puerto Ricans, and working-class whites. And New York's liberal-left coalition came under increasing strain as the anticommunist movement gathered force. On these fronts, defeat in the late forties foreshadowed further retrenchment for New York tenants in the coming decade.

3

"So Much Life"

Retrenchment in the Cold War

Jim Torain still recalls his first neighborhood dance. The year was 1951, and the event was a rite of passage on West 99th Street in Manhattan. "Now, the annual dance, it was just an incredible thing happening. The whole neighborhood got excited about it. And it was the second Saturday of March every year. I first went, I was about nine years old. . . . And Tito Puente was playing! And there were a thousand people there."[1]

That the King of the Mambo would play for a block association was atypical, but so was Torain's block. West 98th and 99th Streets had for decades been home to African American families like Torain's, who formed a stable enclave, socially if not physically integrated with the whites and Latinos who lived nearby.[2] "We were a village within the confines of the greater community," he recalls, "but . . . I never felt isolated." He went to the sound, integrated schools his elders had attended, so "you knew the teacher. You had contact with them. And you couldn't wait to have this teacher or that teacher." He lived among an array of familiar neighbors, mostly blue-collar but including a few artists like the actress Butterfly McQueen. (In earlier decades, Billie Holiday, J. Rosamond Johnson, Bert Williams, and Arturo Schomburg had also made homes on the block.)[3] "It was healthy. Vibrant. And . . . very much connected. People came, as my parents did, from Virginia. The Caribbeans [from] St. Kitts and Nevis. . . . And it was like we were all one family."

"And then, this horrible news came." Torain's block was slated for razing and redevelopment. "Then the realization comes through that [the new housing] is not for us . . . It was hurtful. And, so hurtful, for one, I wouldn't go to school downtown [when we moved], I had to keep coming back. . . . as it's coming down, brick by brick. . . . It's hurtful today when I think of it. You know, just walking around and looking at my neighborhood go. So much life, and the spirit of life, and the quality of life came out of there, that it was such an ugly thing."[4]

Physical and social devastation of this kind would become commonplace in New York City in the 1950s as Title I of the 1949 Housing Act took effect. The venture that uprooted Torain, a six-block upper-income development called Manhattantown, gained special notoriety for the corrupt dealings of its backers. But it was just one of scores of projects that together displaced 500,000 New Yorkers, many from vigorous working-class neighborhoods, in the name of slum clearance.[5]

These dislocations formed one dimension of the tenant experience during the height of the Cold War. The opposition they sparked constitutes a little-studied but important chapter in postwar history. Under assault by influential developers, interested politicians, and a nationwide discourse that cast densely built cities as diseased, New York tenants posed a rare urbanist rebuttal to the postwar ideal of suburban housing. They asserted that dense and integrated city neighborhoods could be, in Torain's words, healthy and vibrant communities. But on this front tenants struggled largely in vain. With business insisting and major liberal players believing that slums would be cleared only on developers' terms; with most of organized labor—a traditional tenant ally—agreeing; and with skeptical liberals barred from the backrooms of power, forceful opposition to Title I projects could come only from the left, which was isolated and disfranchised (though not, as elsewhere, obliterated) during this period.

At the same time, other working-class advocates who allied with power brokers such as Robert Moses were able to accomplish substantial ends. A second generation of labor housing was created by developers who welded some of the spirit of the old Bronx cooperatives onto much larger postwar projects financed by union pension funds. Over a quarter century, the new union developers added nearly forty thousand moderately priced units to New York's housing stock.[6] And by supporting rent control and public housing, labor helped to maintain hundreds of thousands more. Yet union co-ops, like upscale projects such as Manhattantown, were built on the rubble of lower-income communities. Thus organized labor paradoxically championed tenants' worst nightmare—displacement—*and* their prime goal, sound, affordable housing.

That contradiction was symptomatic of a larger political economy in which industrial "segmentation"—the divide between large corporations and small concerns—grew sharper after the war. Industrial segmentation brought labor segmentation: workers diverged into well-paid unionized employees in the "primary" industries on the one hand, and a more vulnerable workforce at small secondary enterprises on the other.[7] The disparity between primary and secondary wage scales, which had remained fairly stable through the early twentieth century, increased steadily from the 1940s on.[8] Thus two strata of workers, union and non-, were separated by a widening economic gap. And people of color fell disproportionately in the lower tier. The distance between their stations became, in New York, the difference between enjoying the new labor co-ops and being uprooted by them. Housing thus served as a critical field on which the class and racial reorganization of the postwar city was accomplished.

The two sides of this unfolding tenant odyssey were distinguished not only by class position, race, and political stripe, but by sex. Labor housing developers and the union leaders they worked with were virtually all men. But opposition to Title I was led by women. During an era of conservative gender norms, this "defensive" dimension of tenant activism became an arena in which a generation of what Frances Goldin called "premature feminists"—women who claimed full citizenship before second-wave feminism organized a large movement around that claim—engaged in no-holds-barred political contests. They did so from a setting, the urban neighborhood, that in its very layout challenged the supposed distinction between domestic and political spheres.

Ideology, Housing, and Gender in the 1950s

New York's tenant struggles of the 1950s played against a background of transformative developments in American politics and society. One was the crusade against the left. Anti-Communists consolidated their power not only within juridical institutions such as the FBI and Congress, but in the ground-level organizations where Americans led their daily lives. Schools, advocacy groups, and professional and artistic associations purged leftists from their rolls in the forties and fifties. Unions were made to forswear Communism under the 1947 Taft-Hartley Amendment. Liberal politicians, long suspected of clandestine socialism, came under pressure to show their anti-Communist patriotism in word and deed. Cumulatively these attacks set narrow limits on the range of ideas that received a hearing in U.S. politics and civil society. Among the excluded concepts were socialized housing, social-democratic provision, and what Communists called "the woman question," known today as feminism.[9]

In New York City, the capital of the American left, anti-Communists were less triumphant but no less energetic. They maneuvered for control of union locals and pushed the CIO to expel left-leaning affiliates. They did likewise with the Democratic Party. For ten years New York's Democrats had been on speaking terms with the American Labor Party, sometimes sharing candidates (Vito Marcantonio and William O'Dwyer appeared on both tickets) and patronage. But in 1947, under pressure from Catholic and other anti-Communist voters, state Democrats joined with Republicans in a campaign to isolate the ALP. In Albany the major parties passed the Wilson-Pakula Act to limit candidates' ability to run on two tickets. In New York City they launched a successful drive to repeal proportional representation.[10] That voting system had allowed minor-party tenant advocates like Ben Davis, Pete Cacchione, and Mike Quill to ride boroughwide votes onto the City Council in the late thirties and early forties. Now such candidates were corralled into local electoral districts, where they were easily defeated, usually by Tammany Democrats.

The ALP held on in an agonal state until 1956; the CP survived as a shadow of its former self; the avowed left presence within the city's labor and electoral arenas was largely expunged. In some ways this mattered less than it might have done, because pieces of the Popular Front agenda were absorbed into mainstream liberalism, and because the Liberal Party—home to anti-Communist social Democrats who marched out of the ALP in 1944—was relatively unscathed by the red-hunts. As well, more than a few Old Leftists stayed active despite the collapse of institutional structures.[11] Tenant struggles would demonstrate both the decline and the resiliency of New York's left in this period.

These ideological clashes reverberated strongly in territory where a second overhaul of daily life was under way: the booming suburbs. Americans had long romanticized rural living, and in the nineteenth century many had moved to fashionable "railroad suburbs."[12] But it was during the Cold War that suburbs achieved a new social and ideological ascendancy through unprecedented government support. Low-interest mortgages were made available—first to veterans, under the GI Bill of 1944, and then more widely through the Federal Housing Administration, which was expanded under the 1949 Housing Act. FHA backing would help nearly eleven million families purchase homes over the next two decades.[13] Those buyers got added bang for their federal buck thanks to new mass-production techniques that slashed construction costs. By the late forties, Levittown's basic Cape Cod model could be had for eight thousand dollars and no money down.[14] Buying became cheaper than renting.[15] And the tax code allowed homeowners to deduct mortgage interest from their taxable income—a break unavailable to renters.[16]

In addition to subsidizing homeowners, Washington directly assumed some costs of suburban development. New towns were reimbursed for the laying of water and sewer lines, while aging cities could get no parallel aid, since the funding was marked for construction, not repair. The Interstate Highway Act of 1956—passed after hard lobbying by the auto, rubber, oil, asphalt, and construction industries—paid for the roadways that new suburbanites needed to get around.[17] Thus an alliance of federal agencies, financial institutions, and major industries directed massive public aid into burgeoning suburban developments—at precisely the time when cities, strapped for housing and services, faced a growing need for investment.

This preferential underwriting of suburban society constituted one of the greatest exercises in social engineering in U.S. history, and it was informed from the start by creeds of capital and caste. From the FHA's racial guidelines, to the agency's backing of Levittowns that excluded black buyers, to the racially restrictive covenants that courts upheld prior to the 1948 *Shelley v. Kraemer* ruling (and that agencies winked at for years afterward), state power sanctioned the making of vast segregated swaths of American society. Local authorities also did their part, as police departments typically condoned (and sometimes led) a wave of white mob terror against blacks who bought homes in white neighborhoods during the forties and fifties.[18] Every stage of development was funded through lending practices and commercial institutions designed, as the Wagner-Ellender-Taft bill's preamble put it, "to maintain the predominance of private enterprise."

Private homeownership and housing segregation received powerful ideological backing from the anti-Communist movement. Much as Jefferson argued that yeoman farmers were the foundation of a democratic polity, new suburban ideologues held that detached, owner-occupied single-family housing was the bulwark of the free world. This notion had been trumpeted as early as 1925, when President Calvin Coolidge declared widespread homeownership the "great[est] contribution [that] could be made to the stability of the Nation and the advancement of its ideals."[19] But such beliefs gained new salience within the Cold War discourse of American freedom. During congressional debates over the Housing Act, realtors cast public housing as "socialistic" and suggested an equation between privately owned homes and American liberty. Developer William Levitt put it bluntly: "No man who owns his own house and lot can be a communist."[20]

At the grassroots, suburbanites themselves elaborated a notion of democracy based on owning a home. Thomas Sugrue's study of white homeowners' associations in postwar Detroit shows that such groups articulated their opposition to integration through a "language of rights" that sustained a pervasive "rhetoric linking homeownership and citizenship."[21] From Washington to Warrendale, suburbanists saw the front lawn as the front line in the battle for global freedom.

Finally, both anti-Communism and the suburban enterprise helped fuel a revival of conservative gender norms. The domestic ideal of womanhood had been gaining in the United States for decades, as the suffrage and Progressive movements gave way to Roaring Twenties conservatism and Depression hardship. War brought a burst of opportunity for Rosie the Riveter and her sisters. But in 1945 those women were thanked and sent home, and the United States embarked in earnest on what might be called second-wave domesticity. Institutions from schools to popular media to the medical and psychiatric professions propagated an ideal of family life in which wives tended the home while husbands went out to work. Elaine Tyler May argues that this gender regime was advanced further by Cold Warriors, who promoted the security of the domestic sphere as an antidote to the insecurity of the global arms race.[22] Federal mortgage and veterans' programs also favored men as homeowners and presumptive heads of household.[23]

The family idyll was typically set in a detached suburban house. Suburbs, where home and work were miles apart, embodied spatially the ideological distinction between domestic and public spheres. In this geography of gender, women's domain included the house, the neighborhood social circle, and motherhood-based civic organizations like the PTA. The worlds of economic agency and political power belonged to men. Betty Friedan wrote of the seductive "dream image" surrounding "the suburban housewife [who was] concerned only about her husband, her children, her home."[24] While this image was indeed dreamful—the proportion of married women who took paid work was actually growing in the 1950s, and those women who stayed home often did so with mixed feelings[25]—it represented a formidable norm.[26]

Still, more than a few women rejected the mystique. Some created activist spaces in the major manufacturing and service unions, where they campaigned for equal pay and workplace rights.[27] Others volunteered or worked on staff with the NAACP, the League of Women Voters, and other civil-rights and advocacy groups. A handful held public office. But if the new domesticity did not stamp out women's political activity, it put such activity on the defensive. And it meant that activist women made most of their contributions *within* organizations—as researchers, educators, and ground-level organizers—rather than as leaders in the public eye.

The venue of female political activism that took the most direct hit from McCarthyism was, of course, the Communist Party, where women had often served as local leaders, and where at least some theoretical attention was paid to "the woman question," notwithstanding a fair amount of sexism in the ranks. Ellen Schrecker writes that Party and Popular Front women "constituted a kind of missing generation within American feminism."[28] That generation, in fact, included Friedan, who studied at the socialist-rooted Highlander Folk School in 1941 and worked as a labor journalist for years before adopting her semi-mythological housewife persona.[29] Kate Weigand has unearthed a whole cohort of Old Left women whose writings in Party publications exposed thousands to feminist perspectives during the forties and fifties.[30] But the new climate of fear and retrenchment meant that fewer and fewer people would encounter such heresies. The House Un-American Activities Committee (HUAC) itself saw to the destruction of one left-wing women's group and sent a message to others.[31]

Taken together, anticommunism, suburban living, and modern domesticity formed a matrix of social order that foregrounded *privacy* as a residential value (homes were privately owned, housed one family each, and delimited the private, or domestic, sphere); that made private ownership a basis of good citizenship; that substantially limited such citizenship to white men; and that defined the private, nonpolitical sphere as woman's place. Against this backdrop, the values of New York's 1950s tenant activists stood out sharply. City tenants asserted that residents, not just owners, had rights to a home. They claimed an urban citizenship based on neighborly and civic ties rather than property holding. And they defended the legitimacy of dense, racially mixed neighborhoods that were the antitheses of tidy suburbs. These positions were typically articulated in terms of community rather than class, but insofar as they challenged the right of politicians and developers to wreak havoc on the poor and blue-collar in order to accommodate the more affluent, they presented an implicit class criticism.

Finally, New York's postwar tenants flouted the domestic ideal of womanhood. Women had long predominated at the grassroots of tenant organizing; in the 1950s they would take on higher, more visible leadership positions. During this era of national suburbanization and urban renewal, tenant activists articulated an alternative vision of home, citizenship, and gender.

Darkness and Blight

While suburbs were celebrated as the ideal American environment, cities were losing ground both symbolically and fiscally. During the 1940s a new rhetoric of urban decay surfaced in news articles, editorials, and civic fora across the country. Urban "blight" and "cancer" were suddenly rampant.[32] This discourse was generated primarily by downtown real estate owners who were lobbying for capital-improvement funds to forestall a drop in property values as the better-off moved out of central cities.[33] But it resonated with other ideological camps: slum reformers who had long equated tenements with pathology; pastoralists who saw urban life as inherently corrupt; Cold Warriors who made the "Communist cancer," ever eating away at democracy, a staple in journalism and political rhetoric.[34] (Susan Sontag observed that cancer replaced tuberculosis as the metaphoric illness of choice in the early fifties, after effective treatments for TB were developed.)[35] Gender was also closely bound with the businessmen's mobilization against urban decay, as retailers took it on faith that white middle-class housewives demanded shopping spaces that were modern, spacious, and pristine.[36]

Urban blight was a metaphor, but it gained power from the reality of northward migration by African Americans and Puerto Ricans seeking jobs. In New York alone the net influx was 353,000 between 1940 and 1950, and 426,000 the next decade.[37] This demographic change intensified the discursive shift in a few ways. Migrants had little choice but to move into already-crowded and deteriorated ghettoes, where their presence provided easy fodder for the belief that people of color were the cause of slum pathology. "Welcome, Paupers and Crime: Porto Rico's Shocking Gift to the United States," ran the headline of a particularly unvarnished expression of this idea in *Scribner's*.[38] (The article, thick with lurid data on dope and depravity, would galvanize New York's Puerto Rican community into protest.)[39] African Americans were the target of similar depictions, not least from white realtors and homeowners concerned with property values.[40] Even ballroom managers who stood to prosper from the mambo craze ignited by Puente's generation of bandleaders worried over racial mixing at dances. One admonished a promoter for drawing too many black customers: "You're gonna ruin my business!"[41]

City officials disavowed such views—a mayoral committee headed by Robert Moses himself declared Puerto Ricans "desirable additions to the city's population"[42]—and liberal advocates and journalists stressed that poverty, discrimination, and dearth of decent housing were the fundamental causes of slum conditions.[43] But there was no denying the strain that the growing population of color placed on long-inadequate ghetto housing. For many liberals the answer was more public housing, which was indeed built in the fifties, but which never cut its waiting list below 100,000, and which became increasingly stigmatized as thousands of black and Puerto Rican tenants moved in.[44] The realities and rhetoric of urban decay also handed ammunition to the slum-clearance coalition, which would open both barrels on blue-collar neighborhoods in the coming decade.

Not many years before, the anti-urban prejudices that pervaded blight discourse had been counterbalanced to some degree by urbanist manifestos.[45] Nineteen thirty-eight saw the publication of Lewis Mumford's *magnum opus, The Culture of Cities*, which celebrated the ideal of the city as "a place in which the social heritage is concentrated, and in which the possibilities of continuous social intercourse and interaction raise to a higher potential the activities of men."[46] Mumford, however, condemned existing cities like New York as overgrown and overly determined by capitalist imperatives. He advocated open space and dispersed towns to replace densely built grids such as Jim Torain's West 90s, which typified the city's working-class precincts. Meanwhile Mumford's chief foil, the 1929 Regional Plan Association report, which did champion New York in all its size and centralization, took a similarly dim view of its existing blue-collar geography. Neither established planning model, therefore, would be much use to working-class tenants who fought for their neighborhoods after the war. Those tenants would have to pick up the flag of a different urbanism to challenge the assumptions behind slum-clearance policy.

Urbanism, Redevelopment, and the Remaking of New York

Title I directed federal funds through "local public agencies" charged with redevelopment planning. In New York that meant Robert Moses, who typically worked with developers to hammer out plans well before they came before his Committee on Slum Clearance. One consequence was that New York's Title I projects conformed to the colossal and car-oriented principles of design that Moses favored. Another was that many local residents and business owners were not consulted or even alerted about proposals in the works. Instead, Moses and backers met behind closed doors and presented the public with a *fait accompli*. Then tenants protested—when it was too late.

This strategy, road-tested with Stuyvesant Town, was soon put to use in the Upper Manhattan neighborhood of Morningside Heights. Here the prime mover was Columbia University. Columbia officials were unsettled by the rooming houses that had proliferated in the area during the Depression, when landlords chopped large apartments into cheap yet lucrative cubbies for the poorest renters. They worried lest "undesirables such as prostitutes and unemployed transients" drive away "professors and other middle-class residents" and infect the neighborhood with "blight." A study commissioned by the university in 1946 confirmed the presence of that urban malady and prescribed heroic treatment: "a long-range, imaginative and bold [redevelopment] plan" to make Morningside Heights "the spiritual, cultural and intellectual center of the world."[47]

Well before passage of the federal housing bill, Columbia was busy assembling ingredients for this plan. It bought up local properties and joined forces with banker David Rockefeller, a trustee of nearby Riverside Church and International House. In 1947, Rockefeller brought those and other local institutions together in a redevelopment consortium, Morningside Heights, Inc. (MHI). MHI's planning director sat on the City Planning Commission, providing a seamless connection to municipal policy making.[48]

Three years later the new federal program was up and running, and Moses' Slum Clearance Committee released a flurry of Title I proposals.[49] Among the glossiest was Morningside Gardens, a middle-income co-op to replace Morningside Heights' cheap rentals. The plan called for the destruction of nearly three thousand units then housing one of New York's few racially integrated communities.[50] To placate critics, MHI promised to lobby for a NYCHA project just north of the co-op site—that is, adjacent to Harlem. This only fueled suspicions that "Negro removal" was MHI's real agenda.[51]

The local ALP club formed a Save Our Homes committee that challenged the project's entire rationale, starting with the presumption of social decay in the targeted area. "We are living there, very happily, Puerto Ricans, Negroes, Japanese-Americans and other minorities," declared committee activist Pedro Quiñones, also a member of the machinists' union. "We don't want those communities broken up."[52] The group collected thousands of petition signatures and mobilized hundreds to protest at hearings. It held a dance featuring Afro-Cuban jazz star Machito, whose shows at the Palladium had sparked controversy over racial mixing.[53] Save Our Homes leader and ALP organizer Elizabeth Barker, a white woman who had turned a vacant lot into a kitchen garden for local families, temporarily stymied the Board of Estimate with an alternate proposal to build low-rent apartments that would rehouse the site residents.[54]

These activists received strong support from Bill Stanley of the Harlem Tenants Council. Stanley, born on a North Carolina plantation in 1904, had moved to New York as a teenager and had begun organizing tenants in 1948 under the auspices of Councilmember Ben Davis. After Davis' fall, Stanley had carried on as head of Harlem's unemployed, welfare, and tenant councils, and also as a member of the Communist Party. He had backed open-housing struggles at Stuyvesant Town and elsewhere.[55] Now he stood with the Morningsiders and cast doubt on the city's vague rehousing promises: "We've had plenty of those. We want deeds."[56] The protests led to several delays at the Board of Estimate.[57]

Meanwhile liberal professionals in the Citizens' Housing and Planning Council, the NAACP, the settlements, and Americans for Democratic Action urged federal officials to pace the project so as to facilitate genuine rehousing of Morningside residents. The CHPC letter also disparaged the Save Our Homes group for its Communist ties.[58] Here again the Stuyvesant Town struggle—in which mainline civil-rights groups excluded grassroots leftists—was prefigurative.

But this time red-baiting did nothing to strengthen the liberals' hand. Instead, Moses deployed his own time-tested strategy: He threatened to scuttle the deal if it were modified or delayed. At his urging, MHI dropped consideration of changes that might appease Save Our Homes and tapped its Washington connections to hasten Title I approval. Federal officials authorized funding for the Morningside Gardens proposal in January of 1953. The following day, New York's Board of Estimate ignored three hundred protesters who packed its chambers and voted in favor of the project.[59] By 1958 the co-ops were built and Moses could file a glowing progress report noting that the city had thoughtfully sent site tenants their eviction letters in both Spanish and English.[60]

Hailed for success, Moses replicated the Morningside Heights method with fifteen other Title I projects. Most were located in Manhattan, where the demand for high-rise housing promised maximum profit. Two in Harlem achieved not Negro removal but, like Met Life's Riverton development, the creation of middle-class enclaves at the expense of the poor. These sparked protests led by an ALP organizer named Jesse Gray, then known mainly in black labor circles but destined for fame as a tenant leader in the 1960s.[61]

Moses and allies also obtained federal subsidy for two nonhousing proposals. One of these, Lincoln Center for the Performing Arts, became the largest Title I project in the country. It remade Central Manhattan in a dazzling new style and by itself displaced seven thousand low-rent families. The sixteen ventures would run up a total cost of more than $700 million.[62]

Competing Urbanisms in the Bronx

The demolition pandemic reached beyond Title I projects through public works such as road building. These, too, were imposed mainly on working-class neighborhoods and sparked desperate efforts at resistance. One of the most storied such efforts, the struggle against a mile-long stretch of the Cross-Bronx Expressway, reveals how the malleability of central concepts in city rebuilding—urbanism, liberalism, and modernism—could serve the dominant growth coalition.

A New York driving aficionado asserts, "If you have ever wondered if you're in Hell, then you are experiencing a rather normal spiritual quandary. . . . If, however, you know without the shadow of a doubt that you are in Hell, then you must be on the Cross-Bronx Expressway."[63] But this road was paved with a good intention: provision of an east–west link within a system of arterials designed to facilitate transport and growth throughout the region. Those goals were central to the urban vision of the Regional Plan Association, which proposed the Cross-Bronx in 1929.[64] By contrast, blue-collar communities and neighborhood walkability mattered little to the RPA, and certainly did not concern Moses, who disdained pedestrians and public transportation. He would serve as the RPA's hatchet man on the highway project when it got started after the war.[65]

The Bronx embodied a different urbanism. Built up with modest, thoughtfully designed five- and six-story attached structures in the early twentieth century, the borough's core neighborhoods joined the cosmopolitan sensibility of Manhattan with human scale and physical amenities made possible by still-open outer-borough land. Bronx developers, writes Richard Plunz, "adopted a modern infrastructure of mass transit, parkways and parks within a nineteenth century outlook in the best sense." "Nineteenth century" here connotes the placing of "nature" and other assets in public spaces rather than private yards, as became the norm in Queens. Indeed, the Bronx set aside 17 percent of its acreage as parkland—far more than did any other borough. And parks abutted block upon block of apartment houses. Thus the area was "characterized above all else by urban density, tempered by a large-scale conception of urban space and urban nature. It [was] not the vertical density of Manhattan, but tight and intense horizontal continuity."[66] The designers had embraced up-to-date technology—elevators, subways, steam heat—without submitting completely to the modernist aesthetics of spatial separation and monumentalism held up by the then-fashionable City Beautiful school of planning.[67]

The Bronx's idiosyncratically modern urbanism was highly appealing to the first- and second-generation Jews who made up most of the core neighborhoods' early residents. As they escaped the tuberculous tenements of the Lower East Side, settlers recreated the communal spaces of Lower Manhattan in their new environs. "The Grand Concourse and Pelham Parkway became the twentieth-century equivalents of Chrystie and Forsyth streets; Third Avenue and East Tremont were the equivalents of Orchard Street."[68] The migrants also transplanted social connections. Often, writes Deborah Dash Moore, they followed friends and family in "chain migrations" to new developments in both the Bronx and Brooklyn, where they "constructed a moral and associational community" of civic organizations much like that on the Lower East Side.[69]

These findings would have surprised eminent sociologists who expected the opposite: a weakening of kinship ties, and a reliance on superficial relationships, in urban settings. "Overwhelmingly the city-dweller is not a homeowner," wrote Louis Wirth, "and since a transitory habitat does not generate binding traditions and sentiments, only rarely is he truly a neighbor."[70] Free-market economists would have been even more befuddled. Columbia professor Robert Haig, who wrote the economic survey that undergirded the RPA's 1929 tome, gave the following account of the urban renter's attitude toward his neighborhood: "[O]ne buys accessibility precisely as one buys clothes or food. He considers how much he wants the contacts furnished by the central location, weighing . . . the various possible combinations of site rent, time, value and transportation costs. . . . The theoretically perfect site . . . is that which involves the lowest costs."[71] In this calculus a concept like "moral and associational community" had no place.

Plunz's and Moore's studies of Bronx development show that urban neighborliness *did* obtain under the right conditions. So does oral history. Reminiscences of midcentury Bronxites portray a kind of cross between Ferdinand Tonnies' archetypes of *Gemeinschaft* and *Gesellschaft*—a social setting in which people enjoyed both urban freedom from traditional social constraints and a place-bound network of familial and neighborly relations. "The neighborhood was very dense," recalled political scientist Marshall Berman, who grew up in East Tremont in the 1940s. "Everybody lived out on the street a great deal of the time in the summer, the kids would play 'til it got dark, parents would sit out in folding chairs and watch us and play cards and gossip. There were always women leaning out of the windows who would comment on the action, on what you were doing, and ask about the family. And say, 'Why are you hanging out with that no-good I saw you walking home from school with?'"[72]

Plunz casts this urbanism as a Jewish proclivity, and he is not alone. Sociologist Marshall Sklare wrote, "[American] Jews . . . do not necessarily experience the proximity of neighbors as an invasion of privacy. Accordingly . . . Jews were characteristically apartment renters rather than home-owners. . . . [I]t is the apartment house that remains the emblem of the Jews' love affair with the city."[73] Poet Grace Paley—daughter of the interwar Bronx and later a tenant activist herself—traced this love affair from the apartment out to the bustling street through the eyes of her alter-ego character, Faith: "To walk in the city arm in arm with a woman friend (as her mother had with aunts and cousins so many years ago) was just plain essential," mused Faith. The piece was titled, "Midrash on Happiness." [74]

But if urban proximity was a Jewish preference, it was not a Jewish franchise. Jim Torain described a similar social fabric on Manhattan's West 99th Street, a black community that enjoyed close ties with neighbors of many descriptions:

> There was a Chinese family in there. There was a Jewish family in 99th Street, who had been there forever, Castle, he owned the store, up near Central Park West, and he lived in the building, Number Nine. And he had been there, and people knew him quite well. And on the other corner, on Columbus Avenue, was the grocer, Comas, a Greek family. In fact my grandmother . . . lived on the top floor of that building . . . They didn't live in the block, but they were part of our community. . . . [If] you needed something, you know, it was free-flowing.[75]

One of Torain's fondest memories involves the explicitly moral dimension of that community. A neighbor lady known as "Miss Purity Harmonious" (she took this name as a follower of Father Divine) spied young Jimmy swiping fruit from Comas' sidewalk bin. With unquestioned *loco parental* authority she summoned him to her apartment and set him to doing chores for the rest of the day. Then she sent him off with a home-baked pie as a sign of goodwill. "She never even had to speak to me about the wrong that I had done," remarks Torain.[76]

While there are elements of nostalgia and romanticism in such descriptions of lost communitiy (as Torain readily acknowledges), this does not mean they are fictitious. Rather, these vignettes point toward an urbanist ideal *and* an urban reality that flourished in New York neighborhoods in the early to mid-twentieth century. Both were compelling for tens of thousands of residents, as can be seen in the protests that Morningsiders, East Tremonters, and others mounted to save their communities, and in the survival of the West 98–99th Street block association to this day—sixty years after the block was razed.

In fighting for their neighborhoods these New Yorkers not only defied the postwar residential ideal of dispersed, segregated suburbs; they expressed particular *affirmative* understandings of concepts—urbanism, liberalism, modernism—that figured strongly in postwar planning and politics. The East

Tremont struggle demonstrates this well, though it merits a word of caution. Robert Caro's account has made the conflict over East Tremont's segment of the Cross-Bronx Expressway the most widely known of all redevelopment controversies, and has drawn fire from historians who charge the biographer with embellishing details to enhance the drama of good versus evil. It is likely that Caro did massage population figures. He also let Moses eclipse the RPA as the highway's author, and exaggerated the ill-mapped road's role in East Tremont's decline.[77] The neighborhood was in trouble anyway because the city was hemorrhaging garment jobs, a chief source of local dollars; over time it would be subject to redlining and other forces of national scope that drove stable blue-collar workers and the middle classes out of many cities.[78] Still, the destruction of the East Tremont mile wrought needless and life-changing havoc on five thousand people while diminishing the area's ability to weather coming economic storms. For tenant history, the essentials of Caro's account stand.

Clashing urban standards appear early in the East Tremont story. In 1938 federal mortgage officials assigned the neighborhood a D rating, as they had done to the Stuyvesant Town area, because surveyors found it "congested" and "getting a steady infiltration of lower class Italians."[79] Yet one man's congestion was another's conviviality. It was the very density of the blocks that fostered the close-knit street life of Berman's memory. And the buildings, even the walkups, remained spacious, affordable, and desirable for the upper working class. Many had been inhabited by the same tenants for decades. Sometimes several generations of a family lived within a few blocks' radius, and young adults who wanted to set up housekeeping on their own waited years for a local apartment to become vacant.[80]

In 1952, 1,530 families living north of Crotona Park were blindsided by official letters telling them their homes were condemned.[81] These residents had assumed that the highway, begun four years earlier, would thread through their neighborhood along the park's edge, a course that would require demolition of only six residential buildings.[82] But Moses had mapped a route that cut diagonally across a mile of densely populated blocks. Desperate residents turned to the Tenant Relocation Bureau, the city's ostensible solution to the problems seen at Stuyvesant Town. The agency sent them on fools' errands to view units that were uninhabitable or beyond their means.[83]

Rejecting those options, East Tremonters formed the Crotona Park Tenants Committee to fight for their homes.[84] Unlike the recently established Morningside Heights group, this committee did not originate in an ALP club, and its spokesperson, Lillian Edelstein, had no political background as far as is known. She was a longtime resident whose sister and widowed mother also lived on the condemned route, and whose children grew tearful at the prospect of changing schools.[85] But "a lot of the [other] people who were involved [in the committee] had political experience," recalled the subsequent president, Vivian Dee. "There was certainly a presence" if not a preponderance of people who "came from the left [and] knew how to organize."[86] Most committee members were women, and most managed family budgets that would be strained by higher rents.[87]

East Tremonters "believed that if the government was doing something that was going to harm us . . . [w]e could organize, and the government would listen," recalls Berman. "We might not win every fight, but at least our needs would be considered."[88] Herein dwelled one incarnation of liberalism: a notion that ordinary citizens play a role in policy-making. It was a civics-class sort of belief—arguably a naive confusion of the electoral with the governing coalition—and it had likely been fostered by Franklin Roosevelt's savvy efforts to project personal concern with "the forgotten man."[89] This understanding of liberal polity and rational process informed the tenants' strategy. They secured pledges of support from local officials. They obtained what they considered powerful ammunition from the Bronx Society of Professional Engineers, which made a *pro bono* study showing the Crotona Park route both feasible and cheaper than the Moses plan.[90]

But at the Board of Estimate and the City Planning Commission the committee ran into a different political creed that also went by the name of liberalism. These government bodies were liberal in the sense of supporting large-scale spending on infrastructure, not in the sense of a meaningful say for the ordinary citizen, or of openness to reasoned debate. Moses had chosen and the matter was closed. At the penultimate hearing, tenants' hopes lay with Deputy Mayor Henry Epstein, who had previously endorsed the alternate route along Crotona Park. To the Bronx women's astonishment, Epstein now did an about-face and voted for Moses' route.[91] (Years later, the retired Moses would admit to strong-arming the deputy.)[92] At the final hearing, the newly elected mayor, Robert Wagner Jr., followed Epstein's example of reneging on his promise to the Bronx tenants. By the fall of 1955, most of the 1,530 families had moved.

The real reason behind Moses' intransigence in this matter never became clear, but certainly it was not what Moses claimed, viz., that the alternate route was "impossible." Not only did numerous independent engineers and planners pronounce the parkside route eminently feasible, but Moses took vast pride in his engineering *tours de force*. He once moved an entire apartment building, while engineers watched slack-jawed, despite the fact that demolition would have been easier, for the simple reason that others had said it could not be done.[93] Had the alternate route posed a genuine challenge it would have drawn Moses as a moth to flame. Further, the HOLC's low mortgage rating did not dictate the highway route, even if it helped Moses depict the condemned buildings as unworthy of preservation. Caro thinks the likeliest explanation is that the alternate route would have required demolition of a bus depot in which powerful Bronx politicians held financial interests.[94]

Berman has argued that the East Tremont saga ultimately demonstrates the seductive power of modernism, in its postwar incarnation of cars and accompanying infrastructure, which convinced New Yorkers that to stand against a Moses project was "to oppose history, progress, modernity itself. And few people, especially in New York, were prepared to do that."[95] This belief was given voice in a 1961 episode of *Car 54, Where Are You?* Guest star Molly Picon—the Yiddish film actress once famous for her cross-dressed performances—played Mrs. Bronson, the last tenant holdout on the Cross-Bronx route. When Mrs. Bronson refused to leave her condemned apartment, it fell to the show's lead characters, Officers Toody and Muldoon, to oust her. That this story was considered comic material—a homegrown *Doña Quixote*—suggests that its tragic dimension was little appreciated, even in New York, much as Berman claims.

But Mrs. Bronson got in the best speech, and it came precisely after Muldoon chided her for "hold[ing] up progress." "The [highway] is *progress*?" scoffed the tenant. "Because some man in New York with Bermuda shorts and fancy socks wants to get to New Jersey ten minutes faster to play golf, I have to get out of my house? Tell him with the Bermuda shorts and the fancy socks, get up ten minutes earlier!" As the audience cheered and guffawed, Toody chimed in, "She makes sense!"[96]

What this exchange shows is two incarnations of modernism vying for the public's heart. The dense, walkable, and intricately sociable neighborhoods of the core Bronx *were* modern, in the turn-of-the-century sense, and for that very reason had attracted forward-thinking settlers from Lower Manhattan. (Berman recalls that his own parents viewed the neighborhood in this way.)[97] The wide support that the tenants' committee garnered among local residents, civic-minded planners, and city officials (before they were intimidated) indicates that that modernism could still stand up to the RPA–Bermuda shorts version. Moses' very resort to strong-arm tactics suggests that in an open contest, East Tremont urbanism might have won out. A generational divide in affinities may have been at work here; Berman believes that younger Jews would have left the area for greener lawns in the 1960s, expressway or no expressway.[98] But those who had reached adulthood by 1950 wanted to stay.

Berman himself points toward the tense coexistence of the two ideals when he comments on the bitter journey of East Tremonters who left the ravaged neighborhood but stayed tied to the city, its backroom politics, and its Cross-Bronx Expressway : "For children of the Bronx like myself, this road bears a load of special irony: as we race through our childhood world, rushing to get out, relieved to see the end in sight, we are not merely spectators but active participants in the process of destruction that tears our hearts. We fight back the tears, and step on the gas."[99]

Urban Villagers and Advocates

Deals, condemnations, and closed-door politics fueled hundreds of thousands of evictions in dozens of New York neighborhoods over the next decade. Many of those neighborhoods, like West 99th Street, Morningside Heights, and East Tremont, were working-class and ethnically mixed.[100] Many of their residents, like the Crotona Park Tenants Committee and the Save Our Homes activists, tried to resist and failed. By the end of the decade, however, two new kinds of opposition to urban renewal were taking shape. One arose among reformist liberals, while the other grew among veterans of the Old Left. Both recognized values of neighborhood and urbanism that went beyond the monetary calculus. And both were led largely by women.

The reformers were a new twist in the long entanglement of city rebuilding and liberalism. From the 1930s on, New Dealers, Fair Dealers, and organized labor had supported "slum clearance" and had been essential to the passage of the 1949 Housing Act. Further, as Joel Schwartz has shown, New York politicians and developers who were understood to constitute the liberal establishment gave crucial support to Robert Moses' postwar redevelopment projects.[101] Yet an undercurrent of liberal dissent from close readers like Charles Abrams had also been present since the 1930s.

In the mid to late 1950s the dissent grew louder. Like urban renewal itself, some of the new criticism built on the lessons of Stuyvesant Town. Council member Stanley Isaacs, a veteran of the Stuyvesant Town open-housing campaigns, was one of the first officials to turn a critical eye on Title I. He went out to visit an early Title I site after hearing complaints from tenants, and was sickened at the sight of people being "hounded out like cattle."[102] On his own he could do little to stop evictions, but he would be a ready ally to those who stepped forward to challenge the city's clearance policies.[103]

State Rent Administration counsel Hortense Gabel, also a Stuyvesant Town activist, would likewise join the battle over Title I. Gabel was born in 1912 and followed her father's footsteps into law, earning her degree from Columbia at a time when the law school graduated only five women per class. But nobody was hiring female attorneys, so she joined the ALP—as a Young Democrat, not a radical—and volunteered on FDR's 1936 campaign. Her break came in 1942, when the wartime labor shortage created an opening in the La Guardia administration. Gabel served there as assistant counsel until O'Dwyer and the resurrected Tammany machine swept out La Guardia's people in 1945; then she decided to write a book about the Wagner-Ellender-Taft bill.[104] A Washington contact offered to introduce her to a housing expert. "And, there was Charlie [Abrams], and I asked the questions and I'll never forget it because Charlie . . . ran down it in the most encyclopedic fashion that only Charlie Abrams could do. And that . . . was the beginning of a friendship that—I don't quite know how to describe it, but there are probably four or five men—ironically, in those days, it wasn't women—who exercised a major influence on me and one of them was Charlie Abrams."[105]

Hooked on housing, Gabel at first floundered in choppy political waters. Henry Holt rejected her manuscript "on grounds that it was a Communist book," yet when she volunteered for the 1948 Henry Wallace campaign, she found herself "cut dead by everybody" after she made a few ill-considered jokes about reds in the office.[106] Snarled at by left and right, taken with Abrams, Gabel soon found her place as a liberal houser.

Through the American Jewish Congress she met Stephen Wise, the organization's founder, and his son-in-law, Shad Polier, a leading attorney in the Dorsey suit. In 1948 Gabel accepted a dinner invitation to the Poliers' and arrived to find "that it wasn't just a social dinner. What Rabbi Wise wanted to do, was to ask me to become the director of the Committee on Discrimination in Housing . . . which was just being organized with the support of the American Jewish Committee, the American Jewish Congress, the UAW, the National Urban League and the NAACP. . . . I said . . ., 'Oh, you mean discrimination in public housing?' He looked at me and he smiled. He said, 'No, Hortense. We mean discrimination in housing. It's time we got rid of the ghetto.'"[107] Gabel assumed the directorship of the New York State Committee Against Discrimination in Housing, which would champion the state's landmark fair-housing laws.

In short order she hired an assistant, Frances Levenson, whose biography in some ways paralleled Gabel's own. Levenson, too, was a Columbia Law graduate who had learned that her degree meant little on the job market because she was a woman. She was also acquainted with Justine Polier, Shad's wife, and it was Polier who referred her to Gabel. "We kind of hit it off." The women's common outlook included the dissident liberal critique of slum clearance that Abrams and fellow housers had been voicing for some time. "The Housing Act had a great promise, you know," recalled Levenson. "All the liberals were in favor of the Housing Act of Forty-Nine. But it soon became apparent that the promise of the Housing Act was being distorted in New York City because of the lack of oversight." Levenson, Gabel, Abrams, NYSCDH chairman Algernon Black, and Robert Weaver—a veteran of FDR's "black cabinet" who was then teaching at NYU and would later serve as federal housing administrator—formed a tight-knit group that met regularly at Abrams' favorite steakhouse. They would collaborate on fair-housing policy for decades. "We were . . . most of us born and bred New Yorkers, and we had a great love for the city and a feeling that it had a great potential."[108]

Gabel ran the NYSCDH until 1955, when she passed the torch to Levenson and began work as counsel to State Rent Administrator Charles Abrams, who had just been appointed by liberal governor Averell Harriman. She was now the highest-ranking, highest-paid woman in the state government. She started receiving "a lot of complaints" about conditions at urban-renewal sites where developers "were doing their best to . . . milk the property." Gabel dispatched her housing inspectors to take Polaroid photos of the apartments.[109] The first time she voiced her concerns, she quickly backed down under pressure from Moses.[110] But a year later she would be well placed to assist reporters who had started to investigate what Title I was doing to New York.

Outside official corridors, the Women's City Club of New York by now constituted the distaff side of professional houserdom. Its officers included Elinor Black, wife of fair-housing activist Algernon; Edith Isaacs, who was married to council member Stanley; and Helen Sachs Straus, wife to federal housing administrator Nathan. Frances Levenson attended one of the club's elegant luncheons in 1949 to solicit support for the NYSCDH and the Wicks-Austin housing bill it was then pushing. "Most of the ladies were wearing hats, and their gloves, and they were being served by the staff," noted Levenson, herself a native of the blue-collar Bronx. "And I was wondering, what are they going to think when I start talking about the evils of slum living and segregated housing? . . . This seems to be so far out of their ken. A hand went right up, and the first question was from this woman. She said in a very meek voice, 'You know, there's one thing I can't understand about what you said. Why are we only looking to outlaw discrimination in housing that received public assistance? Why don't we outlaw discrimination in all housing?' . . . That was Elinor Black."[111] In 1951 the WCC allied with the NYSCDH to make a formal investigation of housing conditions in Harlem.[112] Two years later, having heard rumors like those that spurred Gabel and Isaacs into action, the club resolved on a survey of relocation at a single Title I site. It chose Manhattantown, where Jim Torain lived.

Manhattantown contained in microcosm the bedeviling, contradictory impulses of liberal pro-growth housing politics. It was the brainchild of Herbert Sternau, an insurance salesman who was active in the American Jewish Committee (an advocacy group like the similarly abbreviated American Jewish Congress, to which Gabel belonged, but more aggressively anti-Communist).[113] In 1949 Sternau had put together a West Side redevelopment committee comprising social-welfare advocates and representatives of the local AJC, ADA, and veterans' chapters. It was a classic instance of what Schwartz calls the proclivity of "self-appointed civic groups [to] announce the redevelopment ambitions for an entire community."[114] Sternau himself appears to have been driven by both conventional welfare concerns and a suspicion that anti-Semitism festered among local Puerto Ricans. His committee determined that a stretch of predominantly black and Puerto Rican blocks along Central Park, north of West 98th Street, suffered from blight and should be replaced with modern housing—400 middle-income and 800 low-rent public units.

The proposal thus joined a degree of economic liberalism, in the form of mixed-income neighborhood planning, with a program of Negro removal and a willingness to leave most of the 1,800 site families out in the cold. By the time the plan emerged from the Committee on Slum Clearance, in 1951, it had been doubled in size and sheared of its low-income units.[115] As on Morningside Heights, a residents' group sprang up to protest and was shot down as a Communist front.[116]

The protest group did include leftists—Harlem Communist Bill Stanley and a Morningside Heights ALP leader took part—but it represented a broader constituency with the potential to expose contradictions at the heart of the city's vaunted liberal housing policy. Perhaps the most symbolically significant figure to show up at a Mantattantown protest meeting was Stuyvesant Town resident Raphael Hendrix. Democrats reacted quickly. The local congressman, a Sternau ally, imposed a "gag order" on discussion, and Harlem Council member Earl Brown, sponsor of the city's fair-housing law, sought to quell the rumblings with assurances that tenants would be admitted to Manhattantown on a nondiscriminatory basis. But site residents, Hendrix, the NAACP leadership, and even Harlem moderate Glester Hinds saw clearly that the $30-per-room rents would drive local blacks to the ghettos.[117] They were not buying the brand of liberalism the city was selling.

The Women's City Club's liberalism was a different admixture, one containing a large measure of skepticism drawn from the group's history as a Progressive good-government watchdog. Now the club got a boost from an unlikely source: the Department of City Planning, where career civil servants quietly chafed at Moses' methods. These underlings started feeding the clubwomen information on the realities of tenant relocation. WCC investigators had begun their research on Manhattantown by inquiring at the Bureau of Real Estate, where they ran into a stone wall. So they took a tip from their City Planning contacts and went to see for themselves. The group's trained interviewers, English- and Spanish-speaking, completed thorough questionnaires with over 400 households on the site.[118]

Their survey painted a picture far different from the "slum clearance" and "orderly relocation" promised by Moses' office. For one thing, the condemned site was not what most people meant by a slum. "Although old, many structures were in good condition and well maintained," the investigators observed.[119] For another, 82 percent of the household heads had had no help at all, from either the city or the developer, in obtaining other accommodations.[120] And their own efforts were typically fruitless. "I started looking but no colored people are taken," reported one tenant, "so I stopped looking." Another said, "They expect three months rent in advance, one month as a fee and a three years lease, and you have to pay under the table."[121] Few could afford the rents asked in other Manhattan neighborhoods, let alone those projected for the new Manhattantown apartments, which would run more than three times what the average site tenant had been paying.

But site residents' concerns went beyond low rents. They cherished the dense, urban, integrated environment in which they lived, apparently oblivious to the new suburban catechism. "This preference for urban living was reflected among the larger families too," the clubwomen noted. "Most families seemed to be well satisfied with the neighborhood facilities." Racial orthodoxies did not seem to hold much sway, either, with no recorded mention of the matter by white respondents and "[a] majority of the Negro families . . . expressing a strong preference for mixed neighborhoods, claiming that services such as garbage and snow removal, schools and shopping were far better in non-segregated areas."[122] Manhattantown was mixed—"white, 44%; Negro, 36%; Puerto Rican, 19%; Asian, 1%"[123]—and wanted to stay that way. Indeed, this sense of stable community was what Jim Torain missed most when his family moved to public housing—now predominantly people of color—on the Lower East Side. "My neighborhood was condemned as a slum," he recalled. "And I was moved to a ghetto."[124] Not only Torain but many of his schoolmates mounted their own silent protest against this exile by commuting back to finish their education at Booker T. Washington Junior High rather than at the schools in their new locales.[125]

Still, the Torains were luckier than most. When the clubwomen returned two years later, they found that of the 142 original families who could be traced, only 50 had obtained public-housing slots.[126] The rest had been forced onto the private market, where their rents had increased by a third.[127] These data were especially significant because Moses' official reports routinely cooked relocation numbers down to a palatable mush.[128] Blacks and Puerto Ricans figured disproportionately among Manhattantown's untraceable families.[129]

Figure 4. **Slum or sound community?** Elinor Black took this photo of West 99th Street in 1951 for the Women's City Club study of Manhattantown. Jim Torain, hand on hip, watches the action from beneath a no-parking sign at left. *Courtesy of the Milstein Division of United States History, Local History and Genealogy, The New York Public Library, Astor Lenox and Tilden Foundations.*

Figure 5. **Young residents of West 98th–99th Street community at Comas' produce store.** Left to right: Marvin Robinson, Gloria Evans, and Alex James. *Courtesy of Jim Torain.*

And families of color that *had* gone into NYCHA housing had been placed primarily in Harlem or East Harlem.[130] In other words, such relocating as the city performed served to segregate a formerly integrated population. (As on Morningside Heights, a NYCHA project went up near the Title I site, but it was not completed until two years after Torain and his neighbors were sent packing.) Finally, tenants evicted from Manhattantown paid unquantifiable social costs: "breaking of old contacts, distance from work, church, families, stores, etc."[131] In a public letter the club called upon the city to take direct responsibility for future relocation and to increase the "total supply of housing to meet the needs of all groups."[132]

Preliminary findings from the WCC survey reached the desk of Stanley Isaacs, who used them to leverage a citywide relocation study from of the Board of Estimate in 1952.[133] The troubling data, however, remained in the

Figure 6. **Park West
Village (formerly
Manhattantown)
in 2008.** *Courtesy
of Liz Friedman.*

City Planning Commission office, submerged under a flood of vetoes from
Moses loyalists.[134] But slowly the iceberg hove into sight. In the summer and
fall of 1954 the U.S. Senate Committee on Banking and Currency held hearings
on the use of federal funds in urban redevelopment. The committee spent a
long day in New York interrogating Manhattantown developer and Tammany
crony Samuel Caspert.[135] Caspert was compelled to admit that he had inflated
his land cost fourfold on his FHA filing; had carried out little demolition and
no rebuilding two years after signing a contract, while continuing to collect
rents in neglected site buildings; had put on payroll a remarkable number of
sons, sons-in-law, and other relatives of principals, who drew large salaries
for minimal work; and had paid the principals themselves a total of $649,000,
leaving the company with little money to carry out its contractual obliga-
tions.[136] (An additional $115,000 had been routed through phony rentals and
sales of iceboxes and stoves.)[137] Caspert's grudging testimony was offset by

the crisp presentation of WCC representative Ethel Emerson Wortis, who told the committee what her club had learned about relocation.[138] She was followed by labor co-op developer Abraham Kazan. He testified that his Title I project on the Lower East Side was speeding forward and would be completed five months ahead of schedule.[139]

Although these hearings focused on corruption rather than the harder question of rehousing, they put a tarnish on Title I's public image. (Manhattantown itself was taken under foreclosure by the city and sold to a different developer, who completed the project as Park West Village.) The taint spread in the spring of 1956, when Moses' plan to pave over a Central Park play area for private restaurant parking brought forth a brigade of mothers armed with baby carriages and lawyers.[140] This seemingly trivial face-off marked Moses' first public defeat, and it encouraged two newsmen at the *World-Telegram and Sun* to start snooping around New York's Title I sites.[141]

Fred Cook and Gene Gleason turned out a front-page series showing that Moses had repeatedly handed over prime real estate, at fire-sale prices, to clubhouse developers like Caspert, who spent years "milking" the sites (i.e., collecting rent while letting services degrade). Far from clearing slums, the reporters concluded, Title I projects were "creating new slums."[142] The pair also played a mean game of faux one-upmanship in pursuit of exposure. When the *Telly*'s editor started to bury their stories, Gleason shared his material with a "rival" at the *Post*. Soon a scooping competition was under way, with editors at all the major tabloids obliged to run Title I stories prominently, while the circle of young reporters who wrote them gathered daily with Hortense Gabel to share leads and plot strategy.[143]

These exposés did not directly topple Moses, but they paved the way for Wagner to ease Moses out of housing and toward other projects.[144] Even the *Times*, which had "warmly congratulate[d]" Moses on his sealing the Manhattantown deal in 1951, started to devote ink to the WCC's findings.[145] Moses resigned from the Committee on Slum Clearance in 1960. The chorus of criticism from journalists, tenants, the WCC, and the Citizens' Housing and Planning Council help explain the findings of political scientists Norman and Susan Fainstein that New York broke out of the most antidemocratic phase of urban redevelopment a decade before other cities did.[146]

Indeed, as early as 1958, it seemed that New York might be moving toward a different kind of city rebuilding. Encouraged by a 1954 amendment to the Housing Act that offered funding for housing rehabilitation ("renewal") as well as demolition, Wagner appointed an Urban Renewal Board (URB) headed not by Moses but by James Felt, erstwhile point man for Met Life, who had come to believe that tenant relocation should be managed differently.[147] The URB was charged with "[p]romotion of economically and ethnically integrated neighborhoods" on the Upper West Side.[148] This initiative was threaded through the bureaucratic gears by Hortense Gabel, who would shortly leave her state job to work in the city's new "Neighborhood Conservation" program.[149] Also heartening to housers was a new federal mandate for citizen participation in renewal planning. It had been added in response to mounting evidence of Title I's destructive effects.[150]

The devil of class, however, still lurked in the details of the city's West Side plan, which included far more middle- and high-income than low-rent housing units. Indeed, during the late fifties, when Cold War pundits were stridently declaring America a classless society, Title I developers were starting to embrace and trumpet racial liberalism in a way that distracted attention from their projects' class ramifications.[151] Morningside Gardens and Park West Village both opened on an integrated basis—the former with a 20 percent cap on black occupancy to avert "tipping," the latter eventually becoming home to Coleman Hawkins, Duke Ellington, Tito Puente, Abby Lincoln, and other distinguished figures—even though both were flagrant cases of Negro removal during the demolition phase.[152] In wake of the Stuyvesant Town uprising, poverty was starting to eclipse color as the vector of blight to be eradicated through slum clearance. Racial integration among middle-class cooperators did nothing for the uprooted poor, who usually included large numbers of Puerto Ricans and African Americans.

If nothing else, the 1958 West Side initiative showed that the mayor's office was feeling heat from Title I's critics. Wagner also commissioned a relocation study that affirmed what Abrams, Gabel, and the WCC had now been saying for years: "*Other slums have taken the place of those which have been cleared.*"[153] Prime causes of recurring blight, wrote lead author Anthony Panuch, were inadequate relocation of clearance refugees and chronic shortage of low- and middle-income housing.[154] Panuch urged the city to site future middle-income developments in "deteriorating commercial areas . . . where the residential tenant relocation problem is insignificant," and to cease "tear[ing] down desperately-needed structurally-sound tenements which . . . can be rehabilitated."[155] The Panuch report put City Hall's imprimatur on reforms conceived by tenant advocates.

Intellectuals Reconsider City Rebuilding

Panuch's study was read by a few dozen specialists, but soon a cohort of heterodox intellectuals was bringing criticism of slum clearance to a wide audience. In the late fifties sociologist Herbert Gans conducted field research in the putative Boston slum known as the West End. He found aging but sound buildings, viable small stores, and a close-knit, socially stable community of Italian American working people. Gans published these findings in a 1959 article that directly challenged the equation of blue-collar districts with slums, a definition he said reflected the "value pattern of middle-class [planning] professionals" rather than a valid social-scientific demonstration of harmful environs. Much as Marshall Sklare would later observe of urban Jewish communities, Gans found, "[p]rivacy is not evaluated here as highly as it is in middle-class culture, and West Enders consider it more important to have large numbers of relatives, friends, and neighbors at hand."[156] The article was a prelude to Gans' 1962 classic *The Urban Villagers*.

Gans' research would gain further exposure in Jane Jacobs' *The Death and Life of Great American Cities*, a work of clarity and wit that did to the planning orthodoxy what Moses had done to East Tremont. The arc of Jacobs' career in planning ran somewhat parallel to that of Betty Friedan in feminism. Like Friedan, Jacobs had youthful associations with the Old Left—in her case the ALP and the Federal Workers Union. Like Friedan, she worked as a low-profile journalist (at *Architectural Forum* and other magazines) for years before writing a book that would change the way millions thought.[157] And like Friedan, she got mileage out of a housewife persona that eclipsed her less conventional roles. Although Jacobs drew some examples for her 1961 book from the Greenwich Village block where she lived, she had begun to develop her ideas while on professional assignment uptown in the 1950s. Researching an article on the groves of NYCHA towers that now loomed in East Harlem, Jacobs met with neighborhood social worker Ellen Lurie and others who had undertaken a survey of project residents' views (a venture much like the early Women's City Club studies). The survey revealed widespread demoralization stemming from the city's redevelopment policies: the razing of bodegas and other traditional social hubs to make way for public-housing superblocks; the uprooting that many newer project residents had endured when their previous homes were sacrificed to Title I or NYCHA developments; and the brooding sterility of project architecture. These insights would strongly inform *Death and Life*.[158]

Jacobs aimed her fire at both poles of established city planning. The re-
strictively zoned low-density model embraced by Lewis Mumford, she wrote,
looked toward a future of "self-sufficient small towns, really very nice towns
if you were docile and had no plans of your own and did not mind spending your life among others with no plans of their own."[159] Those with more
vigorous tastes, however, needed the opposite: densely situated dwellings,
diverse people, lively sidewalks, and mixed commercial and residential spaces
that allowed local shopping, adult sociability, and the supervision of playing
children to intertwine. But those very riches were in danger of being plun-
dered by the other urbanists: Moses and his tower-building zealots. Jacobs
reserved special scorn for the Morningside Gardens project, "after [which]
Morningside Heights went downhill even faster."[160] The polemic capped a
decade of grassroots and intellectual questioning of received notions of urban
"blight" and "slums." It forged street-level New Yorkers' insights into a potent
articulation of urbanism that was both new and old, and that took seriously
the role of ordinary city tenants.

Old Leftists, New Tenant Mobilizations

As those ideas built up steam within liberal circles, a separate stirring was
taking place among the embers of the ALP. For a time this left party had
functioned as a venue in which Communists and progressive Democrats could
make common cause. But in the late forties and early fifties it was battered
by internal dissension and McCarthyite attack, and finally cast off by the
CP. The ALP-affiliated New York Tenants Councils—the city's last umbrella
organization for tenants—also came onto the HUAC's radar and ceased to
function.[161] Nothing showed the ALP clubs' weakness more clearly than their
repeated failure to stop Title I projects like Morningside Gardens and Manhattantown. Now an ALP club facing a similar crisis in Yorkville would try a
different tack. Its leader was Jane Benedict.

Benedict was born in 1911 on Riverside Drive to a family of "uptown Jews," a
middle-class, largely German social stratum. Her father influenced her deeply.
He was "very much his own person": a Jew who "made no denial that we were
Jewish" but eschewed overt religious associations; a self-taught scholar; a
corporate lawyer who joined the NAACP; and a liberal who stuck with the left-
leaning Lawyers Guild, despite his doubts about what he called "those mad
young men and women." Jane studied English at Cornell, then sold books at

Macy's and joined the Book and Magazine Guild (a union that the young Jane Jacobs also joined and helped organize in the early forties).[162]

Through the Guild, Benedict "fell into" the CIO and "met a number of left-wingers. And I sort of just found myself very much at home." She joined the Communist Party, where she met fellow CIO organizer Peter Hawley (*né* Horowitz), who was known to "[go] out with every woman around" but soon settled down as Benedict's husband. She stayed with the Guild through the forties, reaching an executive rank and "believ[ing] heart and soul" in the CIO's vision. But with young children to care for, she stepped down from her full-time union job and became a part-time organizer for the ALP.[163] She and Peter both ran for state office on the ALP ticket in the early fifties (as did Frances Goldin).[164]

Benedict and Hawley lived in Yorkville, an immigrant neighborhood located just below East Harlem. In the mid-1950s local tenants started "coming into the ALP [clubhouse] saying, 'Oh my God, the landlord says he's going to tear the house down.'" Urban renewal had arrived in Yorkville. The area had long been a predominantly working-class precinct; now it was being converted into an extension of the posh Upper East Side that it bordered. And there were "a great many Czechs, Slovaks, Poles, Italians . . . whose houses were just being torn down. And there was no legislation to protect them; it was a horror." Unlike redevelopment sites in some other neighborhoods, the condemned buildings in Yorkville were indeed substandard—with shared toilets and no steam heat, Benedict had found, as she made the ALP rounds. But their replacements were all luxury towers. No provision was made for the displaced poor.[165]

The usual overt ALP approach, Benedict and others believed, could not succeed in Yorkville. Most local residents did not want to "feel that they had to go to the American Labor Party. And [they] wouldn't. They were too conservative." But such people might work with "some sort of independent tenant committee, not called the ALP."

> So we set up a nonpartisan, a nonpolitical committee called Yorkville Save Our Homes Committee. And I went to the local minister, just around the corner, in the Lutheran Church, it was a Czech church. . . . . And I said to him just who I was, "chairman of the American Labor Party club, the Eighth A[ssembly] D[istrict]. We want to set up a nonpartisan committee." And he said, "You're sure it's going to be nonpolitical?" I said, "I'm very sure." . . . And he gave us a room, free.[166]

The "nonpolitical" Yorkville Save Our Homes reached out to more conservative neighbors. Frieda Milgrim, a graphic artist, learned about the group because

"Jane . . . rented a truck and got on it and went through all the streets, telling people to come to a meeting of this one area that was being bulldozed. . . . So I saw her and heard her speak. A friend of mine made the signs for her. And then she asked me to do some too." Too shy herself to speak to large groups, Milgrim organized small meetings in people's homes. She had no prior political experience and found in the tenant mobilization an awakening. She was captivated especially by Benedict's fearlessness and charisma. Although Jane Benedict stood well under five feet, Milgrim saw her as "a giant of a woman."[167]

As Yorkville tenants rallied, residents at the city's largest redevelopment site also grew alarmed. Lincoln Center was an explicitly Cold War undertaking. Its backers, led by John D. Rockefeller III (brother to the Morningside

Figure 7. **Yorkville Save Our Homes. "No More Crosses" refers to the marks on condemned buildings.** *Courtesy of Met Council on Housing.*

Heights booster David) and comprising much of the city's corporate and cultural elite, had warned hesitators that without such a symbol of "cultural maturity," America would "grow constantly weaker in its struggle with those who would overturn our way of life." The performing arts center's contribution to the fall of Communism is hard to gauge, but it was certainly a triumph of what *Time* called "monumental modern" over human-scale urbanism—and over 7,000 families and individuals in the area then known as Lincoln Square. Project backers trotted out the usual slum suspects—integration, crime, juvenile delinquency—to cast the neighborhood as unsalvageable.[168] A final dash of salt in the wound was the use of the half-cleared site for the opening skirmish in *West Side Story*, a film about gangs that nonetheless challenged some of the slum stereotypes. ("Them cops believe everything they read in the papers about us cruddy J.D.s," says Jets leader Riff, setting up the satiric "Gee, Officer Krupke!")[169]

Tenant mobilization at Lincoln Square was not led by the ALP, which had just about breathed its last by 1956. Two women at a social-service center organized a committee with moderate aims. "Our program does not oppose slum clearance," they wrote, perhaps seeking to distinguish themselves from Save Our Homes agitators on Morningside Heights. But they maintained that clearance should be contingent on a complete low-rent rehousing program. The nascent group approached Harris Present, a liberal attorney who had recently sat on a relocation reform committee with Stanley Isaacs and representatives of the American Jewish Committee, the CHPC, and the NYSCDH. Present, frustrated by that committee's ineffectiveness, agreed to represent Lincoln Square's residents and business owners.[170]

Present's public letters and the group's eloquent pickets—"Shelter Before Culture"—garnered far more press attention than had the uptown leftists' demonstrations. But they cut no more ice with City Hall. In hindsight this is unsurprising, given the phalanx of titans defending the Lincoln Center project. Yet Present, like the East Tremont liberals, had expected more of Wagner and the Board of Estimate. Now the city's intransigence pushed him and his clients to lose faith in proper channels and to swap their moderate demand—humane relocation—for a call to ax the whole redevelopment.[171] This escalation mirrored a pattern that civil-rights historian Charles Payne notes "would be repeated many times [in the South]—Blacks ask for small adjustments in the system, the authorities refuse, Blacks then make more radical demands."[172] By 1957 Lincoln Square tenants found themselves echoing the Save Our Homes groups' "radical" denunciation of slum clearance after they realized that their own brand of liberalism had been supplanted by a heavy-handed Cold War version.

Bulldozers started to loom on downtown horizons. In 1959 the Committee on Slum Clearance proposed to rebuild Cooper Square, a stretch of twelve low-rent blocks just above the junction of Bowery and Second Avenue, with middle-income co-ops. Unlike Yorkville and Lincoln Square, the Lower East Side already had an established tenant alliance that made no secret of its leftist origins. Seasoned leaders included Frances Goldin—no longer a CP member, but still a socialist at heart—and Esther Rand, a Communist whose organizing passion, legal brilliance, and ornery disposition would become legendary in housing circles. "She could be bitter," recalled Jane Benedict, "she could be nasty. . . . But she was the spirit of that East Side branch."[173] Rand's signature saying, later emblazoned on tenant organizers' T-shirts, was, "Landlords are not the lords of the land; they are the scum of the earth."[174]

Now Goldin and Rand led the charge against the city's plan. The Lower East Side Neighborhoods Association, of which Goldin was secretary, quickly denounced the official site data "as almost unbelievably inaccurate. Hundreds of residents were not included in the totals, hundreds of businesses were not listed in the inventory."[175] The women formed a committee of local residents and business owners. In a significant departure from earlier groups' strategies, they "recognized that a negative approach, one based merely on resisting the city's plan, would not be of much help."[176] They decided to try something new: a full-scale "alternate plan" that promised to rehouse every resident of the site.

Just across town and to the north, Chelsea tenants faced the threat of Penn Station South, a mammoth Title I project that called for replacing low-rent tenements with high-rise co-ops for members of the International Ladies' Garment Workers' Union (ILGWU). Here resistance was led by Jane Wood, a St. Louis native and Smith graduate who had moved to New York in 1930 and become swept up in the city's radical whirl. Wood joined the ALP, and on her door-knocking rounds she learned that tenement conditions were a prime hardship for Chelsea residents.[177] She survived on various jobs—department-store sales, even a brief modeling gig—but eventually her political work drew her fortuitously into a skilled craft. As she was mimeographing tenant handbills one day in the early 1940s, her machine broke down. The repairman who showed up offered to train her in the printing trade, which was short on "manpower" due to the war. Wood became both a skilled typographer and an organizer for the CIO printers' local.[178]

She opened a small printing shop and continued to build up a tenant network. Her college Spanish enabled her to reach out to the many Puerto Ricans who were settling in Chelsea in the 1950s. ("We in the Latino community felt she was one of us," a neighbor and fellow activist later recalled.) The 1957 announcement of Penn South raised the stakes of tenant organizing in the area.[179]

A short ways east of Chelsea, tenants near Gramercy Park also protested a Title I plan for their area. Gramercy Neighbors, like the Cooper Square Committee, called attention to the city's misleading site data and sponsored an independent survey supporting rehabilitation.[180] "We want to see the sound buildings preserved," said chairman Miriam Moody, "and the bad ones replaced by housing within the economic means of people now living here."[181]

As they rallied their neighbors, the activists lent increasing support to one another. Some were already acquainted through the CP or the ALP; Frances Goldin, whose husband managed Vito Marcantonio's election campaigns, had often met party members in other districts.[182] Thus the Old Left parties served as what social-movement scholar Jo Freeman has called a "cooptable communications network," that is, an older social infrastructure linking individuals who launch a new movement.[183] Further connections among neighborhood activists developed from scratch "because if we were interested in housing we went to other housing events and met other housing activists."[184] By 1956, Goldin and Benedict were meeting with Lincoln Square leader Ella Root and representatives of four other neighborhood groups in Manhattan and Queens. They published a detailed study of slum clearance that highlighted the city's "questionable and undemocratic practices" and its utter failure to provide for low-income site tenants.[185] Save for the mothballed 1952 Board of Estimate findings, this was the first report to bring together data from many neighborhoods into a comprehensive rendering of the slum-clearance catastrophe.

From this nucleus grew a network that started meeting at the YMCA on Twenty-Third Street. It included Benedict; Goldin; Rand; Jane Wood; Robert Wood (Jane's husband); Miriam Moody; Harlem organizer Bill Stanley; Juan Sánchez of the Federation of Hispanic Societies; Helen Harris of the Bronx Council on Rent and Housing; and Staughton Lynd, son of the *Middletown* sociologists, who was then a graduate student at Columbia and would go on to become a lifelong historian-activist.[186] In May 1959, these organizers formally constituted themselves as the Metropolitan Council on Housing—Met Council for short. Harris Present spoke at the council's first meeting, and Jane Benedict would soon become the long-serving chair.[187] The founders pledged not just to fight Title I, but to wage a citywide struggle for "decent housing at rentals people can afford to pay." They had their work cut out for them.

Figure 8. **Met Council leaders meet with Governor Nelson Rockefeller in 1963.**
Left to right: Jane Wood, Robert Moore (Parkway-Stuyvesant Council, Brooklyn),
Mamie Jackson (Bronx Council on Rents and Housing), Rockefeller, Jane Benedict,
Lucille Smith (Lower East Side Tenants Council), Frances Goldin, Bill Stanley, Lucille
Flato, Herbert Hinds (Staten Island). *Courtesy of Frances Goldin.*

Labor and Housing: A Second Generation

The Bronx labor co-ops of the 1920s were deeply utopian. Residents saw
collectivist housing as part of a larger struggle for emancipation from the
tyranny of capital. Those values proved more enduring than the projects'
economic arrangements, however. Three quarters of a century after the co-
ops went up, their octogenarian alumni still held reunions to commemorate
their shared cultural heritage. Growing up in the garden-centered communities, they said, bequeathed a commitment to justice and public service that
stayed with them long after they had moved out of the Bronx.[188] Yet in fiscal
terms, most of these developments failed. Only the Amalgamated survived
as a functioning cooperative.[189]

By the end of World War II, organized labor had changed. A decade of legally protected organizing had quadrupled membership. Thick rolls meant steady dues, and election-day turnout meant political muscle. Pension programs, moreover, meant sizable funds to invest. Thus labor entered the late forties and early fifties with the ability to back housing development on a much larger scale than before. At the same time, anti-Communism and the moderating influence of the new Democratic coalition had clipped the movement's left wing. Labor faced its future with an eye toward pragmatism rather than utopia.

In New York, the tenant city, union power and pragmatism birthed a new generation of labor housing cooperatives. The first went up right after the war, but most were launched in the fifties. Their prime mover was Abe Kazan, a longtime garment-trade unionist who had developed the Bronx's Amalgamated co-op in the late 1920s, and who continued to see housing as the foremost need of New York's working people. Kazan's pragmatism showed clearly in his willingness to deal with the tenant's devil himself, Robert Moses. By making a pact with Moses (a pact that stipulated parking garages for workers who did not own cars, in deference to Moses' automobile fetish), Kazan secured city backing for a 1945 plan to replace sixty-five Lower East Side tenements with high-rise co-ops. They were called Hillman Houses after Amalgamated Clothing Workers president Sidney Hillman, and they still house many retirees from the needle trades.[190] Before long other unions began to build co-ops on cheaper land in Brooklyn and Queens. Most ambitious was the International Brotherhood of Electrical Workers' Electchester project. Its 103-acre site would eventually contain 2,300 housing units, a library, a union bank, and a bowling alley.[191]

In 1951 Kazan organized the United Housing Federation, an alliance of existing co-ops and unions dedicated to building more labor housing with Title I funds. The UHF's maiden venture—and the first Title I to be completed anywhere—was an ILGWU project on the Lower East Side called East River Houses.[192] Notwithstanding the differences between Kazan's social vision and those of the Morningside Gardens and Manhattantown developers, East River Houses had an underside like its uptown cousins': It uprooted low-income site residents and accepted few nonwhite cooperators. (The racial exclusion eventually prompted a lawsuit, one of several filed by ILGWU rank-and-filers of color in the sixties and seventies over disparate treatment within the Jewish-led union.)[193] When East River Houses opened in 1956, the UHF was ready to move forward with three larger developments, including Jane Wood's *bête noire,* Penn South in Chelsea. All would be hailed for success. To this day, Penn

South stands out for its inclusive cultural program and its residents' commitment to maintaining the nonprofit status of "housing built with union money for working and moderate-income people."[194]

Such spirit would have surprised onetime union organizer Jane Jacobs, because Penn South—like East River Houses, Manhattantown, and the rest of New York's Title I housing—was a high-rise. Kazan loved them as much as Moses did.[195] Jacobs disdained these towers-in-the-park, believing they disrupted the "intricate sidewalk ballet" that was the lifeblood of organically sociable city blocks.[196] Her disdain was a corollary of her principal insight: attached medium-rise housing does not a slum make. But while Jacobs' rebuttal to the slum stereotype was borne out by evidence—sound buildings, civic engagement, and neighborly bonds in her Greenwich Village area and other aging blue-collar neighborhoods—her tower critique has not fared as well. Not only did cooperators in the new labor developments enjoy communal fellowship; Stuyvesant Town became a beehive of neighborly engagement, and Park West Village (formerly Manhattantown) developed an active tenants' association that confronted the project's disquieting history and forged a relationship with Jim Torain's old block association.[197] Residents of these and other high-rises were able to generate alternative pathways of social engagement within their complexes. Elevators, in fact—unknown on Jacobs' block—served as conduits, encouraging conversation between neighbors as they waited or rode together.[198] But often the towers functioned simultaneously as enclaves, their residents disengaged from nonproject people a block or two away.[199] On that score Jacobs was right.

East River Houses and Penn South capture the paradox of postwar labor: trade unions, which at least espoused solidarity with the working class writ large, built self-identified "communities of working people" for their own members at the expense of working people further down the ladder. They pitted tenant against tenant, worker against worker, and it was the relatively secure tenants and workers who won out. A New York idiosyncrasy also came into play in the advantage enjoyed by unionized workers in *apparel*—New York's largest manufacturing industry—over those in other trades. Garment unions built the labor co-ops that dislocated thousands (as well as the bulk of labor housing generally); their members had first crack at new apartments.[200] The other beneficiaries were building tradesmen, who rallied behind all Title I projects because of the jobs they generated, regardless of social fallout. ("A construction worker," wrote Murray Kempton, "would pave over his grandmother if the job paid $3.50 an hour.")[201] Not surprisingly, tenants evicted from UHF sites saw more than a little hypocrisy in the federation's claim to serve working people.

That contradiction, however, was symptomatic of a postwar political economy characterized by working-class stratification and Taft-Hartley-tamed unions that typically put member benefits ahead of more inclusive social-movement building. Kazan was both a shaper and a creature of labor's twentieth-century transition. He had come of age when garment workers ranked among the city's most exploited and led landmark struggles for shop-floor rights, tenants' rights, contract benefits, and social-democratic provision. Precisely because of those struggles, postwar garment workers were now in a position to buy into his moderately priced co-ops. The labor movement he represented was part of the growth coalition that Moses led. Neither alliance incorporated the poorer economic strata to any great degree.

Joshua Freeman describes labor's postwar housing program as "one of the greatest and least-known achievements of working-class New York."[202] It was that, and simultaneously a great and little-acknowledged hardship for lower-working-class New Yorkers.

Class segmentation, Cold War politics, and a measure of New York exceptionalism also framed the successes and failures of other tenant demands on the state. In the fifties New York tenants continued the major policy battles of the previous decade. They defended rent control, making the pilgrimage to Albany every two years to lobby for renewal of the law. They pushed for public housing, winning an added 75,000 units over the course of the decade.[203] And they enjoyed strong support from local unions, notwithstanding the national labor movement's defection from social-democratic housing policy.[204] Tenants and civil-rights advocates also called for ghetto code enforcement, with the same negligible results as before. Studies told of hundreds of violations per ghetto block, hundreds of thousands living in grim rat-traps.[205]

In other words, the wartime tenant policies that fared best during the Cold War were those that served the upper working and middle classes as well as the poor. Rent control is a clear example. Public housing might appear different, but NYCHA policies continued to favor the steadily working poor over the more precarious, and during the fifties the city added 26,000 units of tax-exempt moderate-rent housing—ideal for middle-stratum workers—to its public stock.[206] Further, public works of any kind directly benefited labor's elite in the building trades. Meanwhile, in 1953, NYCHA started requiring tenants to sign an anti-subversion oath or move out. (Paul Ross, lawyer for the integrationist Stuyvesant Town residents, led the refusers' unsuccessful court challenge.)[207]

Code enforcement was the housing measure needed most particularly by poor and minority tenants, and the one most neglected by public agencies.

Women, Men, and Housing in the Postwar City

Labor co-ops and anti-redevelopment struggles—the offensive and defensive wings of Cold War tenant activism—reveal a gender as well as a class divide within housing politics. Union housing was spearheaded by Kazan and other male visionaries. Not so the fights against demolition. From leftists like Jane Wood, Esther Rand, Frances Goldin, Jane Benedict, and Elizabeth Barker, to faithful liberals like Lillian Edelstein and Ella Root, to professionals like Hortense Gabel, Frances Levenson, and Jane Jacobs, the tenants who tilted at bulldozers were often women.[208] And these women led publicly, breaking the earlier pattern in which housewives organized locally but men served as citywide tenant spokesmen.[209]

Why? One possibility is that the tenant cause's very marginality during the Cold War shaped its leadership. Save-our-homes groups stood much farther outside the fold of power than did labor unions. They commanded no funds; they had limited pull with elected officials; they could never cut a deal with Moses. And they faced an especially Sisyphean task, insofar as tenant unions had always been harder to maintain than labor unions. The leaders most available for save-our-homes groups would come from a class of activists that was also largely excluded from union officialdom and formal politics: women.

But marginality does not explain why women who picked up the anti-eviction banner rather than the co-op planner's pencil reached for an activist implement at all. Many female tenant leaders, especially on the left, showed an inclination toward politics *before* they turned to tenant work. Jane Benedict and Frances Goldin both joined the Communist Party and the ALP prior to taking up housing struggles. Jane Wood, like Benedict, was an ALP member and a CIO organizer. Raphael Hendrix—a critic of Title I clearance as well as a leader at Stuyvesant Town—organized for the Depression-era Domestic Workers Union. And Hortense Gabel, no leftist, broke sex barriers in elite precincts like Columbia Law School and state administration.

The creed these women lived during the forties and fifties might be called "practical feminism." Battling landlords in the courtroom, leading rallies in the street, wielding power in state offices, and speaking with authority on economics and planning, they upended the domestic model of femininity promoted by Cold War pundits. Although the object of their struggles—people's homes—might count as "women's sphere," the terrain on which they fought lay squarely in the political arena. These women did not take up feminism explicitly, or as their primary political commitment. But none of them doubted her fitness to take action in the "man's world" of politics.

How had they arrived at this unorthodox sense of capability? Virtually all the women in this cohort cite the influence of extraordinary, broad-minded men, starting with their fathers. Abe Benedict "taught us early that women have rights," noted Jane.[210] Goldin recalled her father as "my hero, a wonderful man," and the one who encouraged her to become self-reliant and worldly in contravention of her mother's traditionalist outlook. ("'I want you to know what bacon is, [he said], I want you to taste ham. . . . And when you hold a cigarette . . . hold it like this. I don't want you to smoke, but if you smoke you should know what you're doing.'")[211] Gabel was also encouraged by her father and later mentored by Charles Abrams. Meanwhile Benedict was schooled by yet another seasoned houser, Stanley Isaacs. Isaacs was acquainted with Abe Benedict and knew Jane as a child. When Jane became involved with housing in the 1950s, she called on her father's old friend. "And he gave me very good advice. He told me whom to go after, and who was powerful politically, and might do it just for political reasons." This kind of inside information was invaluable for someone with no entrée to City Hall. Benedict was also married to a man who "believed profoundly in the rights of women as equal with men."[212] Peter Hawley was content to work behind the scenes for decades while his wife occupied the public stage.[213]

Beyond their families and mentors, most of these women shared an historical commonality: They were ushered into masculine realms by the lucky breaks of World War II. It was the wartime labor shortage that opened Gabel's job as corporation counsel and Wood's slot in printing. Goldin found employment in the wartime shipping industry, which in turn brought her into the communist movement. And Benedict served as CIO representative on the National War Labor Board (a body created by Roosevelt to avert strikes through mediation).[214] Other women's careers were affected by the war in less obvious but still consequential ways. Frances Levenson's admission to law school was eased by the dearth of male applicants during the early 1940s.[215] Bess Stevenson—not involved in Title I struggles but soon to be a central player in Met Council— was thrown into her first landlord–tenant conflict by her husband's absence for military service. And Bronx organizer and Met Council co-founder Helen Harris was one of three women with prior experience in neighborhood tenant and consumer councils who assumed boroughwide leadership during the war, marking an intermediate stage in women's ascent within housing politics.[216]

In a sense these women belonged to the larger American saga of Rosie the Riveter. Although nearly all the Rosies were laid off from their "men's jobs" after the war, oral histories reveal an "unintended effect of their wartime work experience[:] a transformation in their concept of themselves as women."[217] Those who went back to pink-collar jobs expected rights and dignity at work. Those who retired to homemaking claimed a greater say in household decisions.[218]

The Met Council founders' stories in particular suggest a left variation on this theme: Politically inclined women, drawn further into masculine precincts by the world war, maintained their trajectory through the Cold War—as housing organizers with a particular commitment to poor and working-class tenants. If Schrecker is right that left-wing women were the "missing generation in American feminism," some of those who went missing could be found in the tenant councils of New York City.

Others could be found in labor unions, of course, and the tenant movement's practical feminists both correspond to and contrast with the "labor feminists" that Dorothy Sue Cobble has identified in postwar unions.[219] Both groups of women placed working people's material needs at the top of their agenda. And both demanded a kind of social citizenship: urban citizenship, in the case of tenants who resisted displacement and marginalization, and industrial citizenship in the case of union activists. World citizenship, meanwhile, was the demand of yet another cohort of the missing: the "black left feminists" who mounted protests against racial terror in the United States and abroad during the Cold War, and who had first coalesced as tenant organizers in Harlem during the Depression.[220] But whereas labor feminists and black left feminists fought self-consciously for equality within male-dominated workplaces and political parties, New York's postwar tenant leaders often acted as if sex discrimination were beneath their notice. They appear to have taken their equality as a given, both within the tenant organizations they led and in the courts, legislative chambers, and other political arenas where they demanded tenants' rights.

Like most feminists, they also chose their battles and might still accept the occasional gender distinction. Goldin once took her turn at guarding an elderly neighbor, whose husband worked nights, from a landlord who had tried to burn the couple out with a kerosene bomb. The husband "left a knife. . . . in case we needed it." Sure enough, that night the landlord tried to push his way in. When Goldin told him to leave, "he said, 'Girl!' He wasn't gonna listen to a girl. So I lunged at him with the knife. And he went backward. And like an idiot . . . I ran after him. Until I realized that he was faster than I was." When her watch ended, Goldin went home. "And I saw a mouse. And I ran on the bed. And when my husband came home, I said 'There's a mouse! There's a mouse!' And he said, 'What'd you do tonight?' And I said, 'Oh, I took care of Mamie, and the guy came, and I had a knife, and I almost killed him.' He said, 'And you're standing here afraid of a mouse?' And I was petrified of the mouse. But I did my duty with the landlord."[221]

Vying with vermin was but one way in which these women could both reject and conform to standard gender roles. Adherence to gender convention in the economic sphere, paradoxically, facilitated some of their unconventional work in the political arena. Although Goldin, Stevenson, and some others were breadwinners—Stevenson's marriage did not last, and Goldin's husband was blacklisted—a number of female tenant organizers did not work outside the home, or worked fewer hours than their husbands did. This gave them time for politics. East Tremont's tenant committee was made up of housewives who were able to picket and meet with officials during the day while their husbands were at work. But full-time homemaking was a prerogative of women in the middle and upper working classes; the poorest families needed two incomes just to eat. In a *de facto* segregated labor market, few black men earned a "family wage," and hence few black women stayed home. That may help explain why the sex balance was more even among black tenant activists than among white ones.

Like conventional family arrangements, prevailing gender ideology could paradoxically support women's unconventional political work. Asked why women led the tenant movement, Goldin said, "It's because taking care of the home was the woman's job. . . . [I]t was a tenant *and consumer* movement. You know, buying the milk, and buying the meat, and taking care of the apartment. . . . I think it was natural, that the women felt it more keenly."[222] Benedict disputed this: "I once was talking to somebody about it, who said, 'Well, women *feel* more about houses than men do.' You know, they feel for their families and all that. I don't think that's true."[223] However, even if women did not feel more, the widespread belief that they did—the ideology of domesticity—may have made their tenant work seem to others (and perhaps even to the some of the women themselves) a legitimate form of political participation. In that respect, postwar tenant activists harked back to the municipal housekeepers of the Progressive Era.

Such notions, however, were but an undertone in New York's postwar tenant councils, where most women leaders claimed the political sphere in ways that defied domesticity. It is possible that city geography as well as generational biography played a role here. The physical settings of New York's tenant fights were the antithesis of gendered space as it was constructed in the suburbs. In the city, home and more public areas stood so compactly together that the line between them was fine indeed. This comes through in Marshall Berman's recollection of Bronx window-yentas and Jim Torain's story of Miss Purity Harmonious. Such women could be simultaneously in the home *and* watching over the local store and pedestrian street traffic, precisely because their buildings were not set off by lawns or cloistered away from commercial spaces (the layout that retail boosters believed women preferred). Nor did New York women simply watch the action outside. They claimed, and exercised, full rights to intervene. From their modest apartments in their bustling neighborhoods, New Yorkers created a vital exception to the fifties norms of suburban housing and separate spheres.

By the end of the decade, the ravages of redevelopment had pushed diverse New York to revive a consciousness of tenants' rights and to regroup under that banner. In the 1960s the black freedom movement would draw much greater attention to the depredations of the urban housing market and create opportunities for expanded tenant organizing.

Introduction to Part II

Class, Race, and Housing in the Postindustrial City

New York City in the early 1960s was going through profound shifts in economy and population, shifts that were recasting its political order. The onetime stronghold of organized labor and working-class culture was losing its blue-collar base. Manufacturing had declined steadily in the years since World War II—200,000 jobs moved away or simply vanished—while sectors like finance, real estate, and civil service had grown.[1]

This transformation was driven by corporate practices of automation and capital disinvestment that were remaking many urban centers. But deindustrialization in New York would be pushed further by City Hall, acting at the behest the local planning and business elite. The Regional Plan Association's 1929 recommendations had never wielded the force of law. In 1959 and 1960, however, RPA leaders and downtown real estate moguls crafted a new zoning system which was adopted by the city. It designated the heart of Lower Manhattan for office towers, the most lucrative kind of development. Manufacturing would have to pick up and move to the waterfronts or outer boroughs. The port and its half-million jobs were exiled to New Jersey.[2] The new zoning code was an industrial analog of the city's approach to tenant relocation.

Economic change dovetailed with demographic transformation. Nationally, the decades after 1950 marked a period of urban decline, when American cities registered substantial population losses as millions followed the lure of jobs and mortgages to the suburbs. New York appeared unscathed: Its net population decrease between 1950 and 1960 was just 1.4 percent, nothing compared to the double-digit dropoffs in Boston, St. Louis, and Pittsburgh.[3] Yet New York *was* losing large numbers of people—white people. During the 1950s more than 1.3 million whites moved out of the city; nearly a million more would follow in the next decade. What hid this exodus in the aggregate figures was the large gain, through both natural increase and in-migration, of people of color.[4]

Within the changing city, different kinds of people encountered disparate opportunities. For many of the whites who stayed in New York—some from middle-class families, some the children of postwar workers—the growing white-collar sectors offered upward mobility. (This represented a pyrrhic victory for organized labor, which supported the free higher-education system that opened professional doors for many working-class youths.) And for blue-collar workers in nonmanufacturing fields like construction and civil service, the city's economy could still provide a good paycheck.

But for the new New Yorkers—the hundreds of thousands of African Americans and Puerto Ricans who arrived in the fifties and sixties—the changing economy posed roadblocks. Some could get no jobs at all. Others found low-paid service work, usually nonunion, rather than the unionized manufacturing jobs that had afforded a better future to immigrants before them. And with limited schooling and English, they were ill equipped for the booming white-collar fields. The variegated and semipermeable social spectrum of the postwar years was breaking down. In its place were two castes with increasingly divergent interests.

The middle range might have been preserved, had organized labor reached out to workers in the growing service sector. Instead, established unions in manufacturing concentrated on protecting benefits for their own shrinking memberships. But as those unions dwindled, so did blue-collar political power. New York's left did not die out, but its institutional foundation in strong labor unions grew weaker in the 1960s.

Further, although the city retained a sizable liberal constituency, the social democratic policies this camp had traditionally approved faced mounting fiscal and ideological challenges. Even during the prosperous forties and fifties, city spending had outpaced income, as beholden mayors rewarded supporters with jobs, services, tax breaks, and zoning favors, while creative budget directors "were lauded . . . for making deficits disappear."[5] In the sixties the deficit would grow. Tax-paying people and businesses skipped town just when the tab was rising for New York's distinctive liberal program. Public housing, strong municipal unions, the country's highest per-capita expenditures for welfare and schools—all outgrowths of the midcentury labor-left alliance—cost money. Education and social-service outlays in particular climbed as hundreds of thousands of needy migrants moved to the city. Those outlays would loom as prime budget villains to some observers, including a spokesman for the 1975 fiscal rescue agency who told a reporter, "New York's in trouble because it's got too many fucking blacks and Puerto Ricans [who] use city services."[6] But this vernacular math ignored the more refined variables—dislocation of taxable industry, subsidies to office developers and financiers, federal handouts to the suburban growth machine—that had gutted the revenue line of the city's balance sheet.[7]

Notwithstanding City Hall's own role in creating some of these budget problems, the deficit posed unsavory choices for Robert Wagner as he began his third term as mayor in 1962. The formerly "regular" Democrat had made good on his vow to break with the Tammany machine. But he could not recoup budget losses simply by running a tighter ship. And his appeals for state relief touched few hearts in Republican-dominated Albany.[8] Thus the mayor's circle believed that halting the middle-class exodus was their first task; without middle-class taxes, there would be no money for poor people's needs.

Nowhere did this priority show more clearly than in Wagner's new housing program. In two important ways the mayor had remained loyal to the cross-class tenant agenda of the 1940s: he had supported rent control and continued to build public housing. Yet in other respects he had given short shrift to poor and working-class tenants, even during his first two terms. Prior to 1958 Wagner had done little to restrain Robert Moses' fleet of bulldozers. His inaction had wrought disaster for low-income people, as old low-rent units were knocked down faster than the Housing Authority could put up new ones. Thus the city's housing stock remained 430,000 units short in 1960, and substandard conditions still prevailed in more than a quarter of a million occupied units.[9] Further, according to a study prepared by Met Council leader Jane Wood, the Neighborhood Conservation Program—Wagner's 1959 response to the bulldozer outcry—was serving as a Trojan horse. Rather than protect existing communities, it hastened the removal of people of color from "conservation" areas into segregated precincts and the conversion of low-rent rooms into "luxury efficiency units."[10]

While housing scarcity and redevelopment thus ravaged low-income New Yorkers, the budget-conscious mayor now placed even stronger emphasis on middle-income construction. He created a new agency, the Housing and Rehabilitation Board (HRB), to coordinate urban renewal and expand state-aided middle-income projects.[11] The latter mission found a crucial champion in Governor Nelson Rockefeller, a liberal Republican with eyes for the White House. Rockefeller's strategy for building support among middle-class voters included a creative scheme to channel state dollars into middle-income housing via autonomous "public authorities" rather than voter-approved bonds.[12] This also worked out nicely for real estate investors, another group the governor desired to court.[13]

Developers were enticed through a subsidy arrangement known as the Mitchell-Lama program. Mitchell-Lama (so called after its legislative sponsors) offered low-interest loans and tax abatements for the building of limited-profit rentals and limited-equity co-ops in the moderate and middle-income brackets. It was similar in premise to New York State's 1926 limited-dividend law, which had subsidized the Amalgamated Houses and other modestly priced developments before the war. Mitchell-Lama, enacted in 1955, was little used at first, but Rockefeller pumped new life into the program with his sovereign funding system and legislative revisions. The latter loosened the original law's profit constraints, making it easier for owners to buy out of the program and its 6 percent return cap after fifteen years.[14] With these refinements the low-risk proposition attracted many investors. They would add 140,000 units of middle-income housing to the city's stock by 1978.[15]

Low-income housing, meanwhile, remained subject to voter referendum and was usually killed at the upstate polls. Between 1960 and 1965—when public money subsidized 35,000 new middle-income apartments in New York City—only 21,000 units of low-income housing were constructed.[16]

While Mitchell-Lama put up apartment towers, the Federal Housing Administration continued to subsidize development of single-family homes on vacant land in the outer boroughs. Middle- and upper-working-class buyers could enjoy suburban advantages like square footage and equity while remaining relatively close to urban amenities. This market, like the job market, offered more opportunity to whites than to people of color. True, white homeowners in New York and its suburbs did not mount neighborhood-defense campaigns as virulent as those waged elsewhere, and New York's and New Jersey's pioneering anti-bias laws remained on the books.[17] But realtors and owners found ways to practice what the Congress of Racial Equality called "sophisticated" discrimination by inflating required down payments for minority buyers or telling them houses were already sold.[18] Wage differentials also effectively shut many African Americans and Puerto Ricans out. A 1961 Citizens' Housing and Planning Council study found that the great majority of New Yorkers of color could not afford market-rate housing.[19]

Those who could, moreover, faced exploitative schemes. In 1963 the City Commission on Human Rights investigated block-busting in East New York, Brooklyn. It found that realtors had engaged in "the deliberate parading of groups of Negroes, presumably prospective buyers, up and down a block" of white-owned homes. Such displays would trigger "panic selling," followed by resale "to a Negro or Puerto Rican purchaser at an exorbitant markup." This in turn led to "high cost . . . financing" and a cycle of debt.[20] The American Dream became a financial nightmare. Other white sections of Brooklyn and Queens witnessed similar practices.[21]

In some ways New York's history of civil-rights housing activism did make itself felt in local home-buying markets. Fair-housing laws championed in the fifties by the Stuyvesant Town coalition gave advocates such as CORE, the NAACP, and the Urban League the legal grounds to press, sometimes effectively, for state action.[22] Equally important, white residents in several city neighborhoods and a few Westchester and Long Island towns organized to *support* open occupancy. "This House *Not* for Sale," read the signs these homeowners displayed to foil block-busting. The city's human-rights commission also persuaded the electrical workers to promote integration in their Queens development, which, like most of the labor co-ops, was nearly all-white.[23]

Still, such actions only moderated the racial disparities. In 1960, 40 percent of white households in the city and its suburbs were owner-occupied, while only 17 percent of nonwhite households were.[24] A decade later that gulf remained, with white and black ownership rates of 45 and 20 percent, respectively.[25]

Those figures mattered because housing served as a gatekeeper for economic mobility. Homeowners could build equity, and with an FHA mortgage they might do so for less than they had once paid in rent. Those who bought homes in the suburbs proper often gained access to better-paying jobs and better-funded schools. Racial exclusion from these postindustrial pathways would reinforce economic Jim Crow long after the *de jure* kind was dismantled.

But New York City itself was still a tenant town—solidly so for whites and overwhelmingly so for people of color. (Although nearly half the whites in the wider metropolitan area owned their homes in 1970, only a quarter of those in the five boroughs did.)[26] Therefore New Yorkers' struggles to enjoy the fruits of citizenship *as tenants* would remain central to city politics through the sixties. And tenants' rights still mattered to the middle class as well as the poor. At a time of widening class and racial division, the city's tenant movement faced new opportunities and severe challenges in forging strategies to serve its diverse constituency.

4

"Out of These Ghettos, People Who Would Fight"

Claiming Power in the Sixties

On December 30, 1963, five Harlem tenants walked into Manhattan Civil Court, reached into their coats and handbags, and each pulled out a large dead rat. The judge barred the four-legged exhibits from the rent hearing that followed. But this bit of courtroom theater, captured on film by reporters, reached a larger audience and became an emblem of a new generation of confrontational black- and Latino-led tenant politics in New York. Rats were nothing new, of course; they had long enjoyed star billing in ghetto housing exposés. But in the past, tenants had invited investigators uptown to see the vermin. Now they were laying the problem at government's doorstep and demanding a response.

The rat routine called attention to a rent strike that ghetto residents had launched a few months before. Notice was given in August, when Harlem organizer Jesse Gray castigated city officials for condoning "flagrant housing violations" and urged uptown tenants to hold back their rents until repairs were made. The statement received only brief mention in the *Times*. But alongside it ran a three-column story about an upcoming civil-rights march on Washington that was expected to draw more than 100,000 participants.[1]

The editor who paired these items showed insight. New York's rent-strike movement was a local wave of the rising nationwide tide of civil-rights activity. Historians have been slower to connect those dots, but that project is now well under way. In place of an earlier generation of scholarship that presented a freedom play in two acts—a nonviolent and successful southern movement for integration in the late fifties and early sixties, followed by a nihilistic northern quest for black power—we now have an extensive literature on philosophically and tactically diverse justice struggles across regions and time periods.[2]

New York City's rent rebellion adds to both the narrative continuity and the ideological messiness of this picture. Far from coming as a bolt from the blue, the sixties strikes bore discernible links to earlier characters and chapters in New York's tenant, labor, and civil-rights history. Old Left veterans served as key organizers, and Depression-era legislation provided traction in court. Further, one of the strikes' main achievements was to galvanize tenants throughout the city at a critical moment in the long-term fight over rent control, thus helping to extend that wartime policy into the postindustrial era.

Ideologically, the strikes blur the line between civil-rights liberalism and black power. Rent strikers eschewed the liberal integrationist vision—moving out of the ghetto—that had animated the previous decade's black housing struggles. Instead they sought to improve conditions and build power within the segregated neighborhoods where they, like most African Americans, actually lived. This shift prefigured two better-known rebuffs to liberal reformism in New York, which involved some of the same ideals and people: the 1964 Harlem riot and the late sixties campaign for community control of schools.

Yet rent strikers also allied with liberal and left-leaning whites to demand that a putatively liberal city administration enforce, at long last, existing housing codes. In effect they offered liberal government a chance to redeem itself, to deliver on its promise of economic citizenship for all.

Government did not jump at that chance. Strikers gained some repairs and tighter code enforcement, but their larger demand for sound housing throughout the city's ghettos and barrios could be met only through massive public expenditure. Fearing white flight and a shrinking tax base, New York's municipal and state agencies gave priority instead to building middle-class housing. They offered no program to replace or rehabilitate the mass of deteriorated low-rent stock. This inaction further eroded many blacks' faith in liberal solutions and impelled some to seek new paths to empowerment.

Critics have cast the strike as a failure and laid blame on its leaders and the strategies they embraced. Most famously, social-movement scholars Frances Fox Piven and Richard Cloward, who were involved in the strikes through their service organization, Mobilization for Youth, concluded that organizers erred fatally by leading tenants to work through the courts rather than disrupt state institutions.[3] Historians have pointed as well to confusion among activists with differing notions of where the strikes should lead. Several observers have described Jesse Gray's fondness for publicity as a liability in the long run.[4]

These postmortems offer much insight. There is no denying that strikers failed to alter the basic power dynamics enabling slum exploitation. That was plain to see in Albany, where numerous bills to protect tenants and build public housing were scuttled by legislators who bowed to the landlord lobby.[5] There is also evidence for the position taken by Piven, Cloward, and others that fighting landlords in court made tenants dependent on *pro bono* lawyers, who were never in great supply.[6]

Piven and Cloward's critique, however, written in 1967, assumes that strikers should have prevailed. It is an expression of the same Movement *zeitgeist* that inspired many strike organizers to begin with. Decades later, it is apparent that virtually all incarnations of sixties and seventies radicalism failed to realize their most ambitious goals, particularly those involving redistribution of material resources such as housing. Instead, the black freedom and New Left movements' lasting achievements in the material realm lay in winning what Michael Katz calls "selective incorporation" of marginalized peoples (women, racial minorities) into the privileged strata, and in the establishment of professionally run services for the poor.[7] Indeed, Thomas Sugrue argues that it was precisely through "professionalization of protest" that New York's rent strike gained a degree of institutional longevity, via government and foundation-funded legal services, after Jesse Gray and his tenant council faded from the scene.[8] In other words, the strikes' shortfall attests as much to the adaptability of capital, now evident as a national pattern, as to the missteps of particular protesters.

Further, there are other ways of measuring the strikes' achievement. Rent strikers succeeded in raising the nation's consciousness of ghetto housing conditions and in putting those conditions high on the black agenda at a time when many African Americans were rethinking political strategies. In this way they linked tenants' rights to the nascent community-control movement. As well, the strikes and the legal reforms they did win fostered a sense of agency among New Yorkers who had previously despaired of challenging the system at all. Finally, some strike organizers, women especially, went on to attain a lasting voice in housing and other areas of social policy.

The Package Deal

During the years immediately preceding the rent strike, New York's civil-rights network was reviving its broad Popular Front agenda. Bayard Rustin would later identify 1963 as the moment when "[s]ingle-issue demands of the movement's classical stage gave way to the 'package deal.' No longer were Negroes satisfied with integrating lunch counters. They now sought advances in employment, housing, school integration, police protection, and so forth."[9] This may or may not have been true of the South. But certainly in New York the more ambitious program predominated earlier. "Employment, housing, school integration [and] police protection" were precisely the issues on which New York's early postwar black movement had pushed hardest. Activists had rallied at Stuyvesant Town and called for housing-code enforcement. They had demanded full and fair employment; supported improved and integrated public education; and sought to curtail police abuse.[10]

Like the rest of the left, New York's civil-rights movement was weakened by anti-Communist offensives. But in the late fifties it started surging back. Brooklyn parents, led by African American pastor Milton Galamison and white Communist Annie Stein, organized to demand better schools and an end to *de facto* segregation. A group of uptown mothers dubbed the "Little Rock Nine of Harlem" did likewise. By 1958 a few ghetto residents were boycotting local schools, and by the early sixties, thousands were threatening to do so.[11] In the same years black labor activists renewed the drive for equitable hiring in construction and other skilled trades.[12] The city's left-leaning and heavily black unions sent busload upon busload to the great national civil-rights event of 1963, the March on Washington for Jobs and Freedom.[13] (Indeed, it was Rustin and fellow New Yorker A. P. Randolph who organized the march.) All these efforts gained strength and urgency from continuing migration and population growth. More than three quarters of a million blacks and Puerto Ricans moved to New York during the 1950s and 1960s; by 1970 the city's population of color would surpass 2.6 million.[14]

In this atmosphere of national agitation and local emphasis on socioeconomic disparities, housing was a political tinderbox. Gotham's rental stock was scarce, expensive, and ill maintained, especially in the ghettoes. Thirty-three percent of the city's nonwhites lived in "deteriorating" and "dilapidated" housing in 1960, while only 12 percent of whites did.[15] Half the apartments in Central Harlem were unsound.[16] These figures underscored the failure of successive liberal administrations to deal people of color into postwar economic citizenship.

A Bit of Glasgow in Harlem

Jesse Gray swirled easily into this political ferment. Born and raised in a working-class African American family in Louisiana, he attended Xavier University, and, like many others who would shape the civil-rights movement, served in the military during World War II.[17] The branch he chose was the Merchant Marine, where the left-wing National Maritime Union (NMU) led the struggle for fair employment, and where Gray came under the tutelage of Communist leader Harry Haywood.[18] Gray joined the Party and became active in shipboard committees. After the war he settled in New York, where the union was based, and continued to ship out until he was purged by the NMU's new anti-Communist leadership around 1952. The blacklist did not govern the Harlem Tenants' Council, however, and Gray made that group his new political home. He led several protests against unsafe conditions and illegal evictions in the early fifties. After a two-year hiatus in the South, he returned to New York in 1957 and formed his own organization, the Lower Harlem Tenants' Council.[19]

Gray's ouster from the NMU propelled him into tenant organizing, but his time at sea had primed him for the job. Not only had he learned organizing skills onboard the ships; he had studied housing politics. Activist Jack O'Dell, who met Gray at Xavier and became his NMU brother and Party comrade, recalled that both were struck, in their political education readings, by Engels' treatise *The Housing Question*, "in which he deals with . . . the importance of housing, pivotal to capitalist exploitation."[20] Further, Gray's and O'Dell's travels exposed them to a potential strategy. At port in Great Britain they learned that "the tenant movement in Scotland had made a breakthrough and had elected people to Parliament . . . So we said, 'Well, you know, we ought to be able to do that also.' The fact is that housing isn't just another issue, that housing is like bread and butter and a job." Both men "felt that [the Glasgow residents' accomplishment] was our goal too, to develop a kind of tenants' movement, out of these slums and ghettoes, people who would fight for a national housing policy that guaranteed that working people had decent housing.[21]

Harlem seemed an auspicious place to cultivate this vision when Gray and O'Dell started canvassing there in the late 1950s. "The tenants of Harlem faced a continuous erosion of [housing conditions], with landlords trying to maximize their profit." And "there were still people in their fifties and sixties who had seen [Depression-era upheaval] as teenagers, or even been active in it as teenagers. . . . Boycotts . . ., Adam Clayton Powell leading marches, and that sort of thing. So it was a community that had a rhythm of organization, if you will. It had a sense of organization."[22]

But the rhythm of 1930s street mobilizations did not catch on easily in tenement hallways. As the organizers worked the area south of 118th Street—Lower Harlem, as they called it—the going was slow. Individuals who commanded respect were easy enough to find, noted O'Dell, "but, now, the willingness

to take on responsibility is another whole thing . . . To call the meeting, to
see that the meetings are held, to go around with a committee to check on
the apartments, to see what kind of repairs they needed. There's a certain
initiative that people have to have."[23] By 1961, organizational nuclei were up
and running in perhaps thirty or forty buildings.[24] Maintaining stable tenant
associations in more than a handful, however, would remain a challenge in
coming years.

Sparks to the Tinder

Accordingly, it was through sporadic protests rather than sustained campaigns that Harlem tenants signaled their growing impatience. In 1959 Gray
led a small rent strike that won improved conditions in eight tenements. In
the summer of 1961 he made the papers again with an unofficial block-by-
block code inspection.[25] Months later a Puerto Rican woman from East Harlem brought a live rat into Housing Court to support her complaint against a
negligent landlord. (The judge blandly said "she had seen enough rats in her
time in the courtroom" and accepted the landlord's guilty plea.)[26] A pastor at
Harlem's prominent Abyssinian Baptist Church told reporters, "a city-wide
work stoppage and rent strike by Negroes and Puerto Ricans to protest bad
housing conditions [is] almost inevitable unless something is done."[27]

Neither the rats nor the people of Harlem, then, were novices at housing
protest when Gray issued his strike call in August of 1963. But their actions
would now command greater attention "due to the general civil-rights movement in this country," as Gray put it.[28] Nineteen sixty-three was the year of
the Birmingham showdowns and the March on Washington. It was also a year
in which a handful of young civil-rights activists who had cut their teeth on
the southern campaigns turned their attention to New York's tenements. That
spring the Congress of Racial Equality (CORE), an organization that had historically focused on desegregation, began to organize tenant associations out
of its Harlem office.[29] In July a newer group, the Northern Student Movement
(NSM), won a foundation grant to set up tutoring and other services in Central
Harlem. When a tenant who lived across the street from their Eighth Avenue
storefront organized his neighbors to withhold rent that fall, the NSM workers
would be there to help out.[30]

The ghetto campaigns also drew strength from a second, less publicized
circumstance: code-enforcement policies that the city's older houser network
had put forward at a strategic moment. In 1958 and 1959 a scandal broke over

the widespread palm greasing and false reporting at Mayor Wagner's Buildings and Real Estate Departments; it led to a raft of indictments, resignations, and vows of reform.[31] This provided an opening for tenant advocates to approach the administration proffering new tools. The most important was a receivership bill that pro-tenant legislators had been futilely sponsoring in Albany since 1957. This measure would empower the court to appoint a receiver to contract for urgent repairs when a landlord failed to do so; crucially, it would also authorize the city to advance funds for such repairs when rent revenue was inadequate.[32] The languishing bill gained attention in the 1961 mayoral race between Wagner and State Attorney General Louis Lefkowitz; Wagner was compelled to embrace the receivership remedy as his own and do battle against upstate Republicans until the measure passed in the spring of 1962.[33]

Pressure to use this and other governmental powers mounted the following year, when the Women's City Club released a survey of badly deteriorated buildings in East Harlem.[34] Next, radio station WMCA—headed by Ellen Sulzberger Straus, daughter-in-law of Women's City Club activist leader Helen Straus and member of the *Times* Sulzberger family—ran its own housing exposé and organized a new pressure group, Call for Action, to address the unsavory findings.[35] Two weeks later, Met Council led hundreds of pickets at City Hall. Jane Benedict met with the mayor to demand a code crackdown.[36] Wagner responded with a promise of stepped-up inspections and stricter penalties.[37] He formed a Housing Executive Committee that included James Felt, now president of the City Planning Commission; the directors of NYCHA and the Housing and Redevelopment Board; and, shortly, Hortense Gabel.[38]

Closely related to the code campaign was a struggle over rent control, due to expire during the 1961 legislative session. As maneuvering began, Met Council took on landlords' perennial claim of financial hardship by releasing a study showing the contrary: rent-controlled property paid a hefty 8 percent return, and rent hikes typically brought no improvement to deteriorated buildings.[39] The usual tenant–labor–liberal alliance won extension of the law, but with provisions that would loosen rent restrictions over time. The next year Wagner promoted a different solution: a "home rule" law that gave the city, not the state, authority over rents. With the Republican Governor Rockefeller eager to distance himself from rent wrangling in an election year, the law passed with bipartisan support in February 1962.[40] The mayor also streamlined the city's regulatory apparatus into a single agency, the Rent and Rehabilitation Administration, directed by Hortense Gabel.[41] A year later landlords quietly orchestrated "surprise hearings" on rent control in Albany. Met Council gave

hastily prepared testimony to fend off this attack, then publicized the inci-
dent to mobilize labor and civil-rights groups for the City Hall demonstration
against Wagner's lax code enforcement.[42]

Compelling the administration to use its expanded housing powers was a
principal aim of activists who increased the tempo of ghetto protest in the
summer and fall of 1963. As Gray continued to lead small demonstrations from
his East 117th Street office (now called the Community Council on Housing),
an unaffiliated Central Harlem tenant named Granville Cherry stopped paying rent on his rat-ridden railroad flat and persuaded others in his building to
do the same.[43] Cherry was acquainted with his across-the-street neighbors in
the Northern Student Movement, an organization that had formed two years
earlier to raise money for the southern civil-rights group SNCC (the Student
Nonviolent Coordinating Committee), but that was now developing northern
projects based on SNCC's precept that ordinary people should learn to take
action on their own.[44] "Fannie Lou Hamer, activist sharecroppers, people who
emerged out of the community, who became the voice of that community,"
recalled NSM staffer Danny Schechter. "That's what we believed in, bottom-
up." Granville Cherry came across as a likely carrier of this tradition. "He was
articulate, he was committed, he was a hard worker, he was willing to take
initiative, and distribute leaflets and talk to people. And he was also giving us,
people in the Northern Student Movement, a kind of legitimacy, somebody
in the neighborhood."[45]

One thing NSM could offer in return was publicity. The rent strike launched
by Cherry's group of eight families in September made the front page of the
Times. A reporter described the "falling plaster, broken windows . . . broken
toilet," and ubiquitous rats. Strikers, he noted, "believe[d] that [these] troubles
arise directly from the opportunity for exploitation that a racial ghetto affords
white owners."[46]

NSM also helped to build coalition. It was Schechter, a Jewish labor-re-
lations major from Cornell, who brought together Cherry's nascent tenant
association and Gray's. Schechter came from a family of garment workers
who lived in the Amalgamated co-op in the Bronx. He had learned early about
social democracy. "[M]y father was on the apartment allocation committee.
He was part of the people who were very active in the project. . . . So I grew
up imbued with those values, not only the labor movement, but also living in
a community where people participated, making decisions about housing and
everything else." Schechter gained further exposure to the fifties remnants of

the Old Left at DeWitt Clinton High School, where he befriended a boy named Paul Yergan. Yergan's father, the first African American to teach at City College, was a longtime internationalist and radical with close ties to the Communist Party (which he later renounced stridently). Through Yergan, Schechter met other black leftists, and when he found himself organizing rent strikes in Harlem in 1963, an acquaintance from that network invited him to meet with the union-activist-turned-tenant leader Jesse Gray.[47]

"I went over there, and we said, 'Look, we're doing these rent strikes, we want to help organize and help you.' He said, 'Great.' . . . and suddenly the thing started taking off in the winter."[48] Gray and the students developed a cooperative relationship, sharing organizers and holding joint meetings for Harlem strikers.[49]

Similar convergences of experienced and green activists were taking place on rundown ghetto blocks in other parts of the city. One unusually broad-based effort developed in Bedford-Stuyvesant, Brooklyn. Tenants had been picketing and filing code complaints for two years under the leadership of the Parkway-Stuyvesant Council, a community group that comprised whites and blacks, small homeowners and renters, and that sought a voice in city decisions over redevelopment, cultural provision, and job training as well as housing-code enforcement.[50] At least one of the founders, Hy Bershad, had rubbed elbows with the Old Left in the 1940s.[51] He co-chaired the organization's Tenant Welfare Committee alongside Robert "Skip" Moore, an African American who would go on to hold senior positions in Met Council and the New York Urban League.[52] In 1963 the Parkway-Stuyvesant Council joined forces with Brooklyn CORE to organize rent strikes in the borough's ill-maintained buildings.[53] Meanwhile CORE's NYU chapter collected a truckload of trash from a tenement block in the Puerto Rican section of the Lower East Side and dumped it on City Hall Plaza. A large rat trophy adorned their vehicle.[54] By early November, 110 of 120 families on the block were paying their rent into an escrow account.[55]

In Harlem Jesse Gray now announced exponential (and likely fanciful) growth: three buildings on strike in mid-November, fifty in early December, 1,000 expected by the New Year.[56] By early January, recalled a CORE volunteer, the quickening action and publicity "created what those who experienced it called a 'rent strike fever,' an extraordinary sense of exhilaration and even of historic destiny that drew people to the movement as the initiator of a new stage in the civil-rights movement."[57]

Figure 9. **No rent for rats.** Jesse Gray leads demonstration. *Courtesy of Frances Goldin.*
Powerful photos of strike actions, unavailable for republication here, are, at this writing,
accessible on the Internet. Go to www.books.google.com and enter the following search
term: "Ebony April 1964 'Vol. 19' 'No. 6'." The rent strike story runs on pages 112–20.

Strike Philosophy

At first glance this movement seemed to revive the logic of the early twentieth-century rent strikes, and, indeed, of the labor strikes on which they were
modeled: economic leverage exerted by the masses. Thus *Ebony* reported that
rent-strike organizers had "directed the rage of the community at the slumlords' Achilles heel—their pocketbooks. 'No repairs, no rent,' is Gray's simple
equation."[58] CORE's Marshall England agreed. "We have talked with landlords,
begged landlords," he said. "When the landlord is faced with no rents, then we
get some action."[59] Not since the 1930s had the rent strike figured so prominently as a tenant tactic.

But the 1960s strikers actually wielded little direct leverage over landlords
whose pocketbooks were well protected by the market and the law. Building
owners could claim an annual property depreciation that substantially reduced
their liability for federal income tax. This created a payoff immune to tenant
action. And slum landlords could keep expenses lower than revenue by the
simple expedient of cutting maintenance to nil, a practice effectively condoned
by the city's anemic enforcement. The combination of impunity, tax savings,
and housing scarcity "ma[de] slum ownership and slum maintenance a highly

profitable, risk-free speculation," wrote Anthony Panuch in 1960.[60] Panuch called for legislation to "take the profit out of slums."[61] The 1962 receivership bill was one response to this recommendation.

Organizers seemed to understand these realities, at least some of the time. Gray and the Brooklyn CORE leaders stressed that the strikes were aimed at politicians as much as at landlords. Repeatedly they called on the city to fine and jail negligent owners and to use its new receivership power to effect repairs.[62] Adam Powell and other black officials echoed those demands.[63]

In a sense, then, the strike movement followed in a long line of calls, dating to the Progressive Era, for the policing of slum conditions. What made it different was direct action and a corresponding sense of grassroots agency. The Progressive model had little place for direct demands by the militant poor. Indeed, as late as 1960, the Lower East Side's settlement-house leaders—direct heirs of the Progressive tradition—were appalled at proposals to organize tenants. Mobilization for Youth director Richard Cloward recalled, "Helen [Hall of the Henry Street Settlement] knew that once we started messing around with tenants, we were going to have trouble with landlords. Now, landlords are very important politically in New York. Very important. She knew that once we started organizing welfare clients, well, then we were going to be antagonizing the Commissioner of Welfare, and the next thing she would know, she'd get a call from the Mayor, which is exactly what happened."[64] Mainline civil-rights organizations such as the NAACP were much quicker to embrace the new movement, but it certainly marked a departure from their past emphasis on professional advocacy.

Rent strikers turned away not only from mainline tactics, but from the liberal civil-rights establishment's ranking of priorities. Throughout the postwar period, demands for ghetto code enforcement in New York had taken second place to the push for "fair"—racially open—housing. The program of fire-safety and other improvements sketched out in the early 1940s by the City-Wide Citizens' Committee on Harlem gathered dust as the battle for Stuyvesant Town absorbed all the activists' energy. Nationally, too, the boldest civil-rights housing banner of the fifties and very early sixties proclaimed the right of blacks to rent or buy in predominantly white neighborhoods.

Now rent strikers were taking a different tack. They were not trying to move out of Harlem and into white areas. They were trying to bring the standards upheld in white areas to the ghetto. Behind this shift lay a sense that for the foreseeable future, much of black America would remain in predominantly black neighborhoods. To some this might be a defeatist vision. But to others it signified an ethos, loosely defined, of community self-empowerment.

City Responses

By December 1963, the actions had become regular news. Papers tallied rat bites and ran photos of tenants wearing coats in freezing apartments.[65] Journalists gravitated to the "short, intense slum fighter" Jesse Gray, a "fiery leader" who always had a pithy phrase and an impressive number to punch up leads.[66] "How many buildings do you have on strike today, Jesse?" became their regular query.[67] Gray also kept the story lively with devices like his call for the Red Cross to declare Lower Harlem a disaster area, in need of coal and blankets for hundreds without heat.[68] By the time the rats had their day in Civil Court, the *Times* was heralding the action in advance.[69]

The media spotlight caused some agitation in city agencies. In July the Rent and Rehabilitation Administration—the new consolidated entity headed by Hortense Gabel—quietly granted rent reductions of 33 to 50 percent to CORE-organized tenants on the Lower East Side.[70] When Granville Cherry's Eighth Avenue strikers made the news in September, the agency announced publicly that it would reduce those complainants' rents to one dollar per month.[71] This would render the strike "academic," said officials. But the reductions also gave the strike a certain mayoral imprimatur. Perhaps fearing that implication, RRA officials denied reductions to tenants in other delinquent buildings.[72]

Fundamentally, however, the rent reductions fell short of tenants' demand for proper maintenance. This was not lost on strike organizers and advocates. The Community Service Society—an influential alliance of charitable and reform organizations that dated back to the nineteenth century—did not endorse the strike directly, but it pointedly reminded the mayor that his promises of code enforcement remained unfulfilled.[73] In December several Harlem assembly members and Democratic district leaders met with representatives of the NAACP, CORE, and a nascent community organization, HARYOU-ACT, to form a Rent Strike Coordinating Committee to increase the pressure. (The committee "never particularly performed any coordination," observed one analyst, but "it served for a period to create the impression of cohesion.")[74]

Meanwhile gears began turning in the city's judiciary. The hearing at which Gray's group brandished rats was the strike's first courtroom proceeding, and it ended in a tenant victory when Judge Guy Gilbert Ribaudo recognized the defendants' right to withhold payment on hazard-ridden apartments. He instructed them to deposit their back rent with the court. "[T]he landlord could apply for the money, but only for use to correct violations in the buildings." Thus the court strode into territory from which mayoral appointee Hortense

Gabel had shied: legally sanctioning the strike. Gray quickly prevailed upon Gabel to reduce rents in seven other buildings to one dollar per month.[75]

The ruling signaled the protesters' growing moral authority, but it rested on two generations of tenant lawyering. The statute Judge Ribaudo cited was the 1930 Real Property Actions and Proceedings Law, a section of which allowed tenants in severely neglected units to deposit rent with the court. Although enacted during the Depression, Section 755 had rarely been used. Now it was unearthed by a team of Columbia law professors allied with Mobilization for Youth.[76] The lawyers' linking of the old statute to a new escrow arrangement was important because the 1962 receivership law, in which tenant advocates had placed such hope, was turning out to be a dull weapon. Establishing receivership took a year or longer.[77] Under the Ribaudo ruling a *de facto* receivership—court-controlled spending of rent money for repairs—was to be achieved swiftly through the resurrected property law. Significantly, however, Section 755 would not authorize city funds to supplement the money available for repairs.

On the eve of the nonpayment case, Wagner aides had announced that they were "forging new weapons to combat the slum conditions that have prompted Harlem's spreading rent strike."[78] A week later the mayor unveiled these armaments. They included special housing courts, stepped-up inspections, stiffer penalties, streamlining of the byzantine processes for verifying violations, and, most important, city backing for a state bill to legalize rent strikes.[79] Gray voiced cautious approval.[80] The mayor's well-publicized week of housing proclamations culminated in his Friday announcement of a "million dollar war on rats."[81] The city would arm 148 new inspectors and exterminators with rat poison and the authority to bill landlords for their services.

These moves were not just grudging concessions to tenant pressure. They were also small victories for bureaucrats who wanted to take action (whether to serve tenants, their own public image, or both). Political scientist Michael Lipsky, who interviewed Gabel and others, concluded that these officials both "feared and welcomed" the tenant actions. They feared them, naturally, because such actions showed the inadequacy of existing policy. Especially alarming were what the agencies called "horror cases": fires, rat bites, and the like. But, paradoxically, officials also welcomed the protests and attendant media pressure because these "created a political context in which the mayor and his chief advisors could give high priority to housing maintenance needs."[82] Indeed, Department of Buildings Commissioner Harold Birns, who had been appointed to clean up the scandal-ridden agency in 1959, had been chafing at the fiscal constraints that prevented him from doing his job.[83]

Just as the mayor believed he was making strides, however, another court case forced him to play catch-up. This case arose in Brooklyn, where CORE, the Parkway-Stuyvesant Council, and other neighborhood tenant groups had now formed a joint strike committee. (Its chair, Major Owens, would later serve as Brooklyn CORE director, Met Council vice president, and twelve-term congressman representing Brownsville and Bed-Stuy.) Five tenants in Red Hook had refused to pay rent on their cold, dilapidated apartments. At a hearing in early January, Judge Fred Moritt ruled that the strikers "could live rent-free for as long as landlords failed to correct housing evils that menaced health or safety." According to Moritt, the 1930 property law defined "any act or default on the part of the landlord which deprives the tenant of the beneficial enjoyment of his premises" as an eviction. And "wrongful eviction . . . terminat[es] the tenant's liability for rent." Less technically, he observed, "Some of the buildings aren't fit for pigs to live in." Moritt's decision went beyond the Ribaudo ruling, which had required strikers to pay rent to the court.[84]

Hortense Gabel worried that Moritt had gone too far. Gray retorted that Gabel "acts just like any other slumlord and she has to go."[85] This bit of hyperbole said little about Gabel's actual agenda, but much about the strike movement's rejection of the gradualism that Gabel had come to represent.

Hopes for Expanding the Movement

The Moritt ruling brought forth new endorsements. Gray's next rally featured not only an array of elected officials, but also leaders from the city's leftist unions, Local 1199 and District 65; the Ethical Culture Society's Algernon Black; and writer James Baldwin.[86] An alliance of Lower East Side organizations led by Mobilization for Youth announced its intention to organize rent strikes downtown.[87]

Mobilization had originated two years earlier as something of a shotgun marriage between local settlement leaders and Columbia social workers. The original idea, conceived by the old-line Henry Street Settlement, was to attack juvenile delinquency by expanding the youth services that settlements had traditionally offered. In order to obtain federal funding for the program, however, Henry Street was compelled to accept a "research" component that brought aboard Columbia professors Richard Cloward and Lloyd Ohlin—originators of the theory that economic impediment was the cause of juvenile delinquency—and handed them "considerable leverage in the formation of the program."[88] The grant that Mobilization received would become the forerunner of the War on Poverty, Lyndon Johnson's signature social-welfare program of 1964. In both the Lower East Side agency and the larger antipoverty program, the involvement of social scientists helped to secure funds by "provid[ing] politicians with the scientific legitimacy [to] justify the reforms in urban politics they thought were needed."[89]

But before long Cloward and Ohlin, feeling swept along like "corks on a tidal wave" of civil-rights insurgency, added potentially troublesome housing initiatives to Mobilization's program.[90] In February 1963 they established clinics to help tenants file negligence complaints, apply for RRA rent reductions, and take landlords to court.[91] By fall the clinic data left no doubt about city agencies' impotence. Even with follow-up by the social workers, tenants obtained relief from major deficiencies (defunct plumbing or heating) less than a quarter of the time. Thus Mobilization's academic researchers came to agree with seasoned housing activists: "the only means by which low-income Puerto Ricans and Negroes would achieve . . . better housing was through political action by a mass organization of tenants, such as a city-wide rent strike."[92]

Days after the Moritt decision, Mobilization met with the East Side Tenants' Council, the University Settlement, Met Council, CORE, Puertorriqueños Unidos, and two other black and Puerto Rican organizations to form a Lower East Side Rent Strike Committee.[93] The committee invited Jesse Gray to participate, and at first "it was a very exciting coalition," recalled Lower East Side activist Frances Goldin. "He brought a kind of a gutsiness to the struggle [that] I don't think we would have had otherwise." Gray helped ignite the downtown campaign with a torchlight parade of two hundred people on a freezing night.[94]

Meanwhile, sympathizers from the far rungs of the social ladder sent the movement timely aid in the form of a front-page *Times* piece blasting the city's inspection apparatus. This exposé was generated by the new alliance of society women, Call for Action, which had made a study of code enforcement, and which enjoyed access to the paper of record through its co-chair, Ellen Sulzberger Straus. The copy bristled with charges and retorts. Straus called the Buildings Department a den of "maladministration and nonadministration," while an anonymous official declared, "I wouldn't go to a meeting over there if they paid me. The disorganization is unbelievable." To this the deputy commissioner replied, "Maladministration! With what they give us to work with, we're lucky to get anything done." Even the reporter conceded that pitiful understaffing made the department's new IBM computers "like a Ferrari running on kerosene." He also interviewed Harlem tenants such as Rita Davis, who had taken to knocking on her own bathroom door before entering: "You've got to warn the rats that you're coming or they'll resent the intrusion."[95]

Rhetorical points, however, came more easily than legislative victories. Most code-enforcement bills introduced in Albany that winter went down in defeat. And of two that would have legalized strikes by recognizing "rent-impairing" code violations, it was the weaker version, which stipulated a six-month waiting period, that passed. Of greater value to tenants was a Harlem legislator's bill to create an emergency repair squad and fund it from escrowed rents.[96] Jesse Gray announced a "Rats to Rockefeller" campaign in which tenants would mail rubber rats upstate to prod the governor into supporting the repair-squad bill.[97] Rockefeller forwarded the toys to Wagner.[98] The law, however, was eventually enacted.

By now the mayor's office had girded for its War on Rats. On March 2 an assistant health commissioner "fired the first shots" as he led a brigade of exterminators into combat on 118th Street near Gray's office.[99] Wagner also invited Call for Action to meet with his Housing Executive Committee.[100] The genteel women made a nice foil to Gray's street theatrics as they "presented the assembled Commissioners with a playlet on the theme of the city's inspection services. Using discarded shoe boxes and colored toy soldiers, they showed how 46 inspections had been made by three departments in one building over four years with virtually no results."[101] The group recommended a single agency to address all housing complaints. Mayoral aides promised to study the idea.[102]

Strains on Solidarity

The incipient collaboration between Met Council and the new ghetto organizations reflected a genuine commonality of ideals. Met Council's white leaders had long histories of interracial activism—in the Communist Party, at Stuyvesant Town, and, in Jane Wood's case, in Puerto Rican Chelsea. Further, the organization had been multiracial from the start, with Harlem organizer Bill Stanley and several Puerto Rican activists among its founders. As the black movement caught fire in the early sixties, Met Council was eager to fan the flames. Its 1963 and 1964 conferences centered on desegregation and ghetto problems. Both gatherings featured minority advocates—Granville Cherry was one—and included panels conducted in Spanish.[103] In formal politics, too, Met Council made common cause with the freedom movement. Benedict and Stanley proudly led a tenant contingent to the 1963 March on Washington.[104] Months later Met Council joined the NAACP, the National Association for

Puerto Rican Civil Rights, and Bayard Rustin for a demonstration in Albany. Three thousand marched in the upstate snow to demand an increased state minimum wage, legalization of rent strikes, collective bargaining for hospital workers, a committee on automation, and a "massive program to provide integrated housing for working people at rents they are able to pay."[105] (The platform was defeated by the Republican-led legislature.)

But day-to-day relations between Met Council and the uptown strike leaders were strained. Both of Met Council's senior Harlem organizers, Bess Stevenson and Bill Stanley, kept Gray at arm's length. Stevenson had carried on intermittently as an independent tenant advocate since her World War II baptism and had joined Met Council soon after its formation. (She would be hired as a full-time organizer in 1969, but in the early sixties lived on her day job as an ILGWU staffer.)[106] She believed Gray did little for tenants, often leaving them adrift in court after launching their strikes, and that he even dipped into their escrow funds.[107]

Stanley's history with Gray is murky but suggestive of tension. Both men were Communists; both belonged to the Harlem Tenants Council in the early fifties, before Gray established his own group. Yet by the 1960s they worked entirely separately.[108] In 1964 Stanley was providing legal guidance to tenants in unheated buildings in north-central Harlem, some distance from Gray's beat and completely off the media radar.[109] Gray's friend Jack O'Dell liked Stanley but perceived him as a moderate—"like an NAACP type of organizer"—an impression difficult to square with Stanley's lifelong Party membership.[110] Most likely the cold line between the two Harlem activists had to do less with ideology than with temperament, as Gray's volatility was an ill match for Stanley's measured, soft-spoken demeanor.[111] Certainly Gray's posturing wore on the nerves of Stanley's white comrades at Met Council.[112]

The drawbacks of Gray's appetite for attention were apparent even to some of his allies. Frances Goldin, who got along with Gray better than most Met Council people, noted, "Jesse had to be the chief honcho. That's the way he worked. And when he was, he did really well. He was creative, he was radical, he was gutsy, and I respected him a lot for that. But if somebody else was the chair . . . he was not gonna take a second row seat. . . . . There are some people who are very powerful leaders—he was one of them—who, you follow his leadership or you don't coalesce . . . And that's unfortunate. It's unfortunate for him and it's unfortunate for the movement."[113] NSM organizer Danny Schechter went further, recalling that many civil-rights workers "felt like [Gray] was a real opportunist and a hustler, and to some degree I think that's true."[114] Gray's self-importance must have grated especially on activists schooled in the SNCC ethos of promoting self-reliance and collaborative decision making among the "organized," and attuned to the low-decibel nature of this "slow, respectful work."[115] Still, Schechter continued, "[Gray] was also pretty effective and was a hard fighter for people."[116] In the end, Gray's reception among diverse associates illustrates the competing pulls of charismatic and more self-effacing modes of leadership. More than a few rank-and-file tenants took comfort and inspiration from Gray's forcefulness.

For their part, Gray and his uptown allies were leery of the Met Council leaders, whom they viewed as "older white liberal types, social worker types as opposed to activist types," according to Schechter. "The level of anger was less, the level was more bureaucratic. Here's how you file a complaint with the city."[117] O'Dell, while stressing that he saw Met Council as "good people working in housing," echoed this view: "[T]hey were servicing the tenants like a social service thing. . . . [T]hat's different from trying to build a tenant movement that is trying to empower itself."[118]

Gray aside, the fledgling downtown committee had its own problems. Met Council was by this point ill equipped to contribute much to door-knocking efforts on the heavily Spanish-speaking Lower East Side. The organization's relations with Latinos were generally cordial but well short of sustained partnership. Several Puerto Rican civil-rights leaders took part in Met Council's first meetings, and early records show the executive board's particular concern with Spanish-speaking tenants at Title I sites. The only Latina charter member who stayed aboard, however, was Genoveva Clemente, a protégé and close friend of Frances Goldin. Goldin had spotted Clemente as a "natural leader" at a Lower East Side tenants' meeting and had drawn her into Met Council and the Cooper Square Committee.[119] Clemente sat on Met Council's executive board until 1963, when she withdrew to devote full time to the Puerto Rican independence movement. By then Petra Rosa, a leader of the resistance in the Upper West Side urban-renewal area, had joined the organization. She would serve on its board for a full decade—like Clemente, a sole Latina with a sustained presence there—and would act as ambassador to Puerto Rican groups when joint demonstrations were planned.[120] Years later Goldin would criticize Met Council's failure to recruit more people of color into its central leadership, a failure she believed hampered the organization in the Black Power era.[121] (The Cooper Square Committee, where Goldin held greater sway, took more deliberate and effective steps to build a multiracial corps. Most chairs and vice chairs, including still-active board member Maria Torres Bird, were

Latino.)[122] For the purpose of the rent strikes of 1964–65, Met Council's main contribution was volunteer attorneys.[123]

Civil-rights workers with CORE, Puertorriqueños Unidos, and Mobilization did go out to organize buildings, but they found the work discouraging. Obtaining strike pledges was one thing, bringing off strikes another. Tenants were fearful and only grew more so as Lower East Side landlords racked up eviction and payment orders in court, where the volunteer legal staff was stretched thin.[124] Amid these difficulties, the multiracial Lower East Side coalition disintegrated after less than three months.[125]

The media's interest also waned as spring temperatures made defunct boilers a less compelling story, and as reporters grew disillusioned with Jesse Gray's chronically unverifiable strike figures.[126] Strikers suffered a legal setback in April when the Morritt decision was overruled.[127]

Outside the spotlight, however, city officials who had felt pressure from the protests continued to revise policies for the coming winter.[128] And neighborhood organizers carried on, notwithstanding their disappointment over the strikes' failure to snowball. During the early months of 1964 the Central Harlem campaign achieved a degree of operational stability from NSM funding that paid salaries for Granville Cherry and seven other strike organizers.[129] Uptown tenants also benefited from the volunteer services of a young Upper East Side attorney, Bruce Gould, who instructed them in legal documentation.[130] Some strikes also continued on the Lower East Side as well.[131] At any given time between March and June, tenants in roughly thirty Manhattan buildings were paying rent to the court.[132]

In Brooklyn, meanwhile, Major Owens' committee had four hundred households on strike by April.[133] Here, more than in Lower Harlem, tenant organizing approximated the SNCC model of low-profile, grassroots movement building. Owens believed in that approach, even though it was slow to bear fruit. And he had support from a committee of seasoned CORE members, several of whom were veterans of the Popular Front of the 1930s and 1940s. Brooklyn might have become the rent strike's real hub, but within a few months Owens shifted gears to focus on an (unsuccessful) run for City Council.[134]

Gender and Race in Uptown Organizing

As far as can be told from surviving sources, the Central Harlem cadre comprised an unusually high proportion of men. Six of the eight NSM staffers were male—two white students from Ivy League schools, the others high school–

educated young African Americans.[135] And men made up half the "house lead-ers" in NSM-organized buildings in Harlem.[136] On the Lower East Side, by con-trast, women—Puerto Rican and Jewish, primarily—led the strike organizing, as was more customary in tenant organizations.[137] Brooklyn's committee, half black and half white, was also split evenly between the sexes.

Why was Central Harlem's leadership different? In part because instigators such as Cherry, the NSM leaders, and Gray attracted or recruited other male activists. But there was also a structural factor: the racial and gender contours of the labor market. One reason women had long led in predominantly white tenant groups was that many of them were supported by their husbands' "fam-ily wages." But black men were excluded from most family-wage jobs, making it necessary for many black women to bring home a pay envelope. In 1960 the proportion of black women in New York who held or were seeking jobs was 50 percent—significantly higher than the figures for white and Puerto Rican women, 37 and 38 percent, respectively. (Puerto Ricans would have had a higher employment rate if not for the flight of factory jobs that been their mainstay in earlier years.)[138] Among blacks it was *men* who were hardest hit by deindus-trialization.[139] Thus people like Granville Cherry, a former shipping clerk, were "free" to organize rent strikes, especially when NSM stipends became available.

Gray's council in Lower Harlem, which lacked comparable funding, de-pended more heavily on women. Here the gender arrangements seem to have followed an oft-observed (and criticized) pattern in black church and political organizations, in which men served as spokesmen while women formed the "backbone."[140] Gray lived in the limelight. He shared it with a male "lieuten-ant," Major Williams. Yet women, many of them single mothers, made up at least half the organizers and participants.[141] Much of the daily work inside headquarters was handled by volunteer "secretaries" Florence Rice and Anne Bradshaw.[142]

Little is known of Bradshaw's background, but Rice's story highlights both the connections among labor, consumer, and housing movements that mark other tenant activists' biographies, and the distinctive plight of indigent black women. Rice grew up in foster care during the Depression and was sent out to work at sixteen. She became a runaway. Street life soon left her pregnant, however, and the responsibility of motherhood drove her back to domestic and laundry work. It was World War II that let her into a good job in an aircraft fac-tory, where she learned to read blueprints and use machine tools. In 1945 Rice was cashiered, like nearly all the "Rosies." But now she was determined not to go back to service work. She found a job sewing garments in a union shop.[143]

This led to a political initiation, but one far different from the awakenings that Jane Benedict and Frances Goldin experienced in the labor movement. Rice became union chairlady at her factory and learned that "the blacks and Spanish were getting cheaper work than the white . . . girls." When she objected, "the union [leaders] just told me to keep my mouth shut." Instead Rice testified before a House Committee about the ILGWU's inequitable treatment of black and Latina rank-and-filers. She was blacklisted—by the union itself. (Her testimony, however, paved the way for others, such as Bess Stevenson, who did get their feet on the ILGWU staff ladder.) "And that's when I began to understand how economics works. . . . And once I began to understand economics, that's when I realized that I'd have to fight about it." The 1962 congressional hearing also introduced Rice to two men she admired greatly: committee chairman Adam Powell and NAACP leader Herbert Hill.[144]

She found her main political calling through the retail jobs she picked up after her union ouster. Uptown merchants, she realized, "considered [that] poor people and black people are ignorant, and you can sell them anything. So what I wanted to do is make sure that when my people would shop, they knew what questions to ask." In 1963 Rice founded the Harlem Consumer Education Council.[145] From there it was a short step to volunteering on the rent strikes, even though Rice's own apartment in Washington Heights (just above West Harlem) was in good repair. Anne Bradshaw was already working with Jesse Gray and invited her friend Rice to do the same.

Like a number of other women who organized poor people in the 1960s and 1970s, these "vertebrae" of the rent strike would become significant voices in local and national policy circles.[146] For Rice the strike was an interlude in a career devoted primarily to consumers' and women's rights: She presided for decades at the consumer council, which scored many victories over duplicitous merchants, and she spoke out for reproductive choice, testifying from 1969 onward about the illegal abortion she had had in 1938.[147] Bradshaw remained a housing leader. She headed the tenant association in her NYCHA project, established a youth center there, formed a citywide public tenants' alliance, and participated vigorously in a national affordable-housing coalition until her death in 2010.[148] She became "a walking encyclopedia" of housing law and politics, who always "knew the right people to tap" from Washington to City Hall to Harlem.[149] Another female ally of Gray's, Maxine Green, likewise went on to head up the national tenant federation that Gray cofounded in 1969.[150] As far as is known, none of these able organizers expressed dissatisfaction with the division of labor in Gray's office. Apparently their attitudes in the mid-sixties resembled the views that historian Emilye Crosby has found among contemporaneous Mississippi women who "stepped up to do the [civil-rights] work that needed doing . . . and simultaneously accepted prevailing gender hierarchies."[151]

In February 1964, the *Herald Tribune* published a "Diary of a Rent Striker" that showed just how close to the edge some of Harlem's female activists lived. Innocencia Flores, a divorcée raising four children on relief in a crumbling 117th Street building, waged a daily struggle with rats and cold. For the former she wielded a baseball bat (also handy for driving away junkies who frequented her floor). For the latter she took up a collection from neighbors to buy heating oil. But this did not cover repair costs for the ancient boiler, and often the building went cold. On such days, "I feel miserable," Flores wrote. "You know when the house is cold you can't do nothing. . . . I don't wish no body to live the way I live." (Except culpable landlords, whom she thought should be sentenced to "at least a month in this same conditions.") Flores won a rent reduction from the RRA. From her first reimbursement, "I get some $140 and I pay some $60 for gas and electricity . . . and I spent almost $35 worth of grocery. I get somethings [*sic*] for the fun of it—like ice cream for the girls. . . . We are happy because there is so much food in the kitchen."[152]

Taken together, Gray, Rice, and Flores demonstrate a range of gender roles associated with the Harlem strike; conventional male leadership coexisted with unconventional (divorced, bat-swinging) female initiative. This variety was accommodated not only by Harlem's particular history—the area had long provided spaces for gender nonconformity[153]—but also by the urban neighborhood generally, which geographer Deborah Martin argues can figure as a "third sphere" in which public and private realms, conventionally coded as masculine and feminine, overlap. Thus urban community organizing can accord with the normative roles of both sexes. When the well-being of local children is at stake, for instance, women may take action as "nurturers" while men may be mobilized as "protectors."[154] Jesse Gray made good use of such protean terms when he reminded Harlemites that the strike was about "rats who bite our children."

As Flores' role suggests, Harlem strike organizing also crossed ethnic borders, forming one of the first bridges in a nascent (and fragile) alliance between African American and Puerto Rican New Yorkers.[155] In the very early sixties a young City College graduate, Ted Vélez, began volunteering with Jesse Gray. In 1962 he followed Gray's example and established the East Harlem Tenants Council. As the Central and Lower Harlem protests expanded in 1964, Vélez rallied similar strikes in El Barrio and helped a number of tenants there win repairs.[156] *Ebony* noted the eagerness with which Puerto Ricans joined in the direct actions.[157]

Like Gray's organization and the Northern Student Movement chapter, the East Harlem Tenants Council was spearheaded by men: Vélez and a black friend, Tony Williams. Its roots, however, lay less in the Old Left than in a circle of young, college-educated Puerto Ricans, many of them women, who took up community organizing and advocacy in the 1950s and early 1960s. This cohort felt Puerto Ricans to be "the new kids on the block" in city politics;[158] they sought to empower themselves rather than take direction from East Harlem's white social-service establishment based in the settlements and churches.[159] One of the "new kids'" signature projects was ASPIRA ("Aspire"), a youth leadership program founded by educator Antonia Pantoja, in which young Vélez enrolled.[160] After college the politically keen *aspirante* took readily to tenant organizing.

He also entered the orbit of the city's older liberal network. Summer of 1959 found Vélez teaching swimming at the Educational Alliance, an old-line social-service organization on the Lower East Side. There he met Jane Faulkner, "a nice Jewish girl from Great Neck." She was the daughter of civil-rights attorney Stanley Faulkner, who had represented one of Joseph McCarthy's targets in what became the Army–McCarthy hearings. The young couple dated and decided to marry—a "natural" occurrence as far as the elder Faulkners were concerned. ("If I had come home with a nice Jewish doctor," recalled Jane, "I think they would have been much more surprised.") Jane's parents hosted the tenant council's first fund-raiser, and her father served as its counsel.[161]

From No Heat to Full Boil

In the spring and summer of 1964 the center of drama shifted to two other local race stories: a school boycott and a street riot. Both gave further expression to the feelings driving the rent strikes, namely, profound disenchantment with failed reformism and a search for community self-empowerment. The boycott also drew some of the same rank-and-filers.[162] This action capped a decade-long desegregation campaign that had grown more insistent during the months in which the rent strikes were launched. The very *Times* front page that announced, "Slum Rent Strike Upheld by Judge," also proclaimed, "37 Seized at School Board as They Try to Stage Sit-In."[163] At issue was the quality of schooling: small classes, skilled teachers, and challenging curricula were bestowed overwhelmingly on predominantly white schools, while ghetto classrooms got the leftovers. Black and Puerto Rican parents demanded integration, less as an end in itself than as a way to get their children an equal share of the pie.[164] That was the view taken by rent striker and concerned parent Innocencia Flores: "I doesn't care about integration like that. . . . I agree with the boycott [t]o get better education and better teachers and better materials in school."[165] White parents, however, organized to oppose the integrationists' demands.[166] When the Board of Education stalled, the city's major black and Puerto Rican civil-rights organizations joined school activist Milton Galamison in calling a boycott for February 3. More than 460,000 students stayed home that day in what Joshua Freeman calls "the largest civil rights demonstration ever held in the United States."[167]

That this disciplined display, like the rent strikes, failed to win appreciable change added fuel to the street rebellions that broke out in July after the fatal police shooting of a black teenager. The clashes between black youths and white police in Harlem and Bed-Stuy shook the city as no conflict since the 1943 riot had done. One person was killed; more than one hundred were injured. Bricks rained on white-owned stores, and police beat and shot indiscriminately at black civilians, according to witnesses. City Council President Paul Screvane denounced the uprisings as the work of Communists and "fringe groups." President Johnson dispatched the FBI.[168]

For black New Yorkers, the killing of the teenager, James Powell, symbolized a long-standing system of urban white supremacy that incorporated many discrete means of subjugation, housing included. Jack O'Dell recalled that the rebellion "represented years of frustration with unemployment, bad housing, police brutality, and the political system not responding to it, as if it wasn't there. Putting band-aids on sickness."[169] Among the concerned citizens who were arrested the next day for "loitering" at City Hall after the mayor refused to meet with them were Isaiah Robinson, a leader in the equal-schooling movement, and Raphael Hendrix, black pioneer at Stuyvesant Town and now an officer in the local NAACP.[170]

The day after the fighting began, Jesse Gray, himself bruised from police blows, called a mass meeting titled "Is Harlem Mississippi?"[171] At a time when the South's unbridled Klan terror was finally receiving media attention, Gray strove to connect northern and southern stories in the public mind. President Johnson had just sent FBI agents to search for three civil-rights workers gone missing in Philadelphia, Mississippi. Now Gray called facetiously upon the FBI agents in Harlem to "ARREST ALL THE SLUMLORDS IMMEDIATELY. The FBI can find anyone. The SLUMLORDS violate the law and New York City can not or will not punish them; they freeze women and children . . . ; they allow rats to accumulate and bite our children."[172] By juxtaposing federal action against southern violence with inaction against northern ghetto hazards, Gray highlighted governmental indifference toward black New Yorkers' lives.

Gray also made a melodramatic appeal for "100 skilled black revolutionaries who are ready to die." His call "received a lusty applause" from the crowd of five hundred, *The Amsterdam News* reported, while CORE leaders and nonviolence proponent Bayard Rustin were jeered off the stage.[173] Much as Gray enjoyed rousing an audience, he likely spoke equally for the benefit of a white press establishment fascinated with the violence-versus-nonviolence framework for viewing black activism. "'Guerrilla War' Urged in Harlem," announced the *Times* on cue the following day. (A week later the paper assured readers that its own survey had found black New Yorkers "overwhelmingly [opposed to] violence as a method of achieving equality.")[174]

The specter of a race war probably carried just enough credibility at City Hall to hasten officials' work on the policy revisions they had begun after the previous winter's protests. As the radical democratic city planner Walter Thabit would later observe, "We did our greatest things [in housing] right after a period of great riots."[175]

Thus in the fall, the mayor's Housing Executive Committee took up an idea floated more than a year before: a city program to repair delinquent apartments.[176] Then, in January, Granville Cherry and Vélez's East Harlem group organized thirty tenants from unheated buildings to sit in at the mayor's office.[177] This gave Wagner a final push. The mayor ordered emergency repairs for the sitters-in and shortly announced the creation of a central complaint line and a city repair agency to deal with future exigencies. "In this case," observes Lipsky, "the direct action tactics of the sit-in resulted in early promulgation of a program which the Wagner administration might never have enacted and certainly was not prepared to promulgate at the time."[178] After more than a year of concerted protest, tenants had won a tangible goal.

Rats and Stats

How significant was that achievement? Certainly strikers had scored a moral victory in compelling officials to accept responsibility for "cut[ting] through all the time-consuming red tape to do what has to be done to protect the health and safety of the tenants," as HRB chairman Milton Mollen put it.[179]

Materially, the strike's effects present a bottle-half-full-or-empty question. Lipsky's 1968 study tracked seventeen badly deteriorated Harlem buildings in which tenants had withheld rent.[180] He found that landlords made substantial repairs in four of them, and the city put into receivership five more. The RRA slashed rents in five of the eight unrepaired buildings.[181] Thus striking tenants gained material relief of some type (repair or rent cut) in 80 percent of their actions but won improved housing conditions only half the time. Another drawback of Section 755 sanctions was, as Mobilization researchers had found, the indispensability of legal representation and documentation for successful claims.[182] Over time, however, some laypeople like Met Council's Bess Stevenson developed sufficient expertise in housing law to win Section 755 cases.

More was achieved by the city repair program, which returned heat and hot water to thousands of cold households.[183] The new figures, however much they left to be desired, spelled measurable improvement over the pre-strike repair rates that Mobilization for Youth found in 1963.

Further, the very processes of winning these improvements and using the new city services encouraged tenants to take action on their own behalf. Indeed, strike mobilization and publicity strengthened the city's tenant constituency during a pivotal struggle over rent control. Following the state legislature's 1962 decision to place rent law under home rule in the city, and the landlord lobby's unsuccessful attack on rent control the next year, both sides rallied for an epic City Council battle in 1964. Landlords flew a banner, "Communist Rent Control Must Go." Tenants thronged the street. Jane Benedict, Frances Goldin, Jesse Gray, and CORE all led pickets (Gray one-upped his fellows by scuffling with a landlord and getting kicked out of the hearing). Veteran legislators pronounced the session the most rancorous in memory.[184] The council voted to extend controls (with an exception for high-rent apartments) for two more years.[185]

"Use What's in Your Hand": Seeking Community Power

"Rent strike fever" proved highly contagious. Harlem's example drew national coverage and inspired similar actions in Chicago, Cleveland, Baltimore, and other cities.[186] Locally, the sense of a new day dawning manifested in Gray's budding alliances beyond housing circles, at the intersection of nationalism and the left. "[W]hen Malcolm [X] made that move to try to understand things differently," recalled O'Dell, "and do his own thinking, and went to Africa and came back home and formed the Organization of Afro American Unity, a number of us became active with him."[187] Malcolm presented Jesse Gray to an audience at the Audubon Ballroom, where Gray linked the struggle over "jobs, schools and other basic questions" to liberation battles in Mississippi and the Congo, the subjects of Malcolm's talk.[188] Until a last-minute scheduling conflict arose, Gray and school activist Milton Galamison were slated to appear again with Malcolm on the Sunday he was shot.[189]

These men were trying to forge a tie between black consciousness and tangible power. Some believed that power already resided within black communities, waiting to be recognized and tapped. Malcolm's speeches drew on a long-standing Nation of Islam tenet that blacks were shackled mentally and politically because they lacked "knowledge of self." Self-knowledge would bring power.[190] A Harlem resident and rent striker recalled that both Malcolm's and Adam Powell's public talks stressed this sort of self-realization. "'Look in your hand, right here, [they said]. 'Use it. Make it work. It's right there, use it, what's in your hand.'"[191]

Such expansive rhetoric implied power not just to press bureaucratic buttons, but to bring thoroughgoing material improvements. But tenants' hands had found no lever to compel that kind of change when it came to housing. While Gray and others spoke of a large-scale city takeover of neglected buildings, New York's real estate commissioner pronounced receivership "a good way to go broke unless the city is selective" in acquiring buildings.[192] Thus officials developed the emergency-repair squad as a substitute measure, allowing the city to assume momentary landlord power while avoiding long-term landlord liability. Nor did city or state governments do much to "take the profit out the slums," as Anthony Panuch had urged. True, Wagner's enforcement program made extreme negligence a riskier proposition than it had been before. But the federal tax rewards for minimum-service ownership stayed in place. So did the landlord's market, which had only been tightened by urban renewal's destruction of thousands of low-rent units.

Nothing less than a vastly expanded, state-funded construction and rehabilitation program could alter this formula, as Gray, Flores, and other strike advocates repeatedly pointed out.[193] For a heady moment such a program appeared within reach. "[State] legislation has been drafted this year which was not even dreamed of before the era of Rent Strikes, but which Rent Strikes have put on the order of the day," Met Council chirped in 1964.[194] But Met Council underestimated the leverage needed to wrest that kind of funding from Albany. Two large loans for low-rent housing were defeated in the legislature; a smaller allocation was placed on the ballot and killed at the polls.

The 1965 session—in which Democrats controlled both houses in Albany for the first time in decades—played out in much the same way.[195]

These outcomes are unsurprising in view of landlords' and tenants' relative strength in different jurisdictions. At the city level, Wagner and other officials had reason to tread warily toward reform: they feared reprisal by landlords (often major campaign donors) and budgetary havoc arising from far-reaching management programs. But the cost of doing nothing—bad publicity and consequent electoral vulnerability—was high enough to push these officials toward some concessions.[196] In Albany the calculus was different. City voters made up 42 percent of the state electorate, ghetto voters far less.[197] Upstate legislators were immune to the ire of downstate citizens. Instead they reported to their own districts, where problems such as the flight of industry took priority over hardship in Harlem. Even members of the city's delegation to Albany often depended on hefty landlord contributions. Yet only Albany, or even more distant Washington, could provide the funds required for a large-scale housing program.

Could tenants have gained more? The most influential statement in the affirmative was made by Mobilization researchers Piven and Cloward, who concluded that the strikes' failure owed less to friction among Gray, Met Council, and other players than to the fundamental unworkability of the Section 755 strategy. Organizers made a disastrous error, argued Piven and Cloward, when they opted to follow the city's "elaborate bureaucratic course" for documenting violations and gaining court approval for rent withholding. Filling forms, creating escrow accounts, attending court hearings (often several for each tenant) "turned out to require enormous effort and expertise." Even when all the i's were dotted, the process was sometimes futile because "slum landlords generally do not have the resources to rehabilitate their buildings—not, at least, unless rents are substantially increased." (This last assertion conflicted with Panuch's findings on slum profits.) Ultimately "the bureaucratic rites [of court] exhausted organizers and bewildered tenants."[198] Ego clashes were secondary. "The friction [among people] gets worse—or maybe it just appears to be worse—when things are not going well."[199]

This analysis became the seed of Piven and Cloward's influential thesis that poor people must disrupt the political economy, not work within its approved channels, to bring about meaningful change. Other episodes in the sixties pointed in this direction, Piven recalled, but "the rent strike . . . was an especially vivid case to us, because in a certain way the law and the courts spelled out the organizing strategy."[200] Strikers, Piven and Cloward believed, would have done better to pocket their rents and resist eviction. If thousands had done this, the argument went, they would have overwhelmed the courts, led landlords to abandon properties *en masse*, and forced the state to take responsibility for the buildings.[201]

Jesse Gray's number pumping, in fact, can be understood as an attempt to foment such a groundswell, notwithstanding his continued reliance on the Section 755 defense. Nor was his strategy without a certain logic: Just a few years later, the nascent gay-liberation movement would build courage among its fearful constituency by cleverly cropping a photo of a small demonstration to give the impression of mass participation.[202]

But mass participation in rent strikes had never lasted long, even during the World War I heyday, when Socialist organizers were anything but bureaucratic in their approach. In the sixties as in earlier times, tenants struck over specific grievances: rats, cold, and so forth. Repairs that resolved the grievance dissolved the solidarity. Not only did building councils often collapse when the heat came back on, Mobilization organizers found; erstwhile strikers frequently lost their sense of stake in the larger movement.[203] Labor unions—the original paradigm for tenant organizations—had by now achieved institutional stability through the National Labor Relations Act, contracts with management, and a larger societal "Fordist compromise" on a high-wage, high-consumption, no-strike economy. Tenant organizations, by contrast, had never won parallel accommodation from capital. And by the 1960s their rent strikes put little direct pressure on landlords.

Piven and Cloward thought this problem could be circumvented by small, dedicated "cadres [organized] to resist isolated evictions, defending the lone tenant by pitting the ghetto against the city's marshals." The ghetto had only to be mobilized *ad hoc*, not joined in a stable membership organization.[204] Presumably the cadre would be grassroots organizers not easily distracted by media stunts.

Although the wrath of the ghetto could indeed be potent, as the July upheaval showed, the faith that such militancy could be mobilized at will was a creature of its time, of the "tidal wave" of hope that Cloward later remembered. On dry ground, organizers in the CORE, Mobilization, and Puertorriqueños Unidos offices reported that tenants usually came in for help with more mundane activities, such as applying for public housing and welfare, that would yield more predictable benefits. Volunteers with these organizations and with Met Council felt it was their responsibility to advise help seekers on the known world of bureaucratic procedure rather than the uncharted territory of revolution.[205] In the end it is unknowable whether a different strategy would have won more, but it is evident that the urban political economy posed very formidable barriers.

Community Power, Black Power

Analyzing the rise of Philadelphia's black power movement, Matthew Countryman argues, "[i]t was . . . liberalism's failure that would lead many local black activists to begin a search for alternative approaches."[206] In New York, liberalism had a well-publicized chance to redeem itself through the 1960s rent strikes, with their substantial white support and relatively friendly reception among officials. But as it became clear that these actions were not going to reach the critical mass needed to shake foundations in City Hall or Albany, Jesse Gray began casting about for some other route to black empowerment. His association with Malcolm X was a step along this road. Although his new ventures brought no more tangible results than the strikes had done, in terms of boilers fixed or units built, they shed light on the real quandaries that drove changes in black politics in this period. The special frustrations of a capital-intensive problem like housing impelled ghetto activists' search for an alternative avenue of struggle.

Black power was once understood as a sharp turn away from integrationist civil-rights strategies, with Stokely Carmichael's 1966 speech in Greenwood, Mississippi, serving as the rhetorical hand on the steering wheel. But recent scholars have reconceptualized integrationism and nationalism as overlapping ranges on an ideological spectrum rather than irreconcilable opposites. Many activists "moved between strategies" according to the needs of the moment, and many "ideas implied by the [black power] slogan had been percolating in various activist communities for years" before Carmichael brought them to the attention of white America.[207]

New York further illustrates such percolation and strategic overlap. Here the black power notion of "community control" won attention during the 1968 Ocean Hill–Brownsville school crisis, when African American parents, weary of the city's decade-long refusal to institute educational parity, challenged the heavily Jewish teachers' union for authority over ghetto schools. But similar impulses toward black community self-reliance and ghetto-based empowerment had coexisted and jostled with reformist strategies for years. This can be seen in the attitudes of African American and Puerto Rican parents toward school integration: most declined to participate in the modest transfer program the city initiated in 1960, resentful that their children would have to travel to white neighborhoods to get a decent education.[208] Community feeling surfaced more forcefully in the 1964 riot, which began as a response to police aggression *outside* black territory (James Powell was shot in front of his summer school in Yorkville) but quickly became a contest over who controlled the streets of Harlem and Bed-Stuy.

Rent strikes played a little-recognized part in this evolution of community ideology. Harlem tenants confronted precisely the dilemma that would plague school activists and other black power proponents: how could impoverished ghetto residents transform their socioeconomic conditions within a capitalist polity dominated by whites? Desegregation alone offered little answer, to the poor especially, which was why New Yorkers of color had long decried slum profiteering as well as Jim Crow exclusion. (Indeed, rent strike leaders' own biographies illustrate the intertwining of ghetto-oriented with desegregation struggles: Gray, O'Dell, and Schechter all had picketed the local Woolworth's to support southern lunch-counter sit-ins in the early sixties, and O'Dell served in Martin King's inner circle until he was purged on account of his red past.)[209]

What changed in the 1960s was the battlefronts' relative prominence. Whereas the Stuyvesant Town movement had once siphoned political energy away from Harlem code enforcement, now the ghetto campaigns became the main theater of action in a way that appealed especially to those with little prospect of moving to Long Island. Strikers abandoned integrationism and demanded that public agencies meet the needs of citizens who lived in the ghetto. Their demand did not necessarily signal black power consciousness, but it was certainly compatible, if understood as a call to repay ghetto residents for the decades of exploitation that had left them too poor to fix up the buildings themselves.[210] Further, the thwarting of that demand doused hopes for liberal solutions. In this sense the rent strike would serve as a way station to the campaigns for community control of schooling and other resources.

That rent strikers had to rely ultimately on public agencies, however, also underscored the material limits to community self-empowerment. Scholars of black power in several cities have stressed accomplishments: service programs, independent schools, sharpened criticism of mainstream politics, and, paradoxically, reinvigoration of local Democratic Party organizations.[211] These achievements, while not exactly revolutionary, did represent self-activity that touched people's lives in meaningful ways. But none of them required a fraction of the labor and matériel needed to renovate even a hundred ghetto apartment buildings, or the political muscle needed to make the state step up to that task.

The rhetorical straw grasping that could arise from this predicament was apparent during the strike's decrescendo in late 1964, when Gray challenged a conference of Harlem leaders to build a "revolutionary movement" based on "black power." What was black power? Gray was clearer about what it was not. Black power would not be achieved through the "ins" (sit-ins, etc.), which he said reflected the concern of middle-class blacks "for their own social upward mobility," and which had failed to engage the "black masses." He also took a sideswipe at Met Council, which had titled its recent conference "Bust the Ghetto." "Breaking up the ghetto today," declared Gray, "is the philosophy of white liberals, who continue to attempt to direct and control the movement." Gray urged the opposite: geographical concentration. "If we permit the Man to divide us and scatter us all around . . . we basically would lose our power. . . . The cultures of Chinatown and Little Italy are respected."[212] (He failed to mention that Chinatown's housing was in even worse shape than Harlem's.)

The only tactic Gray offered for transmuting proximity into power, however, was to "enter the political arena," apparently via district-based elections.[213] Students of African American history will find an irony here, for Gray's call prefigured part of the "protest to politics" strategy famously promulgated in 1965 by Bayard Rustin, an outspoken critic of the black power slogan. Rustin urged blacks to begin by "wrest[ing] leadership of the ghetto vote from the machines," just as Gray proposed.[214] Rustin, however, understood that this move would merely gain blacks some leverage within what would inevitably be a coalition with lower-class and liberal middle-class whites.

The next year Gray took his own advice and ran for mayor; he would run unsuccessfully for several more offices before winning a State Assembly seat in 1972. Widely perceived as ineffective, he lost the primary two years later to Morningside Heights tenant leader Marie Runyon, discussed ahead. Neither legislator found in Albany the kind of labor and liberal allies needed to fulfill Rustin's larger vision: an electoral coalition for universal economic enfranchisement. Neither, therefore, was able to win further housing improvements for uptown tenants.

Brooklyn's Major Owens, more modest in tone and even in temper, did establish a career in politics, serving in the city's antipoverty administration, the state senate, and the U.S. Congress. But he, too, would be constrained in his accomplishments by the moderation of the Democratic establishment.

Conclusion

New York's rent strikes, coming amid the national upheavals of the mid-1960s, held a special symbolic potency. Something about Harlem's segregated, profitable, and viscerally disgusting housing conditions captured the very essence of northern racism. Accordingly, the fight against these conditions held great meaning but signified different things to different people: a kind of northern Montgomery Bus Boycott to liberal civil-rights supporters; a revival of the workers' strike to labor veterans; and an exhilarating glimpse of ghetto self-empowerment to those who were losing faith in liberal politics.

Like many such elixirs, the strike movement did not live up to its partakers' highest expectations. The protests publicized ghetto exploitation and raised tenants' own sense of political capacity. But confrontation with the costly task of housing repair also brought home the degree to which the black movement was up against not just Jim Crow but the entire postwar political economy. That the strikes won stronger policing of "horror cases," rather than decent housing for all, underlines the system's overall resiliency.

Ghetto rent strikes formed one front of neighborhood tenant mobilization in the early 1960s. A second front emerged simultaneously in racially mixed areas, where residents fought against urban-renewal proposals that threatened to raze their homes. That is the topic of the next chapter.

5

"A Lot of Investment, a Lot of Roots"

Defending Urban Community

While ghetto strikes tested grassroots power over the rental market, two other neighborhood-based movements challenged redevelopment. Morningside Heights and Cooper Square became policy battlegrounds in the early 1960s as tenants mounted a second round of struggle against urban-renewal schemes. Tenant mobilizations in these areas shared some features with the strike movement, namely tangible contributions from Old Left activists and complicated relations among left and liberal players.

But Cooper Square and Morningside Heights tenants fashioned different ideological tools. They articulated a concept of urban community rights in which "community" signified a racially mixed, predominantly low-income, place-based collectivity bound by neighborly ties—an unusual move at a time when many urban activists defined community along racial lines, and when class-oriented social movements were on the wane.[1] The tenants' assertion of community rights against owners' prerogative also challenged a pillar of postwar American ideology, namely, citizenship based on homeownership.

Ideals of tenant community drew significant support in both Upper and Lower Manhattan. But they fared differently according to the relative roles of city and private interests in each area's redevelopment plan. Morningside Heights was remade, largely to Columbia's liking. Cooper Square was not. Downtown tenants achieved a measure of success that eluded their uptown counterparts, partly because they developed savvier leadership, and partly because they were fighting the city rather than a wealthy private institution.

With these advantages, the Cooper Square community managed to defeat a Title I plan and pioneer a more democratic kind of urban redevelopment.

Institutional Expansion on Morningside Heights

On Morningside Heights the late fifties had brought a string of defeats for low-income tenants, as Columbia University and neighboring educational and religious institutions pursued their ambitious campaign to create an elite enclave by forcing out thousands of black, Latino, Asian, and poor white renters. By 1958 the middle-income Morningside Gardens development was completed. It had displaced over 1,600 families, very few of which were absorbed by the public-housing project that went up nearby.[2] Next the institutions took aim at the area's "single room occupancy" houses, low-rent lodgings that administrators saw as reservoirs for "blight."[3] On this front the institutions enjoyed support from liberal housers at the Women's City Club, the settlements, and the Citizens' Housing and Planning Council, all of which had come to see the often ill-maintained SROs as an affliction on their own residents.[4] The city obliged by vowing to "drive the single room occupancy buildings out of business."[5] In 1960 a federally funded study concluded that with closure of SROs, government financing for repairs, and the "stabilizing influence" of institutional ownership, Morningside Heights could halt the spread of blight.[6] The next year Washington granted the city nearly $200,000 to continue renewal in the area.

Nineteen-sixty and -sixty-one, however, were also years of regrouping for the local tenant movement. It was in 1960 that a fire broke out one August night at 130 Morningside Drive. As firefighters doused the flames, residents discussed their suspicions that faulty maintenance had caused the blaze and talked about what to do. When these tenants and their neighbors in seven nearby buildings received eviction notices the next year, they resolved to fight.[7]

The leader who emerged among them was a forty-four-year-old white woman named Marie Runyon. At first glance she seemed an unlikely organizer in a multiracial neighborhood, and her "baptism by fire" into the tenant movement a mere coincidence. She hailed from a conservative family in North Carolina. "We just accepted, as we grew up, that black people, Negroes, don't ring the front doorbell; they have to go to the back." But in 1930 the teenaged Runyon enrolled in Berea Academy and College, an unusual work-study institution that was affordable to poor students and rooted in the egalitarian Christian idealism of the abolition movement. Berea started her "leaning" toward social change. In 1946 she came to New York, which she loved immediately: "Even then, I knew I was never going to live anyplace else." After a marriage, childbirth, and divorce left her a single mother in need of income, she found a job as assistant membership director at the ACLU. There she learned the skills of organizing and continued to gravitate toward the left. She became a great admirer of Fiorello LaGuardia and Vito Marcantonio. Despite "strong socialist leanings," she never actually joined the Communist Party ("but don't say that, because it's none of anybody's goddamned business"). By 1961 she had taken an interest in tenants' rights and joined Met Council.[8]

Challenging her landlord in 1961 was not a simple matter; first she had to find out who her landlord was. Her lease just said the "130 Holding Corporation." It took digging among city records and running down of leads to determine that the site was owned by the Columbia College of Pharmacy, which was then located downtown and seeking to join its parent institution in Morningside Heights. Learning the owner's identity gave Runyon and her neighbors a legal recourse. They demanded proof that the pharmacy school had the means to proceed with redevelopment, as the law now required in eviction cases.[9] Three years and many court proceedings later, the college admitted that it was $3 million short. It had managed to knock down four of the eight targeted buildings by then. The fiscal disclosure was a victory for residents of the remaining four.[10]

But Columbia made clear its intention to proceed with expansion on other sites. In 1961 the university released a multimillion-dollar building program draped in patriotic purpose. "[T]o sit back [and] do no more than admit the same number of ever more highly qualified applicants each year," the report admonished, "is not the service to the nation that a national institution is obligated to provide." Instead Columbia had "to face squarely the national need for large numbers of men who have had the best possible educational preparation" and increase its capacity through further redevelopment of the neighborhood.[11]

Local residents protested, and the university countered with the creation of a new planning body, the Morningside Renewal Council, "a forum where community organizations and institutions, in cooperation with the City of New York, [can] develop plans for the renewal of this area."[12] But Columbia structured the council to include separate delegates from each religious and educational institution. This ensured that the institutions' development consortium, Morningside Heights, Inc. (MHI), would control a majority of votes.

The stakes of institutional growth rose steeply over the next three years as MHI drew up and lobbied for an urban-renewal proposal, the Morningside

General Neighborhood Renewal Plan (GNRP). In essence the plan equated "renewal" with institutional growth. And "since many properties in these areas are already owned by neighboring institutions," city officials noted brightly, "it would appear that any necessary expansion of the existing institutions may be accomplished without public assistance."[13] In other words, the city would not have to subsidize, but simply to rubber-stamp, the eviction of longtime neighborhood residents. The one project the city would fund was the closing of SROs—another eviction catalyst.[14]

The GNRP roused local residents. In January 1964, Runyon and allies drew a crowd of five hundred to a protest meeting at Riverside Church. From the podium she described the pharmacy site tenants, whose case was still in court, as "120 families who have spent an aggregate of 2142 years in this community, an average of 17 years, 10 months per family. That's a lot of years, a lot of investment, a lot of roots.'" Architecture professor Percival Goodman added, "Universities have lost sight of their humanitarian role in the world." He contrasted Columbia, his employer, with thirteenth-century Oxford, where students had taken up bows and arrows to defend local peasants from the bishop's army. The assembled resolved to form Morningsiders United, a tenant association dedicated to "building-by-building organization of residents . . . to preserve a diversified, integrated community." Met Council's Jane Benedict told the new group that it faced a hard task. In particular she warned that the Morningside Renewal Council—the institutionally dominated "community" planning body—would not save local tenants. In the West Side Urban Renewal area a similar committee was approving the expulsion of low-income Puerto Ricans on a large scale.[15]

By this time Runyon had quit the ACLU and taken a job with the Committee for a Sane Nuclear Policy, a disarmament group, where she worked closely with leftist spokesman Benjamin Spock. But door-knocking around the neighborhood was a tougher kind of activism. Tenants were paralyzed by fear.[16] Still, by the fall of 1964, Morningsiders United had recruited members in 100 buildings. (See map of institutions and disputed sites on page 210.)

Further, the racial implications of the institutions' campaign served to attract widening support for local tenants. At a Met Council meeting, "somebody said, 'Marie, you've got to go and meet Bill Stanley,'" the Harlem-based charter member.[17] Although Columbia was at pains to distinguish Morningside Heights from adjacent Harlem, African Americans saw the institutional threat to black homes on the Heights as very much a Harlem issue.[18] Stanley invited Runyon uptown, where he worked as a super. "And it was a real introduction

Figure 10. **Marie
Runyon, tenant
organizer on
Morningside Heights.**
*Courtesy
of Met Council
on Housing.*

to me. A house in Harlem, the kind that I had never, ever visited."[19] Stanley's
Uptown Tenants Council—quite separate from Jesse Gray's group—joined the
Morningside fight, bringing a contingent of black and Puerto Rican protesters
to a Board of Estimate hearing on the General Neighborhood Renewal Plan
in March of 1965. At the microphone, Stanley deftly linked the Morningside
question to the Harlem struggle that had lately dominated the news. "These
people," he said of Morningside tenants facing eviction, "they know what a rat
or a roach infested home is. Bad as it is, they want to keep it."[20] CORE vowed
to defend the area's low-rent housing, and the local Reform Democrats called
upon the City Commission on Human Rights to investigate the institutions
for "singling out Negroes and Puerto Ricans for eviction."[21]

During the same period a handful of politicized young architects came
together under the guidance of a SNCC veteran, Richard Hatch, to form the

civil-rights-oriented Architects' Renewal Committee in Harlem (ARCH).[22] ARCH prepared a study of Morningside Heights that showed that the GNRP would cause a tidal wave of evictions, even greater than the 6,700 households the institutions admitted would be pushed out.[23]

ARCH also flagged a danger that Jane Benedict had recognized at Morningsiders United's inception: the institution-dominated Morningside Renewal Council, which was being portrayed as a "community group" in the press.[24] But Runyon was slower to see the MRC as a Trojan horse; one of her early newsletters described the council as "an encouraging example of democratic process" and amenable to hearing tenants' concerns.[25] The MRC punctured that illusion in April 1965, when the institutional representatives who formed its majority voted to approve the GNRP. Heeding the voice of the "community," the Board of Estimate quickly followed suit.[26]

This marked a major loss for local tenants. Morningsiders United and ARCH did wring a few concessions. Columbia was compelled to name its projected expansion sites—a move it had fiercely resisted. And the plan was amended to require 50 percent low- and moderate-income rentals in new housing, and to place rehabilitation projects ahead of demolitions. As always, SROs got the short end: their demolition was permitted in full.[27]

Investment and Urban Citizenship

In the teeth of defeat, tenants still articulated important rebuttals to the ideology of institutional expansion. Institutional spokesmen justified growth through a particularly elitist kind of slum rhetoric. Repeatedly they spoke of postwar Morningside Heights as suffering from "blight" and "urban cancer" that made it impossible for the area to "be healthy."[28] Blight—sometimes defined as the presence of addicts and prostitutes, but often left vague—ultimately came to signify extramural life itself. This was clear from MHI's call for a "contiguous" area that would cloister institutional people from the larger neighborhood. A Columbia planner said plainly that the university wanted "a community where the faculty can talk to people like themselves. We don't want a dirty, not a noisy group."[29]

This equation of class homogeneity with social health aligned Columbia ideologically with suburban boosters who idealized tracts of similarly priced homes as the setting for the American Dream. The institutions' rationale also contained snippets of Cold War rhetoric. "[M]inisters and rabbis will go from the [local] seminaries to every part of the free world," proclaimed an MHI newsletter. "Here scholars teach and students learn to live in our complex world. . . . Here the Great Society begins."[30] To fulfill their mission to the free and complex world, budding public servants evidently had to be shielded from the kinds of people who lived there.

Morningsiders United posed a different vision, one informed by the urbanist sensibilities of Jane Jacobs and the Save Our Homes activists who had rallied on Morningside Heights and elsewhere in the fifties. Runyon and her fellows held up the economically and racially "diversified" nature of the Heights as a social good, something to be preserved rather than cured. They denounced the university's expulsion practices as racist social engineering. In lieu of the Great Society they spoke of a good community—one that was not only demographically varied but also enlivened by accessible sidewalks, storefronts, and other venues of unpredictable interaction rather than walled off from the presumptively menacing world.[31]

Most fundamentally, Morningside tenants challenged the assumption that owners' rights to develop land outweighed a tenant community's right to stay in place. "Bureaucracies vs. Families" was how a sympathetic feature in the *Herald Tribune* put it.[32] Tenants in a building owned by the Jewish Theological Seminary deftly cast themselves, rather than the institutions, as agents of neighborhood redemption: "[T]he war [we] are fighting must finally be won if our urban civilization is to escape catastrophe."[33] An elderly resident, afraid of the street crime she said had proliferated when storefronts were razed for co-op construction, asked, "By what right do they . . . move in and annihilate a neighborhood?"[34]

Although homeownership did not figure explicitly in this debate—except in the case of the co-ops, the institutions wanted the land parcels for academic facilities, or to rent to their own personnel—local tenants' appeals implicitly challenged the postwar exaltation of ownership as the foundation of good citizenship. When Runyon spoke of her neighbors' years in the area as "a lot of investment, a lot of roots," she was advancing a provocative claim. Tenants' collective history of living together could stand as a kind of social investment that went deeper than material investment in property. Tenants could claim citizenship, and their communities could claim rights, that were as worthy of public consideration as the prerogatives of property owners.

While that claim was contrarian in the post–World War II era, it was not entirely new. Americans had been debating the proper relationship between citizenship and property for a long time, and arguments over urban political power during the Gilded Age, in particular, prefigured the post–World War II conflict on Morningside Heights. In the 1870s, upper-class New Yorkers took alarm at workers' support for expanded municipal services and tried to quash the labor vote by declaring the city to be a corporation owned by propertied shareholders, in which commoner residents held no franchise at all. The state actually put this idea on the ballot in 1877. Workers, however, mobilized to defeat the disfranchisement measure. And soon a new variety of elite—Progressive social scientists—advanced a counterclaim: modern cities' crying social needs justified "home rule," that is, authority to make regulations and public provisions beyond those established by the state.[35] By extension, urban voters would gain greater say over public policy.

At the national level, competing claims of worker versus property-holder citizenship were reconciled through "social citizenship"—the entitlements extended by New Deal welfare programs such as Social Security and the FHA. The FHA, in fact, revived the possibility of worker homeownership so prized by independent artisans of the Jeffersonian era, when property was a requirement for the franchise. Yet twentieth-century homeownership also bound workers to the market imperative of property values.[36] FHA mortgage policy thus supported the property-based, Cold War-inflected model of citizenship. Such citizenship did not extend to urban renters.

Now Morningside Heights tenants resurrected historical precepts. Their broadsides against institutional landowners recalled generations of working-class attacks on monopoly and privilege. Their appeal to the Board of Estimate echoed Progressive calls for municipal regulation of the market. Their claim to embody "urban civilization" harmonized with both labor and Progressive movements' beliefs in meaningful citizenship for the ordinary city resident.

Morningsiders also reworked old concepts in more inclusive ways. If Progressive reformers recognized a corporate quality to urban social life—Woodrow Wilson called the city "not an aggregation of interests . . . but an organism, whole and vital"[37]—1960s tenant activists provided a close-up view of that organism's connective tissue: neighborly bonds. The centrality they accorded neighborly "community" in their rhetoric of rights underscored the social basis of citizenship at a sidewalk level. Further, whereas most older notions of worker citizenship, as well as New Deal social citizenship, sidelined women and people of color, the Morningside Heights mobilization celebrated racial diversity and rested solidly on the leadership of women. Finally, in contrast to organized labor's focus on the (implicitly male) breadwinner, tenant community citizenship also embraced the unemployed, the retired, and the homemaker.

These views drew growing sympathy from students, community organizations, and even Columbia's own faculty, on whose behalf the school was eradicating "blight."[38] But in court the rhetoric of community was no match for the right of proprietorship. As the Housing and Renewal Board had observed, MHI's expansion plans rested largely on titles the institutions already owned. The years of quietly buying up lots via paper entities like the "130 Holding Corporation" had paid off. All through the late 1960s, institutional evictions went forward, some quietly and some not. Morningsiders United, assisted by Met Council attorney Dick Levenson, helped tenants gain delays.[39] But owners usually won in the end. A 1972 study found that between 1960 and 1968, Columbia alone had acquired 115 local properties; 17 out of 35 SROs had been closed; and roughly eight thousand noninstitution-related tenants—20 percent of the area's total population—had been forced out of the neighborhood.[40] "Already, two-thirds of the population. . . . leaving aside the [NYCHA project]. . . . appears to be institutionally-related," the study noted. "Indeed, the point of no return. . . . [for] the community as we know it. . . . may already have been reached."[41]

Democratic Planning on the Lower East Side

While tenants and wealthy institutions faced off uptown, another redevelopment struggle was taking shape at the far end of Manhattan. Cooper Square's odyssey offers instructive contrasts with Morningside Heights. Like the uptown struggle, the Lower East Side conflict centered on a plan to evict the poor and attract the middle class. But unlike the Morningside plan, the Cooper Square proposal involved Title I condemnation of lots that the developer did not already own. This proprietary discrepancy did not guarantee a different outcome. But it offered leverage to Lower East Siders who would build on the groundwork laid by earlier Title I critics, and on their own distinctive history, to plan a rare victory for democratic urban redevelopment.

For much of the early sixties these residents waged a war of position, not maneuver. The trenches were dug against a series of city-sponsored redevelopment proposals. The first, written by Moses' Committee on Slum Clearance in 1959, aimed to raze most of the twelve-block site so that Abe Kazan's United Housing Federation could rebuild it with middle-income cooperatives. Frances Goldin, Esther Rand, and other neighborhood organizers quickly resolved on the novel strategy of devising a full-scale alternate plan to retain rather than replace the area's low-income population.[42] That did not promise to grease political wheels very richly, however. And even at the level of principle, officials believed that the lofty goals of urban renewal easily trumped the narrow interests of site residents.[43] As a result, the Cooper Square Committee—the new grassroots organization led by Goldin, Rand, and company—spent its first years simply preventing the city from moving forward. Slowly, however, the committee won official support for key elements of their alternate plan.

Democratic planning of this sort was a new endeavor, yet it had recognizable precursors. As early as the mid-1940s, business and civic leaders in Brownsville, Brooklyn, drew up a list of hoped-for postwar improvements to serve current *and* future residents. (The document fell on blind eyes at City Hall.) Around the same time the Citizens' Housing and Planning Council teamed up with the good-government Citizens Union to study citizen participation in district-level planning, a policy already up and running in Chicago and Detroit. The Citizens Union proposal for New York would inspire Robert Wagner to establish "community boards" throughout Manhattan when he became borough president in 1951.[44] Nationally, a new organization of forward-thinking planners known as METCOP (Metropolitan Committee for Planning) called upon localities to make "citizen participation a regular part of the planning process"—a mandate that would be written into federal policy in 1954.[45] Cooper Square's nearest antecedents, however, were the heterodox plans that fellow New Yorkers had put forward in the 1950s: Elizabeth Barker's low-rent housing proposal for Morningside Heights, East Tremonters' alternate highway route, and Ellen Lurie's recommendations, based on local surveys, for more humane design in the East Harlem housing projects. All these had rested on the belief that people should have a say in designing the places in which they lived.

Circumstances favorable to the Cooper Square experiment had also been ripening on the Lower East Side itself. One was a left-wing presence, maintained through organizations such as the East Side Tenants Council, that was substantial enough to have weathered the Cold War and groomed cadre who could jump into action on the alternate plan. Goldin and Rand, both veteran Communists and tenant leaders, played a central role. So did Thelma Burdick, director of the Church of All Nations, which stood on the Cooper Square site. Burdick had grown up among cooperative farmers in Nebraska and considered herself a socialist.[46] No firebrand, she was "a dedicated social worker, a gentle kind person" who enjoyed extensive neighborhood ties through the day-care center her church ran. Her direct stake in the alternate plan made her willing to work with the committee despite her wariness of its "hot radicals" (as Goldin characterized herself and Rand).[47] Whether Burdick knew it or not, she was also carrying on an institutional heritage: the Church of All Nations had served as the first headquarters of the militant City-Wide Tenants Council of the 1930s.[48]

Burdick joined Goldin, Rand, Staughton Lynd (then a settlement-house worker), and four others on a committee under the aegis of the Lower East Side Neighborhoods Association (LENA), a youth-services alliance organized by the Henry Street Settlement. But LENA's leaders were unwilling to oppose Kazan's co-ops, and the Cooper Square Committee broke away.[49] (A few years later, LENA would become the launching pad for Mobilization for Youth, which also ventured into tenant-organizing activities that Henry Street considered too radical.) The now-independent Cooper Square steering committee worked with thirty local activists—eighteen women and twelve men—to solicit the participation and sponsorship of hundreds of individuals and organizations.[50]

A second critical local circumstance was the emergence of a new kind of professional, the "advocacy planner," embodied in a New Yorker named Walter Thabit. Thabit came from a liberal genealogy of housing politics. He had learned early about real estate through the rooming house his mother, a Syrian immigrant, ran in Brooklyn during the Depression. He majored in art at Brooklyn College. He also studied theater and took a course in "Community Design." Then he enrolled in the New School and moved into the University Settlement, where he "took care of groups and things like that" and helped put up a play about the Lower East Side's housing problems. These experiences prompted him to register for a housing course taught by Charles Abrams. Abrams, impressed with Thabit's work, encouraged him to apply to planning school. ("What's planning school?" responded Thabit. "I'd never heard of it.")

The eminent houser, an early prophet against Stuyvesant Town and a founding member of the State Committee Against Discrimination in Housing, "was instrumental in opening [Thabit's] vision to the vagaries of the bureaucracy and to its landlord orientation, to its developer orientation, as opposed to . . . providing for the people. Up and down the line, from the federal levels down to the local levels." Abrams also guided Thabit toward new currents in planning that were emerging from the fifties bulldozer battles. One day he took Thabit to the Washington Square South project—a Title I high-rise near NYU—and shared his opinion "that what was being displaced . . . shouldn't be displaced. And that what they were proposing to do, including . . . cutting a hole through Washington Square Park, was kind of stupid. And the density of the buildings they were intending to put up was not terribly sensible."[51]

After graduate school Thabit joined METCOP, which was collaborating with LENA on some Lower East Side studies. LENA drew him into the first meetings of the Cooper Square Committee. "Then we went to see Hortense Gabel . . . and she said, 'What you should do . . . is develop an alternate plan.' So they hired me to develop an alternate plan."[52]

Thabit stood at a junction in housing politics. His professional training with Abrams reflected an older generation of liberals' accumulated experience with redevelopment, "Negro removal," and urban sensibility. His contacts in the Lower East Side allied him with the left. When Gabel advised the nascent committee to write an alternate plan, Thabit was exactly what they needed: a professionally trained liberal willing to work with outspoken radicals on an ambitious democratic endeavor. Thabit's own democratic disposition went beyond conventional liberalism to a kind of standpoint epistemology with regard to urban planning: Notwithstanding his technical expertise, he believed "there are things that only the community knows."[53] The Cooper Square Committee obtained several small grants from foundations concerned with cities, poverty, and human rights to pay for Thabit's work.[54]

The alternate plan was hashed out over two years in more than 200 committee and neighborhood meetings.[55] Afterward a deadpan Thabit said he would do it again "if I get paid four to six times better."[56] But in truth the plan was a matter of great pride for him and the committee. Far from just an architectural proposal, *An Alternate Plan for Cooper Square* was a political document that crystallized more than a decade of critical thinking about urban redevelopment. It marked a new turn in the quest for urban democracy.

The plan announced a "basic philosophy."

> A renewal effort has to be conceived as a process of building on the inherent social and economic values of a local community. . . . While there is no such thing as a definable neighborhood on the Lower East Side, there are communities of interest, both large and small. There are ethnic, social, cultural and economic associations and dependencies. And there are the individual preferences through which these associations and dependencies are sustained and nurtured—even in the context of a slum community in which people live and do business at least partly because they cannot afford to do it elsewhere.[57]

Here was a direct rebuttal to the slum-clearance rationale of fifties redevelopers. Like the Women's City Club reports and the East Tremont tenants' petitions, the Cooper Square alternate plan looked beneath the "slum" label and traced out the delicate social organism that was a vital city neighborhood. But unlike previous Title I critics, the Cooper Square residents conceded that part of their area *was* a "slum," at least in terms of its housing stock and the many homeless men who frequented the Bowery. That admission just set up a second apostasy: "even in the context of a slum community," there might exist "ethnic, social, cultural and economic associations" worth preserving.

The alternate planners also wrote against the grain of conventional racial politics. Negro removal, "second ghetto" development, and violent white resistance to integration constituted postwar norms to which Cooper Square proudly cast itself as an exception.[58] The plan noted that the Puerto Ricans who moved in after the war had stayed in the area not only because it offered cheap housing, but because "[t]hey have found a welcome, an acceptance which makes them want to stay." Churches, the University Settlement, and other institutions had opened their doors to Spanish speakers. "There have been no gang wars, no outbreaks of juvenile delinquency, no waves of resentment in the Cooper Square area."[59] (This passage was a bit of an exaggeration—LENA had been founded to address the local gang problem[60]—and may have been written to counter the impression left by *West Side Story*, which had just finished a three-year run on Broadway.) Cooper Square's claim to interracial harmony was published in 1961, before civil-rights activity crested nationally, and it prefigured Morningsiders United's embrace of a "diversified community" uptown.

Closely related to this interracial ideal was a seemingly technical planning tenet: the *scale* of redevelopment. Massive projects had become the standard in cities across the country for several reasons: They appealed to public-housing authorities' desire for economy of scale; they brought large profits to private investors; and they suited planning czars' visions of grandeur. But Thabit pointed out that mammoth new developments—be they middle-income Title I's or low-income public housing—"tend to segregate socio-economic groups by concentrating families with similar incomes."[61] The alternate plan favored "vest-pocket" construction and other small-scale designs in the name of class integration.

Finally, the Cooper Square Committee raised the *cui bono* question that urban-renewal proponents had dodged for years. Ever since Stuyvesant Town, slum clearance had meant people clearance. The Cooper Square plan asserted, "it is not inevitable that communities be disrupted through renewal. It is not necessary to tear apart the fabric of the community, or to replace thousands of low-income families with thousands of middle-income families."[62] Reversing the city's principle that evicted residents should accept personal "inconvenience" for the sake of public "progress," the alternate planners declared, "site tenants have an indisputable priority to the new housing on sites from which they are displaced, and it is the city's responsibility to see that this housing is provided for them at rents they can afford. . . . *The physical improvements which will attract a higher income group must . . . benefit those affected by the program*, not cause them to suffer from it."[63]

From this philosophy the plan drew "principles of renewal" such as appropriate scale, affordable rents, staged construction (to let residents remain on-site during redevelopment), and the creation of "visually and socially satisfying" environs.[64] It then summarized Thabit's carefully made findings on Cooper Square's traffic patterns, housing stock, businesses, and community facilities; on the rents its residents could afford; and on its populations with extraordinary housing needs.[65] Thabit devoted special attention to the Bowery homeless. "Perhaps half the Bowery population," he wrote, "can be considered more or less permanent residents. For this half, a great deal can be done. A high percentage are aged persons, a sizable percentage are steady workers, and the number of incorrigible drinkers is lower than suspected."[66] This stable cohort could be housed in regular low-rent units. The more transient homeless, some of them migrant pickers who wintered in the city, would need a different arrangement. In contravention to the city's anti-SRO campaign, Thabit recommended building a furnished rooming house and a large shelter.[67]

The committee's specific recommendations were a far cry from the middle-class takeover proposed by the city.[68] The alternate plan exempted from clearance six blocks of tolerable and densely built low-rent housing that could be rehabilitated with a little-used federal loan program.[69] It proposed 1,440 new units: 620 of low-rent public housing, 300 of state-subsidized moderate rentals, and 520 of middle-income co-ops. Special units for the elderly and 48 studio residences for low-income artists would also be provided. "Altogether, some 1,205 families, 206 furnished room occupants, possibly 2,707 beds for homeless men, and 193 non-residential uses will be displaced and rehoused by the plan."[70] The public housing was to go up on a vacant lot at Houston Street, reducing the need for even temporary displacement of site residents. And the design section specified suitably scaled buildings of varied shape.[71]

In sum, the Cooper Square alternate plan pulled together years of grassroots and professional criticism of urban renewal. It was a descendant of the initiatives taken by Morningside Save Our Homes and East Tremont residents; the many calls from the Women's City Club, Met Council, the American Labor Party, and others for a "demolition moratorium"; and the appreciation of local sociability championed by Ellen Lurie, Herbert Gans, and Jane Jacobs. It set a new standard of urbanism that would inspire similar democratic planning in other cities.

We Can Fight City Hall

The work of surveying the site and sketching its future was dwarfed by the task the Cooper Square Committee now faced: gaining city approval. When the booklet rolled off the presses in the summer of 1961, the committee had high hopes. Chairman Thelma Burdick sent copies to Mayor Wagner and the City Planning Commission.[72] She received support not just from longtime friends at Met Council but from new ones like Columbia architect Percival Goodman—shortly to become a Morningside Heights tenant ally—who had his class build a model of the proposed reconstruction, and from the Ninth Federal Savings and Loan Association, which displayed the model in its Times Square window and found it to be "an eye-stopper [that] has brought numerous people into the office with questions."[73]

Also encouraging was the city's seemingly cordial response. In the year before the alternate plan's release, mounting criticism of orthodox urban renewal had led housing officials to start hedging on their original scheme; this, in turn, prompted a disgusted Kazan to withdraw his bid. ("[T]he bulldozer has been replaced by the peashooter and the slingshot," he fumed.)[74] Now James Felt, Moses' replacement at the City Planning Commission, announced that much of the alternate plan would be incorporated into the city's new proposal for Cooper Square.[75] Through the winter and spring of 1962, the Cooper Square Committee continued to build support. Summer brought more good news: The CPC had designated the Alternate Plan for its Urban Renewal Study Program.[76] Over the next year the committee worked closely with the CPC researchers, and in June 1963, Burdick wrote local residents, "The Alternate Plan for Cooper Square is close to becoming a reality."[77]

But suddenly the wind shifted. CPC officials who had been so talkative went silent when asked about key elements like the Houston Street lot. They especially avoided discussing the "pre-designation statement" of rehousing and redevelopment principles they were preparing for the Board of Estimate. In a July news release Frances Goldin warned, "[T]he whole concept of community participation has been negated by the refusal of the City Planning Commission to discuss the pre-designation statement with us. . . . We charge that this is not true citizen participation."[78]

Goldin's premonition was apt. The CPC's final proposal took no notice of the principle of rehousing site residents. In fact, it promised to make the relocation problem worse by melding Cooper Square with the nearby St. Mark's renewal area, thereby doubling the number of displaced.

Dismayed Cooper Square activists now rallied against the plan their city "allies" had written behind closed doors. Burdick, Thabit, and Rand lit into the commission for its deception of the community and disregard for data. At a CPC hearing in September 1963, Rand called attention to "elderly widows like Mrs. K, for example, who lives in the rehabilitation area on 7th Street. . . . Her pension is $60 per month; her rent, $38, not including gas and electricity. She has no phone, of course. . . . Where is the guarantee that she may continue to live in her apartment?"[79] Thabit revealed that neighborhood people had been swallowing their doubt for months. "During the period of these talks [with city officials, t]he Cooper Square Committee did not once call to *public* attention its criticism and frustrations with the way that dialogue was going. It had many reservations about these talks and came close to stopping them more than once. . . . For a group that includes several of the most outspoken critics of the city's renewal program, this took real forbearance."[80] Perhaps Thabit was the one who had counseled his leftist clients to bite their tongues. Now he felt been duped. Having worked so hard himself to engage in democratic planning, he charged the commission with making a sham of democratic process by acting as though this meant simply reading the "citizens committee's" research. "Your approach to citizen participation," said Thabit, "is to get help to develop the kind of program and to make the kind of decisions you think best for us. . . . We beg to differ. . . . The Cooper Square Committee is nobody's study committee, and it certainly wasn't formed to assist your staff."[81]

Gloves now off, Cooper Square activists mobilized openly against the CPC designation. That cost them some houser allies such as Hortense Gabel and the United Housing Federation; it also made an enemy of Cooper Union, the tuition-free local college that stood to gain space under the city's expanded plan. The Board of Estimate approved the expanded renewal area with a concession in the form of more low-rent housing.[82] Next Cooper Square seemed to win a round: The city approved a public-housing project on the Houston Street lot, as the Alternate Plan urged. But the designation struggle turned out to be just the first in a series of thrusts and parries over citizen participation. Now a second drama unfolded over the fate of the Houston Street site.

The new plot twist tied Cooper Square's future to that of another contested project, the Lower Manhattan Expressway, an analog of the Cross-Bronx. Like the Bronx plan, the downtown highway proposal had been circulating on paper among various Robert Moses agencies since the 1940s. And like the Cross Bronx, the Lower Manhattan Expressway would be a mammoth east–west artery—six lanes in some segments, eight in others—connecting heavily used north–south roads. (The proposed route aligned with Canal Street on the west side and Delancey on the east, where it brushed the southern border of the Cooper Square site.)[83] But unlike the Cross-Bronx, the Lower Manhattan Expressway came up for public hearings in the early sixties, after a decade of dissident planning thought had gelled. And the Lower Manhattan proposal garnered intense scrutiny because it figured in Jane Jacobs' widely read 1961 book. In a chapter on "erosion of cities" by automobiles, Jacobs observed that the expressway "includes a spaghetti-dish of ramps into the city. It will be a [traffic] dumper, and by thus accommodating traffic aimed for the heart of the city, it will actually tend to choke up, instead of aid, city bypass traffic."[84] (For once Jacobs agreed with Lewis Mumford, who had long railed against new highways that stimulated a vicious cycle of driving habits and ultimately worsened traffic congestion.)[85] Jacobs became active in the struggle against the expressway and several other local redevelopment projects, lending publicity to the critics' cause.[86] Wagner shelved the highway plan. Moses, who had been crowbarred out of housing but not fired from other public works, continued to campaign for it vigorously.

One official who came out against the expressway was Cooper Square's State Assembly representative, Louis De Salvio. De Salvio also pledged, in 1963, to support the neighborhood's alternate plan. Thus the Cooper Square Committee was stunned a year later when De Salvio appeared at a Board of Estimate hearing on the Houston Street site, spoke against the public-housing application, and revealed that he was now backing a new bid for middle-income co-ops, to be built on that lot by a fraternal organization in nearby Little Italy.[87]

Cooper Square activists cried foul over what they saw as a land grab by De Salvio (or "Louie the Two-Faced Liar," as they dubbed him in a send-up of "Rudolph" at their Christmas sing-along.)[88] Their tactics took on a new militancy. "[Officials] said that they would negotiate with us," recalled Frances Goldin, "And we tried and tried and tried, and they didn't negotiate with us. So, I don't know how it happened that the lock [to the city's site office] got stuck with epoxy or something, but they couldn't get into the office. And we had a picket line in front . . . and they said that we've gotta disperse. And we said, 'No, this is our neighborhood.'" Another action featured "six feet of garbage, including diapers and rotted food," piled against the basement-level CPC entrance. "It took them a week to get into their offices." Then the Cooper Square Committee took over a hearing of the CPC.

Every month they put it off, and they put it off, and they put it off. And so one month we took the microphone and we said, "No more action of the Planning Commission takes place until [the Houston Street site] is resolved." And they said, "You have to leave, because there are other people waiting to be heard." And we said, "No, we're not going to leave." And I was arrested. And then ten more people were arrested. And then we organized in the room. And [the CPC chair] said, "All right, now the person from Crown Heights will be heard." And they said, "We yield to Cooper Square." And then somebody [else] from Brooklyn was on, and they said, "We yield to Cooper Square." . . . It was wonderful.[89]

In the spring of 1965 *The Village Voice* found a smoking gun—a letter showing that De Salvio had met with Robert Moses to discuss a swap: De Salvio's support for the Lower Manhattan Expressway in exchange for Moses' backing the co-op.[90] At a public hearing packed with Cooper Square activists, the co-op's would-be developer acknowledged the back-room deal and withdrew its bid. "A great feeling of joy and accomplishment swept through those present," Burdick wrote, "when the Board of Estimate . . . announced its decision

Figure 11. **Cooper Square Committee disrupts planners' presentation at Cooper Union.** Frances Goldin center foreground, with arm raised. *Courtesy of Frances Goldin.*

in favor of low cost housing on the vacant lot on Houston Street."[91] The first element of the alternate plan was now secured.

More fights lay ahead, but the Cooper Square Committee had learned from its early struggles. Moreover, the city's slick handling of the predesignation statement had pushed moderate committee members—those who trusted officials to act in good faith—toward the left. Not only Thabit but Burdick, a "perfectly coiffed" churchwoman, found out that public officials sometimes lied, and "just developed over the years into an incredible fighter in her sweet little white-gloved way." Asked about the reasons for Cooper Square's eventual success, Goldin said, "I think it had a good number of either Communists or committed radicals in the leadership that were unbuyable. I think we had a combination of technicians, radicals and troops. We made the technicians do what *we* wanted." Technicians meant Thabit, architects, and lawyers. "We'd get arrested. And [the lawyers] would say, 'Cop a plea.' And we would say, 'Fuck you. We are innocent. And you're defending us as innocent.' . . . We never once pleaded guilty, and we never once lost."[92]

Equally important, the Cooper Square Committee's vision drew neighbors together. Organizers were conscious of the need to build unity among the area's ethnic groups, and they cultivated support among Jewish, Italian, Latino, and Asian groups and individuals.[93] At the winter rally featuring musical lampoons, people also sang serious lyrics about interracial community: "I'm dreaming that by next Christmas / I'll see my new home on that site / We're all kinds of neighbors, and through our labors / We'll live like brothers, black and white."[94] Here, as in the published plan, the committee held up Cooper Square's integration as desirable and viable. In December 1964—just months after the Harlem–Bed-Stuy riots—that was no small thing. The inclusiveness of both the plan and the process also solidified the local movement politically, binding leftists to more mainstream supporters. "We didn't do it alone," said Goldin. "We had the community support. People who went to church regularly got arrested with us. They had dumped the garbage."[95]

Redevelopment Planning as Community Control

Communists and Christians dumping garbage together: this incarnation of "community support" adds breadth and pungency to our understanding of 1960s community discourses. "Community control" is generally understood as a black power demand; in New York it is associated particularly with the embittering Ocean Hill–Brownsville school conflict of 1968. Historian Jerald

Podair has provided an important corrective by showing that decentralized authority over neighborhood schools in New York was first claimed by white anti-integrationists; only later was the idea taken up, and rebranded "community control," by African Americans whose calls for integrated schooling had been denied.[96]

Cooper Square and Morningside Heights, in turn, show that the right of urban community was a protean concept that could, and did, hold yet a third meaning: a democratic entitlement to decentralized decision making arising from neighborly rather than racial ties. When Cooper Square activists told police at the CPC office, "this is our neighborhood," they were asserting a communal right to participate in local planning. Much as black community-control advocates later claimed rights based on their shared history of oppression, multiracial Lower East Siders demanded a say based on their shared history as neighbors.

In this Cooper Square leaders believed they could be a beacon to others. A 1963 news release decrying the City Planning Commission run-arounds declared, "The Cooper Square Community . . . pioneered in drawing up its own plan for the renewal of its neighborhood. . . . [I]f the city won't allow [citizen participation] to work here, then it won't work anywhere."[97] Implicit here was the obverse: Successful citizen participation in Cooper Square could inspire similar processes elsewhere.

And it did. Marie Runyon and Frances Goldin knew each other well through Met Council, and Morningsiders United's 1964 call to preserve "the diversified, integrated community that has always existed here" echoed the philosophy laid out in the Cooper Square Alternate Plan. Walter Thabit is recognized nationally as the father of advocacy planning.[98] Staughton Lynd credits his Cooper Square experience as training for the remarkable "community ownership" campaign he later led among steelworkers facing factory closures in Ohio.[99] Historian Marci Reaven identifies Cooper Square as a critical chapter in a larger story of decentralization of municipal authority that culminated in 1969 with the citywide establishment of community boards that held a designated "seat at the table" in local planning.[100]

Cooper Square also merits attention in the long-running debate over means and ends in city rebuilding. For two decades the urban establishment had accepted the first principle of Stuyvesant Town: Progress meant accommodating the middle class, and progress could be achieved only on developers' terms and at the price of evicting the poor ("inconveniencing" them, in Moses' idiom). Cooper Square said no. The committee's insistence on this point exposed some loose stitching in the seam that otherwise bound middle-class and low-income tenants together on matters like rent control. "[Are] we in the middle class . . . to be constantly overlooked in our critical need for better housing?" asked a woman whose deposit for Kazan's UHF co-op had been returned.[101] But the alternate plan *did* include middle-income co-ops—to be built *around* rather than over the poor.

In the end, however, the woman's fears were realized. Some of the responsibility for this rests with the Cooper Square Committee itself, which split bitterly over a middle-income housing proposal made by a sympathetic church group in 1972. (Goldin and Thabit favored it but Esther Rand's camp blocked it on grounds that the church group's directors included corporate executives. Goldin attributed this "super-revolutionary" bullheadedness to Rand's continued uncritical embrace of the Communist Party, which Goldin had left by then.)[102] In 1990 a new window of official cordiality toward the Alternate Plan was opened under the administration of David Dinkins, but nailed shut when Rudolph Giuliani took office in 1994. The middle-income project did not make it through in time. The Cooper Square Committee did have stellar success at building and rehabilitating low-income co-ops and rentals, which still constitute the majority of housing units on the site. Some of these were won through a trade-off that put up hundreds of new luxury units, but none in the middle bracket.[103]

Divergent Outcomes of Neighborhood Mobilization

Morningsiders United emulated Cooper Square but did not match its achievements. The two neighborhoods' divergence highlights the role of local particularities and legal factors in development struggles. Uptown, the creation of the Morningside Renewal Council—which lent the appearance of community participation to the institutions' plan—weakened the tenant campaign. Joel Schwartz has shown that during the Morningside Gardens conflict of the 1950s, powerful liberals in city and federal agencies ultimately caved in to Moses' pressure and allowed the area's first Title I plan to go forward.[104] In the sixties the institutions were able to orchestrate a second round of liberal collaboration through the MRC, which tenants did not identify as a danger early in the game. Cooper Square activists were also drawn into an illusory vehicle for participation, the City Planning Commission, but the radicals among them were quicker to see it for what it was. Further, the City Planning Commission was a public, not a private, entity. That gave the Cooper Square

Committee standing to tell the higher-ranking Board of Estimate that the CPC had acted fraudulently.

Equally important, the uptown institutions' ownership of redevelopment sites made them less vulnerable than the downtown developers were to political pressure. Possession was nine-tenths of the law. The other major redevelopment struggle in which local tenants ultimately won out was the fight over the Lower Manhattan Expressway; here again it was city policy, not private property rights, that the grassroots groups were trying to thwart. Other redevelopment projects remained in the works and would cause further dislocation of tenants in the late sixties and seventies—especially when, as in the case of Morningside Heights, redevelopers already owned the land.

Cooper Square stands at one end of a spectrum of embattled neighborhoods in the early 1960s, and it shows how many elements had to be in place for a tenant community to prevail. Alert leadership and legal leverage were critical. So was tenants' ability to sustain mobilization. Here not only the neighborhood political heritage, but the severity of the threat—homelessness—helped Cooper Square's cause. In the ghetto rent strikes of the same period, modest concessions by the landlord or the city often eroded tenants' solidarity. But in Cooper Square, a few repairs could not make tenants' main problem go away, or even seem to go away, as long as demolition remained on the agenda. Hence the Cooper Square Committee had a stable committed constituency.

If private redevelopment remained a threat to tenants, at least the tide had turned against massive *state*-subsidized evictions. By the mid-1960s, New York entered what political scientists Norman and Susan Fainstein call a "concessionary" phase of relations between state and citizen. This was characterized by renewal projects of smaller scale and greater accordance with community sentiment.[105] It was ushered in by the local protests tenants had mounted, the urbanist arguments they had advanced, and the political lessons they had accumulated over the preceding decade.

Conclusion

Neighborhood-based tenant struggles of the early to mid-1960s offer insights into both prior and subsequent waves of activism in New York. Looking backward, these efforts show how strongly the Old Left of the thirties and forties reverberated a generation later. The Communist legacy made itself felt from Harlem to Brooklyn as Party veterans like Jesse Gray, Jack O'Dell, Bill Stanley, CORE leaders, Frances Goldin, and Esther Rand brought militance and experience to the challenges of a new decade. Leftist heritage also worked in more subtle ways, leading the Northern Student Movement's Danny Schechter to Gray, informing Marie Runyon's political education, and sustaining a sense of purpose on the Lower East Side.

Equally important, two generations of dissident liberalism gave institutional and technical support to the grassroots movements. The legal and administrative groundwork laid by groups like Met Council (which arguably straddled the liberal-left line by now), the Women's City Club, the Community Service Society, and Call for Action paved the way for city agencies to respond to tenants' needs. The middle-class makeup of some of these groups magnified the political pressure on Albany and City Hall. Strategically placed individuals like Hortense Gabel—protégé of liberal elder statesman Charles Abrams—likewise helped tenants make use of city agencies.

Further, some people who started out with relatively moderate views found themselves "blown back" into alliance with radicals. Walter Thabit, another Abrams student, and Thelma Burdick traveled such a course in Cooper Square. So did Gabel, momentarily, when she suggested that Thabit write an alternate plan. Mobilization for Youth likewise became more militant as civil-rights currents pulled the social workers to the left. It is true that many liberal officials of the thirties, forties, and fifties collaborated with Robert Moses and helped bring about the devastation of working-class tenant communities. By the early sixties, however, liberals with government ties were playing more varied roles. Sometimes they just tinkered with existing bureaucratic mechanisms, but in other instances they helped grassroots groups achieve palpable gains.

Looking forward, the early to mid-sixties actions bring out the complex roots of evolving notions of political community. Far from being a sharp break with civil-rights principles, the idea of community control drew on ideological sources within and without the long black freedom struggle, and continued to develop in response to local conditions. In Harlem, the intransigence African Americans encountered on a constellation of concerns—housing, schools, and policing—pushed many to cast about for more radical paths to community power. Outside the ghetto, different notions of community control emerged. While white community control took hold of school politics in Queens, multiracial tenant communities coalesced behind "community rights" to housing security on Morningside Heights and the Lower East Side. Questions of how to build solidarity in a polarizing city would continue to challenge the tenant movement in the decade to come.

6

"Territorio Libre"

Upheaval in the Vietnam War Era

Seven years after rat-wielding rent strikers made the headlines with their presentation before Judge Ribaudo, New York tenants were back in court for another major hearing. This time a full judicial panel heard testimony from scores of witnesses. "[S]tories of crumbling ceilings, broken fixtures, injuries, lack of hot water, and illness caused by heatless winters began to sound almost routine," *The New Yorker* reported. Several tenants also told of rat bites, lead poisoning, and beatings by landlords' hired thugs. The defendants were found guilty of "permitting slum conditions, maintaining firetraps, . . . criminal neglect, racism and harassment." A judge read the sentence: All rental housing in the city should pass into public ownership under tenant control.[1]

The judge was Jane Benedict of Met Council on Housing, seated on the bench alongside Durie Bethea of the Black Panthers and Iris Morales of the Young Lords Party. The tribunal on which they served was the People's Court, convened by their three organizations for a Housing Crimes Trial that was endorsed by an array of tenant, race, and student groups, and held before an audience of some fifteen hundred in Columbia University's Wollman Auditorium. Representatives from I Wor Kuen, a militant Chinatown youth group, and two more Puerto Rican organizations joined Benedict, Bethea, and Morales on the bench. Met Council's Frances Goldin, Esther Rand, and five others served as prosecutors. Presiding Judge Bethea enforced basic courtroom procedure. But the named defendants—Mayor Lindsay, city housing officials, bank executives—were absent. ("Pig Lindsay and his lackeys did not show," as the *Black Panther* put it.)[2] They were held in contempt of the people.

Figure 12. **Mock trial of landlords and city officials, 1970.** Presiding judge, center, is Durie Bethea of the Black Panther Party. She is flanked by Iris Morales of the Young Lords Party and Jane Benedict of Met Council. *Courtesy of Met Council on Housing.*

This scene from December 1970 captures important elements of the tenant odyssey of the late sixties and early seventies. Central were the dismal conditions that persisted in New York's low-rent housing despite the reforms of the preceding decade. Indeed, the landlord's market, which encouraged neglect, gained strength in this period from ongoing redevelopment of low-income neighborhoods, including expansion carried out by Columbia. Equally important were new political energies among tenants. While seasoned leaders of Benedict's generation continued to play a part in the movement, they were joined by young people rooted in radical race, New Left, and feminist organizations.

The young militants, like the rent strikers before them, held government responsible for ghetto conditions. But they questioned how much help could be gotten from a state wedded to the capitalist order. The device of the people's tribunal, which was adopted by Black Panther branches across the country, underscored the organizers' dim view of the official justice system.

The city these activists were confronting seemed headed toward an abyss. New York in the late sixties saw an ominous rise in housing abandonment; one study found that owners had walked away from nearly 190,000 residential units between 1965 and 1968, leaving their tenants without even minimal services.[3] Federal support for housing declined as the War on Poverty was overtaken by the war in Vietnam. And the city budget, its hour come round at last, slouched toward bankruptcy. Local politics also took on an apocalyptic cast as the school-integration struggle spiraled into the Ocean Hill–Brownsville crisis, a bitter and all-consuming political showdown that pitted parents against teachers, labor against civil rights, and whites against blacks.

In this charged environment, new tenant initiatives gave practical expression to several strands of late sixties liberatory thought. Through alternate planning, organized squatting, and dramatic confrontation with authorities, New York tenants and their allies asserted such ideals as participatory democracy, community control, collectivist property holding, and anticolonial rebellion. In some cases they made those ideals into tangible realities on the ground.

The squatter and alternate planning stories add to a growing literature on diverse grassroots activism at the local level in this period. Recent works on Black Power have explored successful local activities ranging from service provision to curricular reform to electoral campaigns to the building of international awareness; these works challenge the paradigm of nihilism and failure that dominated earlier writing.[4] Still, in New York the prevailing example of Black Power remains the failed effort to improve ghetto schools by placing them under "community control."[5] But the material successes that local tenants achieved in the name of community control, and through groups identified with black and Latino radicalism, reveal another, less heralded side of those ideologies in the very same city. Further, most of the successful squatter actions entailed cross-racial alliance and thus show the continued viability of a multiracial variant of community control that Cooper Square had pioneered a decade earlier.

A second distinctive feature of these New York campaigns was synergy between older and younger participants. Young people mounted their housing actions in the context of an Old Left network and culture that had survived better than most. Old Leftists did not plan most of the new grassroots projects, but they provided a supportive framework.

New York's late sixties and early seventies tenant actions also drive another nail in the coffin of declensionist scholarship on youth movements of the sixties, a body of work that focused on the national career of Students for a Democratic Society (SDS) and its disintegration late in the decade.[6] As it happened, SDS's main contribution to New York's tenant struggles—the 1968 "Battle of Morningside Park"—was effective, precisely because the institution against which students wielded their greatest power, the university, was also the driving force behind redevelopment on Morningside Heights. More importantly, SDS was not the main engine of youth activism in housing in New York. Small local groups did the most significant work.

Finally, tenant activism in New York helped to foster and sustain yet another upheaval of lasting significance: women's liberation. As politicized young women became involved in local housing struggles, they encountered the Old Left cohort that led Met Council and its affiliates. Those senior women became mentors to many of the young people, providing them with an "on the ground" model of female leadership and inspiring them to develop their own abilities as organizers and strategists.

The Revolution Will Not Be Televised: Ghetto Radicalism in the Late Sixties

Late-sixties housing actions in New York took place amid a nationwide escalation of radical movements prompted by the failures of corporate and Cold War liberalism to rectify poverty, *de facto* racial exploitation and antidemocratic foreign policy. Amid the proliferating groups and ideologies, the principle of anticolonialism offered common ground for activists of several stripes. It was fundamental for those who had become politicized protesting the war in Vietnam. And it appealed increasingly to blacks and Latinos focused on racism.

Black America had been captivated from the late 1950s onward by the anticolonial rebellions blazing through Asia and Africa.[7] Not only did these Third World victories against European powers inspire race pride and underscore the slowness of racial progress at home; they also gave African Americans a global context in which to understand themselves and their predicament. In 1967 Stokely Carmichael and Charles Hamilton's *Black Power* channeled this general feeling of identification toward a specific concept: a reinterpretation of the relationship of white to black America as one of colonial domination. Blacks formed a colony within American borders.[8] This idea, an implicit revival of the Communists' "nation within a nation" thesis, gained credence and coherence from U.S. foreign policy. Washington met Africa's (and Asia's) anticolonial movements with wariness in some cases, outright hostility in others. America's tepid support for civil rights at home could be understood as part and parcel of its global imperial project.

"Internal colonialism" recast struggles over urban ghettos in terms of national liberation. Carmichael and other Black Power proponents explicitly defined black liberation as the establishment of community control over ghetto institutions. Quite a few white radicals also came to support this agenda. For all their long-running ideological debates and cleavages, most participants in militant race and left groups saw capitalism, imperialism, and racism as interlocking institutions of exploitation and saw ghettos as the American places most disfranchised by all three. Anticolonialism would resonate strongly with New York's young housing activists.

Further, ghettos were also the places where liberal policy makers hoped to redeem liberalism's good name by waging "war on poverty." Consequently, federal money and a certain amount of institutional support were now available to aspiring ghetto organizers. Several current and former antipoverty workers would play parts in New York's audacious tenant actions of the late sixties and early seventies.

Anticolonial and antipoverty activism in New York took the form of creative housing initiatives for several reasons. Gotham's ghettos and barrios were home to the largest population of color in any American city, and thus supported a wide array of political projects. Further, these neighborhoods were situated within America's leading city for housing politics, where tenants and housers had been confronting property rights, redevelopment, and slum economics for decades. Finally, during the early and mid-1960s New York tenants had developed innovative understandings of community control. From the eviction resisters of Cooper Square and Morningside Heights to the rent strikers of Harlem and Brooklyn, diverse New Yorkers had sought to articulate and enact forms of neighborhood-based democracy defined largely through housing rights. That history would lend impetus to young radicals' anticolonial urban projects.

John Lindsay and the Crucible of Community Control

Like tenant allies Stanley Isaacs and Fiorello La Guardia, John Lindsay was that once-real political unicorn, a liberal Republican. He had served as congressman from the Upper East Side's "silk-stocking district" in the late fifties and early sixties, compiled a strong record on civil rights, and in 1965 won the GOP nomination for mayor. His bid drew crucial support from New York's Liberal Party—the anticommunist rival of the late ALP—leaders of which had little enthusiasm for the Democratic candidate, Comptroller Abe Beame. Beame was a Brooklyn clubhouse fixture who had won a four-way primary after Wagner declined to seek a fourth term. He possessed all the charisma typically associated with the accounting profession. Lindsay was energetic and handsome. With much of the labor vote and a third of the black and Puerto Rican vote defecting from the Democrats, Lindsay narrowly won the race.[9]

But just hours after he took office in January 1966, political disaster struck in the form of a transit walkout. Prompted by the mayor's ill-considered refusal to grant a wage increase, the strike paralyzed the city for twelve days, caused hundreds of thousands to miss work, and created widespread antipathy toward Lindsay and his inept management.[10] The shutdown touched every facet of city life, including housing, as tenants froze while a skeleton Emergency Repair crew struggled to respond to calls.[11]

In other respects Lindsay made an auspicious start, celebrating urbanism and reaching out to people of color in particular.[12] The image of the shirtsleeve-clad mayor walking through Harlem on the night of Martin Luther King's death—much like the figure of La Guardia at the scene of the 1943 riot—would become part New York's social memory.

But the transit strike was a greater omen for his administration, because Lindsay's friendly gestures would soon be eclipsed by labor conflicts and fiscal problems. The city he inherited had already lost thousands of jobs and taxpayers to the suburbs. Now a nationwide recession cracked the remaining pillar of city finance: property taxes based on real estate values.[13] And the revenue messiah that budget planners had counted on—office space—failed to arrive in a market glutted by a new round of tower building.[14] New York began to borrow in earnest.[15] The city's fiscal standing would not become a major public issue until 1975, when banks cut off municipal credit, but the pinch was palpable by the latter part of Lindsay's tenure.[16]

These pressures at City Hall presented opportunities for local activists to advance several programs for "community control," some of the most fruitful being neighborhood housing initiatives. Those initiatives have been eclipsed in popular memory, however, by the Ocean Hill–Brownsville school crisis, a conflict of extraordinary viscerality even in a city where people are not known for soft-pedaling their disagreements. Far from a discrete dispute over educational policy, the 1968 school crisis raised fundamental questions of fairness and democracy and fueled major realignments in New York's class and ethnoracial politics.

The Brooklyn showdown was a product of the city's ongoing refusal to meet ghetto parents' demands for educational parity. The 1964 school boycott had hardly budged officials. This became apparent at the next watershed, Harlem's Intermediate School 201. In 1966 the Board of Education promised to integrate this new school, but instead assigned an all black and Puerto Rican enrollment—and a white principal. As exasperated African Americans took up the demand for a black administrator, the campaign for black "community control" of education was born.[17] The idea struck a chord among veteran school activists, nascent nationalists, white proponents of participatory democracy, and officials and business leaders eager for a low-cost way to appease militants.

Thus, as the dust was settling at I.S. 201, Lindsay appointed a panel to devise an experiment in community control of local schools.[18] But the panel's plan was a recipe for failure. In order to isolate the variable of community control from other factors such as school spending, the Board of Education barred the experimental districts from raising their own funds, thus burdening already poor schools and alienating the teachers' union. The pressure cooker reached a boil in May 1968, when the elected school board in the predominantly black Ocean Hill–Brownsville section of Brooklyn summarily transferred nineteen teachers and administrators. This set off an escalating series of job actions by the union and countermaneuvers by local parents and Brooklyn CORE.[19]

The ensuing teachers' strike created a citywide crisis that made the '66 transit walkout look like an informational picket. Children lost two months of schooling; parents scrambled for day care; political coalitions creaked and split. Images of black parents and Jewish teachers squaring off outside Brooklyn schoolhouses stoked tensions that had long simmered beneath the surface of New York's black–Jewish coalition for civil rights.[20]

The union won reinstatement of the teachers, but historian Jerald Podair argues that the event's lasting effect was to drive a fundamental reconfiguration of New York politics. Whites united across class lines to forge a new ruling coalition, one whose mean-spiritedness toward the black poor would gut the city's once-exemplary schools, hospitals, and other public institutions during the lean years ahead. Podair lays much of the blame for this catastrophe on African Americans who embraced the chimera of community control. Instead of building the interracial coalition necessary for real clout in a city that retained a substantial white electorate, black New Yorkers acted as modern-day Esaus, renouncing their rightful claim on city funds in exchange for a political mess of pottage: nominal control over budget-starved local institutions.

School administration, however, was only one dimension of city life in which New Yorkers demanded a neighborhood-level say over public policy. Housing presented somewhat different challenges and opportunities. Certainly the two issues were related—housing segregation was the basis for school segregation—and they would attract overlapping groups of activists

who saw community disfranchisement and community control in comprehensive terms. But for tenants, community control proved less chimerical
and divisive than it did for educational reformers. Neighborhood tenant
activists of this period did not win every battle, but they scored some tangible victories in housing and achieved a remarkable degree of multiracial
and intergenerational solidarity.

Citizen-Led Planning

The idea that ordinary citizens should determine the fate of their neighborhoods dated back, in New York, to the anti-demolition campaigns mounted
by tenants in East Tremont, Morningside Heights, Cooper Square, and other
areas in the 1950s. A decade later, community control gained ideological currency and revitalized the principle of neighborhood-based citizen participation. The idea struck a chord especially with African Americans and Latinos
who were embracing internal colonialism as a model for understanding their
disfranchisement, and with SNCC and SDS veterans steeped in the ideal of
participatory democracy. It also harmonized with the federal rhetoric (itself
inspired by the civil rights struggle) of "community action" and "maximum
feasible participation" of local people in designing War on Poverty projects.

In the late 1960s, these local precedents and national currents came together in a reinvigorated alternate planning movement. Residents of the
multiracial Cooper Square and Morningside Heights areas continued to push
for tenant participation in redevelopment planning. At the same time organizers in black and Latino neighborhoods took up democratic planning as a
new strategy for racial liberation.

By 1965 the Cooper Square Committee had made one substantive gain: city
approval for public housing on the vacant lot on Houston Street, an essential
element of the democratically formulated Alternate Plan.[21] But each further
step was a struggle. The committee spent years fighting off the city's attempt to
combine Cooper Square with the St. Mark's renewal area. By now the Housing
and Redevelopment Board was trying to project receptiveness toward citizen
participation and opened a branch office that hosted "community" meetings.
These meetings, however, were packed with opponents of the Alternate Plan,
and Cooper Square activists concluded that they were just the latest vehicle
for manipulation. The committee turned to boycotting the city meetings and
stepped up other forms of protest against official flimflam.[22] Committee members picketed the Housing and Home Finance Agency in Washington, which had

written but not enforced a mandate for citizen participation.[23] They pressed Mayor Lindsay, who had endorsed the Alternate Plan during his campaign but had stayed out of the fray since taking office. The committee's position, distilled on a five-inch sticker posted around the neighborhood, was that government had two options: "Support the Cooper Sq. Alternate Plan or . . . CITY KEEP OUT."[24] A 1966 sit-in seemed to turn the tide: Lindsay finally withdrew the city's application for federal funding of the combined area project.[25]

But the "City Keep Out" dictum came back to haunt supporters of the Alternate Plan. Months after backing down on the combination of renewal areas, Lindsay announced that all housing money for the coming year would be directed through Washington's new antipoverty program, Model Cities, into three deteriorated neighborhoods: the South Bronx, Bedford Stuyvesant, and Central Harlem. Everything else would be put on hold.[26] Talks between Cooper Square and the city resumed in 1968, but dissension among officials tied up the Alternate Plan in court. Once again, Frances Goldin and others disrupted a planning commission hearing, warning, as they were taken away by police, "a delay will jeopardize renewal work."[27] They were right. By the time the city affirmed its support of the Alternate Plan, Richard Nixon's budget cuts made such support moot: There was no Title I money to proceed.

After a decade of struggle, then, the Cooper Square Committee had defeated several competing plans but was in no position to implement its own. Its chief accomplishment—not insignificant in light of the usual Title I scenario—was to prevent evictions. Because an immobilized city administration owned the site, rent levels and tenants stayed put. "As a result," a 1986 study noted, "the Cooper Square community is essentially the same one that existed fifteen years ago when the Alternate Plan was approved."[28] Disrepair in the city-owned buildings also remained essentially the same until the late 1980s, when rehabilitation finally began. Decades in crumbling apartments became the price tenants paid for demanding renewal on their own terms.

On Morningside Heights a more complicated saga unfolded. As seen earlier, Marie Runyon's tenant union was outmaneuvered in 1965 by the educational and religious institutions, which had set up their own "community" council to put a veneer of citizen participation on the Title I plan known as the GNRP (General Neighborhood Renewal Plan). By 1968, eight thousand low-income tenants, many of them blacks and Latinos, would be pushed out to make way for institutional expansion.

After the GNRP vote, however, local residents regrouped. Morningsiders United kept up the struggle on the west side of Morningside Park. Meanwhile

Met Council leader Bill Stanley, together with other Harlem residents concerned about the all-black blocks *east* of the park, came together as the West Harlem Community Organization (WHCO). WHCO approached the Architects' Renewal Committee in Harlem—the alliance of civil-rights-oriented planners, including Cooper Square's Walter Thabit—for help in preparing a different proposal.[29]

Like the Cooper Square organizers, ARCH and WHCO wanted not only to increase the area's stock of low-rent housing, but to work out details via neighborhood committees. "It is our contention that [urban renewal] can be made to work effectively only through . . . community planning agencies which can guarantee participation in the renewal planning process of the citizens whom it is to involve," WHCO wrote. The organizers used both the nationally current language of participatory democracy and the local example of Cooper Square. In particular they recognized the lesson that Cooper Square activists learned in their first skirmish with the City Planning Commission: "[P]articipation can be guaranteed only if these [community] agencies are given *statutory power* to decide local planning policy and not if their function remains advisory and consultative."[30]

On campus, meanwhile, Columbia's student left was embracing the tenant cause. If student radicals across the country regarded college administrators as complacent keepers of the corporate flame, Columbia's activists felt caught up in the epitome of corporate evil: a wealthy school that was actively evicting poor people from their homes. Students regularly turned out for Morningsiders United protests against university expansion. By the spring of 1968, their anger at the administration was roiling over both the local tenant question and the national issue of the Vietnam War (which the university supported through military research and draft administration).

The watershed was the university's attempt to build a private gym in Morningside Park, just north of campus and just south of 125th Street, the conventional border of West Harlem. The gym agreement between school and city was another Robert Moses gift dating to 1955. Little notice was taken then, but by the mid-1960s Morningsiders United was loudly protesting this appropriation of public space for private use, and in 1967 WHCO and other black spokespersons added their sharp criticism.[31] The sop Columbia offered, limited public entrée to the gym via a back door, did not go over well in Harlem.[32]

Although the gym was not, strictly speaking, a housing concern, it symbolized Columbia's larger expansion campaign. Accordingly, when bulldozers rolled in the park in February 1968, Stanley and other tenant activists from Harlem and Morningside Heights were there to meet them. Twelve were arrested.[33] Excavation began, but the community outcry had put university officials on edge. The *New York Times* reported that top administrators were fearful "that Negroes might 'burn the whole place down.'"[34]

In late April this volatile mixture of neighborhood and national politics set off a chain reaction. At a noontime anti-gym and antiwar protest called jointly by SDS and the Students Afro-American Society, a black student leader placed the gym at the top of the agenda: "This is Harlem Heights, not Morningside Heights," he told the crowd. "What would you do if somebody came and took your property . . . as they're doing over at Morningside [Park] with this gym?" At that some of the five hundred demonstrators proceeded to the park, broke into the construction site, and scuffled with police who were called to the scene. When the students reconvened on campus, Afro-American Society member Bill Sales praised the white participants, whose actions he likened to "a blow for the Vietnamese people . . . for the freedom fighters in Angola, Mozambique, Portuguese Guinea, Zimbabwe, South Africa."[35] The students then took charge of an academic building, where they were joined that evening by a Harlem contingent including SNCC leader H. Rap Brown. Brown announced, "the black community is taking over," a cue for white sitters-in to leave.[36] This assertion of control was supported by black Columbia students who wanted to maintain "a distinctive identity" in campus politics and to foreground the Harlem issue.[37]

During the six-week campus strike that followed, students and their Harlem allies barricaded the gym site and made the halting of construction there a prominent demand. Columbia backed down. It suspended construction, and the following year abandoned the project for good.[38] Thus an action that marked a milestone in SDS and black student politics nationally also scored a palpable victory for the right of local residents to have a say in redevelopment of the area. (See map of gym and other disputed sites on page 210.)

From Tenant Rebellion to Ghetto Liberation

The Battle of Morningside Park built on ideological groundwork laid by Marie Runyon and other tenants who had insisted that their neighborly ties amounted to an "investment" more compelling than the purchase of private property. Black Power proponents pushed this principle when they declared Harlem the "property" of African Americans. Now a series of tenant initiatives would put the rhetoric of community proprietorship into practice. Through takeovers, squatting, and dramatic street actions, activists asserted moral ownership of both existing tenant communities and vacant homes, especially those located in neighborhoods of color.

Like community control, physical seizure of tenant territory was a strategy that drew on both local precedents and broader ideological currents. Physically assertive tenant action in New York could be traced back to the Communist eviction blockades of the 1930s and the United Negro Veterans' 1946 proposal to appropriate boarded-up buildings in Harlem. More recently, Cooper Square activists had thrown up pickets, thrown down garbage, and thrown out parliamentary decorum after milder tactics failed to bring officials around.

The physical taking of *ghetto* terrain also accorded with the anticolonial *Zeitgeist*, and with an ethos of armed self-defense that had long been part of rural black culture and was now being advocated loudly by a growing urban constituency. Malcolm X and local school activist Mae Mallory were among the many Harlemites who applauded North Carolinian Robert Williams for leading an armed standoff against white supremacists in 1961.[39] Mid-1960s rioters in Harlem and other ghettos likewise understood themselves to be defending their territory against hostile white forces. And the 1966 inauguration the Black Panther Party for Self-Defense in Oakland made the rifle-bearing urban black guardian a household image. Although none of these actions set very appreciable limits on police power in the United States, they did, together with the contemporaneous white youth rebellion, seem like a powerful wave at the time. Certainly that was the perception of Columbia administrators who backed off from Morningside Park.

The people who most dramatically brought together guns, garbage, and ghetto liberation in Gotham were the Black Panthers and the Young Lords. The local history of these groups demonstrates that on the ground, radical bravura could foster constructive activities as well as inflated rhetoric. And it further illustrates the capacity of community control to inspire activists with a range of political concerns and organizational affiliations.

Black Panther chapters cropped up in Harlem and Brooklyn during the summer of 1968, when party branches were proliferating across the country.[40] Soon they began to offer free breakfast programs and health clinics like those the BPP ran in other cities.[41] As early as July of that year, charter member Lumumba Shakur (Anthony Coston) organized a rent strike in a Central Harlem building.[42]

Cleo Silvers joined the Party in 1969. Her path to induction wound through several major chapters of African American history. Her great-grandfather had fled Haiti for the U.S. where he became an abolitionist. Her grandmothers were active in their churches and in black sororal organizations. *The Crisis* and *The Crusader* could always be found around the Philadelphia household where Silvers (*née* Benn) grew up, and her father was one of the first African Americans to get a foot in the door of Philadelphia's building trades.[43]

Silvers herself was an avid reader who devoured the Beatniks and James Baldwin in high school, but her family had no money for college tuition. Waiting tables on the night shift, she felt directionless until one evening at a boyfriend's house she saw a television ad: "'Join VISTA and see the world.'" VISTA (Volunteers in Service to America), conceived during the Kennedy administration as a "domestic Peace Corps" and continued under Johnson's War on Poverty, provided training and stipends for young volunteers on a variety of local service projects. "And [the ad] said, 'You can see the world, and do something to help people.' And I said, 'That's something I might be interested in.'"[44]

She was. Fall of 1966 found Silvers in the VISTA office in Baltimore, where she studied under a protégé of Saul Alinsky and was sent out to organize. "And that's when . . . the whole direction of my life changed." Knocking on doors in a housing project, helping parents there to gain a say over local schools, she found a new kind of satisfaction. After the Baltimore project concluded, Silvers' next assignment was the South Bronx.[45]

"I'd never met Puerto Ricans, I'd never *seen* Puerto Ricans before. And I was like, OK, this is a whole different set of circumstances." New York had some other surprises in store for her, too. As she scrambled to learn street Spanish, Silvers received a crash course in urban exploitation. Her VISTA sponsor in New York was the Department of Buildings, which sent her out with field inspectors and brought her face to face with local housing conditions. "Like rats this big. . . . Like ceilings falling in completely and hitting some old lady in the head. Like no heat and hot water in the wintertime. I was completely and totally appalled."[46]

Silvers' job was to organize tenants in those crumbling buildings. That she would be set to such a task by a notoriously lax city agency underlines the hope for genuine changes in public service that the War on Poverty held out for a time. And it illustrates the role of New York's housing politics in giving local direction to a mutable federal program.

Very likely Silvers' assignment also reflects the vitality of New York's intergenerational left connections and their trace effects on the city's political culture. Silvers' supervisors at DOB were "two Jewish guys in their forties" who "always denied being leftist. . . . And they were so sincere, so nice. . . . Their views always seemed to be in the back of their heads, and they would act kind of like everybody else. And then later on they would take us and say, 'maybe you oughta do this.' . . . They always seemed to point us in the most progressive direction they could." Among other things they pointed Silvers toward Harlem, "to go visit Mr. [Jesse] Gray."[47]

But Silvers' work also took her places her male supervisors didn't know about, into families and local culture. Although the inspectors "had seen as much bad stuff as you could see in housing conditions in New York City, . . . they [lacked] a real sense of how warm and open the people were." That side of tenant work, Silvers and her VISTA roommate found, was more accessible to women. Women were usually the "targets" of their organizing. "Because they're home. They have the ultimate responsibility for taking care of the family." To organize effectively, the VISTA volunteers had to involve themselves in the women's world.

> We would start around eleven o'clock in the day. And lots of the women, the Puerto Rican women, would say, "I can't make a decision until my husband comes home from work." So we would go around and do the social thing. Coffee, lunch, rice and beans, help people cook. We would do whatever it took. Watch the kids while they go to the store. Go to the Welfare with them in the daytime. . . . So that by the time their husbands got home they'd have the dinner ready. And *then* you could have meetings.

In this manner the two women organized seven block associations involving roughly forty buildings, several of which waged successful rent strikes for maintenance and repairs. For Silvers the rewards went beyond the taste of victory to the savoring of local culture. "I learned about Caribbeans, I learned about Haitians. . . . Everybody had different music, they would bring you over to their houses and play their music for you. . . . Block parties were a big deal. . . . I don't think anyone could have these wonderful experiences without knowing that you've been given a great gift."[48]

Silvers' contacts also educated her about neighborhood problems besides housing. Foremost was the quality of instruction at local schools, a grave concern for parents in the Bronx as for those in Harlem and Brooklyn. "That's the wonderful thing about what was going on in New York City at that time, was that there was an *upheaval*. . . . It was not just the tenant organizing going on over in that corner. And there were connections between people." The same women who joined Silvers' tenant councils were also meeting with the United Bronx Parents (UBP), a school-oriented pressure group that had formed a year earlier. Indeed, the UPB's leadership roster showed that when one scratched a leftist organizer in New York, one often enough found a tenant activist. The group's founder was Evelina Antonetty, a Puerto Rican whose organizing re-sume included Vito Marcantonio's 1930s campaigns and the left-wing District 65 union, and who had gotten her first taste of struggle on the anti-eviction brigades she joined in East Harlem during the Depression. The UBP's training director was Ellen Lurie, the social worker who had collaborated with East Harlem tenants on designing better public housing in the 1950s.[49]

Housing and school activism marched easily together under the banner of community control. "We are in our community, in our homes and in our schools, and we have no control," as Silvers put it. "Any [other] community that you go to, parents have some control over the teachers."[50] Here home and school appeared as overlapping arenas within the broader jurisdiction of "community." And community rights such as safe housing and parental authority signified equal citizenship. In this usage, political scientist Claire Jean Kim argues, "community control [functioned] as a place-specific appli-cation of the Black Power frame" that was expansive enough to encompass a range of understandings of self-determination.[51] (For Silvers this frame had room for supportive whites such as Lurie and another Jewish organizer in the predominantly Puerto Rican UPB.)[52] Bronx tenant and school organizing also illustrate historian Rhonda Williams' insight that a locally based, "bread, butter and respect" agenda was often women's point of entry into the Black Power movement.[53]

Silvers' evolving sense of community politics informed her next step. When her VISTA contract expired in the fall of 1967, she resolved to stay in the Bronx. By this time two groups she had organized were receiving Model Cities fund-ing. She accepted a job with one, the Trinity Avenue Block Association, where her responsibilities ranged from helping parents obtain welfare benefits to taking the local kids bowling. She also continued to work on housing because "people would come into the Trinity Avenue Block Association to get help with their housing issues."[54]

More and more, Silvers found, helping tenants meant encouraging them to take control of their buildings. The South Bronx was a prime area in which landlords who had long "milked" ghetto properties were now finding it ad-vantageous to walk away rather than pay debt service and invest in the ma-jor repairs the neglected structures required. At this point tenants' legal recourse, a court-ordered rent reduction, became meaningless. Thus when Trinity Avenue residents consulted Silvers on housing questions, she would help them work with a city agency "if possible. If not, then our suggestion was always, let's call a building meeting . . . and we'd go through . . . what are the barriers to accomplishing this . . . how can we overcome them—and just take over a building."[55]

In the best cases there was "a feeling of community already. . . . So my coming in was just a spark that allowed the buildings to become *formally* organized, because there really already was organization and leadership there." When leadership was sound and participation high, "there were some really nice outcomes." Tenants chipped in to buy materials and did much of the renovation themselves. Operating costs were covered by an escrow account into which residents paid rent. (The majority might even "carry" a few nonpayers who simply did not have the money.) Debt service and profit, which ate up so much revenue in conventional buildings, were gone from the equation. Of course, not every building was a best case. High rates of factionalism or low rates of rent payment could spell failure for tenant control.[56]

But the successful buildings brought a rare measure of reality to the Black Power ideal of community control. Tenants who fixed up dilapidated buildings for their own use wrought meaningful change on one of the most exploitative conditions of ghetto and barrio living. They exercised a degree of control that had eluded rent strikers just a few years before. Stokely Carmichael would exalt tenant seizure of ghetto tenements as one of the most promising "new forms" of black empowerment.[57] Obviously this achievement also depended on factors beyond residents' control, such as the landlord's decision to walk away, the extent of rehabilitation each building required, and the presence of tenants able to meet the material and political challenges of self-management.[58] These factors limited the scope of change, but the *depth* of change enjoyed by successful cooperators would inspire further takeovers in coming years.

After more than a year at the block association, Silvers took a position as mental-health worker at nearby Lincoln Hospital. Health care, like housing and schools, loomed as a community issue: Silvers had often heard from neighbors "that Lincoln Hospital was a butcher shop. And that it was a blight on the Puerto Rican and black community in the South Bronx." Improving Lincoln's service through an innovative "community mental health" program, recently begun with a War on Poverty grant, seemed a natural sequel to the VISTA and Model Cities assignments.[59] But the Lincoln job would also propel Silvers *out* of the War on Poverty and into the next chapter of African American urban history: "revolutionary nationalism."

She went to work in February 1969. "Two weeks later the workers took over the mental health center."[60] Lincoln's community program had become a maelstrom of power struggles, principally between the professional and "paraprofessional" staffs—predominantly white and heavily Puerto Rican and black, respectively—but also among the paraprofessionals of different races, their union, and the Bronx voluntary organizations that advised the program, all of whom claimed to speak for "the community." In early March the firing of four workers prompted more than one hundred paraprofessionals, including Silvers, to evict the administrators and run the mental-health service themselves. The two-week insurrection won a measure of reorganization and shared decision making within the program.[61] It also introduced Silvers to the Black Panthers, who showed up to help with food and other logistics at the request of a paraprofessional leader who happened to be Panthers' karate teacher. Silvers was utterly taken with "these bad, smokin', courageous, intelligent, *fine* black people." When they invited her to join their ranks, she enlisted the next day.[62]

As a Black Panther, Silvers continued to work at Lincoln, organize tenants and volunteer with the parents' group; but she acquired a new political understanding of these activities. "I had never read Marx before. . . . I mean, I was into the education thing . . . and the housing conditions were horrible, and the children were getting bitten by rats, and health care was horrible . . . but I'd never put it all together." The Marxist view of a pervasive capitalist system led many Panthers—some of whom, like Silvers, were employed for a time in War on Poverty agencies—ultimately to adopt a dismissive view of the state and state-funded programs ("poverty-pimps," in their idiom).[63]

Still, many of their activities, like the mid-sixties rent strikes and the Cooper Square protests, were aimed at pressuring the city to live up to its own commitments. When the United Bronx Parents objected to the "white people's nasty food" that their children were being served at school, the Panthers helped the parents collect several garbage bags full and dump them into the middle of a Board of Education hearing.[64] The largest single Black Panther action in New York was a rent strike, organized jointly by the Brooklyn chapter, the Young Lords, and some Ocean Hill–Brownsville activists, in which nearly one thousand tenants withheld rent to demand heat in their ill-maintained city-owned buildings.[65] On a smaller scale, the Harlem chapter, like so many earlier tenant councils, helped people file mundane code complaints with the Buildings Department.[66]

Yet at other moments the Panthers side-stepped governmental agencies completely. In the Bronx, Silvers and Afeni Shakur (Alice Williams) organized a number of extralegal tenant takeovers—similar to those Silvers had encouraged as a Model Cities worker—beyond the Trinity Avenue area.[67] In Harlem, Dhoruba Bin Wahad (Richard Moore) did likewise.[68] The Bronx office also offered extermination services to eradicate the "rats, mice and roaches [that] are a major problem to the oppressed masses."[69] Nikhil Singh has argued that the Panthers' political charge resided in the way their street theatrics— particularly their shadowing of the police with guns and law books—"literally made a spectacle of government authority."[70] The pest control and other "serve the people" programs were lower in voltage, but they likewise pointed up the state's failure to fulfill its self-proclaimed role. Arguably, however, it was the building takeovers—unspectacular actions that had begun during the War on Poverty—that did the most for tenants in the estimated few dozen buildings where they succeeded.[71]

The cross-fertilization that developed among ghetto organizers with different primary concerns also led the Panthers to learn about another housing problem. In the aftermath of the Lincoln takeover, "some [sympathetic] researcher . . . came to the Panthers and said, 'Do you know that kids are getting brain damage from eating lead chips?'" Lead from old paint posed a severe threat to city children, especially undernourished toddlers, who could develop a craving to eat anything. The law required landlords to remove the hazard. But code enforcement in the ghettos was an old story. The Bronx Panthers had already begun to offer free screening for sickle cell anemia and hypertension. Now they added a test for lead poisoning—a housing as much as a health issue—to their program.[72]

Maintaining these service projects, however, became increasingly difficult over the course of 1969 and 1970, when twenty-one of New York's party leaders were charged with conspiring to blow up department stores, train tracks, and police officers, and when relations broke down between the East and West Coast Panther organizations. (The Panther 21 would eventually be acquitted.)[73] Silvers was slightly younger than most of her fellows, and senior members of the chapter wanted to shield her from the meltdown. One day two high-ranking brothers took her aside and "said, 'Let's go.' And I didn't know where they were taking me, to tell you the truth. And they took me over to 111th and Madison Avenue, to the Young Lords' office, and. . . . [t]here was some kind of discussion between . . . Zayd and Lumumba and the [Young Lords] Central Committee. And the next thing I knew . . . they said, 'OK, well, now you're gonna be a Young Lord.'"[74]

The Young Lords Party was a kindred-spirit organization made up primarily of Puerto Ricans. It originated in Chicago, and the New York chapter was started in 1969 by left-leaning college students and VISTA veterans. They made their street debut that summer with a "Garbage Offensive" to protest the city's dismal trash collection in East Harlem. The young activists started by sweeping up garbage themselves. This succeeded in demonstrating a service ethic to neighbors who had complained about the filthy streets, but it failed to shame the Sanitation Department into reforming its operation. So on July 27 the youths piled refuse into a barricade on upper Third Avenue, setting off a series of blockades that snarled traffic repeatedly over the summer.[75] (Garbage was now a favored weapon in the radical armament, having been deployed at Cooper Square, at the Board of Education, and also at Lincoln Center, where a band of alienated artists who styled themselves "The Motherfuckers" dumped bags of rotting trash to symbolize "a culture exchange / garbage for garbage.")[76] The Young Lords' action made uptown sanitation a prominent issue in the 1969 mayoral race between Lindsay and challengers Mario Procaccino and John Marchi.[77]

Amid the housing crisis it was unsurprising that the group's next campaign focused on a tenant problem: lead poisoning. Although this condition afflicted some 25,000 New York children every year, the city's Health Department had no budget or legal authority to police landlords who failed to repair peeling lead paint.[78] The Young Lords may have learned about the epidemic from the Black Panthers, or through Party member Iris Morales' previous experience organizing tenants with a War on Poverty agency.[79] In September 1969, news of a case involving severe brain damage to a Harlem toddler shone a spotlight on the issue.[80]

The YLP's "Lead Offensive," like its garbage campaign, consisted of escalating service actions designed to meet immediate needs while also putting heat on city officials. Although "the Panthers began this whole program," said Silvers, who was assigned to the lead project when she was transferred into the YLP, "The Young Lords took this struggle up and really took it to another level."[81] After forging ties with sympathetic workers at the East Harlem hospital where the gravely poisoned boy was treated, the Young Lords sat in at the Health Department to demand that lead-testing kits be released from storage. Then they went door to door in East Harlem.[82] "People would open the door and we'd have our little things to test, and we'd have someone who had some kind of medical training or related, and people were very open to that," recalled Morales.[83] Through these home visits and accompanying press conferences, the activists generated news coverage and political pressure.[84] *Village Voice* columnist Jack Newfield underscored the municipal negligence with his front-page feature "Young Lords Do City's Work in the Barrio."[85]

By winter the campaign had spurred the city to tighten its lead rule, add lead abatement to the purview of the Emergency Repair Program (the squad that

Wagner had created in 1965 in response to the rent strikes), and increase its screening program tenfold.[86] The Young Lords would continue to raise awareness of lead poisoning in other neighborhoods and make lead screening part of their program for medical care under community control.[87]

Like New York's equal-schooling activists of the 1950s and 1960s, the militant youth parties tackling health and safety problems were ultimately fighting for first- rather than second-class city services; "community control" was their means to that end. But unlike the Ocean Hill–Brownsville movement, the BPP and YLP neighborhood campaigns did not entail a renunciation of poor people's claims on city resources. On the contrary, the parties seized city property (hospitals, lead-testing kits) and established parallel service programs (street-sweeps, health screening) precisely to pressure officials into devoting more resources to ghetto and barrio residents. In the process, historian Johanna Fernández concludes, the YLP "straddled a strange middle ground between traditional social service organization and political organization."[88] In this middle ground they also sought a workable approach to the conundrum that Piven and Cloward identified in the rent-strike movement: how to create disruption that nailed the city, rather than simply the landlord, to the tenement wall. Finally, the BPP's small tenant takeovers, which circumvented government completely, did bring a measure of decentralized citizen control.

Radical Women

Notwithstanding their macho imagery and a certain amount of sexist behavior in-house, both the Black Panther and Young Lords Parties formally adopted feminist planks and cultivated women leaders.[89] On a day-to-day level, sexism often played out alongside egalitarian practices. Silvers recalled being welcomed at the Panther office by a corps of accomplished women who "were very mutually supportive. And fought hard for respect in the organization. And did not take a lot of bullshit off the men."[90] Women and men alike took part in self-defense training and public displays of militance.[91] A flyer for the Bronx pest-control service showed a woman aiming a rifle at a rodent nest, while huge rats menaced her sleeping infant. This image managed to bring together the traditional notion of woman as keeper of the hearth, the reality of single motherhood, *and* the transgressive figure of female armed defender. Several of the party's most effective housing organizers were women.[92]

In the Young Lords, gender relations went through a transformation. At first the party took direction from an all-male Central Committee, and sex-typing was the unwritten rule in work assignments and mundane interactions. Denise Oliver, a Brooklyn-born African American red-diaper baby (a "black red baby," as she put it) who was one of the organization's most politically experienced members, allied with Party sisters to challenge this arrangement.[93] The caucus resolved that the YLP must incorporate feminism into its mission and women into the Central Committee. The party's Thirteen Point Program was eventually amended to include "equality for women," and its newspaper, *Palante*, ran an article, "¡Abajo Con Machismo!" (Down with Machismo!).[94] The YLP further elaborated its gender platform to include Puerto Rican concerns over sterilization abuse and alliance with the nascent gay liberation movement.[95] Women in the party took active part in creating and implementing policy, including the lead-testing program.[96]

Casa Libre

The Morningside Park, Lincoln Hospital, and garbage actions featured physical seizure of "community" space; the lead campaign a less muscular but still-dramatic assertion of quasi-governmental authority by people of color concerned with basic services and conditions. Sound health care, clean streets, safe walls, and open parks defined the minimum standards of modern urban living. But those claims on public assets did not address the lynchpin of slum economics, which was New York's dearth of affordable housing. In 1970 that changed, when a new breed of activists, organized squatters, embarked on the "liberation" of housing itself.

The *casus belli* was a surge in evictions. As housing abandonment started to garner headlines, sharp-eyed New Yorkers were discerning something else below the radar: A surprising number of sound, rent-controlled buildings were vacant. Yet these properties were anything but abandoned; they were being deliberately emptied by their owners in preparation for luxury renovation or redevelopment. Hospital and school expansion fueled some of these assaults on the low-rent housing stock.[97] Residential redevelopment also played a part due to loopholes in New York's rent law. Because rent control applied only to units built before 1947, landlords could boost their profits by demolishing older buildings and replacing them with new, unregulated structures. They could also break free of rent control by converting to co-ops, which sold at handsome prices.[98] Meanwhile they might hold apartments vacant for months or years. Such "warehousing" was volatile news given the citywide shortage and the political times. Twenty years after the dawn of urban renewal, veteran housers were acutely sensitive to schemes for class purging or Negro removal. Younger activists, for their part, were by now well steeped in the theory and practice of direct action and community control.

These conditions set the stage for the squatter movement that seemed to erupt suddenly in the spring of 1970. Yet the movement was not as spontaneous as it appeared. Although most squatters were not experienced in tenant politics, they could draw on the precedent of recent radical takeovers. And they enjoyed support from seasoned tenant leaders, maverick poverty warriors, and dissident city officials.

The dramatic wave of break-ins publicized previously hidden warehousing practices and held strong visceral appeal for New Yorkers who thought putting homeless people into vacant buildings made common sense. Where solid organizing coincided with exceptional proprietary circumstances, squatters were able to establish lasting homes. Where these factors were absent, however, property rights prevailed and squatters lost out.

On Morningside Heights the movement was jump-started by longtime tenant leader Marie Runyon and her contacts in the student left. Runyon knew about warehousing firsthand: Since 1961 she had been fighting eviction from the property that Columbia University wanted to redevelop as a pharmacy school, and by the late sixties she was the last holdout in her building.[99] In 1968 and 1969 Runyon led tenant and student groups in protests over the hundreds of apartments they believed Columbia was holding vacant.[100] Then they broke into a large unit at 130 Morningside, where Runyon lived.[101] Meanwhile the United Bronx Parents put Runyon in touch with Juanita Kimble, an African American mother of ten whose family had been subsisting in dismal Bronx housing for years. The Kimbles moved into 130 Morningside in May 1970, while neighbors helped and reporters looked on.[102] "More important than anything else," Runyon recalled, "was that they had maybe a half a dozen kids who looked like Black Panthers. Big, tough, shades, berets. Scared the bejesus out of Columbia! And they had an around-the-clock guard at that apartment for about three weeks."[103] After two months, Columbia relented so far as to turn on the gas; a year later it offered Mrs. Kimble a lease.[104]

As the Morningsiders courted publicity, a larger group advanced quietly a mile and a half downtown. The West Side area between 87th and 97th Streets had become an urban policy battleground. In 1958 Wagner designated the neighborhood as a showcase for citizen participation in urban-renewal planning. Accordingly, the city's Urban Renewal Board worked with an umbrella organization of neighborhood planners to appoint "community representatives." This set off several rounds of jockeying, first between the two community councils named by the city (one for the whole project area and the other for the initial work site), then among those councils, rival Democratic clubs (Tammany and Reform), business owners, tenants and civil-rights advocates, most of whom regarded the city-sponsored councils as company unions. Aside from legitimacy, the main bone of contention among the groups was the proportion of low-, middle-, and high-income units to be developed.[105]

Puerto Rican civic leaders were especially mindful of the calamities at other slum-clearance sites and demanded that low-rent units make up 30 percent of the project.[106] They received vigorous support from Met Council, where West Side Puerto Rican representative Petra Rosa served on the executive board.[107] To the Puerto Ricans' astonishment, however, the national NAACP's housing secretary claimed that a plan to retain the area's poor tenants would sanction *de facto* segregation.[108] (This argument—an early manifestation of growing tension among disparate civil-rights philosophies—would also be voiced by liberal opponents of the Cooper Square Alternate Plan.)[109] In the end the local NAACP chapter endorsed the Puerto Ricans' demand, and the cumulative pressure moved the Board of Estimate to raise the low-rent quotient from 400 to 2,000—about a quarter of the total units—but not enough to make up for the 5,000 low-rent units to be destroyed.[110] In the spring of 1970 some people took matters into their own hands.

They called it Operation Move-In. Under cover of night, organizers from a local antipoverty group installed low-income families into sound, vacant buildings that the city was planning to raze. These organizers were War on Poverty mavericks—people like Cleo Silvers, and the Young Lords who came out of VISTA—who had concluded that the urban poor would not win their war by following the government's rules. Move-In's leader, Bill Price, had loose ties to Met Council and was acquainted with Marie Runyon. Asked what was the tenant's most effective organizing tool, he said, "a crowbar."[111]

By summer the group had 150 families in place.[112] Most were African American or Latino; some had been precariously housed for years. The Marcanos, for example, had been staying with relatives since they immigrated from the Dominican Republic seven years before; they could not find a landlord who would accept a family with eleven children. Newly installed in a fifth-floor walk-up with twelve rooms, they busily repaired the plumbing, walls, and windows that city crews had sledgehammered in an attempt to drive away residents. Breaking the law, Mrs. Marcano explained, "was the only way our family could stay together."[113]

Veteran tenant leaders were quick to endorse Operation Move-In and instigate similar actions around the city. In Chelsea, Met Council founder Jane Wood helped more than fifty Puerto Ricans settle into a vacant building on West 15th Street, where luxury conversions were underway.[114] Across town, Met Council and Cooper Square leader Frances Goldin did the same with multiracial groups.[115] (One of Goldin's daughters, a lesbian, used her gender-bending skills as an electrician to turn on the lights in the buildings.) A few blocks north, Goldin's friend William Worthy—a longtime radical and the New York correspondent for *The Baltimore Afro-American*—let four families of squatters into the building where he served as tenant committee chairman.[116] Meanwhile Jane Benedict established a "We Won't Move" committee to support tenants resisting eviction, and Met Council's office put aspiring squatters in touch with holdout tenants in half-emptied buildings.[117] The latter had an interest in filling vacant units with responsible squatters, both to forge strength in numbers and to fend off the junkies who would otherwise make themselves at home.[118] Several more sites were opened up that way.[119]

The movement also won support from radical groups of color. Mrs. Kimble was helped into her Morningside Drive apartment not only by the Black Panthers, but also by the Young Lords and a cadre of uptown high school students, one of whom fixed the lights and plumbing.[120] Down in Chinatown, the radical youth organization I Wor Kuen (so named after a band of anticolonial fighters in China's Boxer Rebellion) stepped forward. This group had already taken a page from the Black Panthers and Young Lords by initiating pest control and lead screening services among Chinatown's old law tenements. Now they placed squatters into buildings that had been bought up and purged by the Bell Telephone Company.[121]

In addition to inspiring actions around the city, Operation Move-In also spawned further community organizing on the West Side. The break-ins there drew festive crowds, a volunteer army of furniture movers, and an unexpected second cohort of leaders. Whereas the campaign's first organizers were experienced community workers who had grown disillusioned with the War on Poverty, the second group comprised previously nonpolitical residents who knew one another through sandlot softball. As they took notice of the housing crisis, however, these weekend athletes came to feel that the city's Latino establishment had betrayed them by settling for too little. They joined Move-In and helped expand its scope. Embracing the precepts of Black Power and anticolonialism for barrio residents, the new organizers became the nucleus of El Comité, a voice of New York's Puerto Rican left in the 1970s.[122]

Squatters, Sisters, and Seniors

Squatter actions also sparked strong interest among young, predominantly white women who identified with the women's liberation movement that was flourishing locally as well as nationally. In the West Side renewal area, a feminist collective "liberated" a storefront and set up the West Side Women's Center, a place for Move-In squatters to "rap, exchange information on various women's issues, exchange clothing, enjoy free dinners, and meet their sisters to organize."[123] New York's underground feminist journal, *Rat*—which women had "liberated" from the control of male New Leftists a few months before—devoted extensive coverage to the housing crisis and the move-ins. Photos celebrated the occupied buildings and their banners—*"Territorio libre,"* "Hell no! We Won't Go." Editors invited readers to organize rent strikes and assist squatters.[124]

As the Women's Center action illustrates, young feminists sought not only to support but to emulate the housing insurgents. A *Rat* reporter who interviewed Mrs. Kimble argued that the black woman's ties with local militants underlined "the need that we as white women have to define a community for ourselves." She asked Mrs. Kimble directly about women's role in the struggle. "I just feel that a woman is more stronger," responded the veteran of many battles with housing, school, and welfare authorities. "She can take more, she can do more, a man . . . don't have the ability to fight. . . . Women are being turned down, but we *demand*. I was turned down at housing, and told that I have to stay in the Bronx . . . and I said no this ain't for me. . . ." The reporter quoted Kimble at length to drive home the lessons for *Rat*'s readers.[125]

These squatter–sister interactions cast light on subtle patterns of connection between New York's tenant history and its feminist upsurges of the early 1970s. Although women's liberation sprang from many sources, its New York incarnation gained impetus from the city's unusual tenant infrastructure. Local tenant groups had maintained a predominantly female leadership through what was widely experienced as a feminist nadir in the 1950s and early sixties. In this way they had carved out an exceptional political space where Old Leftists could carry on their work and women's authority was not only tolerated but normal.

Then the 1960s infused new blood from the civil-rights and community-control movements into the tenant struggle, and a new generation of feminists claimed a say within those movements. Most did not see themselves as heirs of the senior tenant leaders who were still on the scene (if anything, the Black Panthers and Young Lords probably believed they could teach Jane Benedict a thing or two about making revolution). Young women like Cleo Silvers and Denise Oliver, whose feminism was of a piece with their racial struggle, turned mainly to party sisters for support, and to their own elders for inspiration.[126] Their trajectory illustrates what sociologist Benita Roth has called the "separate roads to feminism" traveled by white, black, and Latina participants in the women's movements of this period.[127]

Still, those roads sometimes converged, like the irregular streets of northern Manhattan that stray from the standard grid. Oliver traced her gender egalitarianism to her upbringing in a black Old Left household that counted some white comrades (including the Jewish settlement house workers who were her godparents).[128] The United Bronx Parents Puerto Rican leaders, who put Kimble in touch with Runyon, had collaborated with women (and progressive men) of other races at crucial points in their activist careers.[129] More broadly, the ghetto housing actions of the sixties and seventies benefited from a legal, political, and cultural groundwork—rent control, receivership law, "concessionary" planning, and the broad concept of housing entitlement—that a racially diverse, heavily female cast of Old Left and liberal New Yorkers had laid over the previous three decades.

In turn, the feminists who took part in the new ghetto and barrio mobilizations would inspire their white age-peers. (Afeni Shakur in particular received hagiographic coverage in *Rat*.)[130] Finally, in the *multiracial* tenant mobilizations of the sixties—the redevelopment struggles on Morningside Heights and in Cooper Square, the squatter actions in Chelsea and on the Lower East Side—a racially mixed cohort of young activists warmed to the leadership of middle-aged white women like Marie Runyon, Jane Wood, Frances Goldin, and Esther Rand.

Politically awakening young women gravitated toward tenant activism for several reasons. The intensity of New York's housing crisis made the squatter and other tenant campaigns a natural object of interest for politicized youth of all races. And the multiracial character of the squatter actions in particular appealed to white women whose political touchstone was the civil-rights movement of the early sixties. Indeed, the *Rat* writer's admiration for Mrs. Kimble can be seen as a northern analog of the respect that young activists in the South felt toward the local black "mamas" who took some of the greatest risks for the movement.[131] Runyon encouraged this identification when she called for volunteers to help fix up "Ma Kimble's" apartment on Mother's Day.[132] One hundred students showed up.[133]

Young feminists also discerned an economic connection between housing and women's struggles. A 1970 *Rat* article, "Why Housing Is a Women's Liberation Issue," argued that the city's housing shortage weighed most heavily on women, who rarely earned enough to afford decent accommodations on their own, and thus were hard put to move away from parents, leave bad relationships, or—if single mothers—provide for their children.[134] Through housing activism, the Women's Center collective hoped to forge a feminism that went beyond white, middle-class concerns—in other words, to bridge the separate roads.

Drawn by these principles, scores of young women became involved with Met Council and its neighborhood affiliates.[135] And they found in the Old Left strongholds an unexpected feminist apprenticeship. "Practical feminists" such as Benedict, Goldin, Rand, and Wood served as exemplars. "I thought they were amazing," remembered Marge DuMond, who turned to Met Council for help organizing her building in 1971, "and I recognized them as—almost another world. . . . In the way that they would tangle with authority, and the way that they would master the ins and outs of the law, and the history, just in such a rational and bold way. I had not seen women like that before."[136] Claudia Mansbach, another seventies recruit, was similarly impressed. "It was very inspiring to see these older women with gray hair—they were all gray-haired by that time"—who were such adept leaders. Before joining Met Council, "I didn't have very many models of older women who were vital and powerful and unafraid to stand up at meetings and say what had to be said."[137] Susan Cohen, who came into Met Council while taking graduate courses in the late sixties, concurred: "They were wonderful role models, all of them. And they kind of showed you what could be done. In the academic setting, there I was being told that I was a bad risk because I was a woman. And nobody in housing talked about that. They just did it. Here were these women that were doing things that were making a difference."[138]

We Were It

The pragmatic nature of the older tenant leaders' *modus operandi*—their just doing it—set them apart from "maternalist" activists, as scholars have dubbed some other urban female organizers of this era. Maternalists claimed legitimacy for their War on Poverty work because they likened neighborhood organizing to mothering and cast neighborhoods as "nonpolitical" space.[139] New York's senior tenant women did not find it necessary to explain themselves in such separate-sphere terms. Instead, they recognized housing as a thoroughly political arena and took for granted their fitness to do battle there.

This unself-conscious acceptance of women's leadership helps explain something unusual about the intergenerational transmission of values that occurred at Met Council, namely a sort of political unintentionality. Historians of mid-twentieth-century social movements have now identified cohorts of unsung organizers who kept the Popular Front flame from dying out during the Cold War and passed it along to activists who ignited the upheavals of the late fifties, sixties, and seventies. In most of these cases, the struggles young people took up were the very struggles their elders had intended to foster. That is, early postwar civil-rights activists paved the way for subsequent civil-rights campaigns, Cold War feminist strategies informed second-wave feminism, and so forth. In New York's tenant arena, by contrast, senior organizers did not set out in a programmatic way to advance one of the main ideals—women's equality—that would inspire their young protégés. They were concerned with housing. But their housing work nonetheless presented a model of "on-the-ground" women's activism, which complemented the more self-conscious women's liberation movement that was exploding on the American stage just as the squatter actions caught fire. Thus older tenant leaders' contribution to second-wave feminism was largely an unintended consequence of their work for tenants' rights.

Such models impressed not only young women like DuMond, Mansbach, and Cohen, but also a number of young men who joined Met Council during this period. They, too, became protégés of Benedict and her peers.[140] If feminism is about changing society—men as well as women—then these mentoring relationships between older women and young men also count as feminist progress.

In the early seventies, Met Council's board would take up the women's liberation movement's call for abortion rights, much as it joined with the New Left in condemning the war.[141] But the older leaders, again, did not enter into the extended discussions of gender that were taking place in other venues (or at least did not do so at board meetings). "They were certainly feminists, all of them," recalled Cohen. "But they *lived* it rather than talked about it, and studied it and analyzed it. . . . The people who were in the [women's liberation] support groups, I think, were a little more theoretical, perhaps more scholarly. . . . they would read books, they would discuss them, they would talk about how to change that politically, and at some point they took action."[142] Frances Goldin reflected on this in similar terms. One of her own role models was Evelyn Wiener, a CP section organizer who locked horns with Party higher-ups at the end of World War II, "because the guys came back, and they thought they would take over the leadership. And she said, 'No, you won't.' So, she didn't think of herself as a feminist, but she was a feminist." But Goldin and her peers did not explicitly address the topic: "Feminism? We were it. I mean, we didn't strive to do [feminist] things, we just did them."[143]

This sort of unspoken feminism did not suffice for everyone. A case in point is Susan Brownmiller. In 1960, long before she gained renown as the author of *Against Our Will*, the twenty-five-year-old Brownmiller embarked on what would be a brief membership in the decimated Communist Party. (Her interest was cultivated at the Jefferson School, where she enrolled in Herbert Aptheker's course on Negro history after being galvanized by the Woolworth's sit-ins.) Upon signing up—under none other than Evelyn Wiener—she was steered toward the place where the Party's best remaining cadre were at work: Met Council on Housing. "Totally remarkable," was her immediate impression of Goldin and Benedict. "I just loved them." She was also aware that the very first woman she had seen make a political speech, at a 1948 ALP rally for Henry Wallace, was a tenant organizer.[144]

But neither the CP nor the ALP entertained reflection on women's subordination *per se*—a critical omission for Brownmiller. "Before the real start of the feminist movement, no one dared think in those terms. Or if we did," she recalled, the Jefferson School instructors sought to quell the "distraction." "I always bristled at that." In 1964 Brownmiller left Met Council to take part in Mississippi Freedom Summer. Only in 1968, "when I went to my first feminist meeting [with New York Radical Women], I realized I was home. That's when I could talk about my abortions. I suddenly understood that there had been this buried history of women."[145] For Brownmiller it was precisely the "theoretical" analysis of patriarchy, as Cohen put it—an analysis absent at Met Council—that unlocked the door.

The senior tenant leaders' feet-first approach to women's concerns owed not to any lack of a theoretical apparatus—as leftists these women had read their share of theoretical texts—but to an ideology that framed those concerns within class struggle. When a state commission invited Met Council to testify at hearings on women's rights in 1970, the executive board passed a motion "to participate to an extent to include all housing problems relating to women."[146] This rather convoluted phrasing may have been a nod to Party orthodoxy on the part of the still-enrolled Communists at the organization. It may also have

been a genuine reflection of the way board members understood their lives in
the larger scheme of things.

What is the significance of this web of connections between tenant struggles
and emerging women's movements? In New York, as in many other cities, the
feminist upsurge of the late sixties and early seventies was fueled by young
women's prior experiences in civil-rights, antiwar, and campus movements. But
New York City exhibited an unusually dense constellation of influential women's
groups, including Redstockings, New York Radical Women, Radicalesbians, and
the Third World Women's Alliance. This concentration owed significantly to the
city's status as capital of the Old Left, for red-diaper babies played central roles
in the formation of these groups.[147] And New York's left had, in turn, been sustained and reproduced in part through the city's extraordinary infrastructure
of female-led tenant organizations. From the 1904 rent strike committees to
the Popular Front rent clinics to the postwar Save-Our-Homes groups, tenant
organizing had constituted a major field of left-wing activism, one that was
especially important during the Cold War years, when leftists were purged from
so many other venues. In short, women's activism and housing activism had
interacted in symbiotic fashion in New York over many years. The early seventies
squatter and strike campaigns propelled one more revolution in the symbiotic
cycle, providing a reality of "on the ground" women's leadership that inspired
and supported the next generation of activists.

This sort of relationship among social movements over time is difficult to
conceptualize through the prevailing wave metaphor for women's history (viz.
the rhetoric of First and Second Wave feminism), in which Jane Benedict's
cohort appears as an anomaly between the real waves. One solution, proposed
by historian Nancy Hewitt, is to adopt a more nuanced concept of waves based
on radio transmission. Radio energy can travel at many frequencies; it is not
confined to a few big surges.[148] The radio model lets us see that female tenant
organizers of the 1930s and 1940s *did* belong to a wave—a low-frequency,
long-range political broadcast that included labor and race mobilizations and
that aired in many cities. This broadcast was disrupted by the Cold War. But in
New York, local stations run by practical feminists filled the void with short-
range transmissions that remained audible into the 1960s. At that point the
nationwide network crackled back to life.

Met Council did not spark the local women's movement of the sixties and
seventies, but *amplified* it by serving as a parallel space, a venue for people who
were developing a feminist consciousness but did not necessarily see women's

liberation as their primary project. Although *Rat* covered tenant struggles, Susan Cohen doubted that many people really took part consistently in both feminist and tenant organizing: "There just wasn't enough time. . . . People who did the feminist stuff . . .—that was their thing. They might come out for a demonstration if you called them. But their *thing*, the thing they put their time into, was the feminist stuff. I wasn't part of that. I was the person who put my time into the housing stuff." Yet while investing time in housing, Cohen was reaping what she considered a profoundly feminist experience. "My [other women] friends, who became interested in radical politics, they went to all their meetings and stuff, and—it was interesting to get them to talk about it—[they said] everything was very equal, except they always got to get the coffee. . . . And they would say [of the male radicals], 'Underneath it, they're all sexist.' And they would complain. With [housing], it did not happen that way, I have to tell you. We did not have that problem."[149]

That Met Council counted as a feminist space to some but not all young women ultimately underscores the range of ways in which diverse women, all of whom rejected patriarchy, could define and rank their needs. Recent scholarship has shown that poor women and women of color often put welfare rights, freedom from involuntary sterilization, and a broad agenda of racial equality at the top of their list (and often criticized the tendency of predominantly white, middle-class feminist groups to ignore such concerns).[150] For such women, "gender was lived through race and class," as Tamar Carrol has put it.[151] Met Council exhibited a similarly race- and class-conscious activism. The organization addressed a problem that was not exclusively women's—men needed housing too—but was of particular concern to the most vulnerable women.

Met Council's leaders, however, stood apart from those in welfare and reproductive-rights organizations in their apparent unself-consciousness of gender in their own lives. They were disinclined to pursue certain kinds of feminist discussions, discussions that were indeed indispensable for the development of feminism writ large. Yet, paradoxically, their unself-consciousness also *enhanced* the sense of empowerment experienced by some of the young women in the organization. The "other world" that Benedict, Rand, and company represented to DuMond and her fellows was a world in which women's equality was so self-evident that it did not *need* to be discussed. Cohen took satisfaction from the older women's ability to get right down to business—housing business. Before long she learned to "just do it" too.

Gender Pragmatism, Race Principles

Met Council's old guard may have thought and spoken little about gender, but they were highly conscious of race. Indeed, nobody who had been awake through New York's decades of fair-housing and slum-clearance battles could ignore the relationship between race and housing, and Met Council had been integrated from the start. However, because Harlem was not a site of warehousing and upscale redevelopment in 1970, black leaders Bill Stanley and Bess Stevenson were not heavily involved with the squatter organizing. The intergenerational connections, therefore, developed mainly between older white women, a somewhat more mixed group of young organizers, and predominantly Latino and black groups of squatters.

Available evidence indicates this collaboration proceeded amicably, even joyously. Tito Delgado, a young Puerto Rican Lower East Sider, went to Met Council for help with his family's eviction case and immediately felt, "we were *home*." Having stayed on as an organizer, he proudly cast himself as a political descendant of Esther Rand.[152] Norma Aviles and other Spanish-speaking Chelsea tenants considered Jane Wood to be family (Wood was the only bilingual member of Met Council's old guard).[153] Brooklyn CORE director (later congressman) Major Owens, an African American who cut his political teeth on rent strikes and served on Met Council's executive board in the 1960s, beamed years later as he proclaimed himself "a proud carrier of the philosophical DNA of Jane Benedict."[154]

This interracial comity seems to reflect a pragmatic combination of "not talking about" *and* recognizing the centrality of race. In recounting his first meeting at Met Council, Delgado emphasized that some other white people "talked about racism, but these people really *felt* it."[155] That the white women lived out rather than simply articulated their solidarity appears to have been critical to Delgado's sense of fellowship. On the other hand, Wood famously insisted that all Chelsea tenant meetings be conducted bilingually, thereby doubling their length (no small thing given that such meetings tend to be interminable even in one language). Her readiness to counter calls for brevity with an articulated defense of racial inclusiveness—that is, to talk about race—was equally critical to the fellowship she built. In a similar vein, Goldin deliberately recruited a racially diverse lineup for the squatter takeovers she organized and for the leadership of the Cooper Square Committee.[156]

Also important was the older, predominantly white cohort's willingness to play supporting roles in cases where people of color had taken the initiative.

This happened with the Morningside Heights squatter action and the Housing Crimes Trial, both discussed below.

New York and the Nation

Contemporaneous organizing in other cities presents both contrasts and parallels. In New York the main locus of sustained tenant action during this era was privately owned housing (or city property slated for demolition); elsewhere it was public housing.[157] Public tenant councils in at least a dozen cities built substantial pressure for economic protections, better maintenance, and elected representation on management boards.[158] The best-studied case is Baltimore, where predominantly African American women became radicalized by the economic wing of the civil-rights movement and forged public-housing councils into an eloquent voice for equal citizenship for the poor. They also helped launch the welfare-rights movement.[159] Public tenants in Chicago likewise won board representation; their leaders steered a more middling course between advocacy and entrepreneurship, sheltering economic "hustles" within the projects while procuring both vigilante and police protection for their tenant clientele. "Women always controlled men" in these settings, writes sociologist Sudhir Ventakesh, a pattern that was facilitated by the prevalence of female-headed households.[160] Thus two entirely different circumstances—generations of tenant history and left politics in New York, feminization of poverty nationally—made New York's private tenant organizations and other cities' public tenant councils similar venues in which women leaders "did not have that problem" of being undercut by men.

NYCHA residents might look mild-mannered next to public housing militants in Baltimore and Chicago. But New York's public tenants, while not fully satisfied with their housing conditions, did not suffer the extreme levels of disrepair and crime found elsewhere. And NYCHA sometimes met their demands before a major crisis developed.[161] Consequently, activists in NYCHA developments could spend their energy fighting bigger foes: economic changes and social-service cutbacks that were damaging their communities. In 1974, black and Latina public-housing activists in Brooklyn and East Harlem joined with white women from nearby areas to create a remarkable working-class feminist alliance, the National Congress of Neighborhood Women. This group brought college programs, job training, and capital-improvement funds into the low-income neighborhoods that the members had dedicated themselves to saving rather than fleeing.[162]

Over time, the public-housing activists who achieved so much across the country would become vulnerable to backlash as the "welfare queen" was made a demon in conservative discourse—indeed, a rallying point for the Reagan Revolution.[163] Some of the small-scale achievements of New York's ghetto, squatter, and public-project activists were more lasting.

Interestingly, a prominent exception to the pattern of weak private-housing activism outside New York during this period—a coalition of Boston tenant groups that fought bulldozer renewal, challenged negligent landlords, and eventually developed hundreds of affordable units in the South End—also departed from the typical sex pattern in that it was organized by men.[164] This coalition's origins in religious ministries and War on Poverty offices, rather than in long-standing tenant organizations, likely explains its male leadership. (The South End Tenants' Council holds further distinction in housing history for having compelled a major slumlord to make repairs by summoning him before a *beys din*, or rabbinic court—an event immortalized in a 1969 episode of *Mod Squad*.)[165]

Our Neighborhoods, Our Buildings

As they fostered feminism, New York's veteran tenant leaders also contributed to the squatter movement's evolving economic ethos. Squatters and squatter organizers expressed a distinctive view of housing that braided together several ideological threads: Marxian political economy, preindustrial understandings of property, and a locally grounded notion of community rights. Frances Goldin, chair of Met Council's Squatters Committee, brought out the first thread when she called on the city to take over the Lower East Side squatter buildings and convert them to "public ownership with tenant control." The city bore responsibility, she maintained, because municipal agencies had worsened the low-rent shortage by sponsoring urban renewal and luxury redevelopment.[166] Thus she revealed the housing crisis to be a creation of the state rather than a consequence of "natural" market forces.

Squatters, for their part, challenged modern property law with a claim to the fruit of their labor. They invested their own sweat in the extensive repairs that the vacant buildings required, then used that investment to assert a moral right to long-term residency.

Finally, squatters' moral position incorporated a notion of community rights that had been formulated by New York tenants over the last decade and a half of struggle against redevelopment. Sally Goldin (Frances' daughter) declared that warehousing on the Lower East Side concerned the whole neighborhood because tinned-up windows served as "an open invitation for junkies, thieves and drunks to start hanging around." Neighbors who rallied for squatters averred, "we won't let the landlords tear down our buildings in order to build luxury housing that we can't afford to move into."[167] Here tenants were not simply talking about "our buildings" in the mundane sense (i.e., the buildings they lived in); they were asserting communal moral ownership of the neighborhood's resources in rebuttal to the claims of private property.

In the long view these claims picked up on popular traditions of "moral economy" and preservation of the commons. Nineteenth-century New Yorkers had claimed commons rights to the use of undeveloped land for shanty dwellings, and of public streets for grazing hogs.[168] Nowadays, writes David Harvey, "the urban commons is continuously being produced," precisely by processes such as anti-gentrification organizing. "The problem is that it is just as continuously being enclosed and appropriated by capital in its commodified and monetary form."[169] Moral economy, a related preindustrial principle, proscribed hoarding or hard bargaining that would deprive people of necessities such as food and shelter.[170] Warehousing apartments in time of scarcity was a good example.

As the squatter wave gathered momentum over the summer of 1970, the largest action took place on Morningside Heights, where the Episcopal Church had joined the ranks of expansionist institutions. In 1967 the bishop had declared that the Cathedral of St. John the Divine, located a few blocks from Columbia University, would remain unfinished "as a symbol of the anguish of nearby slums."[171] But an Episcopal subsidiary was drafting plans for a luxury nursing home, which called for razing eight structurally sound, rent-controlled apartment buildings across the street. With support from Marie Runyon, tenants in these buildings won a few reprieves.[172] By Saturday, July 25, 1970, however, only three holdouts remained. That evening a couple of young men strolled by the site and struck up a conversation with the guard. Suddenly hearing noises behind him, the guard turned to find that two hundred people had materialized on 111th Street and were entering the condemned buildings. He simply told the decoys, "Fuck Columbia; I want an apartment, too." (For local residents, Columbia had come to symbolize all the institutions.) By the time Sunday's service started at St. John's, fifty families, mostly Dominican and Puerto Rican, had encamped in the buildings where the holdout tenants lived.[173]

These squatters had been organized from the Operation Move-In waiting list by a handful of politicized young Latinos in the area who had met one of the holdouts, a white man named Ames Brown. The youths shared Brown's opposition to the compromise the developer had offered—putting the remaining residents into two of the buildings and demolishing the rest—because they believed all habitable low-rent housing should be preserved. "We didn't see things necessarily in racial terms anymore, but in economic terms," recalled one. "We were very conscious of all these middle-class people living very comfortably in Morningside Heights—in apartments that a lot of poor people could actually afford." By mid-July the developer had begun wrecking the vacant buildings; the move-in was an attempt to defend the remaining three.[174]

The squatters quickly became a *cause célèbre* among tenant groups and Columbia's student left, which gathered endorsements from politicians, civic organizations, and the Young Lords Party.[175] The *Columbia Spectator* ran a sympathetic story featuring this exchange with the canon of St. John's:

CS: Canon Chase, if you want to build an old [people's] home, why did you evict old people to do it?

CHASE: Well, these people were evicted for non-payment of their rent.

CS: You mean to say you evicted old people because they couldn't pay rent, so you could build an old age home that will cost $10,000 a year?

CHASE: Running an old age home is a business like any other. . . .

CS: Would Christ have evicted the old people?[176]

Churchmen were easy targets for such questions in a way that Columbia administrators were not. And a group of sympathetic Episcopalians, including Runyon, began to press the bishop toward compromise.[177] "[The bishop's] own staff, were saying that this is our function in life—to see that [needy] people are taken care of," recalled an insider. "So there it was—the rich against the poor."[178]

Equally important, the squatters showed themselves resolute and capable, establishing an elected council, making repairs, and seeing to the maintenance of the buildings. Many had past experiences that helped them meet the challenges of squatting. "Our people here are very political—the Dominicans, especially," one observed. "They're all in some kind of movement—or have been, in the Dominican Republic."[179] With the memory of the 1965 U.S. invasion of Santo Domingo still fresh, Dominicans must have drawn special satisfaction from "liberating" space in New York.

They also proved adept publicists. Squatter Ana López summed up the local housing crisis when she explained to reporters that the families did not object to paying rent—in fact, they wanted to become legal, paying tenants in their new homes—but were "tired of paying for rats, roaches and junkies."[180] At the Move-In office an anonymous writer posted this verse:

> The door was not open
> It was locked, tinned, cinderblocked, nailed, spiked
> cemented.
> They thought in this way to keep the house empty
> and silent
> And to keep us in the street and in the gutter.
> But we came—quietly in the evening—
> Boldly in the morning—
> Through the tin—the cinderblocks—the nails—
> the spikes and the cement
> Through the locked door.
> And the house welcomed us—
> It sheltered and embraced us.
> The laughter of our children echoed in the
> hallways—
> Love entered the house, and the house rejoiced
> To hear again the long forgotten words—
> *Mi casa.* Home![181]

Here, in the idiom of the Nuyorican cultural movement that was just taking off, was an eloquent statement of moral economy. The house itself rejected the rule of property law; it came to life and took a side in the struggle over economic fairness.

The human drama and political spectacle culminated that winter in the Housing Crimes Trial, an event that brought Black Panthers, Young Lords, El Comité and other young militants of color together with older activists from Met Council, the Cooper Square Committee, Morningsiders United and ARCH. Neighborhood tenant groups, progressive unions and black clergy signed onto the indictments.[182]

Racial inclusiveness and female leadership were on full display. Iris Morales, Jane Benedict and Durie Bethea served as judges alongside a Chinese American and two more Puerto Rican leaders. The poster used to advertise the event also depicted an obviously multiracial assemblage—not a court, but neighbors huddling together, looking toward an uncertain future.[183] This graphic was yet another example of cross-pollination between housing and school activism.

The original drawing was made by Eleanor Magid, a young artist with loose ties to Met Council's East Side branch, while she sat at a local parents' meeting to plan an alternative school during the 1968 teachers' strike. Esther Rand, also present, looked over Magid's shoulder and said, "We could use that at Met Council!" The next thing Magid knew her drawing was plastered around the city, with text in Spanish, English and Chinese, representing tenants.[184]

Intergenerational collaboration was likewise evident at the trial, with Benedict, then nearing sixty, serving alongside the young judges, and Frances Goldin and Esther Rand leading the prosecution. Judge Bethea schooled older witnesses in current argot and expressed judicial approval by saying

Figure 13. **Young, old, and many races band together in this graphic for the Housing Crimes Trial.** It was distributed in Chinese and English as well as Spanish. List of sponsoring organizations at left. *Courtesy of Met Council on Housing.*

"right on." The elders scored back when Morris Goldin (Frances' husband) rose to criticize the prosecution for "a most serious deficiency": omission of "arch-criminal . . . Richard Milhous Nixon."[185]

Significantly, the People's Court heard testimony not only from scores of squatters and tenants, but from several housing professionals. The year before, a revolt of "Young Turks" within the city's Department of Planning had surfaced during a hearing on Cooper Square.[186] Now a former city official acknowledged to the People's Court that urban renewal planners made little provision for the low-income tenants they displaced.[187] Bill Price, the Operation Move-In leader, took the point further: "The way the City can do this is by not acquainting the people in the communities of what the plans are in store for them." He himself, he declared, had spent months going through official channels to obtain a copy of the city's master plan. After many runarounds he had finally stolen one. (Bethea corrected him, "You liberated it for the people. We don't steal.")[188]

People like these—strategically placed sympathizers—sometimes affected the fate of squatter sites. That was the case on Morningside Heights, where the Episcopal Church was filled with parishioners who supported the squatters

Figure 14. **Church members side with squatters in a building owned by an Episcopal subsidiary.** Episcopalians for the Poor pressed the bishop to cancel plans to raze the building. From the third-floor fire escape, squatters fly flags of Puerto Rico, the Dominican Republic and (apparently) Cuba. *Courtesy of Frances Goldin.*

encamped on church-related property. Those squatters also gained leverage from a state policy that made subsidy for the project "contingent on [the developer's] immediate readiness" to build.[189] In the end the Episcopal nursing home scaled back its plans and allowed three apartment houses and their 400 residents to remain.[190]

Two hundred squatter families on the West Side also won a major concession more than a year after Operation Move-In commenced, when officials announced that they could stay as long as they began paying rent to the city. Further, the city added nine hundred low-rent units to the West Side's renewal plan.[191] Here the size of the squatter community, the broad-based support and the political vulnerability of the landlord—New York City, now embarrassed over the failure of "progressive" renewal—added up to a squatter victory.[192]

Some Lower East Side squatters also reached lasting agreements with landlords.[193] Likewise in Chelsea, where Jane Wood's tenacity in bargaining became legendary.[194] But in general, properties owned by individuals, schools and hospitals were inauspicious sites for long-term squatting. Several downtown buildings were cleared by police in a matter of days.[195] Uptown, Columbia likewise ousted thousands of tenants over the years, Runyon and Kimble excepted.

Figure 15. **Chelsea squatters.** Note Puerto Rican flag being raised center-right, between "Power to the Squatters" and "No More Evictions" signs. *Courtesy of Met Council on Housing. Digital editing by Kenneth Chew.*

Figure 16. **Neighbors support squatters in Chelsea.** 233 West 15th Street was occupied in 1970 with help from Jane Wood, far right (holding placard askew). The Chelsea Coalition successfully pressured the city to assume control of the building and recognize the squatters as legal tenants. *Courtesy of Met Council on Housing.*

Conclusion

In New York as elsewhere, the late 1960s saw the combustion of political embers that had been smoldering for years. But New York's extraordinary housing circumstances—inflated costs and massive shortage; a high rate of rentership and a rich tenant history—meant that housing would figure centrally in the work of local radical youth. As one study noted, New York in 1960 contained enough crumbling units to house unsatisfactorily the entire population of Cleveland.[196] (New Yorkers might have considered that a good use for their bad housing.) Here the revolution had to include tenants' rights.

Thus a profusion of audacious tenant actions became part of New York's street-level experience of Black Power, Latino, New Left, and women's liberation movements. Local living conditions, activists' creativity, and an existing framework of tenant politics opened an arena of struggle in which radicalism produced some notably constructive and lasting effects. Here, an SDS strike played out in the Battle of Morningside Park—a victory for local residents that caused shudders among Columbia's planners for decades.[197] Here, the Black Panthers' and Young Lords' campaigns produced the country's strongest laws against lead paint. And here, groups of squatters supported by a broad coalition of revolutionaries, feminists, Old Leftists, and stubborn liberals salvaged some of the city's low-rent stock for the next generation.

This grassroots pressure also placed housing high on the agenda of state agencies. As a result, housing initiatives would become critical tests for the Great Society and other government programs implemented in New York during this period.

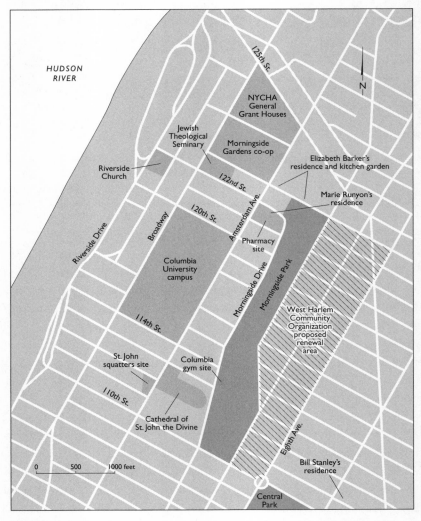

Morningside Heights. Expansionist institutions, disputed development sites, and activist homes in the area, 1950s–1970s.

7

"To Plan Our Own Community"

Government, Grassroots, and Local Development

Months after Columbia shelved its gym-in-the-park plan, two local organizations released a new proposal for Morningside Heights. The West Harlem Community Organization and the Architects' Renewal Committee in Harlem, both formed during the mid-sixties struggles over institutional expansion, remained concerned about the Title I plan that the city had approved in 1964. That plan would redevelop blocks along Morningside Park's eastern border for university use and widen Eighth Avenue to create a "buffer" against Harlem. ARCH and WHCO denounced this agenda in terms that resonated with the principle of ghetto liberation. "For too long," they wrote, "[the institutions] have despised us. . . . smiled in our faces while scheming behind our backs to take what is rightfully ours. . . . The time has come for us to plan our own community."[1]

This declaration reflected not just anger, but hope. By the close of the 1960s, years of tenant and houser protest against orthodox redevelopment seemed to have gotten a hearing in corridors of power. Both Washington and City Hall signaled a desire to forge cooperative planning relationships between government and grassroots. ARCH, in fact, was now supported by a federal antipoverty grant. To many New Yorkers these were welcome signs. Only an overhaul of existing policy could turn back the marauding bulldozers. And only deep-pocketed state agencies could enlarge the stock of decent low-rent housing. "Unless you have government funds," observed East Harlem activist Yolanda Sánchez, who worked with city and federal officials to develop hundreds of affordable housing units during this period, "nothing's going to happen for the poor. Trump ain't comin' in unless he's gentrifying."[2]

Under the new banner of cooperation would march a series of state-funded projects that invoked the War on Poverty mandate of "maximum feasible participation" for community residents. What that mantra meant on the ground, however, varied considerably. Many neighborhoods harbored divided interests. Rivalry among self-proclaimed voices of "the community" had already broken out in the Manhattantown and West Side slum-clearance areas; such competition would proliferate as government authorized new funding for community-led projects. Some local communities thwarted the very types of housing endorsed by longtime advocates of tenant and citizen participation. And, as Cooper Square organizers had learned, even well-organized low-income communities could gain but so much control over officials who held the purse strings.

Financial woes plagued projects of all stripes as the war in Vietnam siphoned public money and boosted inflation, as the city's fiscal crisis intensified, and as Washington withdrew the support that had stabilized cities during previous recessions. By the early seventies, the national shift to neoliberalism—the ideology of slashing public provision in favor of market-driven development—was well under way. (Richard Nixon was philosophical about the effects: "Maybe New York shouldn't survive," he told aides. "Maybe it should go through a cycle of destruction.")[3]

In a few cases, however, grassroots organizing, bureaucratic savvy, and the fortuitous unattractiveness of ghetto areas to conventional developers produced successful, democratically planned state-sponsored projects. These did not entail the comprehensive community control envisioned by the most ambitious Black Power advocates—black-run financing and construction as well as housing[4]—but they offered a meaningful say for the kinds of citizens long excluded from planning decisions. And nationalist sensibilities did play a role by inspiring some of the activists and their housing designs.

The success stories showed that political and economic planets did not just line up by accident. New York's tenant, labor, and civil-rights history helped make that happen. Most of the effective community planners in New York were people whose housing or other grassroots activism predated the new government programs. Several were women, although their leadership was less marked than it had been in the earlier struggles *against* redevelopment. This is unsurprising given that the new community programs targeted the ghettos and barrios, where housing activism had long been more evenly balanced between the sexes than it was in white neighborhoods. The women who did take part in grassroots development planning made that work yet another expression of the broadly defined, race- and class-conscious, community-based feminism that was thriving among welfare, health, and other rights groups during this period.

Federal, State, and Local Initiatives

Federal, state, and local agencies all launched new urban programs in the late 1960s in response to civil-rights mobilizations and riots that called attention to the severity of urban poverty. By 1964 such uprisings had pushed Lyndon Johnson to declare war on poverty and lobby Congress for "community action" funding that would support antipoverty agencies such as Mobilization for Youth on the Lower East Side. The next year the president announced his intention to expand services and entitlements under the rubric of the "Great Society." Central to this package would be the Demonstration Cities and Metropolitan Areas Act, better known as Model Cities. Model Cities promised to join the principle of community action with an array of substantive projects—job training, health care, and housing construction among them—so as to make urban rebuilding "social and psychological" as well as "bricks and mortar."[5] A new cabinet department, the Department of Housing and Urban Development (HUD), would run the program.

New York State, for its part, continued to subsidize middle-income housing construction as it had done since 1955. The chief innovation of the late sixties was the Urban Development Corporation, a public authority created by Governor Rockefeller "in a legendary episode of legislative arm-twisting" in 1968.[6] Rockefeller, a moderate Republican, favored large capital projects as a way to boost the economy; in this instance he may also have been eager to undermine the more liberal Mayor Lindsay.[7] The UDC had legal power to condemn land, override zoning, and sell billion-dollar bonds to support its projects. Thus it bore a strong resemblance to the Robert Moses machine of yore—a similarity noted by Lindsay, wary city lawmakers, and Met Council.[8] Put differently, the UDC was designed precisely to overrule the municipal and neighborhood voices that Rockefeller believed had slowed urban rebuilding to a crawl. The Authority would be hailed in the 1970s for transforming tiny Welfare Island, in the East River between Manhattan and Queens, into Roosevelt Island, a racially integrated community of five thousand low, moderate- and high-rent units. But the UDC's late-sixties ventures were more controversial and demonstrated the authority's ability to capitalize on conservative factions in the communities where it operated.

John Lindsay tried to start off on the right foot with liberal housers. As Wagner's term drew to a close, the mayor-elect named Charles Abrams to chair a task force on housing policy. Not only public officials, but freethinkers Jane Jacobs and I. M. Pei, sat at the table. The group urged consolidation of the city's housing bureaucracy and a vast program to remedy unsound units and build new ones.[9] Lindsay then contracted Ed Logue, the well-regarded director of urban renewal in Boston, to recommend ways of implementing the task force's ideas. Logue titled his report "Let There Be Commitment," a quote from President Johnson's Model Cities speech, to underscore the need for Great Society money to carry out the mission. Ominously, however, Logue refused Lindsay's entreaties to take charge of New York's new program—precisely because he doubted that Lindsay could secure the funds.[10] Instead Logue would serve as director of Rockefeller's UDC.

In the coming years, the three levels of government and their myriad bureaucracies would sometimes clash over use of what money was available. Further, some programs required that each construction project be sponsored by a long-standing community organization, such as a union or church, which would provide grassroots planners with business know-how (and in some cases loan security). Sponsorship added another layer of contingency to housing ventures.

Community and Its Discontents

The most publicized battle over community control of housing development occurred not in a Black Power stronghold but in the predominantly white neighborhood of Forest Hills, Queens. At issue was the Lindsay administration's move to build "scatter-site" public housing—small projects dispersed throughout the city rather than confined to the poverty-stricken areas where NYCHA had traditionally built. Scatter-site was not intended as a community-participation initiative *per se*. But it showed that the mayor had taken to heart a decade's worth of citizen criticism grounded in the community sensibility of Save Our Homes and kindred organizations. In the early sixties Met Council had published a pioneering "Citizens' Survey of Available Land" based on data compiled by volunteers who spent countless hours nosing about city's forgotten corners. They identified 122 small vacant sites on which public-housing could be built. Unlike the conventional NYCHA practice of massive demolition and redevelopment, this "vest pocket" approach would displace no one and increase the *total* housing supply by thousands of units.[11] Vest-pocket development accorded with both the architectural conservationism championed by Jane Jacobs and the integrationist principles advocated by civil-rights groups. It was a signature component of the Cooper Square Alternate Plan. It was also taken up by a progressive caucus within the East Tremont Neighborhood Association (successor to the group that had fought the Cross-Bronx Expressway) when the city signaled interest in redeveloping part of the area with middle-income housing.[12]

Scatter-site, however, foundered on precisely the rock of community voice that Jacobs and allies had also championed. When City Hall proposed thirteen small public-housing projects in the outer boroughs in 1966, it ran into fierce opposition from homeowners. "Low-Income Housing Breeds Slums," declared the critics, who demanded that middle-class communities, like ghetto communities, have a say in local development. With borough presidents exercising effective veto power over NYCHA siting, nearly the entire first crop of proposals died on the vine.[13] Lindsay's planners looked next to the Queens neighborhood of Forest Hills, where they wagered that a liberal Jewish populace would welcome a small public project on a vacant lot.[14]

Figure 17. **Frances Goldin surveys vacant sites for vest-pocket housing.** *Courtesy of Frances Goldin.*

The planners were wrong. Real estate investor and Forest Hills resident Jerry Birbach rallied his neighbors to picket, storm hearings, and file suit against the city. The project was ill-designed and would burden already-crowded local schools, they argued.[15] The Queens borough president had accepted the Forest Hills plan in exchange for the scrapping of a similar one in nearby Corona, so project opponents could not play their usual trump card.[16] But they hoped to stop the project by making City Hall feel the rage of two growing and overlapping constituencies: middle-class citizens who believed that the poor were getting a disproportionate share of government consideration, and Jews who felt that black demands had gone too far.[17]

Jerald Podair argues that Forest Hills was the obverse of the Ocean Hill–Brownsville crisis that crystallized white (especially Jewish) anger at the black community-control movement and the Lindsay liberals who endorsed it.[18] Because blacks and Latinos now constituted the majority of public-housing tenants, scatter-site would necessarily bring racial integration as well as income integration. Civil-rights advocates saw the Forest Hills outcry as New York's iteration of the "neighborhood defense" campaigns waged by white homeowners in Chicago and Detroit. Like blacks in Brooklyn and whites in the Midwest, Forest Hills residents effectively appropriated the language of community rights.

Yet they denied racial animus, often heatedly. A survey in a nearby area found that most Jews who opposed low-income projects said they would welcome middle-class people of color as neighbors.[19] Although the candor of these respondents may be doubted, it is not implausible that some were indeed concerned primarily with class homogeneity. The histories of Morningside Gardens and Park West Village (not to mention Stuyvesant Town) showed that more than a few white middle-class New Yorkers embraced racially integrated, class-segregated housing.

Rancor over Forest Hills owed also to splits within "communities" and among erstwhile allies. Some white residents voiced support for the housing project.[20] Some local African Americans opposed it, for fear that it could "tip" a stable integrated neighborhood.[21] Met Council and its local affiliate strongly endorsed the plan, but another Forest Hills tenant association joined the opposition.[22] Jews divided bitterly. Birbach's camp saw the city's proposal as exploitative of Jewish quiescence—"Impeach Adolf Lindsay!" urged one protest sign—and several Jewish organizations sought to kill the project.[23] But the American Jewish Congress and the Anti-Defamation League of B'nai B'rith allied with the NAACP and other civil-rights groups in backing it.[24] After many rounds of mediation and compromise, a scaled-down project was built, made into a limited-equity co-op, and finally hailed as a success. But the scatter-site policy and Lindsay's career took a beating.[25]

Community Control and Housing in the War on Poverty

The Forest Hills controversy handed some vindication to civil-rights advocates who had long warned that citizen participation in neighborhood planning, a principle idealized in Cooper Square, could work against racial minorities when "the community" was predominantly white. Implicit here was the obverse: when the community was black, community control *would* serve black interests. But ghettos were subject to internal conflicts and competitions (not to mention dependent on funding from white officials). This became clear with two community initiatives in Harlem: HARYOU-ACT and UPACA.

HARYOU (Harlem Youth Opportunities, Unlimited) was New York's highest-profile antipoverty venture and one of the first in the country. Its significance for community-based housing activism lay not with its accomplishments—it had none in this area—but with the early warning it provided regarding the fierce pulls that competing leaders (in this case, elite professionals) and entrenched interests at City Hall would often exert on community projects.

HARYOU was the brainchild of prominent psychologist Kenneth Clark. It began in some ways like Mobilization for Youth on the Lower East Side; both programs were drafted as social-science-based initiatives to combat juvenile delinquency, and both ran on grants from federal agencies that would evolve into the War on Poverty administration. But Clark's 1962 proposal, unlike Mobilization's, proceeded from a community-control ethos. HARYOU's mission would be to throw off the "social work colonialism" of city officials who were accustomed to contracting outsiders to counsel Harlem's youth. And in keeping with Clark's belief that racist disfranchisement was the underlying cause of delinquency among blacks, HARYOU would discard traditional social-service programming in favor of "social action" against injustice.[26] One form of social action was organizing rent strikes, which HARYOU planners discussed with Northern Student Movement organizers early in the summer of 1964.[27] On this point HARYOU and Mobilization overlapped despite their ideological differences.

But HARYOU's social-action program never got off the ground. Clark's bid was taken as a slight by Harlem's existing social-work agencies and, more importantly, as a turf grab by Congressman Adam Clayton Powell Jr., whose office ran its own service-cum-patronage apparatus known as ACT, and who saw himself as the more legitimate community representative because he was an elected official. (Neither leader invited much decision-making by community laypersons, although Clark gave lip service to the idea.) Powell's influence threatened to scuttle the project. City and federal officials finally compelled a merger between HARYOU and ACT, under terms that favored the congressman. Clark resigned in protest. The new agency would be run by a Powell loyalist who hewed to ACT's mission of traditional social-service provision.[28]

The Clark–Powell rivalry became notorious, but it is worth noting that even a unified Harlem leadership would have had a hard time running a rent strike with government funding on Wagner's watch. This could be seen in the fate of Mobilization for Youth, which came under political attack in August 1964, just as HARYOU-ACT was being launched. The mayor's office, furious at Mobilization's rabble rousing among downtown students, welfare clients, and tenants, set in motion a police and FBI investigation of the agency as a "Red honeycomb" which "left-wingers by the score ha[d] infiltrated," as the Daily News lead put it.[29] (Some veteran Communists and Trotskyists did work at Mobilization, as staffers, not directors.)[30] Investigators alleged close ties between Mobilization and Jesse Gray, whose praise for the recent riots had not endeared him to the authorities. This charge must have prompted a snicker from insiders who knew how uneasily Gray and the Lower East Side organizers actually got along; by this time, in fact, Mobilization's rent-strike efforts had ceased. But officials took steps to keep Mobilization's future activities, and by extension HARYOU-ACT's, on a tight rein.[31]

The Upper Park Avenue Community Association (UPACA) differed from HARYOU in several ways: it concerned itself entirely with housing, it was conceived by working-class Harlem residents, and it developed nearly a thousand low- and moderate-rent apartments. In the process, however, it revealed yet more conflicting agendas that different parties brought to the table of "community." UPACA's leaders embraced a populist social conservatism that distinguished between respectable and undesirable community residents. This attitude not only put to rest romantic notions of a unified, organic black community; it also departed from the inclusiveness that was a hallmark of community planning groups like ARCH and the Cooper Square Committee. At the same time, UPACA was a fairly successful instance of black–Jewish cooperation during years when "community control" was widely perceived as an attack on such alliance.

UPACA began in 1965 as a volunteer civic association led by Mary Iemma and Margaret Jenkins, two middle-aged African Americans with little political background, and Jo Adler, a young white leftist civil-rights activist and supporter of Ted Vélez's East Harlem Tenants Council. The women shared a desire to improve the dismal housing on upper Park Avenue, where all three lived, and which straddled the border of black and Spanish Harlem.[32] They had less in common ideologically. Iemma and Jenkins were militant when it came to challenging racism, but, unlike Adler, they sought "a reassertion of older standards of conduct [among local residents] as well as material improvement [in housing]." For example, the black women did not believe landlords were always to blame; they thought tenant misbehavior, such as throwing garbage in courtyards and urinating in hallways, also had to be policed.[33]

In 1966 UPACA obtained War on Poverty funding with which it would build or rehabilitate 441 apartments over the next three years. This accomplishment reflected both Iemma and Jenkins' resourcefulness—the novice activists made a detailed survey of their area's housing stock before they received any funding or expert advice—and the initiative of liberal Jewish networks eager to maintain an alliance with blacks. The latter included Ruth Brod, a Wagner aide who chanced to meet Iemma and Jenkins at a protest led by the East Harlem Tenants Council; the Federation of Reform Synagogues, to which Brod introduced the Harlem women, and which became UPACA's nonprofit sponsor; and Frances Levenson, longtime director of the state and national committees against housing discrimination, whom Lindsay had named as housing advisor when he took office.[34] (She had begun working with the city during Wagner's final term, when Hortense Gabel recruited her to run a pilot program renovating tenements.)[35] These people and groups played a strong role in planning UPACA's ventures and securing funds. When federal antipoverty money dried up at the end of the decade, the synagogue federation in particular helped UPACA stay afloat on funding streams from New York State's new Urban Development Corporation and the Ford and Rockefeller Foundations.[36]

Paradoxically, these liberal supporters warmed to UPACA in part because of Iemma and Jenkins' conservative streak. UPACA's first plan, in which Levenson had a strong hand, promised staged construction and rehousing of residents— progressive principles pioneered by Cooper Square downtown. But Iemma and Jenkins felt no obligation to involve area residents in planning as the Cooper Square Committee had done. They aimed for efficient management, an orientation that appealed to sponsors who wanted to get things done. (It did not appeal to co-founder Jo Adler, who shortly resigned.) Jenkins became manager in the buildings UPACA completed and won admiration for her tough, effective dealings with maintenance workers and tenants alike. UPACA's leaders also learned to guard their turf. Having won their first antipoverty grant, they quickly enlisted their new friends in city government to fend off the East Harlem Tenants Council—the very group UPACA had so recently supported—when it tried to set up shop nearby.[37]

Iemma and Jenkins' determination to steer their own course in community development showed in their 1968 proposal to the UDC: a monumental high-rise, just what Save Our Homes groups, Jane Jacobs, and other Title I critics had been denouncing for the past decade. Nor did the similarities with Title I end there. The eight blocks under UPACA's jurisdiction had long been home to different kinds of residents: an SRO population of "single Black men, some drug addicts, some alcoholics, some simply alone," as a team of sociologists put it—and a cohort of "nuclear families and female-headed families."[38] Iemma and Jenkins belonged to the family cohort and desired not just to upgrade dwellings, but to upgrade people, by razing the SROs, ousting the single men, and attracting middle-class families in their stead. They also raised rents beyond most site tenants' means. Thus only 20 percent of the original residents ended up living on-site after the reconstruction, notwithstanding the leaders' talk of rehousing "the community."[39] This outcome differed little from those at Title I projects like Manhattantown and Morningside Gardens.

Not only the population but its power relations were transformed. One of the sociologists' interview subjects was a woman who had lived in UPACA's area for forty years. She "described the contrast between the old and new area in terms that romanticized the earlier area but captured a good deal of truth about UPACA: before UPACA, this had been a neighborhood. People had known one another, talked and worked together, frequently across ethnic lines. Now, all were clients, united only by their dependency on the UPACA leaders."[40]

This street-level resentment emerged just as the organization's finances were becoming strained. First inflation drove up maintenance costs. Then news broke that Rockefeller's beloved UDC had taken foolish gambles and was deeply in debt. The state legislature struck back by freezing the UDC's projects. Finally President Nixon axed federal housing funds, and UPACA broke with the Ford Foundation over the latter's demand for more rationalized management.[41]

Under these pressures "the community" imploded. Iemma fired Jenkins' management staff; the maintenance union walked out; tenants sided with the workers; a street gang told Iemma she had better get the boiler running. Tenants also formed their own union to push back against UPACA's imperious management. Black politicians, whose support Iemma and Jenkins had successfully courted in the past, now refused to take sides. In the end, Albany intervened and control of the buildings reverted to the state; UPACA itself dissolved.[42]

It is important to recognize that the financial crises would have been damaging no matter what UPACA's ideology and internal relations. What UPACA's story illustrates is the adaptability of late-sixties community rhetoric to a variety of purposes, including the very sort of "people clearance" that had done so much to galvanize the participatory community-planning movement in the first place. It also demonstrates the attractiveness of Iemma and Jenkins' relatively conservative norms and management style to politicians and bankers who were eager to garner some community cachet while avoiding the headaches they associated with more inclusive decision making.

In fairness, those headaches were not imaginary. Soon after it teamed up with UPACA, the UDC also started working with another Harlem group that had adopted a more participatory structure. But this group, the Milbank–Frawley Circle Housing Council, overplayed its hand. After UDC director Logue had already accepted such progressive planning fundamentals as low- and moderate-rent construction and minimal relocation, the Frawley Circle group demanded a $2 million job-training program that the UDC, for all its other powers, was not authorized to support. Logue gave up on the collaboration and recruited Mamie and Kenneth Clark, eager for a comeback after HARYOU. The Clarks established a rival organization that ran Frawley Circle's redevelopment. The final project included new space for the psychologists' guidance clinic.[43]

In Pursuit of Inclusive Planning

If HARYOU-ACT and UPACA represented community advocacy as brokering, and the Frawley Circle group participatory but ill-advised brinksmanship, the Architects' Renewal Committee in Harlem tried to chart a third way. In 1966 ARCH obtained foundation funding and a federal antipoverty grant and sought to move abreast of the Cooper Square Committee as a force for inclusive neighborhood planning.[44] The two groups maintained personal connections through Walter Thabit and Frances Fox Piven, who sat on both boards. Other ARCH leaders were Harlemites such as Isaiah Robinson, parent activist at I.S.

201; Marshall England, HARYOU-ACT chair and former CORE director; and the writer John Killens.[45] The ARCH professionals, now an all-black corps, worked with a handful of lay organizers to survey local residents' views. Their mission was to combine community control and state funding in concrete, workable fashion.

ARCH's principal plan grew out of its three-year collaboration with the West Harlem Community Organization (WHCO) on the Morningside Heights struggle. By the time this plan came out in September 1968, Columbia and allied institutions already controlled most of the space west of Morningside Park between 125th and 110th Streets. ARCH and WHCO called attention to the other half of the federally designated renewal area—east of the park and west of Eighth Avenue—which contained a nearly all-black population and a "horrible" stock of housing.[46] It was here that ARCH and WHCO sought to preempt further institutional expansion and seize "[t]he time . . . to plan our own community."[47]

That sense of moral ownership informed ARCH's final document. The authors proposed rebuilding the abandoned Columbia gym site in Morningside Park as a community sports and cultural complex.[48] They called for new affordable housing to be developed on adjacent blocks with state and federal funds. (The existing tenements were unsuitable for rehabilitation due to poor interior layouts.) According to ARCH, the local mood toward bureaucratic state programs was summed up by a resident who told the surveyor, "MAN, DON'T HAND ME ALL THAT JIVE ABOUT 221D3, 221H, XYZ AND ALL THAT. JUST TEAR THIS SHIT DOWN AND PUT UP SOME GODDAMN HOUSES!" The planners, however, recognized that "the task ahead is mobilization of community residents to become aware of existing programs [and] fight for their implementation."[49]

It never came to pass. No funding was allocated to realize the plan, and the conflict over West Harlem reached a draw, with neither Columbia nor the residents redeveloping the area to their liking. Most of the old housing remained; Eighth Avenue was left alone; Morningside Park languished until it was renovated in 1989.[50] As in Cooper Square during this period, a democratically minded community-planning organization was able to fend off the development it didn't want, but not to win state support for its own vision. The city's failure to move ARCH's proposal past the drafting table stands out especially alongside its allocation of millions to the more conventionally managed and politically connected UPACA.

Under what circumstances would city agencies put their money where their participatory-planning rhetoric was? The story of East New York, Brooklyn, suggests one answer: an absence of affluent players with their own development schemes. Through the early 1960s, East New York had been a stable working-class neighborhood of 100,000 residents, 85 percent white (mostly Jews and Italians) and 15 percent African American and Puerto Rican.[51] The area was one of several in New York that exhibited a civil-rights housing culture: As more people of color moved in in the sixties, local whites posted "not for sale" placards to fend off blockbusters and signal welcome to the newcomers. But it did not take long for redliners and predatory realtors to gain the upper hand. By 1966 the area was predominantly black and Latino, mostly poor, and filled with rental properties in the last stages of milking. The final exodus of whites and better-off people of color was hastened by a riot between blacks and Puerto Ricans. Within days, whole buildings stood vacant (save for the looters who stopped by to strip the plumbing).[52] The area, remote from Manhattan, was now notorious. Private developers did not come knocking on the city's door.

In this investment vacuum, and in wake of the riot, the Lindsay administration now proposed a Vest Pocket and Rehabilitation Program for East New York and hired Walter Thabit to design it. ("We did our greatest things right after a period of great riots," the planner noted later.)[53] Thabit proceeded as he had at Cooper Square, taking stock of local incomes, housing, and other needs and meeting repeatedly with neighborhood committees. The process was more complicated in East New York because the area's sudden demographic shifts meant that it had few long-standing community organizations.[54]

But able leaders emerged. The planning committee was co-chaired by Sara Ross, a middle-aged white Communist with many years in the neighborhood, and Leo Lillard, a young black Tennessean and veteran of the 1961 Freedom Ride. Lillard's story demonstrates the appeal that community-based development held for activists experienced but not fully satisfied with what Bayard Rustin had called "classical" civil rights activism. Lillard, the son of a Garveyite, had known even while risking his life to desegregate bus stops that "it couldn't end with a toilet and a hamburger." After the Freedom Ride he struck out for New York in search of "a new theater and a new paradigm" of struggle. He enrolled in an engineering program at City College and easily "plugged in" to the local movement. When rent strikes took off in 1963, he rallied pickets near his Lower East Side apartment. But he kept his distance from groups like

CORE—the originator of the Freedom Ride—because "civil rights was too limited." To him it signified "an attempt to gain approval . . . begging . . . as opposed to developing grassroots power. And it wasn't black power [I wanted]. It was *people* power in the community. Where everybody is a leader, rather than having a single leader." (This was the SNCC ethos in a nutshell.) When Lillard heard through the grapevine about the East New York project, he saw a chance to pursue "a new way of struggle, in terms of property values and land control."[55]

He moved to the neighborhood and consulted his networks to find the people involved. By now he had earned his degree and was supervising the emergency repair squad that Mayor Wagner had created in response to the rent strikes. His construction knowledge and organizing skills made him a natural person for Thabit to tap. Before long Lillard found himself working with "a beautiful coalition" invested in the same kind of moral ownership claimed by tenant activists in Harlem, Morningside Heights, and the Lower East Side. Brooklyn boasted black leaders like Miss Lillie Martin, one of "the female giants of East New York." And "we had Puerto Ricans, we had old Jewish people who were still there, and . . . radical Catholic priests. . . . They [all] had this New York sense that 'this belongs to me, I draw the line in the sand here.' And I was so excited about that kind of feeling, that I had never seen in the south."[56]

Over five months the residents and Thabit hashed out a thoughtful plan for 1,270 new housing units (two-thirds public, one-third middle-income); 1,020 rehabilitated ones; a health center; a library; and parks. Consensus was no small feat. "Many nights we left meetings confused, angry, or just uncertain," Lillard noted. "[B]ut we stimulated each other and kept pushing for understanding. Maybe understanding was helped by dispensing with formal agendas, Roberts Rules of Order, and petty disputes." The written plan was just one fruit of this labor. "People in contact with each other produce not only better ideas but also better people. I certainly am better for the world than I was before this process."[57] The city approved most of the housing and ignored the rest. Coalition members began talking to churches and other potential sponsors.[58]

Here, in further testament to the difference made by the absence of upmarket real estate interests, the public-housing question came out like a photo negative of Forest Hills. East New Yorkers approved hundreds of public-housing units. It was Thabit, the liberal, who urged the city to stop referring welfare clients to a neighborhood already bearing its share of the schooling and social-service costs that the very poor imposed. And it was the landlords—the same ones who excoriated welfare tenants as dirty and destructive—who insisted, "We NEED the welfare tenants. They're the only ones who will live here!"[59]

In the end, East New York demonstrated both the possibilities of state–community partnership and the constraints it faced in a dizzyingly bureaucratic city and an increasingly inflationary and neoliberal political economy. The neighborhood gained 2,300 new or rehabilitated housing units—there would have been more had the Buildings Department not erroneously demolished several structures slated for rehabilitation—and residents eventually won their campaign for health and child-care centers. But inflation pushed even the well-managed developments over budget, resulting in rents that surpassed the means of poorer tenants.[60] Government did not make up the difference. As historians David Goldberg and Michael Katz have observed of other cities, white officials and investors were willing to cede a degree of control, along with financial responsibility, in an area that decades of exploitation had turned into a money pit.[61]

Further, while most of the nonprofit sponsors operated aboveboard, one of them proceeded to pilfer Vest Pocket monies while cloaking itself in the language of black community control. The result was four hundred poorly built, overpriced units. Subsequent investigation led Thabit to conclude that HUD officials, who were supposed to be monitoring the books, were on the take.[62]

Community and Economic Development

One of the most portentous signs of the challenges that loomed for New York's low-income tenants was not a housing project at all. It was a state office tower at 125th Street and Seventh Avenue. This project, the Urban Development Corporation's largest Harlem endeavor, served as an uptown herald for a postindustrial economic-development program that would soon remake parts of the city as dramatically as Title I had done. Unlike UPACA, the office tower sparked a very public debate over black community needs and who was authorized to identify them. Like UPACA, it showed how community divisions could be useful for promoters of relatively conservative schemes. Ultimately the State Building, as it was called, became a victory for Harlem's up-and-coming centrist politicians.

The project was conceived as a way to deal African Americans into the game of economic development embodied in the World Trade Center. In 1966, when Governor Rockefeller announced that New York State would lease offices in the new downtown towers, Urban League director Whitney Young called for Harlem to get a share of the state's business and the jobs and investment presumed to go with it. Other black leaders and then the governor endorsed the idea for an uptown office tower, complete with "community cultural" spaces to appease the Black Power camp.[63]

Then state lawmakers axed the cultural provision, prompting cries of betrayal from community-control advocates and opening the way for an argument that was less about the cultural facility *per se* than the process by which it had been decided to bless Harlem's main commercial street with a massive stack of office space for predominantly white public employees who lived elsewhere. Jesse Gray, Marshall England, Adam Clayton Powell Jr., and ARCH denounced what they saw as a scheme "fostered far from the Harlem community by those who were completely divorced from any and all comprehension of Harlem's needs." They proposed other uses for the site, such as housing or a school. Meanwhile the NAACP, the black business establishment, the black ministry, and rising Harlem politicians such as Percy Sutton and Charles Rangel all endorsed the project on grounds that "some pie is better than no pie."[64] They insisted that the radicals did not represent Harlem.[65] (Neither side paid much heed to the small shop owners who had long made livelihoods on the site—a cobbler, an S&H Stamp trader, ninety in all—and were bitter at being evicted, or to the three hundred residential tenants, one of whom was forced into a nursing home.)[66] In the summer of 1969 the conflict blossomed into a full-fledged public drama, with anticolonial protesters encamping on the site to block construction and a supportive public bringing them food.[67]

But the decisive action took place behind closed doors, where the state consolidated ties with ambitious politicians by offering them a capacious pie server for future occasions: a new Harlem subsidiary of the UDC. The squatters were hauled away, construction sped forward, and the project became a clean sweep for the big businessmen and centrists. At the 1974 dedication, Sutton praised the political "maturing" that the tower represented, while hecklers asked where the jobs were and a sidelined Gray sniped, "People can't sleep in this building."[68] Rangel and his ally H. Carl McCall continued to climb the ladder, reaching the offices of congressman and state comptroller, respectively. The new Harlem UDC would function as a patronage machine. (A million-dollar award went to a project headed by Sutton himself.) The leaders capped their victory in 1983 when they renamed the building after Adam Powell—symbolically bringing the outspoken critic onboard eleven years after his death.[69]

Although supporters and critics alike saw the State Building as a Harlem issue, it also signaled the citywide reconfiguration of development policy that had spawned the World Trade Center and would beget even larger progeny in coming years. Young's linking of the uptown and downtown projects was astute. The Twin Towers, like the Harlem tower, were made possible through a public authority (the Port Authority) endowed with enormous financial and legal leverage. And they required razing of a small business district that had filled mundane but vital niches, such as the cluster of electronics shops known as Radio Row.[70] There is no comparing the two projects' scales, of course. Indeed, the World Trade Center was just part of a colossal redevelopment program rammed through by the Downtown Lower Manhattan Association—an alliance of the Rockefeller brothers and other real estate and finance titans—that cleared more than one hundred downtown acres and filled them with offices and luxury apartments. This program went beyond Title I in its brazen handing of massive state subsidies to private concerns serving the very rich. (Even Robert Moses balked at using slum clearance monies for the Rockefellers' plan, which was implemented instead by the UDC and other agencies.)[71] Harlem's State Building was modest by comparison. But its backers drank from the same postindustrial chalice—"revitalization" as the replacement of mom-and-pop with tie-and-briefcase enterprises—that the Lower Manhattan alliance served up to the public to consecrate its plan.

Social and Psychological Rebuilding: Model Cities

The urban initiative that was supposed to transcend all these contradictions, to engage "the community" by inviting neighborhood participation in planning and attacking many problems at once, was Model Cities. This program, enacted in 1966, raised particular hope among housers who recognized that federal action was more crucial than ever. Privately financed housing starts in New York had reached a virtual standstill. What little was being built was for the luxury market. The 93 percent of New Yorkers who were priced out of that stratum required middle-, moderate-, and low-income housing built with public aid.[72] Now Washington promised not only to launch a new gravy train, but to put local people at the switch.

The train, however, was pretty well sabotaged by both inadequate funding and unworkable administration. Model Cities had been conceived as an

experiment to test the effect of generous, targeted support in a few locales.
Historian Frank Stricker has pointed out that this plan, even as drafted, lacked
a job-creation component and hence would have left in place the high unemployment rate that kept wages down and poor people poor.[73] In any event,
the plan was not implemented as drafted. Congress authorized $1.3 billion
instead of the $2.3 billion Johnson requested.[74] Then pork-barrel dynamics
drove legislators to multiply tenfold the number of participating cities. Consequently, no locality received enough to mount the comprehensive attack
on housing, employment, and social deprivation envisioned by the program's
authors. And the law naively mandated cooperation among federal, state and
municipal agencies that had their own entrenched interests.[75] Small surprise
that Model Cities' accomplishments fell short. In New York, Mayor Lindsay
finally concluded that community control itself was the culprit and regeared
his Model Cities administration for efficient, centralized decision making.[76]
Lindsay was succeeded in 1973 by centrist Abe Beame, who, like Richard Nixon,
was lukewarm toward the antipoverty operations he had inherited. Congress
would put the entire program to rest in 1974, replacing it with "community
development block grants" that gave localities wide latitude in using funds
and were less targeted toward cities and the poor.[77]

The ambitions and failings of Model Cities made it a lightning rod for ideological disagreement over poverty and disfranchisement in America. Conservatives held up the program as proof that well-intentioned government
meddling did no good. Even many liberals, including those who had worked
within Model Cities agencies in good faith, concluded that it was ill conceived.
Newer scholarship has begun to challenge that failure consensus, pointing out
that War on Poverty programs ultimately enlarged the role of poor people in
policy making by setting templates and raising expectations for community
participation that would outlast the sixties programs.[78]

There is little debate, however, over the paucity of the program's material achievements in New York City. After the federal pie was slivered, New
York's allocation amounted to one-tenth of 1 percent of the city's annual
budget, or "one twentieth of what was needed to make it effective," by Walter Thabit's reckoning. That grant was then divided among three areas—the
South Bronx, Central and East Harlem, and Central Brooklyn—comprising
three hundred separate projects.[79] Finally, the inadequate slices of pie were
distributed by unwieldy serving knives: the city's mindboggling antipoverty
and social-service bureaucracies. "It is doubtful there is any other American

government . . . where red tape is as prevalent," wrote one expert. Discord between city and state agencies compounded the trouble.[80]

If these problems were detrimental to job-training and youth-service efforts, they were nearly fatal for housing.[81] More expensive, slower to show results, and subject to higher levels of corruption than other program components, housing projects drafted under New York's Model Cities rarely became brick-and-mortar reality. In the worst cases, such as Brownsville, money was simply absorbed by old-fashioned patronage as members of the "community" committee awarded jobs and contracts to their friends, who did not build housing. In nearby East New York, the city again retained Walter Thabit, but the Model Cities administrator circumvented Thabit's neighborhood meetings and dealt instead with a set of instant "community representatives" looking, in Thabit's words, for "a piece of the action."[82] By the time a plan emerged, it had to be shelved due to Nixon's cutbacks.[83] Clashes among claimants to the "community" mantle—particularly between African American and Puerto Rican groups—were also rife in Manhattan and the Bronx.[84] East Harlem witnessed a protracted antipoverty war between the East Harlem Tenants Council and a rival Puerto Rican organization, Massive Economic Neighborhood Development (MEND).

And yet a few projects took off. Generally these required stitching together of Model Cities grants with other support. And they depended largely, as East New York's Vest Pocket initiative had done, on the work of activists and professionals who had cut their teeth *before* the Great Society era. The most striking example is the East Harlem Tenants' Council.

By the mid-sixties this group, born in 1962 amid the uptown rent strikes, had adopted a broader mission and leadership that would help it become a much longer-lived institution than Jesse Gray's tenant council, the prototype that EHTC founder Ted Vélez had embraced. Yolanda Sánchez was invited onto the EHTC's board in 1965. An East Harlem native and college-educated social worker, she was, like Harlem's Florence Rice, already experienced politically before she became involved with housing. But unlike Rice, she had begun her career in civic organizations—ASPIRA and the Puerto Rican Association for Community Affairs (PRACA)—in which women were well represented among the leadership. She was mentored by the remarkable teacher and institution builder Antonia Pantoja.[85] She did not come into the tenant council as a secretary.

A self-described "pit-bull," Sánchez established a good working relationship with "the guys." And "once I got on that board, then I became a major player." Most notably she led the team that developed Taino Towers, a complex of 656 low-rent housing units on upper Third Avenue. Vélez, Sánchez, and a progressive architectural firm began planning this project in 1965. The tenant council incorporated—filing courtesy of Vélez's father-in-law, Stanley Faulkner—and thus became eligible for government support. Funding was to come from Model Cities, city grants, and a low-interest federal mortgage.[86]

The final design joined race pride with an assertive claim on postwar economic citizenship. The four high-rises memorialized the Tainos, a Caribbean tribe that was virtually annihilated by the Spaniards. At thirty-four stories, they clashed sharply with the local cityscape—a cardinal sin in the new progressive planning orthodoxy—and were sheathed in horizontal bands of glass and concrete that signaled modernism and glamor. One critic likened them to "rich people's housing in Caracas," but that was the point: The tenant leaders were determined that the complex not replicate the grim ambience of public housing. Or the discomforts. At one meeting Sánchez pushed hard for central air-conditioning, which could be included in the new heating ducts at little cost. "But this was housing for the poor. . . . And [public officials'] whole notion was, 'Why do you need air conditioning?'" Sánchez replied, "Because the poor sweat too."[87]

In keeping with Model Cities' comprehensive mission and Sánchez's own sense of interconnected community needs, the towers also provided multibedroom apartments for large families, a day-care program, and a health clinic—the latter an amplification of the free medical service that ran out of Vélez's storefront on East 123rd Street as early as 1964.[88] None of this happened easily. Many bureaucrats considered the EHTC's demands unreasonable, and a combination of management snarls, inflation, and budget cuts necessitated post–Model Cities funding infusions and delayed the project's opening until 1979.[89] But Sánchez stressed the remarkable circumstances that allowed the tenant council to develop the ambitious project at all.

"The sixties was a whole different world," she recalled. "Because of the civil-rights movement and other things that were happening, there was a move by the established liberals in New York to help the new arrivals. . . . People were willing to be helpful to 'those little natives from the island.'" Not only Vélez's in-laws, but the architectural firm, the Lindsay administration, "the white liberal community," took a chance on Taino Towers. Thus Sánchez found herself, "a kid who grew up on welfare, [heading] a forty-million-dollar housing project." Equally important was backing from moderate Republicans such as Jacob Javits, New York senator, and George Romney, HUD secretary under

Nixon.[90] It is also likely that here, as in East New York, officials' willingness to support the grassroots initiative reflected not only genuine liberal sentiment, but the absence of interest by private developers.

Further, the tenant council was able to reach détente with most other uptown community groups (the exception being MEND). Areas west and north of the East 120s were the "turf" of UPACA and another African American organization, the East Harlem Triangle Association. "Everyone accepted that, acknowledged it and let it be." The black organizations, in turn, left Taino Towers alone. On the local Community Board, Sánchez enjoyed "cordially combative" relations with African Americans such as rent-strike veteran and public-housing activist Anne Bradshaw. "They know they've gotta deal with Yolanda, I know I've gotta deal with them. Great relationships. Socially and otherwise. . . . But it was a constant, constant fight."[91]

Nation and Gender in Barrio Development

As the Taino moniker suggests, an anticolonial sensibility pulsed beneath the Barrio planners' pragmatic reliance on federal money. By this time the Popular Front left heritage had faded from East Harlem; few remembered Vito Marcantonio's electric presence on the platform. Many Puerto Ricans had become disaffected from the CPUSA in the early 1940s, when the Party disavowed the island's militant independence movement in the name of antifascist unity with the United States. (Marcantonio remained faithful to the *independistas*.)[92] But Popular Front radicalism was survived by national liberationism, both a Black Power–New Left tenet and as old as *el Grito de Lares*. "A lot of the activists [in the East Harlem Tenants Council]," recalled Sánchez, "were people who in their heart of hearts believed in the independence of Puerto Rico." To this day, "they're very much alive and kicking and staffing programs."[93]

In the 1980s the council would follow Taino Towers with Casabe Houses for the Elderly. For this project Sánchez recruited an organizer who *was* a surviving link between Old and New Lefts: Lower East Sider Ernesto Martínez, a veteran of the Lincoln Brigade, the National Maritime Union, the ALP, and Vito Marcantonio's staff. Like civil-rights leader Ella Baker, Martinez worked by drawing together people with common concerns and posing questions rather than giving orders. In his own neighborhood he had organized the Coalition for Human Housing in 1968. Like the Cooper Square Committee a few blocks away, the Coalition was born in struggle against an urban-renewal plan to replace low-rent with middle-income apartments and went on to become a lasting voice for affordable housing development. And like the East Harlem Tenants' Council, the Coalition took pride in its distinction status as the first Latino housing organization in its area. Through advocacy and grantsmanship, the coalition and its successor organizations would bring in funds for 1,600 subsidized units downtown. (HUD even approved Martínez's proposal to name a development after Pedro Albizu Campos, the Puerto Rican independence leader whom the U.S. government had imprisoned as a "terrorist." Martínez and Sánchez had a good laugh over that.)[94] Martínez's diasporic Puerto Rican identity mixed comfortably with a deep feeling for the multiracial New York neighborhood where he lived most of his adult life. He was strongly aware of the area's long left heritage, still palpable when he settled there after World War II, and one of his closest comrades was fellow Lower East Side nationalist Frances Goldin.[95]

Yolanda Sánchez was not in contact with the senior leaders at Met Council, although she "thought they were doing great work." But her *modus operandi* as a politically active woman was not so different from the "practical feminism" of the Old Left veterans. Sánchez had come of age in Puerto Rican community organizations where "there were a lot of women in the forefront." She knew that male leaders still got most of the recognition, and that in-house custom followed a "classic" gender pattern: "The women set up the meetings, make sure the food is ordered, that the coffee pot is on. And when the meeting is over, it's not the guys who stay behind and clean up. . . . I think people almost do it without thinking. We're aware of it, I'm aware of it . . . but I don't correct it. . . . [T]here are certain things you don't want to bother with, it's not worth the fight." No amount of coffee making, however, prevented Sánchez from taking full part in "guys'" work such as securing development funds, choosing contractors, deciding on structural particulars (which she learned about along the way), and managing programs.

When women's liberation "arrived," Sánchez saw it as a worthwhile movement—to a greater degree, probably, than did Met Council's old guard. Yet much as the Met Council leaders folded women's issues into their concern with housing, Sánchez regarded the new movement through a politics grounded in El Barrio (the place name she preferred to "New York City" in her mailing address). "I sat in on a lot of meetings" with the likes of Gloria Steinem and Bella Abzug. "Part of the reason I sat in was because we used to bitch about, 'Hey, you're calling a meeting, you're not including Puerto Ricans.' And the answer would be, . . . 'We couldn't find Puerto Ricans who would participate.' So a group of us said, 'Oh, hell, that means we've gotta show.'" Sánchez and the handful of other Latinas and blacks who attended these feminist gatherings "were reacting because we knew it was an important issue and . . . we were demanding Puerto Ricans be involved in whatever was happening in New York City."

Looking back, "I think I am and was [a feminist]. But I would never have described myself as a feminist, no. . . . 'Cause it was not in my world. Living in East Harlem and operating with a whole bunch of other Puerto Ricans, it wasn't the word that came up. [When] I crossed that line from downtown, midtown Manhattan meetings into East Harlem, that was not something that followed me into East Harlem."[96] On these trips along what might be called "separate subway lines to feminism," Sánchez claimed autonomy to choose among competing political pulls. She considered the feminist meetings important enough to attend despite the many other demands on her time. That did not stop her from making pragmatic choices about what to import from those meetings into her principal field of activism.

Sánchez did fight hard for women on the terrain that mattered to her. In the mid-1970s, she and others in her circle established a New York chapter of the Washington-based advocacy organization the National Conference of Puerto Rican Women. A decade later they would form the harder-driving National Latinas Caucus. The caucus built links among organizers in different neighborhoods and provided campaign backing for Council member Lucy Cruz ("the guys wouldn't let her run") and Congresswoman Nydia Velásquez. Sánchez also broke ground in another area of importance to women in her community: foster care. Outraged that charity administrators were sorting Puerto Rican children by complexion—sending the light ones to Irish families, the dark ones to Italians, separating siblings in the process, and all the while claiming there were no suitable Puerto Rican foster parents—Sánchez and her PRACA fellows "got all uppity" and obtained foundation funding to create the city's first Puerto Rican foster-care agency: *Criaremos los Nuestros* ("We shall raise our own").[97] Through their work in affordable housing and Latina institution building, Sánchez's generation of Puerto Rican New Yorkers gained a say in public policies of immediate concern to the neighborhoods with which they felt their deepest affinity.

Taino Towers was a grassroots affair; the Betances public-housing project in the Bronx was planned by bureaucrats who heard little from the poorly functioning Model Cities residents' committee. (Ultimately that committee did learn to navigate the bureaucracy and assert itself in other matters, such as tenant relocation.)[98] The housing project, however, bore the stamp not only of nationalist pride—Ramón Betances was a Puerto Rican independence leader

Figure 18. **Yolanda Sánchez (back row, center, in V-neck) takes part in Latino Leadership Institute, 2012.** *Courtesy of George Jorge Carva.*

and an abolitionist—but also of alternative design principles that previous citizen activists had worked hard to advance.

NYCHA's planners had long suffered migraines as they endeavored to meet New York's high construction costs and astronomical land prices while bound by federal spending rules. Through the early sixties they had managed with cost-efficient slabs and superblocks. By Lindsay's day, however, inflation was making even this impossible. Projects that had conformed to guidelines when planned became too expensive by the time bids were taken. In middle-class areas this gave leverage to opponents of scatter-site housing, because simply delaying a project meant killing it.[99] Even in the ghettos, public-housing starts ground to a halt.

The South Bronx Model Cities Administration enabled NYCHA to slip through these neoliberal shackles by directing part of its grant toward new public housing. The resulting Betances development showed that planning ideals set forth by Ellen Lurie, Jane Jacobs, Met Council, and the Cooper Square Committee had gained a toehold at City Hall. The vest-pocket project was built on vacant lots around the new Lincoln Hospital complex (another Model Cities undertaking). It left through-streets intact and included low-, medium-, and high-rise structures with multi-bedroom apartments needed desperately by local families.[100]

A final housing legacy of Model Cities in New York is a paradoxical one: the constructive work undertaken in opposition to the program, or arising from its ashes. The chief oppositional initiative was the Bedford-Stuyvesant Restoration Corporation, established in 1966 by Senators Jacob Javits and Robert Kennedy. Kennedy aimed to help his poorest constituents while stealing some of Johnson's Great Society thunder by funding the Brooklyn venture through the older antipoverty apparatus crafted in Jack Kennedy's White House. Free of Model Cities' administrative labyrinth, and enriched by private aid, the corporation built and rehabilitated 660 housing units.[101] Bed-Stuy Restoration became the template for a slew of community development corporations (CDCs), some of which would mount successful, democratic housing renewal in other poor neighborhoods in the 1970s and after.[102]

One such was the Banana Kelly Community Improvement Association. This South Bronx group was organized in 1977 by Kelly Street residents who were fed up with the vacant lots pocking their neighborhood—residua of Model Cities projects that never made it off the drafting table. The block association, organized a decade before by VISTA volunteer Cleo Silvers, had ossified into a Model Cities bureaucracy.[103] So Banana Kelly sidestepped the block association and launched its own renewal program. It thus exemplified something revisionist scholars of public policy have stressed: a lasting *expectation* of citizen participation that was fostered by War on Poverty and Great Society programs even when those programs failed to meet their immediate goals. Banana Kelly "liberated" and rehabilitated several abandoned buildings. It also created the South Bronx's first community garden out of a rubble-strewn Model Cities site.[104] As a CDC, the organization would rehabilitate and manage thousands of affordable units on properties that the city had taken in foreclosure.

Banana Kelly also illustrates the potential of informal community-building to address the problem of commitment that so often plagued tenant organizations. The rescue of Kelly Street was conceived by a social worker and a block resident who had met through pickup basketball. They were familiar with the idea of citizen participation but had a hard time convincing neighbors who had come to feel helpless about the area's decay. Then they seized upon the garden project. Neighbors were willing to haul rubble and plant vegetables, and the quick transformation of the empty lot "g[a]ve them something to see and keep [their] spirits up" as they undertook more ambitious work on apartment buildings.[105] A similar idea had been floated ten years earlier by CORE organizers dismayed at the fizzling out of the rent strike. Tenant associations, they suggested, might have more staying power if built on the foundation of neighborhood recreational groups.[106] Banana Kelly's history indicates that a sense of political capacity could indeed be developed incrementally through collective social endeavors. Two decades later, labor advocates would also adopt this approach, working through informal soccer leagues to establish self-advocacy programs among "hard-to-organize" Latino immigrants.[107]

By 1974, Model Cities had built or rehabilitated six thousand housing units in New York—a drop in the city's six-figure bucket of need.[108] (Twenty-six thousand additional units were constructed during the same period under HUD's mortgage program for small-scale, low-rent projects, but this program carried no requirement for participatory planning.)[109] Leo Lillard, involved centrally in both East New York's successful Vest Pocket project and its Model Cities fiasco, concluded that inefficacy was built into the federal program. In a 1969 article, "Model Cities, Model Airplanes, Model Trains," he criticized the "hobby shop mentality" through which white policymakers tinkered with ghettos while relinquishing few resources and no power. Meaningful change would require "proportionate" distribution of tax monies and a program whereby land and development were "owned, managed and maintained by us." "Us" meant blacks—the collectivity specified a few sentence before—*and* alliances like the Vest-Pocket coalition that Lillard had characterized, a page earlier, as "a rainbow."[110]

Model Cities' best cases demonstrate that democratic planning and rebuilding are possible, but they are proof as well that decent housing is insufficient to establish economic citizenship. The program's authors failed to foresee how completely the neighborhoods would remain at the mercy of a national political economy hurtling toward ever greater inequality. Planning successes such as Taino Towers and Betances Houses became hellholes of poverty and crime in the 1980s and 1990s, just as other ghetto areas did. (Ernesto Martínez, visiting New York after his retirement, wept to see what had become of his beloved East Harlem project.)[111] East New York and Bedford-Stuyvesant slid into the same abyss, notwithstanding the Restoration Corporation's strong track record of training and hiring local residents as construction workers.

In 1970, New York street poet Gil Scott-Heron handed up an indictment in the killing of the Great Society. His verses gave a litany of ghetto housing realities: rat bites, no heat, no lights, and "the man just upped my rent last night." Every one was answered with the tagline that showed where America's funding priorities lay: "And Whitey's on the Moon."[112]

Labor Housing in a Postindustrial Era

Ideals of community participation and realities of inflation and economic contraction manifested also in a third generation of labor-sponsored cooperative housing. The recession-era co-ops stood apart from their predecessors most clearly in their siting: they were built on vacant or nearly-vacant land, signaling developers' retreat from bulldozer confrontation. But their fates rested largely on their sponsors' ability to navigate late-sixties political and economic tides. This can be seen in the contrasting fates of two projects: 1199 Plaza, in El Barrio, and Co-op City in the Bronx. While the former succeeded, the latter became "the Vietnam of the nonprofit cooperative housing movement."[113]

Both developments were made possible by the state's Mitchell-Lama subsidy program. Abe Kazan's United Housing Federation, which built Co-op City, took full advantage of Mitchell-Lama as it had done with Title I. The UHF's first large-scale Mitchell-Lama development, Rochdale Village, was built in 1965 on a disused racetrack in Queens (Kazan's first concession to the slum-clearance outcry). It was notable not only for its siting but for its racial integration, which the UHF promoted and Robert Moses pragmatically accommodated.[114] Rochdale Village's success boded well for further nonprofit housing ventures.[115]

1199 Plaza was conceived by different players: progressive architects, City Hall, and Local 1199, the health-care workers' union that had become labor's leading voice for civil rights. The idea was sparked in 1963 when a building-supply company sponsored a competition for the design of subsidized housing on a mostly uninhabited strip along the upper East River. The jury, which included sociologist Herbert Gans and the chairman of the city's Housing and Redevelopment Board, had clearly come around to Jane Jacobs' way of thinking. It chose a plan for densely situated five- and six-story buildings in keeping with East Harlem's architecture, set along streets that would extend the existing grid. Rents would range from low to middling. Funding was to come from Washington and City Hall, as well as from New York State's Mitchell-Lama program.[116]

But when the city found a sponsor—the health-care union—a second phase of design was set in motion. Hospital workers wanted housing, but not exactly as the architects had imagined. Like Taino Towers, 1199 Plaza revealed a gap between professional and blue-collar aesthetics. Specifically, 1199 members rejected two of the plan's hallmark progressive features: medium-rise architecture and an open street grid. Many of these union members lived in El Barrio already. They wanted things the old housing lacked: sunlight, security, and the river views prized by residents of middle-class and luxury high-rises. "If the union could only put up apartments—if they could not influence the quality of life," recalled the lead architect, "they were not interested in proceeding."[117]

Thus in 1968 the union and the architects hammered out a hybrid plan. Four towers would rise thirty-two stories, providing excellent views and increasing the number of units to 1,594; but rather than loom as towers in the park, these structures would join with medium-rise segments in a stepped slope that eased the discordance with local architecture. A modified grid struck a similar compromise between street access and seclusion. The development included space for storefronts, health- and day-care centers, a meeting hall, a gym, and a pool.[118]

Local residents also gained a say in the project, largely through the efforts of a community activist and city employee named Shirley Jenkins. Jenkins, an African American with a degree in teaching, had lived in an East Harlem public-housing development since 1957. She was president of the tenants' association there and had prevailed on management to provide residents with unusual improvements: doors on closets, replacement of ugly floor tiles, accessible grounds in lieu of "keep off the grass" signs. Backing from the local Democratic club was crucial to her success here. Jenkins' alliances also extended to nearby settlements and youth programs with which she had volunteered for years. In all these institutions—not just the housing project and youth associations, but also the Democratic club, headed by a tenant supporter named Hilda Stokely—"the women were the leaders, as we usually are."[119] Jenkins' political education was not unlike Yolanda Sánchez's.

When her youngest child turned four, Jenkins went to work for the city. She was assigned to a job-training program during Wagner's final years, then to Lindsay's antipoverty division. (In the latter role she supported MEND, one of the East Harlem organizations vying for antipoverty funding.) When 1199 Plaza got under way, Jenkins was asked to direct the preparation of the site.[120]

A veteran tenant leader managing an urban-renewal site: Times had changed. Jenkins reconciled her roles by finding ways to deal local residents into the perquisites. Concerned that the existing blueprint "turned its back on the community" by orienting buildings toward the river, she persuaded union leaders to "turn the project around [so] it embraced the community." With this "embrace" came neighborhood access to the health- and day-care services. Jenkins also convinced 1199 to add two representatives from a nearby community center to the project's board of directors. With these allies in place, she hitched the site preparation to a jobs program for local teenagers. "I had them visit with the architects. I had them work with the maintenance [department] . . . in the hopes that the young people would develop careers as a result." (Some did.) Jenkins also involved neighborhood people in relocating the small number of site residents. "We had a major concern . . . especially [with] the senior citizens. Because we found in studies that when you removed senior citizens . . . into other areas, they didn't live so long." Jenkins and her fellows ensured that elderly site residents were placed in nearby public housing.[121] Arrangements of this kind would later become known as "community benefit agreements," a strategy adopted in the early 2000s by workers, local residents, and others seeking to mitigate the effects of development schemes.

These collaborations, in turn, worked to 1199's advantage by speeding construction. During planning the project had fallen two years behind— an ominous sign at a time of runaway inflation. Jenkins brought it back on schedule. "In any kind of construction anywhere in the city, when the total community is not involved from the ground up, it delays the project several years." By contrast, "when you start involving the young people in the community planning, by the time the first shovel goes in the ground, those young people are adults, and . . . would not stop the development." Timely completion enabled 1199 Plaza to stay within budget and hence fee projections.[122] Units were snapped up in 1974. At this writing, many original cooperators still live in the complex.[123]

Co-op City faced harder going. This project was a last dance between UHF president Abe Kazan and Robert Moses, who had been ousted from his Title I position but still headed the Triborough Authority, one of the state's politically insulated "public authorities." In 1964 Moses and Governor Rockefeller conceived of putting a vast middle-income co-op on a tract of swampland in the north Bronx. They hoped to stem the borough's exodus of middle-class families while also bailing out the site owner, whose amusement park there had become a monumental flop. Moses coaxed Kazan onboard, and when the plan went public in 1965, the UHF was flooded with applications.[124] The 15,000-unit Mitchell-Lama complex would become the largest housing development in the country.

Although it was situated on vacant land, Co-op City paid little heed to other principles of progressive planning. Its gigantism fostered class segregation; its

bulky towers looked like "filing cabinets for people," according to one architectural critic.[125] But the project's real problems were financial and political. By
1971, spiraling inflation and unexpectedly high costs of stabilizing the swampy
ground pushed carrying charges far beyond projected levels. Then the UHF
appointed a board of directors (normally chosen by shareholder vote).[126] And
the board, rather than allying with residents to lobby for state relief, slammed
them with the entire cost increase.[127]

This mix of inflation and autocracy sparked revolt. Co-op City residents sued
the UHF for stock fraud. As the case dragged on and the OPEC oil embargo
drove costs and tempers to new heights, residents finally called a "rent strike."
The drama verged on the John Sayles satire, "At the Anarchists' Convention,"
with the veteran leftist strikers stowing escrow money in secret caches and
the UHF striving vainly to persuade them that they were owners, not tenants,
and their fees were carrying charges, not rent.[128] But the results were hardly
comic. The aid that finally trickled from Albany was too meager to rectify the
project's financial and structural flaws.[129] The UHF never recovered. It sold its
last, unfinished complex to a private owner and got out of the development
business for good.[130]

Ironically, the revolt that did so much to demoralize UHF directors also
showed that workers and "tenants" had not lost their fighting spirit. Many
Co-op City residents were union members, and the solidarity they maintained
for thirteen months would have been the envy of Jesse Gray. (Strike leader
Charles Rosen helped reinforce unity by holding strike meetings in Spanish,
English, and Yiddish.) The problem was that the rebels aimed their fire at the
developers, who, however much they had brought it on themselves by cutting residents out of decisions, were nonetheless powerless to fix the balance
sheets. Historian Tony Schuman concludes, "In reality it was not the strike
but the disequilibrium between worker wages and housing costs that drove
the UHF out of business."[131]

With fifteen thousand units amid an invincible landlord's market, Co-op City
still boasts a long waiting list. But the complex marked a turning point. Like its
street names—Debs, Darrow, Bellamy—Co-op City belongs to a bygone era of
the left. The ambition and political power to build nonprofit housing on a large
scale were crushed under the new regime of conservative budgeting. Schuman
points out that over time, working people themselves would help inter the affordable co-op movement: In the 1990s, privatization factions emerged within
several UHF developments, urging abandonment of the limited-equity rules

designed to keep the apartments affordable for future generations of workers.[132] Here again, however, neoliberal politics set the parameters. Privatization became a "hot topic" at Co-op City in the early 2000s, explained a manager, because "[w]e have a mortgage for $220 million and construction problems requiring $210 million, and the state has told us there will be no new money coming to us."[133] At this writing, some labor co-ops have gone market-rate and others have withstood the pressure to do so.[134]

Conclusion

New York housing became the terrain of defeat for most large-scale liberal programs in the late sixties and early seventies. Although War on Poverty initiatives had contributed to the city's upsurge of community organizing—Cleo Silvers, Iris Morales, the ARCH professionals, and the Move-In organizers were all on the antipoverty payroll for a time—the Great Society programs failed to bring more than a few community-housing endeavors to fruition. This owed in part to local hurdles such as the city's exorbitant costs and vast bureaucracy. It owed also to the real difficulties of forging community agreement; even successful groups like the East New York coalition had their share of heated meetings, which required great diplomacy to cool down. But the short half-life and limited scope of federal support set the ultimate limits on the achievements of community-based planning in this period.

The successful projects showed not only that democratic state-sponsored urban renewal was possible, but that New York's tenant history made a difference. Virtually all the fruitful community-based housing ventures were led by people and groups—the East New York Coalition, the Cooper Square Committee, Local 1199, Shirley Jenkins, the East Harlem Tenants' Council—whose political heritage traced back to tenant and labor mobilizations of the early 1960s or before. The experience in organizing, negotiating, and sustaining citizen participation that these advocates had accumulated *before* there was much federal "action" to get a piece of, helped them navigate the new environment of state-supported grassroots planning.

8

"A Piece of Heaven in Hell"

Struggles in the Backlash Years

In 1974, the Staple Singers released a track that showed how far urban hopes had fallen since the Great Society days. For years the gospel crossover group had served in the black freedom movement. But "City in the Sky" expressed little faith in earthly justice:

> There's too many children with tears in their eyes
> We're gonna have to build them a city in the sky
> Where they can fly away . . .
> They sure ain't gonna miss the city they leave behind

Like the Stapleses, many Americans now questioned whether cities could be made livable in this life.[1]

Certainly in New York it had become clear that sixties visions of urban transformation would not be fulfilled anytime soon. The War on Poverty had been starved of funds. City finances were in even sorrier shape. And rental housing had reached an unprecedented crisis. More than 200,000 units stood abandoned by owners in 1970, their occupants bereft of basic services like heat and hot water.[2]

Circumstances like these were conducive to the enactment of neoliberal policies throughout the country, and in New York they created an opening for propertied interests to advance on turf they had been eyeing for decades: rent control. The early seventies saw intense struggles in city and state legislatures over rent regulation and associated housing policies. Tenants lost heavily, due in part to their own disarray.

But within a few years, a combination of fresh organizing and realigned politics had won back some legislative ground. Equally important, both despite and because of the severe economic contraction, activists were able to fashion ideals from the late-sixties radical movements into tangible state-supported programs for tenant empowerment through limited-equity cooperatives. Finally, the new generation of activists helped to extend the tenant movement's lasting contributions to feminism and left politics.

Vengeance Is Mine, Saith the Landlord

The debate over rent control in New York in the late sixties and early seventies epitomized the growing dominance of free-market ideology in public discourse. Landlords had long blamed the city's housing woes on rent control, claiming that the system denied them a fair return and hence the means for proper maintenance. Tenants had countered that exploitative landlords were the problem, and for a time this position had a measure of support from public officials who felt some obligation to the tenant electorate. It was Mayor Wagner who commissioned the 1960 Panuch report, which showed that tax write-offs and milking could make rent-controlled slum properties very profitable indeed.

In the late sixties, as housing abandonment started to generate alarming headlines, landlords grabbed the chance to reset the terms of argument. "Just today I abandoned a 30 family house," one owner told a public panel in 1968, going on to explain that low rents had left him no choice.[3] Absent from the discussion was much attention to the city's history of weak code enforcement, which had allowed owners to milk buildings to the point where they required prohibitively costly repairs; or to the role of increasing poverty, which meant that some tenants simply could not cover their apartments' operating costs. Present but unspoken was the assumption that banks and landlords must not be allowed to lose out on their investments.[4] In sum, as planning scholar Peter Marcuse argues, dominant voices told the story of urban crisis in a way that hid the state's role in economic dislocation—its lax regulation of housing, subsidies to redevelopers and sidelining of industry—and hence legitimated hands-off policies that left the urban poor bearing the costs.[5]

In this ideological environment, City Hall straddled the question of rent regulation. On the one hand, in 1969 Mayor Lindsay took up the important problem of *un*controlled units—those built after 1947—where rents were skyrocketing. He and City Council Democrats worked out a compromise whereby rents in the newer buildings would be "stabilized." Increases would be determined annually by a Rent Guidelines Board appointed by the mayor. Met Council and more liberal lawmakers assailed this deal, arguing that all apartments should be brought under the more stringent rent-control system.[6] The rent-stabilization law, however, did provide a measure of relief to 400,000 tenants previously at the mercy of the landlord's market.

On the other hand, Lindsay's Housing and Development director, Jason Nathan, gave owners powerful ammunition for their crusade against rent control by commissioning studies that correlated low rents with poor upkeep. These findings persuaded not only the mayor but the *New York Times*, the Citizens' Housing and Planning Council, and a substantial number of rent-controlled tenants themselves that rent control was making things worse.[7]

Accordingly, in May 1970, Lindsay's office introduced a bill that would raise controlled rents by up to 15 percent and ultimately revise them using a calculation of operating costs known as "maximum base rent" (MBR). Met Council put out a study showing that landlords and city consultants had skewed their figures to conceal profits, but to no avail. The City Council passed the MBR bill by a wide margin.[8]

These city clashes opened the way for further struggle in Albany in 1971. Asserting that tenant interests had blocked "responsible" rent policy in New York City, Governor Rockefeller and upstate Republicans rammed through legislation that ended the home-rule arrangement in place since 1962. Now the state legislature, not the City Council, would regulate rent. Albany also enacted "vacancy decontrol," lifting rent limits from apartments whenever a tenant moved out.[9] The new state laws represented tenants' worst legislative defeat since Congress ended federal rent control in 1947.

The Party's Not Quite Over

The assaults on rent control came at a moment when the city's umbrella tenant organization, Met Council, was particularly ill equipped to fight back. Met Council's weakness at this juncture stemmed, ironically, from one of its longtime assets: the Communist heritage. In the 1950s, when bulldozers began looming over Yorkville, Chelsea, Cooper Square, and other blue-collar neighborhoods, CP and ex-CP members emerged as the most compelling leaders of the resistance. These organizers were not afraid to challenge the liberal mantra of slum clearance, and they were typically "unbuyable," as Frances Goldin put it. Left-led Save-Our-Homes groups served as the building blocks for Met Council, and Met Council, in turn, became one of the few venues where Communist cadre continued to function effectively through the 1960s. Jane Benedict credited Party culture for Met Council's stable leadership: The CP "put people in a spirit [to] plant their feet" and remain involved.[10] But in the early 1970s—paradoxically, just when the anti-Communist hysteria was ebbing—the CP's doctrinaire side came back to haunt the tenant federation.

In the years preceding Lindsay's rent initiatives, Met Council had tacked several times on the question how to engage formal politics. Through the mid-1960s the organization had tried to lobby city and state officials. But in 1967, legislation committee chair Frances Goldin told the executive board that her trips to Albany were not working: Even Democrats had failed to advance public housing and other tenant causes. Only a full-time lobbyist could "cope with the massive details involved in steering a bill from its inception to passage."[11] If Met Council could not hire a professional, it "should abandon its role of formulating new legislation." Goldin's peers grudgingly conceded her point. In 1968 the board voted to "press . . . for only one or two bills per year of a 'vanguard' nature . . . [and to] use the [legislative] committee as a propaganda mechanism to publicize MCH programs."[12] Rent strikes would replace lobbying as Met Council's main strategy.

The decision to elevate strike organizing probably reflected not only a dearth of cash to hire lobbyists, but also regrets over the missed opportunities of 1963–65.[13] Piven and Cloward's postmortem on the mid-sixties strike wave had underscored the failure of Mobilization and Met Council to build a mass movement. Now Met Council would try again. The organization's second generation of strikes did not become a mass movement either, but it was fairly successful in helping many tenants win better conditions.[14] Met Council sometimes had strikes going in two dozen buildings at a time during these years. Organizers helped strikers protect themselves by gaining court approval for rent withholding.[15] Passage of the MBR bill in 1970, however, showed how vulnerable the entire legal framework of tenant protections had become.

In this crisis, Met Council made an ill-considered decision to put the strike weapon to double duty by urging all city tenants to withhold their rents until legislators repealed MBR.[16] Michael McKee was then one of the group's energetic young organizers, having "stumbled into" the tenant movement when his landlord in Chelsea refused to replace the building's blown boiler. McKee turned to Met Council for help, then came aboard as a volunteer. Like most of his cohort, he was awed by Jane Benedict. Thus when the executive board announced the rent strike to repeal MBR, "I was right in there. 'Oh, a citywide rent strike!' We were all so naive, it was pathetic, it was ridiculous. And we learned the hard way . . . that people were not going to go on rent strike against their landlord for political reasons." Rent strikes could be maintained for repairs only.[17] Previous generations, from the early twentieth century Socialists to the 1960s CORE and Puerto Riqueños Unidos organizers, had also learned this the hard way.

The citywide strike fiasco and the subsequent Rockefeller maneuvers spurred McKee's cohort at Met Council—"the young people," as they were known in-house—to reflect further on their lesson. These youths constituted a recognizable cluster of nine organizers, half of them men, most of them white and middle-class, who by 1971 had committed themselves to the tenant cause. Several had prior experience in the antiwar movement, but only one, a red-diaper baby named Joan Brown, knew much about the CP and its tendencies toward closed ranks and dogmatism.[18]

For those with eyes to see, those traits were surfacing. Early in 1971 the executive board's majority turned against charter member Frances Goldin. Ostensibly the dispute was over tactics: Met Council policy called for striking tenants to put their rent in escrow, but Goldin shared her friend Frances Piven's view that playing by every legal rule was a losing game. She advised strikers to "take your rent money and use it to put oil in the burner and fix the room. And when you go to court, bring your receipts." Beneath that disagreement, however, lay unspoken resentments: Benedict's and Rand's displeasure over Goldin's having left the Party, and Benedict's sense that Goldin had received a disproportionate share of publicity for her squatter organizing.[19] In June, Goldin submitted a pained resignation letter that cited innuendo, lies, and overt hostility from longtime comrades, and a refusal to consider seriously the advantages of "illegal" strikes. Months later, Benedict arranged for Met Council's general assembly to denounce Goldin's ongoing extralegal strike work on the Lower East Side.[20]

Much of this went over the heads of the young people, uninitiated in left infighting, who now began analyzing membership records with a view to stabilizing the organization's finances. They found that rent strikes brought in dues-paying members—Met Council required that tenants seeking strike support join up—but that annual turnover approached 60 percent. People "d[id]n't see Met Council as relevant once they g[o]t their individual problem solved in their building." The young people suggested a reassessment of membership policy. To their surprise, this sat ill with Benedict. McKee later concluded that senior leaders saw his position—viz. that membership was generally driven by personal or building-level crises—as an attack on the CP model of movement building, which called for enlightening tenants as to the general machinations of capitalism.[21]

Membership discussions were shelved, but young people and old guard soon locked horns over a proposal to establish a statewide lobbying coalition. Such an alliance would fill the void left by Met Council's abandonment of lobbying a few years earlier. McKee and his peers first raised this idea in 1971 and got hearty approval from the executive board.[22] They began forging links with upstate tenant groups. Then, in the fall of 1972, the board reversed itself. Met Council could *head up* a lobbying campaign, but it could not form a caucus with independent tenant councils. Joan Brown understood this flip-flop as compliance with a new CP directive against coalition with outside groups.[23] The young people rejected the senior leaders' dictate, and in a series of vinegary board meetings characterized by use and misuse of parliamentary procedure, they were censured. At that point the nine resigned rather than get kicked out. They were pained as well as stunned by this sudden turn, because they had "thought the world of Jane."[24]

It is worth noting that in the years leading up to this rupture, Met Council's senior leaders had taken occasional liberties with the party line. Their endorsements of abortion rights and the women's liberation movement deviated from CP orthodoxy.[25] Whether this rankled Party higher-ups is impossible to know. One can only speculate that in 1972 some pressure was brought to bear at CPUSA headquarters on West 26th Street over the coalition heresy. Perhaps the senior tenant leaders, most of whom were then in their sixties and had, at no small cost, made Party loyalty the central moral principle of their adult lives, found the prospect of breaking with the CP too much to bear.

Ugly as this episode was, it was less damaging than it might have been. The next three years brought political realignments that helped city tenants recoup some ground. The young people's ouster from Met Council left them free to follow their own strategic inclinations, and they joined with their upstate friends to found a statewide lobbying group, the New York State Tenants Legislative Coalition (NYSTLC). In New York City the coalition attracted several relatively new tenant councils that had sprung up in middle-class neighborhoods where residents stood to lose heavily from the relaxation of rent law. By January 1973, the rookie lobbyists had begun weekly visits to Albany.[26]

Events there soon gave them leverage. Governor Rockefeller resigned in order to seek the Republican presidential nomination. His departure left his low-profile lieutenant, Malcolm Wilson, in the executive seat with less than

twelve months to build a constituency before the next election. Wilson established a working relationship with the NYSTLC. This unusual Republican
support enabled the coalition to sponsor several successful state bills in 1974.
One required that 35 percent of tenants in a prospective markekt-rate co-op
building buy in before conversion—and consequent eviction of nonbuyers—
could take place. A second imposed limits on the razing of rent-controlled
structures. These measures set moderate brakes on demolitions and evictions.
A third measure, the Emergency Tenant Protection Act, tempered the 1971
vacancy-decontrol statute. Under the new law, rent would rise to market level
when an incumbent tenant moved, but after that the unit would come under
the 1969 rent-stabilization provision, which would slow subsequent hikes.[27]
Over time, nearly all rent-controlled units in New York City would follow this
path into the weaker rent-stabilization system. In 1975 the NYSTLC's allies
also enacted the Warrant of Habitability, which codified full rent abatements
for uninhabitable apartments.[28]

Meanwhile Met Council continued to let lawmakers know its own views,
sometimes at odds with the NYSTLC's more moderate ones, and relations between the two organizations remained bitter for years. But paradoxically, the
older group's uncompromising stance sometimes strengthened the NYSTLC's
hand by exerting what sociologists call a "radical flank effect," making politicians eager to negotiate with the moderate camp. As well, NYSTLC organizers
were in some ways still stamped by Benedict's early mentoring, which had built
up their sense of political capacity if not governed their strategic choices.

Generational Bridges and Divides

While the nine Young Turks split off from Met Council, some of their age-
peers stayed aboard, and new ones joined (often after getting help with their
own landlord problems, as had happened with McKee). Young people who
had not been burned by the 1972 coalition dispute still found Met Council
a welcoming environment. Thus the senior leaders continued to cultivate
new organizers

Yet Met Council did develop a kind of generation gap over what might be
called political lifestyle. Benedict, Rand, and their contemporaries came from
an Old Left culture in which the struggle absorbed virtually every waking
hour—and limited sleeping hours, too. As a CP slogan put it, "Every Evening
to Party Work."[29] For this cohort there was no such thing as a nine-to-five
activist. Remarkably, the senior Met Council women continued to live that

way, devoting every evening and weekend to tenant politics, into their sixties and beyond. (If anything, their age enhanced their ability to put in late hours, since they no longer had children to tuck in at home.) The young folks just couldn't keep up. Claudia Mansbach spoke of "a huge burnout factor" among younger Met Council workers, especially those seeking to balance their political activities with family life.[30] Joe Hyler, another young organizer from this period, likewise recalled that many of his generation "got worn out. Because we're talking about people who could work—particularly Esther, and Jane, and Bess. . . . these were powerful people. Hard to even describe. Larger than life. . . . [Other] people just could not keep up with [their] pace. I certainly could not." (The older cohort's commitment to politics was so complete, Hyler said, that Benedict's husband, Peter, "worked at Met Council [in part] because he wanted to be with his wife. . . . That was the way [they] could have dinner together every night.")[31] Young people who could not meet the elders' standard drifted away.[32]

The high rate of turnover among young volunteers and staff produced paradoxical effects. For one thing, it delayed by many years the passing of the torch of leadership that Benedict was by now eager to carry out.[33] For another, it meant that while Met Council served as a link between two generations of feminists, it also imposed one of the very burdens that modern feminism would seek to throw off: a standard of full-time work that left few moments for home and family. ("Full-time" at Met Council, Mansbach noted, meant "9:30 a.m. to 11:00 p.m. every day.")[34] Finally, however, Met Council's high turnover may also have *increased* the organization's ripple effect. As new members joined up and then left every few years, the organization churned out scores of young people who had been affected by mentoring relationships with the senior women. The turnover rate made these alumni more numerous than they would have been if a single younger cohort had simply come aboard and stayed.

Further, if some activists' careers were shortened by burnout, others' were lengthened by a sort of shock-absorber effect created by Met Council's federated structure. This is what happened to Susan Cohen when she and Esther Rand butted heads. Rand was a formidable figure even among her contemporaries. "An absolute pisser," laughed McKee. "They broke the mold with her."[35] A subsequent Met Council's director remembered the time in the late 1980s when a landlord, having agreed to meet over a tenant's case, added, "Just one more thing: please, whatever you do, don't bring Esther Rand.' I told him, 'You'll be happy to know she's been dead for several years.'"[36]

Rand would have been pleased at this epitaph, and some younger organizers like Tito Delgado were proud to be her protégés.[37] But her forcefulness could cause problems. While other Met Council leaders "would never steam-roll me," said Cohen, "Esther would roll right over you." At one meeting chaired by Rand, Cohen found herself "getting less and less shy" and offered an idea about the tactical question at hand. "And she goes, 'OK,' and she goes on like I never said anything. So I . . . wait for my moment, and raise [my idea] again. And it never got acknowledged and discussed. . . . And I finally realized over time that Esther didn't *like* the idea. . . . And she was not even going to entertain discussion on it. And so I said to myself, what am I doing here?"[38]

Rand's behavior, Cohen believed, reflected her peculiar disposition rather than any generational pattern. Other senior leaders, such as Jane Benedict, "understood process. Jane might, in the end, not accept your idea. But Jane would let you talk about it, let everyone else talk about it, would tell you why she didn't agree, and be done with it. So would Jane Wood." Thus Cohen was able to handle the problem by simply shifting gears and devoting herself to the Chelsea Coalition on Housing—the organization that emerged from that neighborhood's squatter campaign—where she worked closely and amicably with Wood.[39]

As in the past, moreover, the mundane "servicing" of tenants with legal problems recruited new activists. Delgado is a case in point. He had first come to Met Council when he learned that the city planned to raze his family's apartment building. "I didn't know nothing from nothing" about the housing movement, he recalled, but he had heard through the grapevine that Met Council "would fight like hell for you." With Met Council's guidance, the Delgados challenged the city and won. Delgado stayed on, working under Rand to become an accomplished organizer in his own right. He still delights in telling of the day a housing judge chided a lawyer who questioned his mentor's knowledge of a statute: "If Esther Rand says that's the law, that's the law!"[40]

Over time, these individual experiences at Met Council and its neighborhood affiliates added up to a larger process of political reproduction. While Benedict supervised volunteers at the main office, Rand trained young organizers on the Lower East Side, Bess Stevenson did likewise in Harlem, and Jane Wood mentored a generation of new leaders in Chelsea. "She got that bit in her teeth and she did not let go," remembered Cohen. "And she was very dynamic and very charismatic. And people followed her. It was amazing: one minute I was this naive little shy kid, and the next minute I was getting arrested! What happened to me? It was very liberating to finally put your body where your mouth was. And she gave you the courage to do that. . . . Somehow, you got into it with her, and you saw those connections, and you just followed. And then you learned the stuff and you led."[41]

Private Ownership with "Tenant" Control

The most distinctive development in housing rights during this period was a hybrid of radical and insider strategies: the establishment of legalized tenant control over deteriorated buildings. This innovation, created by tenant advocates and sympathetic officials, built on precedents set by tenants' direct-action community campaigns of the 1960s and early 1970s. Now new laws and technical support would make the ouster of negligent landlords and the formation of limited-equity cooperatives an alternate route of empowerment for low-income New Yorkers.

Workers' housing co-ops dated back to the Finnish and Jewish labor developments of the early twentieth century, but the late-twentieth-century crop grew up differently. The Amalgamated, the Coops, and their contemporaries had been planned as cooperative housing; the late-sixties and early seventies collectives were formed by tenants who took control of conventional rental buildings.

The legal basis for takeover was a 1965 amendment to the state property law, enacted in response to the ghetto strikes. This amendment, Article 7-A, permitted tenants in badly deteriorated buildings to petition for relief in Civil Court. If one-third of a building's households joined the petition, and if they showed that a dangerous condition had persisted for five days, they could deposit their rents with the judge. Further, the court could designate an administrator to spend the rent monies on repairs.[42] This latter provision was critical, for it was here that the 7-A amendment went beyond mere legalization of the rent strike. The court-appointed agent's legal power to collect and spend rent took away the landlord's authority to run the building. A handful of tenant associations went through the legal hoops of 7-A management in the late 1960s.

The economic contraction of the early 1970s, however, expanded the horizon for tenant-based management by precipitating a collapse of the real estate market.[43] Now thousands of buildings contained serious code violations. Thousands of landlords had walked away. Their abdication made way not just for temporary 7-A management, but for lasting cession of landlord control. In 1974 the state legislature further amended Article 7-A to permit tenants themselves to become managers.[44]

As important as the new market and legal leverage was the ideological and practical groundwork laid by earlier activists. By the 1970s, grassroots neighborhood mobilizations had made "community control" a part of New York's political culture in housing as well as education. The rent-withholding practiced by ghetto strikers; the quiet building takeovers organized by VISTA and the Black Panthers; the Battle of Morningside Park; and the squats launched by Move-In, El Comité, and Met Council affiliates had made tenant seizure of home turf an on-the-ground reality. Further, the rhetoric of "our community" and "our buildings" had circulated a notion of moral ownership. Mainstream policy makers might not accept such moral claims, but they could not be unaware of them.

Amid these legal, material, and ideological pressures, city officials now offered unprecedented support for tenant control. In the early spring of 1970, HDA head Jason Nathan authorized deputy commissioner Robert Schur to begin making low-interest rehabilitation loans to tenant associations as well as to landlords.[45] Schur, like Nathan, was a housing moderate; both men were architects of the Lindsay bill to raise controlled rents. (So, for that matter, was longtime tenant advocate Hortense Gabel.)[46] But both also supported the novel idea of subsidizing ten2ant-led co-op conversions, which were being pioneered extralegally by squatters not far from Schur's own residence on the West Side. By March of 1971, Schur reported city-subsidized cooperatives in a dozen buildings, comprising more than a thousand units, near completion.[47]

This example drew interest from other government agencies and advocacy organizations, where liberal impulses and networks still survived to some degree, despite the country's rightward turn. The South Bronx Model Cities Administration, Albany, and the FHA all started to provide loans for the purchase and repair of abandoned buildings. Legal services established by War on Poverty agencies helped tenants with requisite filings and negotiations. (One of the lawyers involved also wrote grants for Yolanda Sánchez's East Harlem projects and was a prime example of the supportive "white liberal establishment" she credited.)[48] New nonprofit organizations joined in as sponsors.[49] In 1972, residents in one of the first buildings to complete the process proudly displayed the new boiler, fresh paint, and rat-free interior that distinguished their home in the South Bronx from neighboring structures. Organizer and cooperator Domingo Calderón remarked, "At first everybody in the neighborhood says, 'Forget it, forget it.' Now they see and I think they do the same thing."[50]

Calderón was right. By the fall of that year, dozens of deteriorated buildings had entered state-subsidized programs for limited-equity co-op conversion. Tenants in still more buildings were blazing a parallel trail without the legal niceties, forcing negligent owners out through rent-strikes or 7-A petitions and establishing "*de facto* ownership."[51] By the mid-seventies, several nonprofits specializing in limited-equity financing and "sweat equity" conversions (in which residents carried out gut rehabilitation themselves) had sprung up to assist New York's tenants through the legal, technical, and financial thickets of co-op conversion. Some grew out of activist churches; others were led by secular professionals with political backgrounds. Met Council, at first wary of such initiatives (because they raised the specter of some tenants' evicting others for nonpayment) also began to steer tenants through these programs.[52]

New York's new co-ops stood out not only from surrounding buildings, but from parallel efforts in other cities. Detroit, for example, was home in the late 1960s and early 1970s to an impassioned Black Power movement that tried to establish collectively owned housing in the ghetto; but the movement's efforts were scuttled by undercapitalization.[53] New York City's unusually supportive funding and advising structures, products of its long-standing tenants'-rights movement, made for unusual accomplishments.

At their best, limited-equity co-ops did not just provide shelter. They helped to secure intangibles cherished by the street-level urbanists who fought for East Tremont, West Ninety-Ninth Street, Cooper Square, and other neighborhoods. A study of Harlem residents who tried to form co-ops in abandoned buildings in the seventies and eighties underscored the critical role of mutual aid and social ties among neighbors. Time and again, researchers found, successful cooperators said their buildings were "like a family." Neighbors knew one another, ran errands for the elderly and sick, watched over other residents' children as well as their own.[54] A Bronx study yielded similar findings. Limited-equity co-op residents prized their buildings' physical soundness *and* their social vigor, both of which contrasted sharply against the miserable conditions on nearby blocks. One Bronx cooperator said the successful buildings were "a piece of heaven in hell."[55] In buildings with struggling or failed co-ops, by contrast, residents reported far less social interaction and neighborly help.

Women predominated among the leadership of the thriving co-ops. The Harlem researchers hypothesized that the "household skills" women were socialized to develop—conflict resolution, listening, patience with ongoing tasks—were essential to effective tenant organizing.[56]

Such organizing was necessary but not sufficient for success. Two other essential ingredients were expert assistance and adequate funding. Most of the stable co-ops received technical advice on legal proceedings, construction, and other unfamiliar tasks, usually from Legal Aid, Met Council, a church, or the nonprofit group UHAB (Urban Homesteading Assistance Board).[57] All the failed ones did not. Low-interest loans were necessary for major repairs, and some of the initial funding dried up during New York's fiscal crisis of 1975. (A few new sources appeared in subsequent years, however.)

Further, the social fallout of economic contraction—poverty, drugs, high rates of incarceration—posed additional burdens on aspiring cooperators. Sweat investment, for instance, had to come mainly from the young and healthy, who were not always numerous in slum buildings. And even buildings with viable corps of participants might be put at risk by a few severely troubled tenants. This problem afflicted low-income rental housing, too, as Yolanda Sánchez learned during her brief stint with Taino Towers' management team. "I'm a social worker and a bleeding heart," she said, "but if I get a tenant who I know is selling drugs . . . or it's their kids messing up the hallways, or their dog . . . I am willing to put their ass in the street."[58] Tenants seeking control of abandoned buildings sometimes had to decide whether they were similarly willing.

But amid the abandonment epidemic of the 1970s, and the rent hikes and market-rate co-op evictions that followed, the establishment of limited-equity co-ops remained a meaningful route of empowerment for low-income New Yorkers. It offered shelter from one front of the harsh economy. And New Yorkers' pioneering achievements in this field inspired federal assistance for similar programs in several other cities.[59]

Grassroots housing actions also lent impetus to a vibrant community gardening movement that took off in New York as residents of abandoned neighborhoods turned vacant lots into oases of greenery and creative landscaping, then forced the city to give its blessing after the fact. Sometimes gardeners and squatters were the same individuals. More broadly, garden and squatter movements rested on the same moral principle. According to Lower East Side ethnographer Miranda Martínez (daughter of downtown housing organizer Ernesto), community garden activists believed that negligent city administrations had "lost the right . . . morally, if not legally . . . to decide unilaterally what would happen to local land.[60]

The 1970s chapter in affordable co-op history contains paradoxes. For one, the political-economic conditions that disposed officials to endorse the new programs—recession and the neoliberal attack on direct state interventions like rent control—were devastating low-income New Yorkers in every other way. For another, although the co-op programs grew out of earlier struggles for tenants' rights, they empowered participants precisely by letting them take title to their homes—and thus cease being tenants at all. In this way they reinscribed the privilege of ownership that had been tenants' bane all along. Thus the new limited-equity co-op programs were both an achievement of the tenant movement and a sign of its weakness, of tenants' dwindling ability to protect themselves *as tenants*. This paradox can be seen as the housing counterpart of labor's postindustrial predicament, which left insecure blue-collar workers more determined than ever that they, or their children, would move up out of the working class.

In theory, and sometimes in practice, the new co-ops can be seen as small fulfillments of the long struggle against commodification of land and housing— that is, the struggle for the urban commons. Planning scholar Tom Angotti writes that progressive advocacy planners seek to redefine land "not as simply a physical object but as a set of social relations." Their mission is to constitute "community land," a form that "sustain[s] the human relations and cultures associated with places while progressively eliminating inequalities."[61] Cooper Square's Alternate Plan exemplified this principle, and on a smaller scale, individual limited-equity co-ops also sustained existing neighborly relations while removing the inequality of landlord–tenant relations. But this achievement did not always last beyond the first generation. Some co-ops' legal arrangements contained loopholes that eventually enabled shareholders to escape the equity limits and sell units at a profit.

Conclusion

The early 1970s witnessed recession and conservative backlash across the country. In New York, where fiscal troubles and capital concentration were particularly acute, it is not surprising that the tenant movement lost ground. More remarkable was the movement's ability to reproduce itself under fire. Not only did new organizing campaigns build the ranks of Met Council, the NYSTLC, and other groups—thus amplifying the movement's intergenerational ripple effect—but new programs, supported by well-placed professionals, extended the legacy of late-sixties radicalism by institutionalizing "sweat equity" and tenant control of housing. Together—if not always cooperatively—activists preserved a modicum of security for working and middle-income New Yorkers in an era of neoliberalism and growing class division.

Afterword

In the winter of 2001, Marie Runyon's building loomed over weeds and rubble. With Manhattan's real estate market humming all around, 130 Morningside was a throwback, its boarded windows and graffiti reminding passersby of the fiscal crisis thirty years before.

Today the marble gleams. And 130 nestles against a modern high-rise on the neighboring lot. After what journalist Clyde Haberman called the Forty Years War, Columbia University completed a handsome renovation of upper Morningside Drive and made peace with its senior resident. Most buildings are dedicated to institutional uses, but 130 itself houses a mix of institutional and noninstitutional tenants.[1] Columbia set the facade with a brass plate proclaiming the building's new name: Marie Runyon Court.

Jane Wood died in 2004. The walk from the subway to her memorial service led through a jungle of big-box stores and luxury co-ops that were remaking blue-collar Chelsea. Yet inside the old church on West 25th Street, a different Chelsea showed through. Neighbors filled the aisles. In Spanish and English they told of Wood's courage and compassion. Their presence attested to the close-knit community that had struggled to stay in place. Some were squatters from 1970. Some were their children and grandchildren.

Wood's friends were launching a campaign to rename West 19th Street, where the organizer had lived for more than fifty years, "Jane Wood's Way." Susan Cohen drew guffaws when she explained to the assembled, "If you worked with Jane, in the end you always did things Jane Wood's Way."

On plaques and street signs and in many other texts, the gains and losses of tenant struggles are written everywhere on today's New York. The losses are in bolder print. Laws enacted in the 1990s and after have weakened the rent-stabilization system. The city's homeless population climbs ever higher. Whole neighborhoods have gentrified with a vengeance. (Morningside Heights is a prime example, and the renaming of Runyon's building was, among other things, a smart publicity move by a victorious landlord who could afford a little *noblesse oblige*.) Behind the direct authors of these changes lie the invisible hands of free-market dogma and superheated real estate values.[2] Even the ghost of Jane Jacobs has played a part, as affluent newcomers in search of the "authentic" urban village have driven rents in erstwhile blue-collar areas far beyond blue-collar budgets.[3]

Spiraling prices have impelled particularly consequential changes in co-operative housing. The late 1970s and 1980s saw a boom in conversions of moderate-rent buildings to market-rate co-ops, deals that turned handsome profits for departing landlords. "The co-oping craze was a death knell for se-rious [tenant] lobbying," said Cohen, because the middle-class people who bought into co-ops dropped out of the movement. And those could not afford to buy in were turned out of their homes. Sunset clauses have allowed many Mitchell-Lama and other limited-equity co-ops (along with Mitchell-Lamas limited-dividend rentals) to buy *out* of their affordability programs and go market-rate.[4] Several labor-sponsored co-ops have joined this exodus. And some of the limited-equity co-ops formed in abandoned buildings have loos-ened income caps and resale restrictions. Thus the co-operative apartment building, a socialized form of property holding, now serves in some cases to dispossess poorer tenants.

Another institution that held out hope for such tenants, the community-board system, has also fallen short of its purported mission. The establishment of community boards during the 1950s and 1960s seemed a response to the many calls—from good-government groups, the racially identified commu-nity-control movement, and multiracial tenant organizations—for citizen participation in local planning. The boards, however, were granted "advisory" rather than actual say over redevelopment. Ira Katznelson calls New York's community-board program a "mimetic" reform, one characterized by adoption of revolutionary rhetoric alongside failure to redistribute power.[5]

Community-development corporations were likewise supposed to give peo-ple a voice in the rebuilding of their own neighborhoods. Many did so; some still do. But most have now adapted to the neoliberal environment by trading in participatory planning and sweat equity for corporate boards, city contracts, budgets balanced on for-profit subsidiaries, and professional staffs that treat residents as clients, not constituents. This transformation has enabled material growth—New York CDCs have developed or managed some eighty thousand housing units, many below market rate—at the price of what sociologists call "social capital," the bonds of neighborly trust and association at the heart of the tenant movement's formulation of citizenship.[6]

But when we read between the charades and high-rises, we can see that the tenant movement has not quite expired. Half the city's two million renters still benefit from rent stabilization or control. Renters still make up most of New York. Tenant councils continue to dot the boroughs, and umbrella groups like Met Council, Tenants and Neighbors (successor to the New York State Tenants Legislative Coalition), and the Mitchell-Lama Residents Coalition soldier on in legislatures, courtrooms, and residential hallways. Indeed, old rifts have healed, and Tenants and Neighbors founder Michael McKee is back on the board of Met Council at this writing. Tenants in neglected buildings still use 7-A petitions and limited-equity co-op programs to better their conditions. And some of the older affordable co-ops have kept faith with their mandate,

Figure 19. **Dedication of Jane Wood's Way.** Susan Cohen, right foreground, in profile. *Courtesy of Met Council on Housing.*

Figure 20. **Limited-equity co-op, Edgecombe Avenue, Harlem, 2012.**

resisting the call of the market-rate siren. The family sentiment among neighbors can still be found if one looks in the right places. A research visit to East Harlem's Casabe Houses—Ernesto Martínez's and Yolanda Sánchez's final project—led into a bustling lobby where residents, managers, and security guards all greeted one another as "*mami*" and "*papi*."

The survival of New York's large public-housing stock stands out starkly against a national background in which demolition and privatization have become the order of the day. Credit goes to savvy management, high demand, and NYCHA's renewed—and controversial—preference for job-holding tenants. But it belongs also to "an activist core of tenants willing to travel and protest in Albany . . . and Washington."[7]

Beyond specific buildings and laws, the political culture of housing rights has reproduced itself in the lean years. "Housing Notebook," Met Council's weekly radio show, has passed the thirty-year mark on New York's noncommercial radio station. Tenants and Neighbors airs a public-access cable show. For a few years these staid productions were joined by *Rent Wars Ronin*, a pro-tenant cable series that presented "realistic legal principles set in a kung fu meets swords and sorcery motif."[8]

Glimmers of movement history appear even in defeat. In 2002, city lawyers finally won an eviction order against descendants of the West 15th Street squatters in Chelsea. But the tenants sued back and gained a compromise: They would leave the building when the city found them other affordable housing. After several offers, they were satisfied with city-renovated apartments in Upper Manhattan.[9] Four years later, Stuyvesant Town again became a testing ground for tenants' rights. At a time when property owners were stampeding through the new gaps in rent regulation, Met Life put the complex up for sale. The tenant association submitted a modest bid, calling for special consideration in light of the project's *raison d'être* as a haven for the lower middle class. But the deal was closed with a high-bidding speculator—a shining victory for the free market. Nonetheless, when the new owner jacked up rents, the tenants won refunds under the rent-stabilization law. The speculator, unable to meet mortgage payments, surrendered the complex to the lenders, reviving the possibility of sale to the residents.[10]

In feminism the movement's shadow is long. Women still make up much of the membership and leadership of tenant organizations, though not as disproportionately as before. Paradoxically, this "decline" reflects the success with which earlier generations of women, whose feminist careers benefitted directly and indirectly from tenant activism, claimed the political terrain as their own. Women's breaking into traditionally male political precincts left more room for men in tenant organizations. One of the city's first female judges, as well as the second woman to serve as Manhattan borough president, credited Jane Benedict as a crucial exemplar and mentor.[11] The first female speaker of the City Council cut her teeth as a tenant organizer. (At this writing, she also stands accused of selling out her old constituency in pursuit of the mayoralty—arguably another step into traditional political territory.) Latinas in public office have become more commonplace thanks to the spadework of Yolanda Sánchez and her peers. The Brooklyn-based National Congress of Neighborhood Women continues to support low-income communities fighting for a decent life. And at a time when female-headed households bear the greatest risk of poverty, public and rent-regulated housing answer one of the foremost needs of New York women.

Tenant history is also palpable in contemporary community organizations that have advanced both the concept and the reality of "community land." In the 1990s the Cooper Square Committee established a mutual-housing association, a form of ownership in which tenants collectively direct the management but do not own shares that can be bought and sold. The association's buildings sit

Figure 21. **Park West Village Tenants, Association gathering, 2007.** *Courtesy of
Liz Friedman.*

on lots owned by a "community land trust" charged with serving low-income
residents in perpetuity. These legal devices close off the escape hatch through
which other limited-equity co-ops have fled their original fee strictures. Other
neighborhoods have organized for nonprofit development through progressive
CDCs. A Bronx group called We Stay! ¡Nos Quedamos! was established in the
1990s by two Melrose residents, Pedro Cintrón and Yolanda García, who were
determined to stop a renewal venture that would have replaced their neighborhood's affordable rentals and small businesses with incongruous suburban-
style houses for the middle class. We Stay! forged alliances and mounted protests that finally made the city accept an alternate proposal. The alternate plan
was democratically formulated to retain the existing Melrose community, much
in the tradition of Cooper Square. It also took on the environmental racism
embodied in noxious local waste facilities. Hundreds of new affordable units
have now been built.[12]

    As in the past, housing politics reveal two sides of New York, and America,
squaring off for a fight. During his 2001 mayoral run, Fernando Ferrer spoke
of "the other New York," the New York of working people and people of color,

that he hoped to represent. New York is indeed a bifurcated city. It is at once a flagship of the left—a stronghold of labor, feminist, and racial justice movements—and the capital of capitalism. It is the nation's leading city for tenants' rights, and the domain of fantastically wealthy owners and developers.

The tenant movement has spoken unabashedly for that other New York. In the process it has also imagined an "other America," a set of political and social alternatives to the mainstream. During an era in which private home ownership became the foundation of American society—driving the economy, structuring daily life, grounding a sense of entitled citizenship, and reinforcing class, racial and gender divisions—the postwar movement for renters' rights went against the American grain. It helped to create and defend other realities: multiracial neighborhoods, women's political empowerment, collective ownership, and an ideal of citizenship based on neighborly ties.

Through these processes the movement played a part in regenerating the left. "I think that the struggle is a long one," said Frances Goldin, discussing the role of tenant organizing in the unfolding of political history.

> And I think that if people can eat when they're hungry and if they can have a roof over their head when they're homeless, that you don't wait for the Millennium, for the Revolution. You do what you can [now] to make life easier. . . . But when people feel that their lives, or the lives or their children are threatened, or their roof is threatened, and they're organized in a way that is not just for this thing, or for themselves alone—you know, not only might you win, but *people are changed*. Which is the whole point.[13]

Fostering and maintaining that kind of transformation has always been the movement's greatest challenge. But Goldin and the generations she has mentored are evidence that some people *have* been changed, and that the movement has carried on to a significant degree. The tenant agenda that was central to New York's civil-rights and working-class struggles of the 1930s and 1940s became, during the Cold War, a venue of ongoing activism for leftists and women in particular. Amid the upheavals of the late 1960s, the tenant movement fostered a second round of political reproduction. The Old Left had helped make New York uncommonly fertile soil for the people of color, New Leftists, and feminists who sought to put ideals of community and democracy into practice. And the still-active older leaders trained a new generation of organizers, transmitting Popular Front precepts to the children of postwar prosperity.

That affinity across generations and that resonance among struggles were manifest at the packed memorials for Jane Benedict and Jane Wood, where

Figure 22. **From mambo to line dance.** Former residents of West 98th and West 99th Streets demonstrate their command of modern steps at the 2012 reunion. *Courtesy of Marione "Deno" Lawrence Jr.*

all ages came to pay tribute. At Wood's service the high point came when the leader of an ecumenical peace group, with whom Jane had traveled illegally to Cuba many times, called her name on the roll. "*¡Presente!*" thundered the crowd.

It is a cliché that the dead are present in spirit. But surviving activists are committed to keeping Wood, Benedict, Sánchez, Bess Stevenson, Jesse Gray, Walter Thabit, and many other now-lost tenant voices present in brick and mortar and social fabric. Susan Cohen said one of the most important things Wood bequeathed her was the courage "to put your body where your mouth was." In time she concluded that even with courage, "you can't save the world. But you can save little pieces of it." In New York those pieces include the still-populous co-ops, rentals, street corners, bodegas, gardens, and democratic planning alliances where neighborly ties make people "like a family," and also like citizens. There New York's tenant history is *presente*.

List of Abbreviations

Newspapers and Magazines

BAA	Baltimore Afro-American
BHN	Bronx Home News
BP	Black Panther
CD	Chicago Defender
CDS	Columbia Daily Spectator
CL	City Limits
CT	Chicago Tribune
DW	Daily Worker / Daily World
HC	Hartford Courant
LAT	Los Angeles Times
MS	Morningside Sun (Box 6, Folder 14, CCC)
MT	Manhattan Tribune
NYAN	New York Amsterdam News
NYDN	New York Daily News
NYHT	New York Herald Tribune
NYP	New York Post
NYT	New York Times
TN	Tenant News
TNAT	The Nation
TNY	The New Yorker
VV	Village Voice
WP	Washington Post

Journals

AANY	Afro-Americans in New York Life and History
AF	Architectural Forum
AHR	American Historical Review

CA   City Almanac
JAIP   Journal of the American Institute of Planners
JOUH   Journal of Urban History
PA   Progressive Architecture
SSR   Social Service Review

Manuscript Collections

ABP   Algernon Black Papers, Rare Book and Manuscript Library,
         Columbia University
BPP   Black Panther Party, Harlem Branch, Collection, Schomburg Center
         for Research in Black Culture
CAP   Charles Abrams Papers (microfilm)
CCC   Christiane Collins Collection, Schomburg Center for Research
         in Black Culture
JHC   James Haughton Collection, Schomburg Center for Research
         in Black Culture
MCH   Metropolitan Council on Housing Collection, Tamiment Library*
NSM   Northern Student Movement Collection, Schomburg Center
         for Research in Black Culture
OHC   Oral History Collection of Columbia University
WCC   Women's City Club Collection, Hunter College Archives

Organizations and Housing Terminology

ACLU   American Civil Liberties Union
ADA   Americans for Democratic Action
AJC   American Jewish Congress; also American Jewish Committee
ARCH   Architects' Renewal Committee in Harlem
BPP   Black Panther Party
CHCR   City Commission on Human Rights
CHPC   Citizens Housing and Planning Council
CIO   Congress of Industrial Unions
CPC   City Planning Commission
CSC   Cooper Square Committee
CSCDCBA   Cooper Square Community Development Committee
          and Businessmen's Association
CSS   Community Service Society
CWCCH   City-Wide Citizens' Committee on Harlem
CWTC   City-Wide Tenants Council
FHA   Federal Housing Administration
HAG   Harlem Action Group

*Citations to this collection refer to the folder numbers in the Tamiment's inventory, not to the handwritten numbers on the folders.

HOLC	Home Owners' Loan Corporation
HRB	Housing and Redevelopment Board
HUAC	House Un-American Activities Committee
ILGWU	International Ladies Garment Workers Union
LENA	Lower East Side Neighborhoods Association
MHI	Morningside Heights, Inc.
MRC	Morningside Renewal Council
MU	Morningsiders United
NAACP	National Association for the Advancement of Colored People
NSM	Northern Student Movement
NYCHA	New York City Housing Authority
NYSCDH	New York State Committee against Discrimination in Housing
OPA	Office of Price Administration
RPA	Regional Plan Association
SNCC	Student Nonviolent Coordinating Committee
SRO	Single Room Occupancy
UHF	United Housing Federation
UTL	United Tenants' League
UPACA	Upper Park Avenue Community Association
WCC	Women's City Club of New York
YLP	Young Lords Party

Notes

Introduction

1. See especially David Harvey, "The Right to the City," *New Left Review* 53 (2008): 37.

2. United States Department of Commerce, Bureau of the Census, *Sixteenth Census of the United States: 1940. Housing, Volume II, Part 4* (Washington, D.C.: United States Government Printing Office, 1943), table 1, 269.

3. Ibid.; United States Department of Commerce, Bureau of the Census, *Sixteenth Census of the United States: 1940. Housing, Volume I, Part 1* (Washington, D.C.: United States Government Printing Office, 1943), table 10, 12. New York City's total of occupied rentals, 1.7 million, surpassed the numbers of occupied housing units in all states save California, Illinois, New York, Ohio, and Pennsylvania.

4. United States Department of Commerce, Bureau of the Census, *Sixteenth Census of the United States: 1940. Housing, Volume II, Part 2* (Washington, D.C.: United States Government Printing Office, 1943), table 1, 213, and table 1, 763.

5. Maurice Isserman, *If I Had a Hammer: The Death of the Old Left and the Birth of the New Left* (Urbana: University of Illinois Press, 1987), xvii.

6. See, for example, Isserman, ibid.; Charles Payne, *I've Got the Light of Freedom: The Organizing Tradition and the Mississippi Freedom Struggle* (Berkeley: University of California Press, 1995); and John D'Emilio, *Lost Prophet: The Life and Times of Bayard Rustin* (New York: Free Press, 2003).

7. See especially Barbara Ransby, *Ella Baker and the Black Freedom Movement: A Radical Democratic Vision* (Chapel Hill: University of North Carolina Press, 2003); Dorothy Sue Cobble, *The Other Women's Movement: Workplace Justice and Social Rights in Modern America* (Princeton, N.J.: Princeton University Press, 2004); Erik S. McDuffie, *Sojourning for Freedom: Black Women, American Communism, and the Making of Black Left Feminism* (Durham, N.C.: Duke University Press, 2011); and Danielle L. McGuire, *At the Dark End of the Street: Black Women, Rape and Resistance* (New York: Knopf, 2010).

8. Jerald E. Podair, *The Strike That Changed New York: Blacks, Whites and the Ocean Hill–Brownsville Crisis* (New Haven, Conn.: Yale University Press, 2002).

9. Coined in the nineteenth century, the phrase was revived by King and other civil-rights activists. See Casey Nelson Blake, *Beloved Community: The Cultural Criticism of Randolph Bourne, Van Wyck Brooks, Waldo Frank, and Lewis Mumford* (Durham: University of North Carolina Press, 1990); Martin Luther King Jr., *Stride toward Freedom: The Montgomery Story* (New York: Harper and Row, 1958), 102, 220; Diane Nash, "The Beloved Community: Origins of SNCC," in Cheryl Lynn Greenberg, ed., *A Circle of Trust: Remembering SNCC* (New Brunswick, N.J.: Rutgers University Press, 1998).

10. Frances Goldin, interview with author, February 11, 2001.

11. Kathleen A. Laughlin, Julie Gallagher, Dorothy Sue Cobble, Eileen Boris, Premilla Nadason, Stephanie Gilmore, and Leandra Zarnow, "Is It Time to Jump Ship? Historians Rethink the Waves Metaphor," *Feminist Formations* 22, no. 1 (2010).

Chapter 1. "A Time of Struggle"

1. "'Peace Is Hell,'" *NYT*, November 29, 1945; Anthony Jackson, *A Place Called Home: A History of Low-Cost Housing in Manhattan* (Cambridge, Mass.: MIT Press, 1976), 221, 227; Joshua B. Freeman, *Working-Class New York: Life and Labor since World War II* (New York: The New Press, 2000), 105; J. Anthony Panuch, *Building a Better New York: Final Report to Mayor Robert F. Wagner* (New York, 1960), Chart after 16, 35.

2. Jared N. Day, *Urban Castles: Tenement Housing and Landlord Activism in New York City, 1890–1943* (New York: Columbia University Press 1999); Anthony Jackson, *A Place Called Home*, 202.

3. United States Department of Commerce, Bureau of the Census, *Sixteenth Census of the United States: 1940. Housing, Volume II, Part 4* (Washington, D.C.: United States Government Printing Office, 1943), table 1, 269. Rentals also formed a majority of occupied units in each of the outer boroughs.

4. Lizabeth Cohen, *A Consumers' Republic: The Politics of Mass Consumption in Postwar America* (New York: Alfred A. Knopf, 2003).

5. Max Page, *The Creative Destruction of Manhattan, 1900–1940s* (Chicago: University of Chicago Press, 2001), 5–6. "Creative destruction" was coined by Joseph Schumpeter, *Capitalism, Socialism and Democracy* (New York: Harper and Brothers, 1942).

6. Plunz, *A History of Housing*, 131.

7. An introduction to the range of definitions and distinctions can be found in Christopher Silver, "Neighborhood Planning in Historical Perspective," *Journal of the American Planning Association* 51, no. 2 (1985); Deborah Martin, "'Place-Framing' as Place-Making: Constituting a Neighborhood for Organizing and Activism," *Annals of the Association of American Geographers* 9, no. 3 (2003); Margarethe Kusenbach, "A Hierarchy of Urban Communities: Observations on the Nested Character of Place," *City & Community* 7, no. 3 (2008). That acknowledged, I have followed the common practice of New Yorkers in using the term imprecisely. In some instances, such as Cooper Square, "neighborhood" refers to what Kusenbach calls a "walking distance neighborhood." In others, such as Harlem or East New York, it means a much larger district.

8. Jenna Weissman Joselit, "The Landlord as Czar: Pre–World War I Tenant Activ-

ity," in Ronald Lawson and Mark Naison, eds., *The Tenant Movement in New York City, 1904–1984* (New Brunswick, N.J.: Rutgers University Press, 1986).

9. Lawrence Glickman, *Buying Power: A History of Consumer Activism in America* (Chicago: University of Chicago Press, 2009), 5, 120, 130, 162–63, 180; Paula E. Hyman, "Immigrant Women and Consumer Protest: The New York City Kosher Meat Boycott of 1902," *American Jewish History* 70, no. 1 (1980); Joselit, "The Landlord as Czar"; Dana Frank, "Housewives, Socialists, and the Politics of Food: The 1917 New York Cost-of-Living Protests," *Feminist Studies* 11, no. 2 (Summer 1985).

10. Joselit, "The Landlord as Czar," 41.

11. Joel Schwartz, "The New York City Rent Strikes of 1963–1964," *SSR* 57, no. 4 (1983): 546.

12. Joseph A. Spencer, "New York City Tenant Organizations and the Post–World War I Housing Crisis," in Lawson and Naison, eds., *The Tenant Movement*, 56, 58, 68; Mark Naison, "From Eviction Resistance to Rent Control: Tenant Activism in the Great Depression," in Lawson and Naison, eds., *The Tenant Movement*, 103; Joel Schwartz, "Tenant Power in the Liberal City, 1943–1971," in Lawson and Naison, eds., *The Tenant Movement*, 137.

13. Ira Katznelson, *City Trenches: Urban Politics and the Patterning of Class in the United States* (New York: Pantheon Books, 1981), 65, 71.

14. Spencer, "New York City Tenant Organizations," 56–58.

15. *Ibid.* 59, 66, 72–73, 83, 85–89

16. Naison, "From Eviction Resistance to Rent Control," 95–101, 103, 107.

17. Joel Schwartz, "The Consolidated Tenants League of Harlem: Black Self-Help vs. White, Liberal Intervention in Ghetto Housing, 1934–1944," *AANY* 10, no. 1 (1986).

18. Xsusha Carlyann Flandro, Christine Huh, Negin Maleki, Mariana Sarango-Manaças, and Jennifer Schork, "Progressive Housing in New York City: A Closer Look at Model Tenements and Finnish Cooperatives," Columbia Graduate School of Architecture and Planning, 2008, http://www.scribd.com/doc/2963635/Progressive-Housing-in-New-York-City-A-Closer-Look-at-Model-Tenements-and-Finnish-Cooperatives (accessed June 3, 2013), 41–42.

19. Plunz, *A History of Housing*, 151–59.

20. Anthony Jackson, *A Place Called Home*, 184.

21. Plunz, *A History of Housing*, 150–51.

22. Tony Schuman, "Labor and Housing in New York City: Architect Herman Jessor and the Cooperative Housing Movement," http://urbanomnibus.net/main/wp-content/uploads/2010/03/LABOR-AND-HOUSING-IN-NEW-YORK-CITY.pdf (accessed November 28, 2011), 2.

23. Anthony Jackson, *A Place Called Home*, 12–14.

24. Ibid., 122.

25. Ibid., 92–94, 114–15.

26. Paula Baker, "The Domestication of Politics: Women and American Political Society, 1780–1920,"*AHR* 89, no. 3 (June 1984): 641; Daphne Spain, *How Women Saved the City* (Minneapolis: University of Minnesota Press, 2001), 13.

27. Spain, *How Women Saved the City*, 24–26.

28. Betty Boyd Caroli, "Settlement Houses," in Kenneth Jackson, ed., *The Encyclopedia of New York City* (New Haven, Conn.: Yale University Press, 1995), 1059–61.

29. Alice Kessler-Harris, *Women Have Always Worked: An Historical Overview* (New York: The Feminist Press, 1981), 117. Florence Kelley, Jane Addams, Lillian Wald, and Frances Perkins are examples.

30. Terry Jane Ruderman, *Stanley M. Isaacs: The Conscience of New York* (New York: Arno Press, 1982), 50–55.

31. "Children Starved," *NYT*, October 19, 1923; "Women's City Club," *NYT*, February 18, 1928.

32. "Housing for the Family,"1936, Series XI, Box 41, Folder 22, WCC.

33. Estelle B. Freedman, "Separatism Revisited: Women's Institutions, Social Reform, and the Career of Miriam Van Waters," in Linda K. Kerber, Alice Kessler-Harris, and Kathryn Kish Sklar, eds., *U.S. History as Women's History: New Feminist Essays* (Chapel Hill: University of North Carolina Press, 1995), 173.

34. Plunz, *A History of Housing*, 88–112; Schwartz, "Tenant Unions," 415.

35. Alan Brinkley, *The End of Reform: New Deal Liberalism in Recession and War* (New York: Vintage Books, 1995), 10.

36. Kenneth T Jackson, *The Crabgrass Frontier: The Suburbanization of the United States* (New York: Oxford University Press, 1985), 195–201.

37. "Why You Should Vote Communist" (1934), 22, Communist Party of the United States of America Printed Ephemera Collection, Box 5, Folder 4, Tamiment Library; "A Brief Review of the ALP in 1938–1939–1940," 1–2, Printed Ephemera Collection on Organizations, Box 8, Folder 6, Tamiment Library; Nicholas Dagen Bloom, *Public Housing That Worked: New York in the Twentieth Century* (Philadelphia: University of Pennsylvania Press, 2008), 24–25.

38. Nita Jager, ed., *Charles Abrams: Papers and Files, A Guide to the Microfilm Collection* (Ithaca, N.Y.: Cornell University, 1975), 8–10.

39. Eugenie Ladner Birch, "Woman-Made America: The Case of Early Public Housing Policy," *JAIP* 44, *passim* and 136, 141.

40. Bloom, *Public Housing That Worked*, 22, 25–26.

41. Plunz, *A History of Housing*, 125–26 and 209–10; Anthony Jackson, *A Place Called Home*, 211–12.

42. "'First Houses' Open," *NYT*, December 4, 1935.

43. Naison, "From Eviction Resistance to Rent Control," 118–27.

44. CHPC papers, Reel 11, Charles Abrams Papers, Cornell University Department of Manuscripts and University Archives.

45. Harvey Klehr, *The Heyday of American Communism: The Depression Decade* (New York: Basic Books, 1984), 366, 379; Maurice Isserman, *Which Side Were You On? The American Communist Party during the Second World War* (Chicago: University of Illinois Press, 1993), 19, 120, 167.

46. Freeman, *Working-Class New York*, 56–60, 77; Gerald Meyer, *Vito Marcantonio: Radical Politician, 1902–1954* (Albany: State University of New York Press, 1989), 1, 25–27, 54, 65, 81–83.

47. Frances Goldin, interview with author, January 8 and February 11, 2001.

48. Gilberto Gerena Valentín, interview with Amílcar Tirado Avilés, *Centro* 2, no. 5 (1989): 35.

49. Freeman, *Working-Class New York*, 61–62, 65–68.

50. Naison, "From Eviction Resistance to Rent Control," 129; Ronald Lawson, Stephen Barton, and Jenna Weissman Joselit, "From Kitchen to Storefront: Women in the Tenant Movement," in Gerda Wekerle, ed., *New Space for Women* (Boulder, Co.: Westview Press, 1980), 258–62.

51. Thomas Angotti, *New York for Sale: Community Planning Confronts Global Real Estate* (Cambridge: MIT Press, 2008), 44–45, 61–63, 69.

52. "Freezing of Rents," *NYT*, June 13, 1942. The city's 1940 vacancy rate was 7 percent. United States Department of Commerce, Bureau of the Census, *Sixteenth Census of the United States: 1940. Housing, Volume I, Part 2* (Washington, D.C.: United States Government Printing Office, 1943), table 4, 71. But the majority of vacant units almost certainly fell among the 1.9. million units "needing major repairs or [having] no private bath." Even those substandard dwellings were filled as defense production increased. "Population Down, Apartments Full," *NYT*, February 16, 1944.

53. "No Time," *NYT*, August 4, 1943.

54. Naison, "From Eviction Resistance to Rent Control," 128–30.

55. Anthony Jackson, *A Place Called Home*, 164–68.

56. "Rent Gouger," *NYT*, March 16, 1946.

57. "Evicted Veteran," *NYT*, February 7, 1946.

58. State of New York, *Ninth Annual Report of the Judicial Council* through *Fourteenth Annual Report of the Judicial Council* (Albany, N.Y.: Williams Press, and New York: Publishers Printing, 1943–48).

59. "Tenants League," *NYAN*, February 16, 1946; "Harlem's Tenants," *NYAN*, October 5, 1946; "Falling Ceiling," *NYAN*, February 1, 1947; David Shannon, *The Decline of American Communism* (New York: Harcourt, Brace, 1959), 94.

60. "Tidying-Up Drive," *NYT*, April 4, 1946; "Dirty Tenements," *NYT*, June 13, 1946.

61. "Tenants Piling Up," *NYT*, October 30, 1948.

62. Goldin, interview. The 1940 census shows small numbers of "non-white persons" on most blocks on the Lower East Side. United States Department of Commerce, Bureau of the Census, *Sixteenth Census of the United States: 1940. Housing, Supplement to the First Series, Housing Bulletin for New York, Manhattan Borough, Block Statistics* (Washington, D.C.: United States Government Printing Office), 8–14.

63. Goldin, interview.

64. Bess Stevenson, interview with author, February 27, 2001; "Bess Stevenson," *CL*, June 1985.

65. Bess Stevenson, interview with author, February 27, 2001.

66. Jenny Laurie, conversation with author, 2004.

67. Goldin did volunteer with a settlement in the 1960s, long after her political initiation.

68. Susan Lynn, *Progressive Women in Conservative Times: Racial Justice, Peace and Feminism, 1945 to the 1960s* (New Brunswick, N.J.: Rutgers University Press, 1992), 5.

69. Ibid., 6.

70. "Rent Rise Asked," *NYT*, March 10, 1945.

71. "Wants Rent Control," *NYT*, October 22, 1945.

72. Cohen, *A Consumers' Republic*, 23, 31, 70–77, 112–14.

73. Ibid., 127.

74. Ibid., 122, 126–27.

75. Ibid., 66, 102.

76. "Thousands Rally" and "Mayor to Head," *DW*, April 25, 1946; "Pleas to Keep OPA," *NYT*, June 6, 1946; "Bronx Price Protest," *BHN*, July 24, 1946; "Consumer Strike" and "Buy-Buy Blues," *DW*, July 24, 1946.

77. "Congress Warned," *NYT*, July 26, 1946; "OPA Dies," *NYT*, May 27, 1947.

78. Freeman, *Working-Class New York*, 62; "Truman Gets Bronx," *BHN*, June 20, 1946; "OPA Bars Rise," *NYT*, September 1, 1946.

79. "Truman Signs Bill," *NYT*, July 1, 1947.

80. Schwartz, "Tenant Power," 151.

81. "State Takes Over," *NYT*, March 30, 1950.

82. Schwartz, "Tenant Power," 152.

83. Ibid., 148, 137–53.

Chapter 2. *"The Right to Lease and Occupy a Home"*

1. Richard Plunz, *A History of Housing in New York City: Dwelling Type and Social Change in the American Metropolis* (New York: Columbia University Press, 1990), 214–16.

2. Ibid., 233–34; Anthony Jackson, *A Place Called Home: A History of Low-Cost Housing in Manhattan* (Cambridge, Mass.: MIT Press, 1976), 219–20; Nicholas Dagen Bloom, *Public Housing That Worked: New York in the Twentieth Century* (Philadelphia: University of Pennsylvania Press, 2008), 35–36.

3. Anthony Jackson, *A Place Called Home*, 216; Plunz, *A History of Housing*, 207–8.

4. Joel Schwartz, "Tenant Unions in New York City's Low-Rent Housing, 1933–1949," *JOUH* 12, no. 4 (1986): 415.

5. Ibid., 421; Joel Schwartz, "The Consolidated Tenants League of Harlem: Black Self-Help vs. White, Liberal Intervention in Ghetto Housing, 1934–1944," *AANY* 10, no. 1 (1986): 39.

6. NYCHA, *First Houses* (New York: NYCHA, 1935), 31.

7. Schwartz, "Tenant Unions," 420–21.

8. Ibid., 417–28.

9. Studs Terkel, *Hard Times: An Oral History of the Great Depression* (New York: Pantheon Books, 1970), 384.

10. Schwartz, "Tenant Unions," 428–29.

11. Plunz, *A History of Housing*, 209–10; Anthony Jackson, *A Place Called Home*, 211–12.

12. Bloom, *Public Housing That Worked*, 50.

13. Plunz, *A History of Housing*, 210, 216.

14. Plunz, *A History of Housing*, 216–27; Samuel Zipp, *Manhattan Projects: The Rise*

and Fall of Urban Renewal in Cold War New York (New York: Oxford University Press, 2010), 15.

15. Bloom, *Public Housing That Worked*, 55–57.

16. Ibid., 6, 70.

17. Ibid., 59, 62, 74.

18. CHPC papers, Reel 11. CAP.

19. Franklin Roosevelt, "Message to the Congress," January 11, 1944.

20. Peter Dreier, "Labor's Love Lost? Rebuilding Unions' Involvement in Federal Housing Policy," *Housing Policy Debate* 11, no. 2 (2000): 341; Andrew Edmund Kersten, *Labor's Home Front: The American Federation of Labor during World War II* (New York: New York University Press), 206, 212; Joshua B. Freeman, *Working-Class New York: Life and Labor since World War II* (New York: The New Press, 2000), 61, 63.

21. Jo Ann E. Argersinger, "Contested Visions of American Democracy: Citizenship, Public Housing, and the International Arena," *JOUH* 36, no.6 (2010): 792–813.

22. Lee F. Johnson, "How They Licked the TEW Bill," *Survey Graphic* (November 1948): 445–49.

23. "New Housing," *NYT*, May 19, 1946.

24. "City to Oust 2,769," *NYT*, January 16, 1947; Schwartz, "Tenant Unions," 430–31.

25. "Tenants Fight," *NYT*, March 22, 1949.

26. Schwartz, "Tenant Unions," 431–32.

27. Plunz, *A History of Housing*, 261–65.

28. "Low Rentals," *NYT*, December 6, 1948; Bloom, *Public Housing That Worked*, 64–68.

29. "Supports Housing," *NYT*, February 6, 1944; "Housing Week," *NYT*, April 30, 1944; "Housing and Trade Rent," *NYT*, April 1, 1945; "Favors Housing Subsidy," *NYT*, November 3, 1946; "Favors Increases," *NYT*, March 9, 1947; "Community Group," *NYT*, February 22, 1948.

30. Donald Craig Parson, *Making a Better World: Public Housing, the Red Scare, and the Direction of Modern Los Angeles* (Minneapolis: University of Minnesota Press, 2005), *passim* and 17, 33–43, 106–9, 130–35.

31. Project completion dates, Development Data Book 2010, http://www.nyc.gov /html/nycha/html/resources/development-data-book.shtml, accessed July 5, 2010.

32. Parson, *Making a Better World*, 75.

33. Bloom, *Public Housing That Worked*, 110.

34. Parson, *Making a Better World*, 51.

35. Plunz, *A History of Housing*, 219–20.

36. NYCHA, *Development Data Book* (New York: NYCHA, April 1950), 10.

37. NYCHA, *Development Data Book* (New York: NYCHA, 2012), 63.

38. Bloom, *Public Housing That Worked*, passim.

39. Dreier, "Labor's Love Lost?," 343.

40. "Federal Housing Activities, 1918–1946," *Congressional Digest*, November 1946, 269.

41. Harry Truman, "Special Message to Congress," September 6, 1945; "Continued Shortage," *NYT*, March 30, 1945; Steven Fraser, *Labor Will Rule: Sidney Hillman and the Rise of American Labor* (Ithaca, N.Y.: Cornell University Press, 1991), 506–7.

42. "Federal Housing Activities," 260.

43. Lizabeth Cohen, *A Consumers' Republic: The Politics of Mass Consumption in Postwar America* (New York: Alfred A. Knopf, 2003),122.

44. Kenneth T. Jackson, *The Crabgrass Frontier: The Suburbanization of the United States* (New York: Oxford University Press, 1985), 203–18; Thomas Sugrue, *The Origins of the Urban Crisis: Race and Inequality in Postwar Detroit* (Princeton, N.J.: Princeton University Press, 1996), 43–44, 60–63; Douglas S. Massey and Nancy N. Denton, *American Apartheid: Segregation and the Making of the Underclass* (Cambridge, Mass.: Harvard University Press, 1993), 115–60.

45. Alan Brinkley, *The End of Reform: New Deal Liberalism in Recession and War* (New York: Vintage Books, 1995), 6–8, 267.

46. Housing Act of 1954, Public Law 560, *U.S. Statutes at Large*, Vol. 68, Part I, 622.

47. NYCHA, *First Houses, op. cit.*, 5.

48. Joel Schwartz, *The New York Approach: Robert Moses, Urban Liberals, and Redevelopment of the Inner City* (Columbus: Ohio State University Press, 1993), 50.

49. Martha Biondi, "The Struggle for Black Equality in New York City, 1945–1955." PhD diss., Columbia University, 1997, 342.

50. Congress, Senate, 79th Cong., 2nd sess., S. 1592, November 14, 1945, 3062.

51. "Ask Housing Units," *NYT*, August 2, 1945.

52. "Realty Men," *NYT*, March 28, 1947.

53. *Congressional Digest*, November 1946, 268; "Kings Legion," *NYT*, July 17, 1948.

54. Dreier, "Labor's Love Lost?," 343; "Federal Housing Activities," 260.

55. Johnson, "How They Licked the TEW Bill," 445–46.

56. Zipp, *Manhattan Projects*, 282.

57. Housing Act of 1949, Public Law 171, *U.S. Statutes at Large*, Vol. 63, Part I, 414.

58. Dreier, "Labor's Love Lost?," 331.

59. Zipp, *Manhattan Projects*, 12–14, 23–25, 79, 166, 275.

60. Housing Act of 1949, *op. cit.*, 416–21; Schwartz, *New York Approach*, 132. Charles Abrams advocated such a provision. *CHPC*, "Minutes of the Post-War Planning Committee Meeting," October 24, 1942, Reel 11, CAP.

61. Robert Caro, *The Power Broker: Robert Moses and the Fall of New York* (New York: Vintage Books, 1974), *passim* and 172–73, 260, 360–62, 411, 471, 610–13.

62. Jane Benedict, interview with author, June 1, 2000.

63. Robert Moses, "What Happened to Haussmann?" *AF*, July 1942.

64. Eric Darton, *Divided We Stand: A Biography of the World Trade Center* (New York: Basic Books, 2007), 27.

65. Robert Murray Haig, *Regional Survey of New York and Its Environs* (New York: Regional Plan Association, 1929), 1:33.

66. Kenneth T. Jackson, in Kenneth T. Jackson and Hillary Ballon, eds., *Robert Moses and the Modern City: The Transformation of New York* (New York: W. W. Norton, 2007), 68.

67. Haig, *Regional Survey of New York*, 41–44.

68. Hillary Ballon and Kenneth T. Jackson, "Introduction," in Jackson and Ballon, eds., *Robert Moses and the Modern City*, 66; Kenneth T. Jackson, "Robert Moses and the Rise of New York, " in Ibid., 68.

69. Schwartz, *New York Approach*, 86–87.

70. Caro, *The Power Broker*, 705.

71. Zipp, *Manhattan Projects*, 78–82; Martha Biondi, *To Stand and Fight: The Struggle for Civil Rights in Postwar New York City* (Cambridge, Mass.: Harvard University Press, 2003), 122; "Slum Bill," *NYT*, February 20, 1942.

72. Schwartz, *New York Approach*, 90.

73. Abrams to Governor Dewey, April 3, 1943, Reel 11, CAP. See also Schwartz, *New York Approach*, 93.

74. Oliver Ramsay, "Governor Fails," *The New Leader*, May 8, 1943.

75. Zipp, *Manhattan Projects*, 81–82; Biondi, *To Stand and Fight*, 122.

76. "Dewey Signs," *NYT*, April 4, 1943.

77. Plunz, *A History of Housing*, 255; "East Side," *NYT*, April 19, 1943.

78. "Negroes and Whites," *NYAN*, May 29, 1943.

79. Biondi, "The Struggle," 311.

80. "Negro Families," *The Survey*, n.d, 502, Box 8, Folder 6, ABP.

81. "Gas-House District," *NYHT*, April 19, 1943.

82. "City Has Its Displaced," *NYHT*, December 16, 1945.

83. Schwartz, "Tenant Unions," 423–24.

84. "East Side," *NYT*, April 19, 1943; Zipp, *Manhattan Projects*, 97–98.

85. Zipp, *Manhattan Projects*, 98–99.

86. Arthur Simon, *Stuyvesant Town, U.S.A.* (New York: New York University Press, 1970), 49–50.

87. Zipp, *Manhattan Projects*, 79, 88.

88. Dominic J. Capeci Jr., "Fiorello H. La Guardia and the Stuyvesant Town Controversy of 1943," *New York Historical Society Quarterly* 62., no. 4 (1978).

89. Biondi, *To Stand and Fight*.

90. CHPC, statement to City Council, May 19, 1943, and telegram to Board of Estimate, June 2, 1943, Box 8, Folder 6, ABP.

91. "Sues Stuyvesant Town," *NYT*, June 8, 1943; "Suit to Enjoin," *NYT*, August 16, 1943.

92. "Stuyvesant Town Upheld," *NYT*, March 18, 1944.

93. Biondi, *To Stand and Fight*, 123.

94. Biondi, "The Struggle," 318.

95. Biondi, *To Stand and Fight*, 124.

96. Brinkley, *The End of Reform*, 10.

97. A. Scott Henderson, *Housing and the Democratic Ideal: The Life and Thought of Charles Abrams* (New York: Columbia University Press, 2000), 139.

98. Mark V. Tushnet, *Making Civil Rights Law: Thurgood Marshall and the Supreme Court, 1936–1961* (New York; Oxford University Press, 1996).

99. *Dorsey v. Stuyvesant Town Corp.*, 190 Misc. 187 (1947).

100. *Dorsey v. Stuyvesant Town Corp.*, 299 N.Y. 512 (1949), 515.

101. Ibid., 518.

102. Biondi, *To Stand and Fight*, 127–28.

103. *Dorsey v. Stuyvesant Town Corp.*, 299 N.Y. 512 (1949), 518.

104. Sugrue, *Origins of the Urban Crisis*, Chapter 8; Massey and Denton, *American Apartheid*, 92–94; Jonathan Rieder, *Canarsie: The Jews and Italians of Brooklyn against Liberalism* (Cambridge, Mass.: Harvard University Press, 1985), 179; Joseph Rodriguez, *City against Suburb: The Culture Wars in an American Metropolis* (Westport, Conn.: Greenwood, 1999), 110; Robert O. Self, *American Babylon: Race and the Struggle for Postwar Oakland* (Princeton, N.J.: Princeton University Press, 2003), 104, 167.

105. "Integration Troubles Beset Northern Town," *Life*, September 2, 1957, 43.

106. David Harvey, *Consciousness and the Urban Experience: Studies in the History and Theory of Capitalist Urbanization* (Baltimore, Md.: Johns Hopkins University Press, 1985), 42, 56.

107. Biondi, *To Stand and Fight*, 128.

108. *Dorsey v. Stuyvesant Town Corp.*, 299 N.Y. 512 (1949), p. 536; *Hirabayashi v. United States*, 320 U.S. 81 (1943).

109. *Dorsey v. Stuyvesant Town Corp.*, 299 N.Y. 512 (1949), p. 536.

110. "Stuyvesant Town," *NYAN*, January 26, 1952; "Battle in Black and White," *NYT* March 26, 2006.

111. "Negro Couple," *NYT*, August 12, 1949.

112. "Negroes to Stay," *NYT*, September 12, 1949; "Stuyvesant Town Barriers 'Broken,'" *NYAN*, November 5, 1949.

113. "Stuyvesant Town Acts," *NYT*, September 13, 1949.

114. "Group Hails Negroes," *NYT*, September 14, 1949.

115. "Munoz Marin's Foe," *NYT*, October 27, 1949.

116. Lee Lorch, email, September 24, 2011.

117. Biondi, *To Stand and Fight*, 129.

118. NYSCDH narrative, Box 8, Folder 12, ABP; NYSCDH Statement of Policy, Box 9, Folder 2, ABP. The initial members included the NAACP, the Urban League, the ACLU, the American Jewish Committee, the American Jewish Congress, the Citizens' Union, the Women's City Club, the International Ladies' Garment Worker's Union, and the Japanese American League.

119. "The Housing Act of 1949," Box 9, Folder 1, ABP.

120. Executive board minutes, September 7, 1950, Box 9, Folder 5, ABP; "Color Line Talks," *NYT*, June 30, 1950; "City Bills," *NYT*, March 2, 1951; "Bill Barring Housing Bias," *NYT*, March 15, 1951.

121. "Housing Unit," *NYT*, August 9, 1950.

122. "Teacher Fighting Bias," *NYT*, April 10, 1950. Metropolitan Life had refused Lorch's rent the previous fall. "Negro 'House Guests,'" *NYT*, October 22, 1949.

123. "Teacher Fighting Bias," *NYT*, April 10, 1950.

124. Charles Abrams, *Forbidden Neighbors: A Study of Prejudice in Housing* (Port Washington, N.Y.: Kennikat Press, 1955), 336.

125. Ibid., 335.

126. "Stuyvesant Town Drops Evictions," *NYT*, January 21, 1952; Biondi, *To Stand and Fight*, 135.

127. "Tenants against Discrimination," 16, Box 9, Folder 5, ABP.

128. Biondi, *To Stand and Fight*, 184–85.

129. "Tenants against Discrimination," 17–18, Box 9, Folder 5, ABP.

130. Biondi, *To Stand and Fight*, 134.

131. Patricia C. Kenschaft, *Change Is Possible: Stories of Women and Minorities in Mathematics* (Providence, R.I.: American Mathematical Society, 2005), 17–21; Karen Anderson, *Little Rock: Race and Resistance at Central High School* (Princeton, N.J.: Princeton University Press, 2010), 2, 82–83.

132. Frances Goldin, interview with author, February 11, 2001.

133. Ronald Lawson, Stephen Barton, and Jenna Weissman Joselit, "From Kitchen to Storefront: Women in the Tenant Movement," in Gerda Wekerle, ed., *New Space for Women* (Boulder, Co.: Westview Press, 1980), 262.

134. Biondi, *To Stand and Fight*, 127, 130, 134.

135. Caro, *The Power Broker*, 707.

136. "Brown's Housing Bill," *NYAN*, June 15, 1957; Virginia Sánchez Korrol, *From Colonia to Community: The History of Puerto Ricans in New York City, 1917–1948* (Westport, Conn.: Greenwood Press, 1983), 33–35; Peter Kwong, *Chinatown, New York: Labor and Politics, 1930–1950* (New York: Monthly Review Press, 1979).

137. "Subcommittee on Housing," 3, Box 8, Folder 11, ABP.

138. "Let's Get at the Source," *NYAN*, November 29, 1941.

139. CWCCH, "The Beginnings," 1–3, 10–22, and "Purpose and Method," Box 7, Folder 1, ABP.

140. "Subcommittee on Housing," second document so titled, Box 8, Folder 11, ABP; "Report of the Sub-Committee on Housing of the Citizens City-Wide Committee on Harlem," Reel 11, CAP.

141. "Subcommittee on Housing," 13, Box 8, Folder 11, ABP.

142. "Report of the Sub-Committee on Housing," CWCCH, Reel 11, CAP.

143. "Financial problems," and correspondence from spring 1947, Box 8, Folder 12, ABP.

144. "Landlords Warned," *NYT*, June 4, 1946; "Rent Cuts," *NYT*, June 5, 1946; "Wagner Suspends," *NYT*, June 13, 1947; "Man Killed," *NYT*, January 13, 1948; "Harlem Fire," *NYT*, April 5, 1948; "4 Children," *NYT*, November 4, 1948; "One Killed," *NYT*, December 18, 1948.

145. "Harlem Tenants," CD, June 1, 1946.

146. "3-Day Conference," *NYT*, May 20, 1948.

147. "Hinds Is 'Unsung Hero,'" *NYAN*, March 20, 1965; "Harlem Mourns," *NYAN*, January 30, 1988.

148. "Civic Association," *NYAN*, September 7, 1946; "Group Airs," *NYAN*, May 10, 1947; "Clean-Up Drive," *NYAN*, October 11, 1947; "Let's Keep Harlem Clean," *NYAN*, January 15, 1949.

149. John Christopher Walter, *The Harlem Fox: J. Raymond Jones and Tammany, 1920–1970* (Albany, N.Y.: State University of New York Press, 1989), 86, 94–96; "Officials Outline," *NYAN*, January 18, 1947; "Find Violations," *NYAN*, October 16, 1948.

150. "A Phony 'Racial Issue,'" *NYAN*, March 11, 1950.

151. "Four at Hearing," *NYT*, April 9, 1949.

152. Freeman, *Working-Class New York*, 75.

153. Gerald Horne, *Black Liberation/Red Scare: Ben Davis and the Communist Party* (Newark: University of Delaware Press, 1994), 208, 225.

154. "Subversion Laid," *NYT*, May 29, 1948.

155. Biondi, *To Stand and Fight*, 139, 167.

156. "The Shame of New York," *TNAT*, October 31, 1959, 276.

157. Thomas Farrell, "Object Lesson in Race Relations," *NYT Magazine*, February 12, 1950.

158. New York City Housing Authority, *Annual Report 1941* (New York: NYCHA, 1941), 11, 22–23; Ira Rosenwaike, *Population History of New York City* (Syracuse, N.Y.: Syracuse University Press, 1972), 117.

159. Bloom, *Public Housing That Worked*, 86–89.

160. "Low Rentals," *NYT*, December 6, 1948.

161. "Projects Become Home," *NYT*, June 21, 1949.

162. Farrell, "Object Lesson," 16.

163. Morton Deutsch and Mary Evans Collins, *Interracial Housing: A Psychological Evaluation of a Social Experiment* (New York: Russell and Russell, 1951), 125, 127, 131.

164. Ibid., 25–28.

165. Schwartz, "Tenant Unions," 427.

166. "Seizure of Houses," *NYT*, December 22, 1946.

167. "O'Dwyer Rebukes," *NYT*, December 4, 1946.

168. "Barring of 4," *NYT*, March 13, 1947; "50 in Sit Down," *NYAN*, March 15, 1947; "Mix-Up on Housing," *NYT*, 14 March 1947.

169. "Housing Project," *NYT*, September 18, 1944; CWCCH news release on Riverton, n.d., Box 8, Folder 6, ABP; "20,000 Seek Homes," *NYT*, July 29, 1947; "Meeting notes, October 25, 1944," Box 8, folder 6, ABP.

170. Roi Ottley, "New York vs. Chicago," *Ebony* (December 1952), 16–20.

171. Ibid., 18.

172. Ted Poston, "New York vs. Chicago," *Ebony* (December 1952), 16, 23–24.

173. Ibid., 23.

174. Ibid., 23.

175. Ibid., 23.

176. Ibid., 24.

177. Rosenwaike, *Population History*, 133.

Chapter 3. "So Much Life"

1. James Torain, interview with author, October 17, 2001.

2. Census data show the blocks bounded by West 98th Street, Central Park West, West 100th Street, and Columbus Avenue with over 600 "nonwhite" households in 1940, and over 900 in 1950. U.S. Department of Commerce, Bureau of the Census, *1950 United States Census of Housing* (Washington, D.C.) New York City, Manhattan Borough, 31; U.S. Department of Commerce, Bureau of the Census, *16th Census of the United States, 1940, Housing Supplement to the First Series* (Washington, D.C.) New York City, Manhattan Borough, 31.

3. Donald Clarke, *Billie Holiday: Wishing on the Moon* (New York: Da Capo Press, 2002), 112; James Weldon Johnson, *Along This Way; The Autobiography of James Weldon Johnson*

(New York: Da Capo Press, 2000), 252; Camille Forbes, *Introducing Bert Williams: Burnt Cork, Broadway, and the Story of America's First Black Star* (New York: Basic Civitas, 2008), 153; Elinor Des Verney Sinnette, *Arturo Alfonso Schomburg, Black Bibliophile & Collector: A Biography* (Detroit, Mich.: Wayne State University Press, 1989), 34–35.

4. Torain, interview. Similar reminiscences from other ex-residents may be heard in Jim Epstein, *The Tragedy of Urban Renewal: The Destruction and Survival of a New York City Neighborhood* (New York: Reason.TV, 2011).

5. Norman Fainstein and Susan Fainstein, "The Politics of Urban Development: New York since 1945," *CA* 17, no. 6 (1984): 2–3. The figure covers 1946 to 1960.

6. Joshua B. Freeman, *Working-Class New York: Life and Labor since World War II* (New York: The New Press, 2000), 124.

7. David M. Gordon, Richard Edwards, and Michael Reich, *Segmented Work, Divided Workers: The Historical Transformation of the Labor in the United States* (New York: Cambridge University Press, 1982), 165–90.

8. Ibid., 197.

9. Ellen Schrecker, *Many Are the Crimes: McCarthyism in America* (Princeton, N.J.: Princeton University Press, 1999), *passim* and 196–200, 203, 206–9, 383–89; *Dennis v. United States* 341 U.S. 494 (1951).

10. Freeman, *Working-Class New York*, 74–85.

11. Ibid., 93–94.

12. Kenneth T. Jackson, *The Crabgrass Frontier: The Suburbanization of the United States* (New York: Oxford University Press, 1985), Chapter 5.

13. Ibid., 205.

14. Ibid., 236.

15. Ibid., 205–6.

16. Alex F. Schwartz, *Housing Policy in the United States* (New York: Routledge, 2006), 72.

17. Jackson, *Crabgrass Frontier*, 248–49, 293.

18. Raymond A. Mohl, "Race and Housing in the Postwar City: An Explosive History," *Journal of the Illinois State Historical Society* 94, no. 1 (2001): 8–30. Mohl's examples are drawn from owner-occupied districts of cities as well as suburbs proper.

19. "Better Homes Week," *Building Age* (May 1925): 103.

20. Eric Larabee, "The Six Thousand Homes That Levitt Built," *Harper's*, September 1948, 84.

21. Thomas Sugrue, *The Origins of the Urban Crisis: Race and Inequality in Postwar Detroit* (Princeton, N.J.: Princeton University Press, 1996), 218–19.

22. Elaine Tyler May, *Homeward Bound: American Families in the Cold War Era* (New York : Basic Books, 1988).

23. Lizabeth Cohen, *A Consumers' Republic: The Politics of Mass Consumption in Postwar America* (New York: Alfred A. Knopf, 2003), 141, 147.

24. Betty Friedan, *The Feminine Mystique* (New York: Norton, 1963), 18.

25. William H. Chafe, *The American Woman: Her Changing Social, Economic and Political Roles, 1920–1970* (New York: Oxford Press, 1972), 218; May, *Homeward Bound*, 178–81.

26. This is not to say it was the only norm. See Joanne Meyerowitz, "Beyond the Feminine Mystique: A Reassessment of Postwar Mass Culture, 1946–1958," in Joanne

Meyerowitz, ed., *Not June Cleaver: Women and Gender in Postwar America, 1945–1960* (Philadelphia: Temple University Press, 1994).

27. Dorothy Sue Cobble, *The Other Women's Movement: Workplace Justice and Social Rights in Modern America* (Princeton, N.J.: Princeton University Press, 2004); Dennis A. Deslippe, *"Rights, Not Roses": Unions and the Rise of Working-Class Feminism, 1945–80* (Urbana: University of Illinois Press, 2000).

28. Schrecker, *Many Are the Crimes*, 386.

29. Daniel Horowitz, *Betty Friedan and the Making of the Feminine Mystique: The American Left, the Cold War and Modern Feminism* (Amherst: University of Massachusetts Press, 1998).

30. Kate Weigand, *Red Feminism: American Communism and the Making of Women's Liberation* (Baltimore, Md.: Johns Hopkins University Press, 2001).

31. Amy Swerdlow, "The Congress of American Women: Left-Feminist Peace Politics in the Cold War," in Linda K. Kerber, Alice Kessler-Harris, and Kathryn Kish Sklar, eds., *U.S. History as Women's History: New Feminist Essays* (Chapel Hill: University of North Carolina Press, 1995).

32. Robert A. Beauregard, *Voices of Decline: The Postwar Fate of U.S. Cities* (Cambridge, UK: Basil Blackwell, 1993), Chapter 6; Amanda I. Seligman, *Block by Block: Neighborhoods and Public Policy on Chicago's West Side* (Chicago: University of Chicago Press, 2005), 54.

33. Jon Teaford, *The Rough Road to Renaissance: Urban Revitalization in America, 1940–1985* (Baltimore, Md.: Johns Hopkins University Press, 1990), 26 and Chapter 1; Beauregard, *Voices of Decline*, 86; Alison Isenberg, *Downtown America: A History of the Place and the People Who Made It* (Chicago: University of Chicago Press, 2004).

34. On "Communist cancer," see Schrecker, *Many Are the Crimes*,144; Joanne Sharp, *Condensing the Cold War: Readers' Digest and American Identity* (Minneapolis: University of Minnesota Press, 2000), 99; Philip Jenkins, *The Cold War at Home: The Red Scare in Pennsylvania, 1945–1960* (Durham: University of North Carolina Press, 1999), 163.

35. Susan Sontag, *Illness as Metaphor* (New York: Farrar, Straus, and Giroux, 1977), 35, 74.

36. Isenberg, *Downtown America*, Chapter 5.

37. Ira Rosenwaike, *Population History of New York City* (Syracuse, N.Y.: Syracuse University Press, 1972), 135–36.

38. Charles Hewitt, "Welcome, Paupers and Crime: Porto Rico's Shocking Gift to the United States," *Scribner's Commentator* (March 1940): 11–17

39. Angelo Falcon, "A History of Puerto Rican Politics in New York City: 1860s to 1945," in James Jennings and Monte Rivera, eds., *Puerto Rican Politics in Urban America* (Westport, Conn.: Greenwood Press, 1984), 37.

40. Sugrue, *Origins*, 79, 217, 227; Thomas Sugrue, *Sweet Land of Liberty: The Forgotten Struggle for Civil Rights in the North* (New York: Random House, 2008), 205, 226; Wendell E. Pritchett, *Brownsville, Brooklyn: Blacks, Jews and the Changing Face of the Ghetto* (Chicago: University of Chicago Press, 2002), 83, 89–90.

41. Federico Pagani in Carlos Ortiz, *Machito: A Latin Jazz Legacy* (New York: Icarus Films, 1987).

42. "Steps to End Peril," *NYT*, July 7, 1952.

43. See, e.g., "Better Care," *NYT*, November 12, 1947; "City Puerto Ricans," *NYT*, October 3, 1949; "City Puerto Ricans," *NYT*, October 4, 1949; "Segregation Rise," *NYT*, February 11, 1953; "Puerto Rican Will," *NYT*, February 25, 1953.

44. Anthony Jackson, *A Place Called Home: A History of Low-Cost Housing in Manhattan* (Cambridge, Mass.: MIT Press, 1976), 235–36; Pritchett, *Brownsville, Brooklyn*, 159; Fainstein and Fainstein, "Politics of Urban Development," 10.

45. Beauregard, *Voices of Decline*, 96–100; Robert Fishman, "The Metropolitan Tradition in American Planning," in Robert Fishman, ed., *The American Planning Tradition: Culture and Policy* (Washington, D.C.: The Woodrow Wilson Center Press, 2000), 65–76; John L. Thomas, "Holding the Middle Ground," in Fishman, *American Planning Tradition*, 33–35.

46. Lewis Mumford, *The Culture of Cities* (London: Secker and Warburg, 1938), 161.

47. "Depression, War," *CDS*, November 30, 1960.

48. Joel Schwartz, *The New York Approach: Robert Moses, Urban Liberals, and Redevelopment of the Inner City* (Columbus: Ohio State University Press, 1993), 155–57.

49. Ibid., 175.

50. U.S. Department of Commerce, 1950, op. cit., 31, Tract 211, Blocks 3 and 4.

51. "Force Delay," *DW*, October 26, 1951.

52. "Housing Conference," *DW*, January 19, 1953.

53. James Glanz and Eric Lipton, *City in the Sky: The Rise and Fall of the World Trade Center* (New York: Henry Holt, 2003), 19; Ortiz, *Machito*.

54. "School for Gardeners," *NYAN*, September 22, 1951; "Manhattanville Tenants," *DW* 25, April 1952; Senate Committee on the Judiciary, Subcommittee on Immigration and Naturalization, *Communist Activities among Alien and National Groups: Hearings on S. 1832* 81st Cong., 1st sess., Part 2, 583.

55. "Bill Stanley," *DW*, January 2, 1980; "Hunger March," *NYAN*, December 17, 1949; "Jobless Plan," *NYAN*, March 4, 1950; "Builders Plan," *NYAN*, June 17, 1950; "Stichman Picketed," *NYT*, July 23, 1952 . The organizational names oscillated; sometimes Manhattan Tenants Council was used.

56. "Force Delay," *DW*, October 26, 1951.

57. "Eviction Project Blocked," *DW*, November 16, 1951.

58. Joel Schwartz, "Tenant Power in the Liberal City, 1943–1971," in Ronald Lawson and Mark Naison. eds., *The Tenant Movement in New York City, 1904–1984* (New Brunswick, N.J.: Rutgers University Press, 1986), 158.

59. Ibid., 159.

60. New York Committee on Slum Clearance, *Title I Slum Clearance Progress* (New York: Committee on Slum Clearance, 1958), 9.

61. "Harlem Tenants," *Freedom*, March 1, 1953; "Tenants Council," *NYAN*, December 3, 1955.

62. Joel Schwartz, *The New York Approach*, 175.

63. Jeff Saltzman, quoted in Steve Anderson, "Cross Bronx Expressway," http://www.nycroads.com/roads/cross-bronx/ (accessed August 11, 2004).

64. Ray Bromley, "Not So Simple! Caro, Moses and the Impact of the Cross-Bronx Expressway," *Bronx County Historical Society Journal* 35, no.1 (1988): 15–16.

65. Robert Caro, *The Power Broker: Robert Moses and the Fall of New York* (New York: Vintage Books, 1974), 19, 171, 318, 492, 545–46, 562–63.

66. Richard Plunz, *A History of Housing in New York City: Dwelling Type and Social Change in the American Metropolis* (New York: Columbia University Press, 1990), 131.

67. Ibid., 40–41.

68. Ibid., 132.

69. Deborah Dash Moore, *At Home in America: Second Generation New York Jews* (New York: Columbia University Press, 1981), 61, Chapters 2 and 3.

70. Louis Wirth, "Urbanism as a Way of Life," *American Journal of Sociology* 44, no. 1 (July 1938): 17.

71. Robert Murray Haig, *Regional Survey of New York and Its Environs* (New York: Regional Plan Association, 1929), 1:39–40.

72. David McCullough, Edward Gray, and Mark Oberhaus, "The World That Moses Built" (Washington, D.C.: PBS Video, 1988).

73. Marshall Sklare, "Jews, Ethnics and the American City," *Commentary*, April 1972, 72.

74. Grace Paley, "Midrash on Happiness," in *Long Walks and Intimate Talks* (New York: The Feminist Press at the City University of New York, 1991), 6. Paley's participation in the tenant movement was reported by Frances Goldin, interview with author, January 8, 2001, and August 23, 2002.

75. Torain, interview.

76. Ibid.

77. Caro, *The Power Broker*, 886–94.

78. See Bromley, "Not So Simple!," 17–19.

79. Ibid., 18.

80. Caro, *The Power Broker*, 853–55.

81. Ibid., 859.

82. Ibid., 878.

83. Ibid., 860–62.

84. Caro gives the organization's name as "East Tremont Neighborhood Association," but that was its later moniker, according to Vivian Dee, cited below. See also Bromley, "Not So Simple!," 16–17; and "Engineers Charge," *NYP*, November 28, 1954.

85. Caro, *The Power Broker*, 865; McCullough, Gray, and Oberhaus, "The World That Moses Built."

86. Vivian Dee, interview with author, October 16, 2012.

87. Caro, *The Power Broker*, 855.

88. McCullough, Gray, and Oberhaus, "The World That Moses Built."

89. Robert S. McElvaine, ed., *Down and Out During the Great Depression: Letters from the Forgotten Man* (Chapel Hill: University of North Carolina Press, 1983), 5–7.

90. "Engineers Society," *NYP*, May 14, 1953.

91. Caro, *The Power Broker*, 874.

92. Ibid., 876.

93. Ibid., 846.

94. Ibid., 878.

95. Berman, *All That Is Solid*, 294.

96. Gary Belkin and Nat Hiken, *Car 54, Where Are You?*, Episode 5, "I Won't Go," original air date October 15, 1961 (Los Angeles: Republican Home Pictures Video, 1990).

97. Berman, *All That Is Solid*, 295.

98. Marshall Berman, "Buildings Are Judgment," *Ramparts* 13, no. 6 (1975): 57.

99. Berman, *All That Is Solid*, 291.

100. Schwartz, *New York Approach*, 175; "Demolitions Pose Housing Problem," *NYT*, June 26, 1955.

101. Schwartz, *New York Approach*.

102. Jeanne R. Lowe, *Cities in a Race with Time: Progress and Poverty in America's Renewing Cities* (New York: Random House, 1967), 83.

103. Jane Benedict, interview with author, June 1, 2000; Goldin, interview.

104. "Reminiscences of Hortense W. Gabel" (1983), 1.1–2.31, OHC.

105. Ibid., 2.32.

106. Ibid., 3.34–36.

107. Ibid., 3.42.

108. Frances Levenson, interview with Jim Epstein, September 16, 2007; Wendell E. Pritchett, *Robert Clifton Weaver and the American City: The Life and Times of an Urban Reformer* (Chicago: University of Chicago Press, 2008), 154–55, 159.

109. "Reminiscences of Hortense W. Gabel" (1983), 5.71., 5.85.

110. Schwartz, *New York Approach*, 270–71.

111. Levenson, interview with Jim Epstein, September 16, 2007, and interview with author, June 23, 2012.

112. WCC, *Tenant Relocation at West Park* (New York: WCC, 1954), 1.

113. Stuart Svonkin, *Jews against Prejudice* (New York: Columbia University Press, 1997), 12, 23, 133, 145, 172.

114. Schwartz, *New York Approach*, 162.

115. Ibid., 161–62, 190–91.

116. Ibid., 191–92, 194; "Opposes Housing," *NYT*, October 8, 1951; "Hecklers Disrupt," *NYT*, December 8, 1951.

117. Schwartz, *New York Approach*, 191, 344; "Two Groups," *NYAN*, December 8, 1951; "League Wants" and "Manhattantown Debate," *NYAN*, December 15, 1951.

118. WCC, *Tenant Relocation at West Park*, 2; Levenson, 2012 interview.

119. Ibid., 6.

120. Ibid., 13.

121. Ibid., 10.

122. Ibid., 8.

123. Ibid., 4.

124. Torain, interview.

125. Jim Torain, email to author, June 6, 2012.

126. Elinor Black, "Manhattantown Two Years Later,"1956, Series XI, Box 42, Folder 8, WCC.

127. Ibid., 4.

128. Caro, *The Power Broker*, 967–69.

129. Black, "Manhattantown Two Years Later," 9.

130. Ibid., 5, 20.

131. Ibid., 5.

132. "Developing Housing Plans," *NYT*, June 7, 1956.

133. "Hardships Studied," *NYT*, November 18, 1952.

134. Caro, *The Power Broker*, 977.

135. Fred Cook and Gene Gleason, "The Shame of New York," *TNAT*, October 31, 1959, 287.

136. U.S. Congress. Senate. Committee on Banking and Currency, *FHA Investigation: Hearings* (Washington, D.C.: U.S. Government Printing Office, 1954), 3,097–3,122, 3,145–46.

137. Ibid., 3,123.

138. Ibid., 3,149.

139. Ibid., 3,163–66.

140. Caro, *The Power Broker*, Chapter 42.

141. Ibid., 1,005–7, 1,019–21.

142. Gene Gleason and Fred Cook, "Few Homes Built," *New York World-Telegram and Sun*, July 30, 1956.

143. Caro, *The Power Broker*, 1021–22.

144. Ibid., 1,055, 1,059–62. Fainstein and Fainstein, "Politics of Urban Development," 9.

145. "Partnership for Housing," *NYT*, September 22, 1951; Sarah Vogel, "Taming the Hydra," unpublished paper in author's possession, 2007, 18.

146. Fainstein and Fainstein, "Politics of Urban Development," 7.

147. "Mayor Sets," *NYT*, May 28, 1958; Samuel Zipp, *Manhattan Projects: The Rise and Fall of Urban Renewal in Cold War New York* (New York: Oxford University Press, 2010), 359; J. Clarence Davies III, *Neighborhood Groups and Urban Renewal* (New York: Columbia University Press, 1966), 119.

148. Anthony Jackson, *A Place Called Home*, 250–51.

149. Gabel, "Reminiscences of Hortense W. Gabel" (1983), 6.96–102.

150. *Housing Act of 1954*, Public Law 560, *U.S. Statutes at Large*, Vol. 68, Part I, 623; Charles S. Rhyne, "The Workable Program. A Challenge for Community Improvement," *Law and Contemporary Problems* 25, no. 4 (Fall 1960): 686–87, 691.

151. Cohen, *A Consumers' Republic*, 125–26.

152. Schwartz, New York Approach, 203; Winifred Armstrong and Barbara Earnest, *Park West Village: History of a Diverse Community* (New York: Park West Neighborhood History Group, 2007).

153. J. Anthony Panuch, *Building a Better New York: Final Report to Mayor Robert F. Wagner* (New York, March 1960), 35. Emphasis in original.

154. Ibid., 35–36.

155. Ibid., 6, 7, 12.

156. Herbert Gans, "The Human Implications of Current Redevelopment and Relocation Planning," *JAIP* 25 (February 1959): 16–17.

157. Jane Jacobs to Conrad Snow, March 25, 1952, in Max Page, ed., *Ideas That Matter:*

The Worlds of Jane Jacobs (Owen Sound, Canada: Ginger Press, 1997), 171–78; Peter Laurence, "The Unknown Jane Jacobs: Geographer, Propagandist, City Planning Idealist," in Max Page and Timothy Mennel, eds., *Reconsidering Jane Jacobs* (Chicago: American Planning Association, 2011), 20–35.

158. Jane Jacobs, "The Missing Link," *AF* 104 (1956): 132–33; Zipp, *Manhattan Projects*, 299–311.

159. Jane Jacobs, *The Death and Life of Great American Cities* (New York: Random House, 1961), 17.

160. Ibid., 6.

161. Committee on Un-American Activities, *Report on the National Committee to Defeat the Mundt Bill; A Communist Lobby*, 81st Cong., 2d sess., 1950, 8–9.

162. Benedict, interview; Laurence, "The Unknown Jane Jacobs," 23. The guild had become the Book and Magazine Union by Jacobs' time.

163. Benedict, interview.

164. "Composition of New Congress," *NYT*, November 8, 1950; "Candidates in the City's Primaries," *NYT*, August 17, 1952; "List of Candidates," *NYT*, August 11, 1954.

165. Benedict, interview.

166. Ibid.

167. Frieda Milgrim, interview with author, June 22, 2000; "Yorkville Tenants," *NYT*, January 18, 1956.

168. Zipp, *Manhattan Projects*, 166, 173–78, 184, 224.

169. Jerome Robbins and Robert Wise, dirs., *West Side Story* (United Artists, 1961); James Gilbert, *A Cycle of Outrage: America's Reaction to the Juvenile Delinquent in the 1950s* (New York: Oxford University Press, 1986), 193–94.

170. Zipp, *Manhattan Projects*, 214–15; Joel Schwartz, "Tenant Power," 158–59.

171. Zipp, *Manhattan Projects*, 216–30.

172. Steven F. Lawson and Charles Payne, *Debating the Civil Rights Movement, 1945–1968* (Lanham, Md.: Rowman and Littlefield, 1998), 100.

173. Benedict, interview.

174. Edwin "Tito" Delgado, interview with author, April 16, 2004.

175. "U.S. Challenges City," *NYT*, April 14, 1959; CSCDCBA, *An Alternate Plan for Cooper Square* (New York: 1961), 1.

176. Ibid., 1 and *passim*.

177. Jane Wood, interview with author, October 10, 2001. Wood was probably a Communist as well. Susan Cohen, interview with author, June 14, 2004.

178. Wood, interview; testimony of Tim Wood at Jane Wood memorial service, June 6, 2004.

179. Wood, interview; Norma Aviles, conversation with author, June 6, 2004.

180. "Gramercy Group," *NYT*, March 5, 1949; "Relocation Rule," *NYT*, May 2, 1959.

181. "4 Buildings," *NYT*, May 5, 1959.

182. Jane Benedict believed that she met Goldin through the CP or the ALP before they joined forces on housing. Benedict, interview with author, November 13, 2001.

183. Jo Freeman, *The Politics of Women's Liberation: A Case Study of an Emerging Social Movement and Its Relation to the Policy Process* (New York: David McKay, 1975).

184. Goldin, interview.

185. Minutes, December 9, 1957, Box 26, Folder 23, MCH; *New York City's Slum Clearance Committee: A Critical Study*, Box 2, Folder 2, MCH.

186. Minutes, April–July 1959, Box 4, Folder 6, MCH.

187. Ibid. Minutes of early meetings list several co-chairs, including Lynd, Sánchez, and Moody. Zipp, *Manhattan Projects*, 355.

188. Discussion at "New York/Utopia: The Labor Cooperative Housing Movement, 1919–1972," panel at the First Gotham History Festival, October 6, 2001, City University Graduate Center, New York, New York.

189. Plunz, *History of Housing*, 162–63.

190. Freeman, *Working-Class New York*, 112; author site visits.

191. Ibid., 112–13.

192. Ibid., 115.

193. Herbert Hill, "Black-Jewish Conflict in the Labor Context: Race, Jobs and Institutional Power," in Maurianne Adams and John Bracey, eds., *Strangers and Neighbors: Relations between Blacks and Jews in the United States* (Amherst: University of Massachusetts Press, 1999), 603.

194. Gloria Suckenick, "Miracle on 24th Street," *Tenant/Inquilino* (May 2001); "Penn South Mural," http://www.artmystic.com/psps.html (accessed August 12, 2004).

195. Freeman, *Working-Class New York*, 118.

196. Jacobs, *Death and Life*, 50–54, 394.

197. "A Community Erased," *NYT*, October 10, 2011. See also Peter Eisenstadt, *Rochdale Village: Robert Moses, 6,000 Families and New York's Great Experiment in Integrated Housing* (Ithaca, N.Y.: Cornell University Press, 2010), 121–23.

198. J. S. Fuerst and Roy Petty, "High-Rise Housing for Low-Income Families," *The Public Interest* 103 (1991): 120–23.

199. Win Armstrong, conversation with author, September 28, 2012.

200. East River, Penn South, and Seward Park together drove out over 5,000 households. Public-sector union co-ops at Park Row displaced about 400. Joel Schwartz, *New York Approach*, 175.

201. Quoted in Caro, *The Power Broker*, 738.

202. Freeman, *Working-Class New York*, 105.

203. "CIO Urges State," *NYT*, January 20, 1950; "State C.I.O. Seeks Curb," January 16, 1952; "Easing Rent Curbs," *NYT*, February 2, 1952; "CIO Denounces Albany's Record," *NYT*, March 25, 1955; "Harriman Plan," *NYT*, January 5, 1957; Nicholas Dagen Bloom, *Public Housing That Worked: New York in the Twentieth Century* (Philadelphia: University of Pennsylvania Press, 2008), 110; NYCHA, *Project Statistics December 1949*, 10; NYCHA, *Project Statistics December 31 1959*, 17.

204. Hilary Botein, "Labor Unions and Affordable Housing: An Uneasy Relationship," *Urban Affairs Review* 42, no. 6 (2007): 801–3.

205. "665 Violations," *NYT*, January 30, 1960; "Slum Tour," *NYT*, March 12, 1960.

206. NYCHA, *Home, at Last; The 1959 Annual Report of the New York Housing Authority*, 30.

207. "U.S.-Aid Tenants," *NYT*, May 19, 1955.

208. Barker's leftism is strongly suggested in "Congress Pressed on Red Labor Curb," *NYT*, June 5, 1953.

209. Here I disagree with an otherwise strong article by Lawson et al., which works the Save Our Homes phenomenon into the earlier pattern by arguing that men took the reins at Met Council. Ronald Lawson, Stephen Barton, and Jenna Weissman Joselit, "From Kitchen to Storefront: Women in the Tenant Movement," in Gerda Wekerle, ed., *New Space for Women* (Boulder, Co.: Westview Press, 1980), 263. Male chairmanship at Met Council was a short-lived anomaly in the life of an organization directed primarily by women.

210. Benedict, interview.

211. Goldin, interview.

212. Benedict, interview.

213. Jenny Laurie, conversation with author, 2001.

214. Benedict, interview.

215. Levenson, interview, 2012.

216. Lawson, Barton, and Joselit, "From Kitchen to Storefront," 263.

217. Sherna Gluck, *Rosie the Riveter Revisited: Women, the War, and Social Change* (Boston: Twayne, 1987), 265.

218. Ibid., 266; Cobble, *Other Women's Movement*, 13.

219. Cobble, *Other Women's Movement*.

220. Erik S. McDuffie, *Sojourning for Freedom: Black Women, American Communism, and the Making of Black Left Feminism* (Durham, N.C.: Duke University Press, 2011), 44–46, 85, 131, 160–92.

221. Goldin, interview.

222. Goldin, interview.

223. Benedict, interview.

Part II. Introduction to Part II

1. "Poor Hard-Hit," *NYT*, May 26, 1965; Joshua B. Freeman, *Working-Class New York: Life and Labor since World War II* (New York: The New Press, 2000), 143–47, 149; Jerald E. Podair, *The Strike That Changed New York: Blacks, Whites and the Ocean Hill–Brownsville Crisis* (New Haven, Conn.: Yale University Press, 2002), 9–13.

2. CPC, *Zoning Maps and Resolution* (New York: CPC, 1961), especially maps 8b, 12a, 12b, and 12c. Preliminary versions were drawn up starting in 1956. S. J. Makielski Jr., *The Politics of Zoning: The New York Experience* (New York: Columbia University Press, 1966), 85–92; Robert Fitch, *The Assassination of New York* (New York: Verso, 1993), 134–35; Joe Flood, *The Fires: How a Computer Formula Burned Down New York City and Determined the Future of Cities* (New York: Riverhead Books, 2010), 143–45. Robert Fishman argues that the damage to manufacturing industries was not inflicted deliberately. See "The Metropolitan Tradition in American Planning," in Robert Fishman, ed., *The American Planning Tradition: Culture and Policy* (Washington, D.C.: The Woodrow Wilson Center Press, 2000), 74–75.

3. Jon Teaford, *The Rough Road to Renaissance: Urban Revitalization in America, 1940–1985* (Baltimore, Md.: Johns Hopkins University Press, 1990), 124.

4. Ira Rosenwaike, *Population History of New York City* (Syracuse, N.Y.: Syracuse University Press, 1972), 136–37.

5. Esther R. Fuchs, *Mayors and Money: Fiscal Policy in New York and Chicago* (Chicago: University of Chicago Press, 1992), 19, 81–83; Teaford, *Rough Road*, 72, 80, 127, 141; "How New York Became a Fiscal Junkie," *NYT*, August 17, 1975.

6. Fitch, *Assassination of New York*, vii.

7. Ibid., 136–38; Flood, *The Fires*, 232; Peter Marcuse, "The Targeted Crisis: On the Ideology of the Urban Fiscal Crisis and Its Uses," *International Journal of Urban and Regional Research* 5, no. 3 (1981): 338–41.

8. Teaford, *Rough Road*, 124–25, 139, 141–43.

9. J. Anthony Panuch, *Building a Better New York: Final Report to Mayor Robert F. Wagner.* (New York, 1960), chart after 16, 35; Norman Fainstein and Susan Fainstein, "The Politics of Urban Development: New York Since 1945," *CA* 17, no. 6 (1984): 2–3.

10. "Summary of Fourth Annual Housing Conference," 11, Box 3, Folder 1, MCH.

11. Anthony Jackson, *A Place Called Home: A History of Low-Cost Housing in Manhattan* (Cambridge, Mass.: MIT Press, 1976), 256.

12. Hilary Botein, "New York State Housing Policy in Postwar New York City: The Enduring Rockefeller Legacy," *JOUH* 35, no. 6 (September 2009): 835–36.

13. Thomas Angotti, *New York for Sale: Community Planning Confronts Global Real Estate* (Cambridge, Mass.: MIT Press, 2008), 73.

14. Botein, "New York State Housing Policy," 838–40.

15. Office of the Comptroller, *Affordable No More: New York City's Looming Crisis in Mitchell-Lama and Limited Dividend Housing* (New York: 2004), 3.

16. Jackson, *A Place Called Home*, 258–59. Figures are rounded to the nearest thousand.

17. Black home buyers did encounter substantial animosity on Long Island. Martha Biondi, *To Stand and Fight: The Struggle for Civil Rights in Postwar New York City* (Cambridge, Mass.: Harvard University Press, 2003), 236–37.

18. "L.I. Realty Men," *NYT*, August 7, 1962.

19. "Minority Income," *NYT*, October 22, 1961.

20. City Commission on Human Rights of New York, "Report on Blockbusting," CORE Papers, Reel 15, Document 69, 4–5.

21. Freeman, *Working-Class New York*, 197; Podair, *Strike That Changed New York*, 18 and *passim*; Jonathan Rieder, *Canarsie: The Jews and Italians of Brooklyn against Liberalism* (Cambridge, Mass.: Harvard University Press, 1985).

22. "L.I. Group," *NYT*, October 11, 1961; "Integration Forces," *NYT*, March 19, 1962; "L.I. Realty Men," *NYT*, August 7, 1962.

23. City Commission on Human Rights, "Report on Blockbusting," 1, 4; Jack Wood to Members of the Civil Rights Housing Advisory Council, April 15, 1964, CORE papers, Reel 15, document 70, 0070; "Great Neck Housing," *NYT*, May 25, 1961; "L.I. Fight," *NYT*, October 23, 1961; "Integration Forces," *NYT*, March 19, 1962; "185 in Bronxville," *NYT*, November 13, 1963.

24. U.S. Bureau of the Census, *U.S. Census of Housing, 1960*, Vol. I, *States and Small Areas, Part 6: New Jersey–Ohio* (Washington: U.S. Government Printing Office, 1963), Table 12, 34–24. Calculated from New York–Northeastern New Jersey Standard Consolidated Area figures.

25. U.S. Bureau of the Census, *Census of Housing: 1970*, Vol. I, *Housing Characteristics for States, Cities and Counties Part 34, New York*, Table 8, 34–15. Calculated from New York–Northeastern New Jersey Standard Consolidated Area figures.

26. Ibid., table 8, 34–19.

Chapter 4. "Out of These Ghettos, People Who Would Fight"

1. "Rights March" and "Harlem Housing Ills," *NYT*, August 4, 1963.

2. For a start on this voluminous literature, see Steven F. Lawson, "Freedom Then, Freedom Now: The Historiography of the Civil Rights Movement," *American Historical Review* 96, no. 2 (April 1991); Charles Payne, *I've Got the Light of Freedom: The Organizing Tradition and the Mississippi Freedom Struggle* (Berkeley: University of California Press, 1995), 413–41; Komozi Woodard and Jeanne Theoharis, eds., *Freedom North: Black Freedom Struggles Outside the South, 1940–1980* (New York: Palgrave Macmillan, 2003); Jacquelyn Dowd Hall, "The Long Civil Rights Movement and the Political Uses of the Past," *JOUH* 91, no. 4 (2005); Thomas Sugrue, *Sweet Land of Liberty: The Forgotten Struggle for Civil Rights in the North* (New York: Random House, 2008).

3. Frances Fox Piven and Richard A. Cloward, "Rent Strike: Disrupting the Slum System," *The New Republic*, December 2, 1967, and *Poor People's Movements: Why They Succeed, How They Fail* (New York: Vintage Books, 1977).

4. Joel Schwartz, "The New York City Rent Strikes of 1963–1964," *SSR* 57, no. 4 (1983): 547, 556. See also Goldin and Schecter interviews *infra*.

5. "Legislative Bulletin—May 4, 1965," Box 12, Folder 4, MCH.

6. Schwartz, "Rent Strikes," 554.

7. Michael B. Katz, "Why Don't American Cities Burn Very Often?," *JOUH* 34, no. 2 (2008): 192–93.

8. Sugrue, *Sweet Land of Liberty*, 409–10.

9. Bayard Rustin, "From Protest to Politics," *Commentary* (February 1965): 25.

10. Martha Biondi, *To Stand and Fight: The Struggle for Civil Rights in Postwar New York City* (Cambridge, Mass.: Harvard University Press, 2003).

11. Adina Back, "Up South in New York: The 1950s Desegregation Struggles," PhD diss., New York University, 1997, 320–39; Joshua B. Freeman, *Working-Class New York: Life and Labor Since World War II* (New York: The New Press, 2000), 186, 190–91.

12. Freeman, *Working-Class New York*,189–90.

13. Ibid., 187–88.

14. Calculated conservatively from Ira Rosenwaike, *Population History of New York City* (Syracuse, N.Y.: Syracuse University Press, 1972), 136–37, 139–41. Figures are approximate because many Puerto Ricans were counted as white.

15. Joseph Kelley, "Racial Integration Policies of the New York City Housing Authority, 1958–1961," DSW diss., Columbia University, 1963, 224.

16. Harlem Youth Opportunities Unlimited, Inc., *Youth in the Ghetto: A Study of the Consequences of Powerlessness and a Blueprint for Change* (New York: HARYOU, 1964).

17. "Closeup: Rent Strike Leader," *NYP*, December 18, 1963. Jack O'Dell, interview with author, February 18, 2003.

18. O'Dell, interview; Gerald Horne, *Red Seas: Ferdinand Smith and Radical Black Sail-*

ors in the United States and Jamaica (New York: New York University Press, 2005), 71–74; Gwendolyn Midlo Hall, *Harry Haywood: A Black Communist in the Freedom Struggle* (Minneapolis: University of Minnesota Press, 2012), xxii.

19. Horne, *Red Seas*, 188; "Harlem Slum Fighter," *NYT*, December 31, 1963; "Rent Office," *NYAN*, December 19, 1953; Joel Schwartz, "Tenant Power in the Liberal City, 1943–1971," in Ronald Lawson and Mark Naison, eds., *The Tenant Movement in New York City, 1904–1984* (New Brunswick, N.J.: Rutgers University Press, 1986), 162; Schwartz, "Rent Strikes," 547; O'Dell, interview.

20. O'Dell, interview; Frederick Engels, *The Housing Question* (New York: International Publishers,1935).

21. O'Dell, interview.

22. Ibid.

23. Ibid.

24. O'Dell, conversation with author, June 29, 2004.

25. "Angry Tenants," *NYAN*, July 4, 1959; "Rent Strike," *TNY*, January 25, 1964, 20; "Harlem Volunteers," *NYT*, April 9, 1961.

26. "Live Rat," *NYT*, October 20, 1961.

27. "Pastor in Harlem," *NYT*, March 3, 1961.

28. "Rent Strike," *TNY*, January 25, 1964, 20.

29. Schwartz, "Rent Strikes," 548. On CORE's housing desegregation efforts, see Biondi, *To Stand and Fight*, 82–84, 237–39; Sugrue, *Sweet Land of Liberty*, 411–12.

30. "Collegians Help," *NYT*, July 14, 1963; "Harlem Back Lot," *NYT*, July 14, 1963; Danny Schechter, interview with author, February 5, 2003.

31. "City Buildings Aide," *NYT*, February 27, 1958; "Ex-Building Aide," *NYT*, "City Reorganizes," *NYT*, January 8, 1959; "City Is Reforming," *NYT*, March 11, 1959; "Slum Maneuvers," *NYT*, May 27, 1960.

32. CSS of New York, *Housing Legislation in New York State, 1958* (New York: CSS, 1958), 22–24; CSS of New York, *Housing Legislation in New York State, 1959* (New York: CSS, 1959), 96–99; CSS of New York, *Housing Legislation in New York State, 1960* (New York: CSS, 1960), 57–64; CSS of New York, *Housing Legislation in New York State, 1961* (New York: CSS, 1961), 53–56.

33. WLIB press release, October 22, 1961; Statement of Edward Dudley, November 1, 1961; Statement of Mayor Wagner for WLIB, n.d., all in Subject Files III Sub Series, Box 060303, Folder 8, Robert F. Wagner Papers, LaGuardia Community College. MacNeil Mitchell to Jane Benedict, March 15, 1962; Hortense Gabel, undated testimony; *Albany Report* 1, no. 1 (1962), Box 12, Folder 1, MCH; Act of Apr. 14, 1962, ch. 492, 1962 N.Y. Laws 2388.

34. "Building Violations," *NYT*, April 5, 1963.

35. "Women Spur City," *NYT*, April 15, 1963; "Ellen Sulzberger Straus," *NYT*, February 26m 1995; Rebecca Straus, conversation with author, March 5, 2003.

36. "Slum Complaints," *NYT*, April 26, 1963.

37. "Wagner Orders Stiff Slum Plan," *NYT*, June 27, 1963; "Inspection Begun," *NYT*, July 16, 1963.

38. Michael Lipsky, *Protest in City Politics: Rent Strikes, Housing and the Power of the*

Poor (Chicago: Rand McNally, 1970), 90; "Wagner Sets Up Housing Agency," *NYT*, February 27, 1962.

39. "Rentals Pay," *NYT*, February 28, 1961.

40. "Power over Rent," *NYT*, February 15, 1962.

41. "Wagner Sets Up Housing Agency," *NYT*, February 27, 1962.

42. Flyers and correspondence, March and April 1963; list of rally participants, Box 2, Folder 4, MCH.

43. "Harlemites Picketing," *NYAN*, July 27, 1963; "Tenants Picket," *NYAN*, October 19, 1963; "Only 200," *NYAN*, November 2, 1963; Joel Edelstein, "Rent Strike: What When How," Box 24, Folder 1, NSM. *Pace* the NSM account cited below, Edelstein and Schechter say Cherry started organizing independently before he allied with NSM.

44. Jennifer Frost, *An Interracial Movement of the Poor: Community Organizing and the New Left in the 1960s* (New York: New York University Press, 2001), 10–11; Payne, *I've Got the Light*, 103.

45. Schechter, interview.

46. Ibid.; "A Brief History of the Rent Strike in Harlem," n.d., Box 24, Folder 1, NSM; "Harlem Tenants," *NYT*, September 28, 1963.

47. Schechter, interview.

48. Ibid.

49. Ibid., "Join the Rent Strike," Box 8, Folder 14, NSM, and flyers in the Helen Garvy Collection, International Instituut voor Sociale Geschiedenis, refer supporters to both organizations and announce joint meetings.

50. "Tenants Picket," *NYAN*, March 18, 1961; "Say City's Taking," *NYAN*, October 13, 1962; "Leaders Question," *NYAN*, February 16, 1963.

51. Committee on Un-American Activities, House of Representatives, *Hearings on Communist Methods of Infiltration (Education, Part 9)*, 83rd Cong., 2nd Session, June 28 and 29, 1951, 5772.

52. "Brooklyn Increased," *TN*, December 1963.

53. "Spotlight," *TN*, June 1963; "July 4 Deadline," *NYT*, June 4, 1963; "Rents Withheld," *NYT*, December 1, 1963; "A Rent Strike Grows in Brooklyn," *Community News*, March 1964, Box 66, Folder 29, MCH; "Tenants Mount," *NYAN*, December 14, 1963. The Parkway-Stuyvesant Council's role in the Brooklyn escrow case can be deduced from the involvement of its officer, Stanley Leyden, who represented the tenants in court.

54. "8 Seized," *NYT*, August 22, 1963.

55. "110 Tenants," *NYT*, November 2, 1963.

56. "Harlem Boycott," *NYT*, November 5, 1963; "Rents Withheld," *NYT*, December 1, 1963; "Rent Strike," *NYT*, December 18, 1963.

57. Mark Naison, "The Rent Strikes in New York," *Radical America* 1., no. 3 (November–December 1967): 28.

58. "Rent Strike," *Ebony*, April 1964, 112.

59. "Rents Withheld," *NYT*, 1 December 1963.

60. Panuch, *Buliding a Better New York: Final Report to Mayor Robert F. Wagner* (New York, 1960), 35.

61. Ibid., 6.

62. "Closeup: Rent Strike Leader," *NYP*, December 18, 1963; "Rent Strike," *NYT*, December 18, 1963; "Rents Withheld," *NYT*, December 1, 1963.

63. "Powell Urges City Hall March," *NYT*, December 16, 1963.

64. Noel A. Cazenave, "Ironies of Urban Reform," *JOUH* 26, no. 1 (1999): 31.

65. "Bleak Day," *NYT*, December 26, 1963; "Harlem Tenants," *NYT*, January 1, 1964; "Rat Bites Son," *NYT*, January 3, 1964.

66. "Closeup: Rent Strike Leader," *NYP*, December 18, 1963; *NYT*, December 31, 1963.

67. Lipsky, *Protest in City Politics*, 80.

68. "Rent Striker Bids," *NYT*, December 25, 1963.

69. "Intensified Attack," *NYT*, December 30, 1963.

70. "110 Tenants," *NYT*, November 2, 1963.

71. "Harlem Rents Cut," *NYT*, October 12, 1963.

72. "150 Harlem Tenants," *NYT*, October 29, 1963; "Rents Withheld," *NYT*, December 1, 1963.

73. "City Action Urged," *NYT*, November 17, 1963.

74. Lipsky, *Protest in City Politics*, 62; Edelstein, "Rent Strike."

75. "Slum Rent Strike," *NYT*, December 31, 1963.

76. Lipsky, *Protest in City Politics*, 63–64.

77. Ibid., 92; Richard Carlton, Richard Landfield, and James Loken, "Enforcement of Municipal Housing Codes," *Harvard Law Review* 78, no. 4 (February 1965): 829.

78. "Intensified Attack," *NYT*, December 30, 1963.

79. "Wagner to Urge Albany," *NYT*, January 6, 1964.

80. "Reaction Is Mixed," *NYT*, January 7, 1964.

81. "City Plans Drive," *NYT*, January 11, 1964.

82. Lipsky, *Protest in City Politics*, 91.

83. Harold Birns to William Shea, December 19, 1962, Box 2, Folder 4, MCH.

84. "Court Halts Rent," *NYT*, January 9, 1964.

85. "March Is Planned," *NYT*, January 13, 1964.

86. Ibid.

87. "Lower East Side," *NYT*, January 12, 1964.

88. Frances Fox Piven, "Dilemmas in Social Planning: A Case Inquiry," *Social Service Review* 42, no. 2 (1968): 197, 201; Cazenave, "Ironies of Urban Reform," 36.

89. Noel Cazenave, *Impossible Democracy: The Unlikely Success of the War on Poverty Community Action Programs* (Albany: State University of New York Press, 2007), 39–40.

90. Ibid., 15.

91. Harold H. Weissman, "The Housing Program 1962 to 1967," in Harold H. Weissman, ed., *Community Development in the Mobilization for Youth Experience* (New York: Association Press, 1969), 46.

92. Ibid., 46–50.

93. Ibid., 50–51; "Lower East Side," *NYT*, January 12, 1964.

94. Frances Goldin, interview with author, January 31, 2003; "Lower East Side," *TN*, February 1964.

95. "Slum Complaints," *NYT*, January 20, 1964.

96. Lipsky, *Protest in City Politics*, 68.

97. "200 Rubber Rats," *NYT*, February 16, 1964.

98. "Governor Sends 'Rat,'" *NYT*, February 26, 1964

99. "Rent Cuts," *NYT*, March 3, 1964.

100. "Mayor Sets Parley," *NYT*, February 20, 1964.

101. Lipsky, *Protest in City Politics*, 71.

102. "City Officials Seeking," *NYT*, April 28, 1964.

103. "Who's Who in the Conference" and 1963 program, "Conference #4" folder, and 1964 program, "Conference #5" folder, Box 2 MCH.

104. Photo, Met Council archive.

105. Manual, March on Albany, Box 12, Folder 3, MCH; "Umbrellas Join Protest," *NYT*, March 11, 1964.

106. "Bess Stevenson," *CL*, June 1985; Jenny Laurie, conversation with author.

107. Bess Stevenson, interview with author, February 27, 2001. Marie Runyon had similar reports from tenants who entrusted Gray with money. Runyon, interview with author, February 7, 2001. Naison corroborated the charge of weak legal follow-up. Naison, "Rent Strikes," 33.

108. Although news clippings (cited in Chapter 3) document both Stanley's and Gray's activism through the 1950s, I have found no document that shows them working together.

109. "Met Council Diary," *TN*, October 1964.

110. O'Dell, interview; Goldin, interview.

111. Goldin, interview.

112. Minutes, August 10, 1964, Box 4, Folder 6, MCH; Benedict, interview.

113. Goldin, interview.

114. Schechter, interview.

115. Payne, *I've Got the Light*, 264.

116. Schechter, interview.

117. Ibid.

118. O'Dell, interview.

119. Goldin, interview.

120. Executive Board minutes, March 8, 1965, and correspondence with Pepe Sánchez, Box 4, Folder 6, MCH.

121. Frances Goldin to Executive Board, June 9, 1971, Box 4, Folder 2, MCH.

122. Goldin, interview, and email to author, July11, 2012; "45th Anniversary," *Cooper Square News*, Winter 2005.

123. Schwartz, "Rent Strikes," 554–55.

124. Ibid.

125. Weissman, "Housing Program," 52, 54.

126. Lipsky, *Protest in City Politics*, 79–80.

127. Ibid., 83.

128. Ibid., 72.

129. "Staff Personnel" sheet, Box 8, Folder 14, NSM.

130. Mandi Isaacs, "Harlem's Rent Strike and Rat War, 1958–1964," unpublished

manuscript in author's possession, 18; Minutes of Meeting at Mount Morris, March 1, 1964, Box 8, Folder 14, NSM.

131. Lipsky, *Protest in City Politics*.

132. Ibid., 138.

133. "400 Families," *NYAN*, March 29, 1964.

134. Brian Purnell, "A Movement Grows in Brooklyn: The Brooklyn Chapter of the Congress of Racial Equality (CORE) and the Northern Civil Rights Movement During the Early 1960s," PhD diss., New York University, 2006, 398–401, 436.

135. "Staff Personnel" sheet, Box 8, Folder 14, NSM.

136. "Buildings in the H.A.G. Area," n.d, but including dates up to June 1964, Box 8, Folder 14, NSM.

137. "Rent Strike Gets a Woman's Touch," *NYT*, March 20, 1964. On women's leadership in Puertorriqueños Unidos, a member organization in the strike committee, see Daniel Kronenfeld, "A Case History of a Block Association," in Weissman, "Housing Program," 35.

138. United States Department of Labor, Bureau of Labor Statistics, *A Socio-Economic Profile of Puerto Rican New Yorkers* (Washington, D.C: G.P.O., 1975), 63; Rosemary Santana Cooney and Alice Colón Warren, "Declining Female Participation among Puerto Rican New Yorkers: A Comparison with Native White Nonspanish New Yorkers," *Ethnicity* 6 (1979): 284, 288; Rosemary Santana Cooney, "Intercity Variations in Puerto Rican Female Participation," *The Journal of Human Resources* 14, no. 2 (1979): 232–33.

139. Freeman, *Working-Class New York*, 144.

140. For a seminal critique, see Jacquelyn Grant, "Black Women and the Church," in Gloria T. Hull, Patricia Bell Scott, and Barbara Smith, *All the Women Are White, All the Men Are Black, but Some of Us Are Brave* (New York: The Feminist Press, 1982).

141. Photos of organizers and protesters, "Rent Strike," *Ebony*, April 1964; Mandi Isaacs Jackson, "Harlem's Rent Strike and Rat War: Representation, Housing Access and Tenant Resistance in New York, 1958–1964," *American Studies* 47, no. 1 (2006): 61; O'Dell, interview.

142. Ronald Lawson, Stephen Barton, and Jenna Weissman Joselit, "From Kitchen to Storefront: Women in the Tenant Movement," in Gerda Wekerle, ed., *New Space for Women* (Boulder, Co.: Westview Press, 1980), 263.

143. Gillian Aldrich and Jennifer Baumgardner, *I Had an Abortion* (New York: Women Make Movies, 2005); Florence Rice, interview with Gerda Lerner, in Gerda Lerner, ed., *Black Women in White America; A Documentary History* (New York: Vintage Books, 1972), 275–84.

144. Florence Rice, interview with author, January 20, 2012; Subcommittee on Investigation of the Garment Industry, Committee on Education and Labor, *Hearings*, 87th Cong., 2nd Session, August 17, 18, 23, 24 and September 21, 1962, 166–68.

145. Rice, interview; Pamphlet, "Harlem Consumer Education Council," Florence Rice personal archive; "Black Womanpower," *New York Magazine*, March 10, 1969.

146. Laurie B. Green, "Challenging the Civil Rights Narrative: Women, Gender and the 'Politics of Protection,'" in Emilye Crosby, ed., *Civil Rights History from the Ground Up: Local Struggles, a National Movement* (Atlanta: University of Georgia Press, 2011), 56–57.

147. "A Friend of the Consumer," *NYT*, October 26, 1991; Aldrich and Baumgardner, *I Had an Abortion*.

148. "In Memoriam: Anne R. Bradshaw," *Tenant Talk* 2, no. 2 (2011): 4.

149. Ruby Kitchen, conversation with author, January 27, 2012.

150. "Queensbridge Committee," *NYAN*, November 7, 1964; "Housing Tenants Beware," *NYAN*, November 8, 1986; Rhonda Y. Williams, *The Politics of Public Housing: Black Women's Struggles against Urban Inequality* (New York: Oxford University Press, 2004), 175; Peter Marcuse, "The Rise of Tenant Organizations," *TNAT*, July 19, 1971, 51. Green's association with Gray can be traced in news articles including "Backstreet Demonstrate," *NYAN*, August 27, 1966, and "The Story of Youth," *NYAN*, 18 July 1970; "Housing Tenants," *NYAN*, November 8, 1986.

151. Emilye Crosby, *A Little Taste of Freedom: The Black Freedom Struggle in Claiborne County, Mississippi* (Chapel Hill: University of North Carolina Press, 2005), 137–38.

152. "Diary of a Rent Striker," *NYHT*, February 16, 1964.

153. Eric Garber, "A Spectacle in Color: The Lesbian and Gay Subculture in Jazz Age Harlem," in Martin B. Duberman, Martha Vicinius, and George Chauncy Jr., eds., *Hidden from History: Reclaiming the Gay and Lesbian Past* (New York: Meridian, 1989).

154. Deborah Martin, "Constructing the 'Neighborhood Sphere': Gender and Community Organizing," *Gender, Place and Culture* 9, no. 4 (2002): 336, 339, and *passim*.

155. Sonia S. Lee and Ande Diaz, "'I Was the One Percenter': Manny Diaz and the Beginnings of a Black-Puerto Rican Coalition," *Journal of American Ethnic History* 26, no. 3 (2007): 65 and passim.

156. Schwartz, "Tenant Power," 177.

157. "Rent Strike," *Ebony*, April 1964, 116–17; "E. Harlem Leader," *NYAN*, May 2, 1964.

158. Yolanda Sánchez, interview with author, February 6, 2012.

159. Vicki L. Ruiz and Virginia Sánchez-Korrol, *Latinas in the United States: An Historical Encyclopedia* (Bloomington: University of Indiana Press, 2006), 11–12; Arlene M. Dávila *Barrio Dreams: Puerto Ricans, Latinos and the Neoliberal City* (Berkeley: University of California Press, 2004), 33.

160. Arlene Harris Kurtis, *Puerto Ricans: From Island to Mainland* (New York: Simon and Schuster, 1969), 57. It is possible that this passage refers not to ASPIRA proper, which was incorporated in 1961, but to one of its precursors such as PRACA (Puerto Rican Association for Community Affairs) or the Puerto Rican Forum.

161. Jane Vélez, interview with author, February 17, 2012.

162. Flores, "Diary of a Rent Striker"; Lee and Diaz, "I Was the One Percenter," 65.

163. *NYT*, 31 December 1963.

164. Jerald E. Podair, *The Strike That Changed New York: Blacks, Whites and the Ocean Hill–Brownsville Crisis* (New Haven, Conn.: Yale University Press, 2002), 25; Lee and Diaz, "I Was the One Percenter," 68; Back, "Up South," 319.

165. Flores, "Diary of a Rent Striker."

166. Podair, *Strike That Changed New York*, 23–30.

167. Freeman, *Working-Class New York*,191.

168. "Violence Flares," *NYT*, July 20, 1964; "Screvane Links Reds," *NYT*, July 22, 1964.

169. O'Dell, interview.

170. "Screvane Links Reds," *NYT*, July 22, 1964; "Sutton Heads," *NYAN*, October 31, 1959; "School Walkout," *NYAN*, August 24, 1963.

171. Flyer for July 19 rally, Box 5, Folder 9, JHC; "'Guerilla War' Urged," *NYT*, July 20, 1964.

172. Jesse Gray, "Tenant News," Box 5, Folder 9, JHC.

173. "James Powell's Funeral," *NYAN*, July 25, 1964; "'Guerilla War'" *NYT*, July 20, 1964.

174. "Negroes' View," *NYT*, July 27, 1964.

175. Walter Thabit, interview with Matthew Lyons, Cornell University Libraries, 1989, 23.

176. Lipsky, *Protest in City Politics*, 72.

177. "Harlem Sit-In," *NYT*, January 22, 1965; "City Plans Single Phone," *NYT*, January 28, 1965.

178. Lipsky, *Protest in City Politics*, 72–73.

179. "City Will Force Repairs," *NYT*, January 24, 1965.

180. Lipsky defines the sample as a set of twenty buildings but notes that three did not harbor severe violations. Lipsky, *Protest in City Politics*, 154.

181. Ibid., 154–55.

182. Ibid., 143.

183. Weissman, "Housing Program," 61, 67.

184. "City Hall Crowds," *NYT*, January 24, 1964.

185. "City Rent Control," *NYT*, January 29, 1964; "City Council Ends Control," *NYT*, February 19, 1964.

186. Sugrue, *Sweet Land of Liberty*, 405; "Westsiders Wage," *CD*, December 7, 1963; "CORE in Rent Strike," *CD*, June 13, 1964; "Tenants Call Rent Strike," *WP*, March 17, 1964; "NECAP Is Considering," *HC*, January 6, 1964; "Settlement in North End," *HC*, June 30, 1964; "Rent Strikers' Case," *BAA*, March 10, 1964; "In Cincinnati," *BAA*, September 8, 1964.

187. O'Dell, interview.

188. George Breitman, ed., *Malcolm X Speaks: Selected Speeches and Statements* (New York: Grove Weidenfeld, 1965), 88–89.

189. O'Dell, interview.

190. Dean E. Robinson, *Black Nationalism in American Politics and Thought* (New York: Cambridge University Press, 2001), 37–38; Ula Taylor, "Elijah Muhammad's Nation of Islam: Separatism, Regendering, and a Secular Approach to Black Power after Malcolm X (1965–1975)," in Woodard and Theoharis, *Freedom North*.

191. Ifabayo Muhammad, interview with author, February 6, 2001.

192. "City's Slum Plan," *NYT*, February 13, 1964.

193. Isaacs Jackson, "Harlem's Rent Strike," 59–62.

194. State Legislative Bulletin, February–March 1964, Box 12, Folder 3, MCH.

195. CSS of New York, *Housing Legislation in New York State, 1964* (New York: CSS, 1964), v, 38–39; "Most Bond Issues," *NYT*, November 5, 1964; "5 Amendments," *NYT*, November 4, 1965.

196. On these dynamics in the abstract, see Joseph E. Luders, *The Civil Rights Movement and the Logic of Social Change* (New York: Cambridge University Press, 2010), 2–10.

197. Peter W. Colby and John Kenneth White, eds., *New York State Today: Politics, Government, Public Policy* (Albany: State University of New York Press, 1989), 11.

198. Piven and Cloward, "Rent Strike," 12. See also Naison, "Rent Strikes," 44.

199. Frances Fox Piven, interview with author, March 20, 2003.

200. Piven, interview.

201. Piven and Cloward, "Rent Strike," 13.

202. Martin Duberman, *Stonewall* (New York: Penguin Books, 1993), 273–74.

203. Schwartz, "Rent Strikes," 555–57.

204. Piven and Cloward, "Rent Strike," 13–14.

205. Schwartz, "Rent Strikes," 550, 554, 558.

206. Matthew J. Countryman, *Up South: Civil Rights and Black Power in Philadelphia* (Philadelphia: University of Pennsylvania Press, 2006), 57.

207. Jeanne Theoharis, "'I'd Rather Go to School in the South': How Boston's School Desegregation Complicates the Civil Rights Paradigm," in Woodard and Theoharis, *Freedom North*, 135; Angela D. Dillard, "Religion and Radicalism: The Reverend Albert B. Cleage, Jr., and the Rise of Black Christian Nationalism in Detroit," also in Woodard and Theoharis, 155.

208. Podair, *Strike That Changed New York*, 25.

209. O'Dell, interview; Schechter, interview; "Northern Pickets," *CD*, 12 March 1960.

210. See Countryman, *Up South*, 268–69.

211. Robert O. Self, *American Babylon: Race and the Struggle for Postwar Oakland* (Princeton, N.J.: Princeton University Press, 2003); Woodard and Theoharis, *Freedom North*; Countryman, *Up South*; Devin Fergus, *Liberalism, Black Power, and the Making of American Politics, 1965–1980* (Athens: University of Georgia Press, 2009).

212. Jesse Gray, Federation for Independent Political Action Conference, December 19, 1964, Box 15, "Housing/Tenants Rights" folder, JCH.

213. Ibid.

214. Rustin, "From Protest," 29, and "'Black Power' and Coalition Politics," *Commentary*, September 1966; see also Countryman, *Up South*, 296.

Chapter 5. *"A Lot of Investment, a Lot of Roots"*

1. Enrique Laraña, Hank Johnston, and Joseph R. Gusfield, eds., *New Social Movements: From Ideology to Identity* (Philadelphia: Temple University Press, 1994), 6–9.

2. Only 10 percent of the site families found new apartments in the neighborhood. Morningside Heights, Inc., *Relocation: Critical Phase of Redevelopment; The Experience of Morningside Gardens, New York City* (New York: Morningside Heights, Inc., 1957), 12.

3. Walter Thabit, *Morningside Renewal Progress*, 1972, report in author's possession, 22; "Depression, War" *CDS*, November 30, 1960.

4. "Progress Toward End," *The Morningside Citizen*, September 27, 1959, Box 6, Folder 9, CCC.

5. New York State Temporary State Housing Rent Commission, *Prospects for Reha-*

bilitation: A Demonstration Study of Housing in Morningside Heights, New York City (New York: 1960), 21; "City Decides to Take Over," *NYT*, February 10, 1960.

6. New York State, *Prospects for Rehabilitation*, 3, 6, and *passim*.

7. *Westsider*, June 28, 1979, in Box 5, Runyon folder, CCC.

8. Marie Runyon, interview with author, February 7, 2001, and March 18, 2003.

9. Ibid.

10. *Morningsiders United Newsletter*, July 1964, Box 6, Folder 13, CCC.

11. "The Next Six Years," 29, Box 1, Folder 1, CCC.

12. Eugene Laubach to MRC, June 4, 1968, "MRC 1969–78" folder, Marie Runyon personal archive.

13. HRB, "Summary Statement," January 11, 1963, Box 6, Folder 7, CCC.

14. "CU May Still," *CDS*, March 1963.

15. "Protest Columbia," *Morningsider*, January 30, 1964; "Morningsiders United," *Morningsider*, March 26, 1964.

16. Runyon to Collinses, August 12, 1964, Box 1, Folder 1, CCC.

17. Runyon, interview.

18. Jerry Avorn, *Up Against the Ivy Wall: A History of the Columbia Crisis* (New York: Atheneum Press, 1969), 39.

19. Runyon, interview.

20. "Morningside Tenants," *NYT*, March 12, 1965.

21. "CORE Founds," *CDS*, April 8, 1965; "Columbia Named," *NYT*, February 28, 1964.

22. Robert A. M. Stern, Thomas Mellins, and David Fishman, *New York 1960: Architecture and Urbanism between the Second World War and the Bicentennial* (New York: Monacelli Press, 1995), 858; "ARCH: Black Advocates," *PA* 49 (September 1968): 107.

23. Ronald Kolbe, "A Review of the Morningside General Neighborhood Renewal Plan," Spring 1965, Box 6, Folder 7, CCC.

24. Ibid.; "Uptown Renewal," *NYT*, April 23, 1965.

25. "Morningsiders United," *Morningsider*, March 26, 1964.

26. "Uptown Renewal," *NYT*, April 23, 1965.

27. "CU's Urban Renewal," *Morningsiders United Newsletter*, May 24, 1965, Box 6, Folder 13, CCC.

28. "Chamberlain Seeks," *CDS*, October 9, 1964.

29. Thabit, *Morningside Renewal*, 47; *Morningsiders United Newsletter*, April 13, 1967, Box 6, Folder 14, CCC.

30. MHI statement to Board of Estimate, March 11, 1965, Box 6, Folder 7, CCC.

31. MU newsletters and flyer, "A Residential Neighborhood / Nuestro Barrio está en Peligro!" Box 6, Folder 14, CCC.

32. *NYHT*, March 28, 1965.

33. *Voice of MOSTA*, September 12, 1967, Box 11, Folder 3, MCH.

34. "CU vs. Morningside Heights," *Columbia Owl*, March 20, 1968.

35. Thomas Bender, *The Unfinished City: New York and the Metropolitan Idea* (New York: The New Press, 2002), 204.

36. T. H. Marshall, *"Citizenship and Social Class" and Other Essays* (Cambridge, UK: Cambridge University Press, 1950). On New Deal social citizenship and its limitations,

see Nelson Lichtenstein, *State of the Union: A Century of American Labor* (Princeton, N.J.: Princeton University Press, 2002) and Alice Kessler-Harris, *In Pursuit of Equity: Women, Men and the Quest for Economic Citizenship in 20th-Century America* (New York: Oxford University Press, 2001); David Montgomery, *Citizen Worker: The Experience of Workers in the United States with Democracy and the Free Market during the Nineteenth Century* (New York: Cambridge University Press, 1993), 15, 50–51.

37. Bender, *Unfinished City*, 210.

38. Faculty Civil Rights Group, "The Community and the Expansion of Columbia University," 1967, Box 1, Folder 7, CCC.

39. Runyon, interview; "Morningside Tenants' committee" folder, Marie Runyon personal archive.

40. Thabit, *Morningside Renewal*, 24, 48.

41. Ibid., 55, 57.

42. CSCDCBA and Walter Thabit, *An Alternate Plan for Cooper Square* (New York, 1961), 1.

43. Marci Reaven, "Citizen Participation in City Planning: New York City, 1945–1975," PhD diss., New York University, 2009, 203.

44. Wendell E. Pritchett, *Brownsville, Brooklyn: Blacks, Jews, and the Changing Face of the Ghetto* (Chicago: University of Chicago Press, 2002), 67–72; Reaven, "Citizen Participation," 135–44.

45. Quoted in Reaven, "Citizen Participation," 170. METCOP's paper came out in 1949.

46. Reaven, "Citizen Participation," 87.

47. Goldin, interview.

48. Mark Naison, "From Eviction Resistance to Rent Control: Tenant Activism in the Great Depression," in Ronald Lawson and Mark Naison. eds., *The Tenant Movement in New York City, 1904–1984* (New Brunswick, N.J.: Rutgers University Press, 1986), 120.

49. Reaven, "Citizen Participation," 85, 111–14.

50. CSCDCBA and Thabit, *An Alternate Plan*, inside front cover.

51. Walter Thabit, interview with Matthew Lyons, Cornell University Libraries, 1989, 1–6.

52. Ibid., 6–7; Reaven, "Citizen Participation," 168.

53. "There Are Things," *VV*, November 1961.

54. Reaven, "Citizen Participation," 184.

55. Statement of Walter Thabit before CPC, September 23, 1963, Box 3, Folder 8, MCH; Reaven, "Citizen Participation," 185, 187.

56. "There Are Things," *VV*, November 1961.

57. CSCDCBA and Thabit, *An Alternate Plan*, 3.

58. On second ghettoes, see Arnold Hirsch, *Making the Second Ghetto: Race and Housing in Chicago, 1940–1960* (Cambridge, UK: Cambridge University Press, 1983).

59. CSCDCBA and Thabit, *An Alternate Plan*, 4.

60. Reaven, "Citizen Participation," 164.

61. CSCDCBA and Thabit, *An Alternate Plan*, 5, 6, 10.

62. Ibid., 6.

63. Ibid., 5–6. Emphasis added.

64. Ibid., 7.

65. Ibid., 11–37.

66. Ibid., 27.

67. Ibid., 28, 36.

68. "Cooper Square," *NYT*, October 25, 1961.

69. CSCDCBA and Thabit, *An Alternate Plan*, 47.

70. Ibid., 48.

71. Ibid., 64.

72. Thelma Burdick to Mayor Wagner, July 31, 1961, front matter, CSCDCBA and Thabit, *An Alternate Plan*.

73. Jane Benedict to Robert Wagner, August 30, 1961; Alfred Genung to Jane Benedict, April 4, 1962, Box 3, Folder 8, MCH.

74. Quoted in Reaven, "Citizen Participation," 121.

75. "Cooper Square," *NYT*, October,25 1961.

76. CSC *Newsletter*, July 1962, Box 3, Folder 8, MCH.

77. *CSC News*, June 1963, Box 3, Folder 8, MCH.

78. News release, July 29, 1963, Box 3, Folder 8, MCH.

79. Statement of Esther Rand before the CPC, September 23, 1963, Box 3, Folder 8, MCH.

80. Statement of Walter Thabit before CPC.

81. Ibid.

82. Reaven, "Citizen Participation," 241–44.

83. Steve Anderson, "Lower Manhattan Expressway," http://www.nycroads.com /roads/lower-manhattan/ (accessed August 13, 2004).

84. Jane Jacobs, *The Death and Life of Great American Cities* (New York: Random House, 1961), 377.

85. Lewis Mumford, "The Roaring Traffic's Boom," *TNY*, March 19, April 2, and June 16, 1955; "Cities Fit to Live In," *TNAT*, May 15, 1948. See also John L. Thomas, "Holding the Middle Ground," in Robert Fishman, ed., *The American Planning Tradition: Culture and Policy* (Washington: The Woodrow Wilson Center Press, 2000), 34–36.

86. Christopher Klemek, "From Political Outsider to Power Broker in Two 'Great American Cities': Jane Jacobs and the Fall of the Urban Renewal Order in New York and Toronto," *JOUH* 34, no. 2 (2008): 315–16.

87. CSC Newsletter, July 1964, Box 3, Folder 8, MCH.

88. "Songsheet," Box 3, Folder 9, MCH.

89. Goldin, interview.

90. "How to Get a Housing Project," *VV*, March 25, 1965; "Expressway 'Deal,'" *NYT*, March 25, 1965.

91. CSC Newsletter June 24, 1965, Box 3, Folder 9, MCH.

92. Goldin, interview.

93. CSCDCB and Thabit, *An Alternate Plan*, inside front cover.

94. "Songsheet," Box 3, Folder 9, MCH.

95. Goldin, interview.

96. Jerald E. Podair, *The Strike That Changed New York: Blacks, Whites and the Ocean Hill–Brownsville Crisis* (New Haven, Conn.: Yale University Press, 2002), 21.

97. News release, July 29, 1963, Box 3, Folder 8, *MCH*.

98. Lily M. Hoffman, *The Politics of Knowledge: Activist Movements in Medicine and Planning* (Albany, N.Y.: SUNY Press, 1989), 67; Thomas Angotti, *New York for Sale: Community Planning Confronts Global Real Estate* (Cambridge, Mass.: MIT Press, 2008), 275; Paul Davidoff, "Democratic Planning," *Perspecta: The Yale Architectural Journal* 11 (1967): 158.

99. Reaven, "Citizen Participation," 87.

100. Reaven, "Citizen Participation," 290–91, 314.

101. Quoted in Reaven, "Citizen Participation," 122.

102. Goldin, interview; Reaven, "Citizen Participation," 256–57.

103. Reaven, "Citizen Participation," 356–57; Angotti, *New York for Sale*, 121–23.

104. Joel Schwartz, *The New York Approach: Robert Moses, Urban Liberals, and Redevelopment of the Inner City* (Columbus: Ohio State University Press, 1993).

105. Norman Fainstein and Susan Fainstein, "The Politics of Urban Development: New York since 1945," *CA* 17, no. 6 (1984): 4–5.

Chapter 6. *"Territorio Libre"*

1. Trial transcript, Box 30, Folder 2, MCH; "Mock Trial," *TNY*, January 9, 1971, 22; "A Common Grievance," *TBP*, December 26, 1970.

2. "A Common Grievance," *TBP*, December 26, 1970; trial transcript, Box 30, Folder 2, MCH; "Mock Trial," *TNY*, January 9, 1971, 22.

3. Ira S. Lowry, ed., *Rental Housing in New York City: Confronting the Crisis* (New York: Rand Corporation, 1970), 6. A HUD study put the figure at 100,000. United States Department of Housing and Urban Development, *Abandoned Housing Research: A Compendium* (Washington, D.C.: HUD, 1973), 5.

4. Peniel E. Joseph, "The Black Power Movement: The State of the Field," *Journal of American History* 96, no. 3 (2009). Other studies of local activism include Jennifer Frost, *An Interracial Movement of the Poor: Community Organizing and the New Left in the 1960s* (New York: New York University Press, 2001); John MacMillan and Paul Buhle, *The New Left Revisited* (Philadelphia: Temple University, 2003); Annelise Orleck and Lisa Gayle Hazirjian, eds., *The War on Poverty: A New Grassroots History, 1964–1980* (Athens: University of Georgia Press, 2011).

5. Jerald E.Podair, *The Strike That Changed New York: Blacks, Whites and the Ocean Hill–Brownsville Crisis* (New Haven, Conn.: Yale University Press, 2002).

6. MacMillan and Buhle, *The New Left*, 3–4.

7. James Hunter Meriwether, *Proudly We Can Be Africans: Black Americans and Africa, 1935–1961* (Chapel Hill: University of North Carolina Press, 2002).

8. Stokely Carmichael and Charles Hamilton, *Black Power: The Politics of Liberation in America* (New York: Random House, 1967), 5.

9. Joshua B. Freeman, *Working-Class New York: Life and Labor since World War II* (New York: The New Press, 2000), 209.

10. Ibid., 210–11.

11. "Heating Protests," *NYT*, January 10, 1966.

12. Jon Teaford, *The Rough Road to Renaissance: Urban Revitalization in America, 1940–1985* (Baltimore, Md.: Johns Hopkins University Press, 1990), 170, 176. Freeman, *Working-Class New York*, 209.

13. Esther R. Fuchs, *Mayors and Money: Fiscal Policy in New York and Chicago* (Chicago: University of Chicago Press, 1992), 154, 161–62.

14. Robert Fitch, *The Assassination of New York* (New York: Verso, 1993), 122–23.

15. Teaford, *Rough Road*, 223.

16. "Mayor Warns," *NYT*, January 9, 1969.

17. Podair, *Strike That Changed New York*, 34–35.

18. Ibid., 36–42.

19. Freeman, *Working-Class New York*, 218–23.

20. Ibid., 222–25.

21. "Estimate Board Approves," *NYT*, May 21, 1965.

22. CSC position papers; CSC to Herbert Evans, December 9, 1965; CSC newsletter, December 20, 1965; press release, February 15, 1966, Box 3, Folder 7, MCH.

23. "East Side Group," *NYT*, October 13, 1965.

24. Agenda for Lindsay, May 11, 1966; sticker and flyers, Box 3, Folder 7, MCH.

25. "2 Groups," *NYT*, July 21, 1966; "Cooper Sq. Plan," *NYT*, July 26, 1966.

26. "The Square," December 25, 1966, Box 3, Folder 6, MCH.

27. "9 Arrested," *NYDN*, September 25, 1969.

28. *The Cooper Square Plan: Report for Discussion* (New York: CSC, 1986), 1, Box 3, Folder 6, MCH.

29. "Memorandum: Creation of a Community Planning Agency in West Harlem," May 4, 1966, Box 1, Folder 2, MCH.

30. Ibid. Emphasis added.

31. "Morningside Park Chronological History," Box 3, Folder 9, CCC; Stefan M. Bradley, *Harlem vs. Columbia University* (Urbana: University of Illinois Press, 2009), 58–59.

32. Columbia shared the park's playing fields fairly equitably in the early 1960s but then increasingly monopolized them. Stefan Bradley, "'This Is Harlem Heights': Black Student Power and the 1968 Columbia University Rebellion," *Afro-Americans in New York Life and History* 32, no. 1 (2008): 105.

33. "Columbia U Gym," *NYAN*, February 24, 1968.

34. "Community Discontent," *NYT*, March 3, 1968.

35. Jerry Avorn et al., *Up Against the Ivy Wall: A History of the Columbia Crisis* (New York: Atheneum, 1970), 39, 48.

36. Bradley, *Harlem*, 74.

37. Ibid., 77.

38. "Columbia Halting Work," *NYT*, April 26, 1968; "Trustees Drop Gym," *CDS*, March 4, 1969. Eventually the university built a gym on campus, below ground.

39. Timothy Tyson, *Radio Free Dixie: Robert F. Williams and the Roots of Black Power* (Chapel Hill: University of North Carolina Press, 1999), 190, 204–5, 283–84, 287–88.

40. "Black Panthers," *NYT*, July 28, 1968; "Historical Note," BPP. A short-lived Harlem organization calling itself the Black Panther Party was established two years earlier by a nationalist group, the Revolutionary Action Movement, which adopted the logo created by voting-rights activists in Alabama. Komozi Woodard, *A Nation within a Nation: Amiri Baraka (LeRoi Jones) and Black Power Politics* (Durham: University of North Carolina Press, 1999), 72; "Black Panthers," *NYT*, September 13, 1966. The New York Panther organization launched in 1968 was a branch of the nationwide party based in Oakland.

41. Alondra Nelson, *Body and Soul: The Black Panther Party and the Fight against Medical Discrimination* (Minneapolis: University of Minnesota Press, 2011), 90, 92; Brooklyn clinic, http://www.itsabouttimebpp.com/Chapter_History/images/New_York/nyork10_2.html and http://www.itsabouttimebpp.com/Chapter_History/images/New_York/nyork8_9.html (accessed March 31, 2012).

42. "2nd Police Spy," *DW*, January 27, 1971.

43. Cleo Silvers, interview with author, January 30, 2004.

44. Ibid.

45. Ibid.

46. Ibid.

47. Ibid.

48. Ibid.

49. Adina Back, "'Parent Power': Evelina López Antonetty, the United Bronx Parents, and the War on Poverty," in Orleck and Hazirjian, *War on Poverty*, 188–89, 195; Nancy A. Naples, *Grassroots Warriors: Activist Mothering, Community Work, and the War on Poverty* (New York: Routledge, 1998), 133.

50. Silvers, interview.

51. Claire Jean Kim, *Bitter Fruit: The Politics of Black-Korean Conflict in New York City* (New Haven, Conn.: Yale University Press, 2000), 61.

52. Silvers, interview.

53. Rhonda Y. Williams, "Black Women, Urban Politics and Engendering Black Power," in Peniel E. Joseph, ed., *The Black Power Movement: Rethinking the Civil Rights–Black Power Era* (New York: Routledge, 2006), 94.

54. Silvers, interview; Jonas Vizbaras, *Bronx Plan 1968–72: A Report on the Bronx Model Cities Neighborhood* (New York: Bronx Model Cities, 1972), 36.

55. Silvers, interview.

56. Ibid.

57. Stokely Carmichael and Charles Hamilton, *Black Power: The Politics of Liberation in America* (New York: Vintage Books, 1967), 172.

58. Graham Towers, *Building Democracy: Community Architecture in the Inner Cities* (London: UCL Press, 1995), 163.

59. Silvers, interview.

60. Ibid.

61. Seymour R. Kaplan and Melvin Roman, *The Organization and Delivery of Mental Health Services in the Ghetto: The Lincoln Hospital Experience* (New York: Praeger, 1973), xvii, 18–58; "Community Takes Over," *NYT*, March 6, 1969.

62. Silvers, interview.

63. Ibid.

64. Ibid.

65. "Rent Is Withheld," *NYT*, November 8, 1970.

66. Cheryl Foster notebooks, Box 1, Folder 12, BPP.

67. Silvers, interview.

68. Dhoruba Bin Wahad, "The War Within," in Jim Fletcher, Tanaquil Jones, and Sylvère Lotringer, eds., *Still Black, Still Strong: Survivors of the U.S. War against Black Revolutionaries* (New York; Semiotext(e), 1993), 30; Abiola Sinclair and Klytus Smith, *The Harlem Political/Cultural Movements, 1960–1970* (New York: Gumbs and Thomas, 1995), 65. See also Safiya Bukhari, *The War Before* (New York: The Feminist Press, 2010), 97, and Curtis J. Austin, *Up Against the Wall: Violence in the Making and Unmaking of the Black Panther Party* (Fayetteville: University of Arkansas Press, 2006), 277–78.

69. "People's Free Extermination Service," http://www.itsabouttimebpp.com/Chapter _History/images/New_York/nyork7_8.html (accessed August 22, 2010).

70. Nikhil Pal Singh, *Black Is a Country: Race and the Unfinished Struggle for Democracy* (Cambridge, Mass.: Harvard University Press, 2004), 203.

71. Figures are elusive, since no records were kept. Silvers estimates that more than one hundred buildings came under tenant control through VISTA, Model Cities, and Black Panther organizing in the Bronx.

72. Silvers, interview; Nelson, *Body and Soul*, 87.

73. Peter L. Zimroth, *Perversions of Justice: The Prosecution and Acquittal of the Panther 21* (New York: Viking Press, 1974).

74. Silvers, interview.

75. Johanna Fernández, "Between Social Service Reform and Revolutionary Politics: The Young Lords, Late Sixties Radicalism, and Community Organizing in New York City," in Komozi Woodard and Jeanne Theoharis, eds., *Freedom North: Black Freedom Struggles outside the South, 1940–1980* (New York: Palgrave Macmillan, 2003)258–64; Iris Morales, *Palante, Siempre Palante! The Young Lords* (New York: Columbia University Station, 1996).

76. Osha Neumann, *Up Against the Wall Motherf**ker: A Memoir of the '60s, with Notes for Next Time* (New York: Seven Stories Press, 2008), 63–64.

77. Fernández, "Between Social Service Reform," 264–69; Morales, *Palante*. On an early direct action campaign for sanitation, see Brian Purnell, "'Taxation without Sanitation is Tyranny': Civil Rights Struggles Over Garbage Collection in Brooklyn, New York during the Fall of 1962," *AANY* 31, no. 2 (2007).

78. Fernández, "Between Social Service Reform," 270–74; "Paint-Poison," *NYT*, March 2, 1969.

79. Silvers, interview; "Reminiscences of Iris Morales" (1984), 25–26, 87, OHC.

80. Fernández, "Between Social Service Reform," 270.

81. Silvers, interview.

82. Fernández, "Between Social Service Reform," 271–72.

83. "Reminiscences of Iris Morales" (1984), 87, OHC.

84. Jack Newfield, "Young Lords Do City's Work," *VV*, December 4, 1969; "Criticism Rising," *NYT*, December 26, 1969.

85. Newfield, "Young Lords."

86. Fernández, "Between Social Service Reform," 274; "New City Unit," *NYT*, March 18, 1970.

87. "Service Reduced," *NYT*, January 28, 1970; "Young Lords Seize Lincoln Hospital," *NYT*, July 15, 1970; Latino/a Education Network Service, "The Lincoln Hospital Offensive," http://www.palante.org/04LincolnOffensive.htm (accessed August 22, 2010); "Think Lincoln," *Rat*, October 6, 1970.

88. Fernández, "Between Social Service Reform," 276.

89. Tracye Matthews, "'No One Ever Asks, What a Man's Role in the Revolution Is': Gender and the Politics of the Black Panther Party, 1966–1971," and Angela D. LeBlanc-Ernest, "'The Most Qualified Person to Handle the Job': Black Panther Party Women, 1966–1982," in Charles Jones, ed., *The Black Panther Party Reconsidered* (Baltimore, Md.: Black Classic Press, 1998); Robyn Ceanne Spencer, "Engendering the Black Freedom Struggle: Revolutionary Black Womanhood and the Black Panther Party in the Bay Area, California," *Journal of Women's History* 20, no. 1 (2008).

90. Silvers, interview.

91. "Free the Panther 21," http://www.itsabouttimebpp.com/Chapter_History /images/New_York/nyork3_5.html (accessed August 21, 2010).

92. "People's Free Extermination Service"; Silvers, interview, and email March 5, 2004.

93. Johanna Fernández, "Denise Oliver and the Young Lords Party," in Dayo Gore, Jeanne Theoharis, and Komozi Woodard, eds., *Want to Start a Revolution? Radical Women in the Black Freedom Struggle* (New York: New York University Press, 2009), 273–74, 287–88.

94. Ibid., 288; Morales, *Palante*. See also "Young Lords Position Paper on Women," reprinted in *Rat*, October 6, 1970.

95. Fernández, "Denise Oliver," 289; Morales, *Palante*.

96. "Reminiscences of Iris Morales" (1984), 87, OHC.

97. "Institutions' Growth," *NYT*, October 20, 1969.

98. "The Great Co-op Boom," *MT*, April 25, 1970.

99. Marie Runyon, interview with author, February 7, 2001.

100. "Sit-in Delays," *TN*, September–October 1968, 2; "A Rally Urges Seizure," *NYT*, May 4, 1969; flyer, "500 Vacant Apts," Box 6, Folder 14, CCC.

101. Flyers, "We Just Took One Vacant Apartment," and "The Story of This Apartment," May 2, 1969, Box 1, Folder 8, CCC.

102. "Welfare Refugees," *NYDN*, May 2, 1970; "Hey!, Hey!," *MS*, May 18, 1970.

103. Runyon, interview.

104. "Squatter Movement," *NYT*, July 22, 1970; "CU Offers Tenancy," *CDS*, May 10, 1971.

105. Clarence Davies II, *Neighborhood Groups and Urban Renewal* (New York: Columbia University Press, 1966), 110–41; Robert A. M. Stern, Thomas Mellins, and David

Fishman, *New York 1960: Architecture and Urbanism between the Second World War and the Bicentennial* (New York: Monacelli Press, 1995), 725–30; "Segregated Slum," *NYT*, July 21, 1970.

106. Davies, *Neighborhood Groups*, 132–33; Rose Muzio, "The Struggle against 'Urban Renewal' in Manhattan's Upper West Side and the Emergence of El Comité," *Centro Journal* 21, no. 2 (2009): 121.

107. Senate Special Committee on Aging, Subcommittee on Involuntary Relocation of the Elderly, *Hearings*, 87th Cong., 2nd Session, 1962, Part 2, 229–30.

108. Davies, *Neighborhood Groups*, 138.

109. Marci Reaven, "Citizen Participation in City Planning: New York City, 1945–1975," (PhD diss., New York University, 2009), 204–5.

110. Davies, *Neighborhood Groups*, 142.

111. "Operation 'Move-In,'" *MT*, May 23, 1970; "The Other West Side Story," *TN*, November–December 1968, 2; "Don't Move Out," *TN*, April–May 1970, 6. ("Community Development, Inc." is likely an erroneous reference to Price's "Community Action, Inc."); Jane Benedict to Executive Board, June 29, 1970, Box 4, Folder 3, MCH; Housing Crimes Trial transcript, *op. cit.*, 13–14; "Police in Chelsea," *NYT*, July 21, 1970. Price's acquaintance with Runyon can be inferred from his plan to move families into 130 Morningside.

112. "Squatter Movement," *NYT*, July 22, 1970.

113. "A Large Family," *NYT*, October 11, 1970; *Society*, July/August 1972, 51.

114. "Police in Chelsea," *NYT*, July 21, 1970.

115. "Squatter Movement," *NYT*, July 22, 1970; "They Shall Not Be Moved," *WIN*, September 15, 1970.

116. Frances Goldin, interview with author, January 8 and February 11, 2001; "150 Police" *NYT*, August 3, 1970.

117. "We Won't Move," *TN*, May–June 1969; "No More," *TN*, October–November 1969; "On the Squatter Front," *TN*, June–July 1970; "Tenants Picket," *NYT*, December 16, 1969.

118. Martin S. Allen, "A Frontier Challenge to the Urban Landowner: Squatters in New York," *Urban Law Journal* 49 (1971–72): 330, 336.

119. "Squatter Movement," *NYT*, July 22, 1970.

120. "My Fighting Community," *Rat*, October 29, 1970.

121. William Wei, *The Asian American Movement* (Philadelphia: Temple University Press, 1993), 212–14; Silvers, interview; Carmen Chow, "I Wor Kuen in Chinatown New York," *Hawaii Pono Journal*, Special Issue, "Ethnic Studies Interim Conference," April 1971, 63; Rocky Chin, "New York Chinatown Today: Community in Crisis," *Amerasia Journal* 1 (March 1971): 13–14; "Chinatown and Its Problems" and "Serve the People," in *Getting Together*, February 1970; Carmen Chow, "I Wor Kuen: Righteous Harmonious Fist," *Gidra*, June 1971.

122. Muzio, "Struggle against 'Urban Renewal,'" 122–23, 129. Furniture installation and celebration can be viewed in Newsreel, *Break and Enter: (Rompiendo Puertas)* (New York: Third World Newsreel, 1970).

123. "Sisters Squatting," *Rat*, October 29, 1970.

124. "Women Take Over," *Rat*, February 6, 1970; "Pa Bell," *Rat*, July 15 –August 5,

1970; "Apartments for Rent," *Rat*, October 6, 1970; "Sisters Squatting," *Rat*, October 29, 1970; "How to Organize a Rent Strike," *Rat*, November 17, 1970.

125. "My Fighting Community," *Rat*, October 29, 1970.

126. Silvers was clearly influenced by her activist mother and grandmothers, and Oliver by her leftist parents.

127. Benita Roth, *Separate Roads to Feminism: Black, Chicana, and White Feminist Movements in America's Second Wave* (New York: Cambridge University Press, 2004).

128. Fernández, "Denise Oliver," 273–74, 285.

129. Back, "Parent Power," 188–89, 195; "New Parent Unit," *NYT*, October 4, 1963.

130. "Afeni Shakur," *Rat*, January 7, 1970; "To Those in Exile," *Rat*, February 6, 1970;

131. Charles Sherrod, quoted in James Forman, *The Making of Black Revolutionaries: A Personal Account* (New York: Macmillan, 1972), 276.

132. Pink flyer, Box 11, Folder 2, MCH.

133. "100 Rally," *CDS*, May 13, 1970.

134. *Rat*, December 17, 1970.

135. Extant minutes show a spike in new memberships averaging more than one hundred per month in the early 1970s. Minutes of Assembly, June 21, 1971, attributes this to strike actions. Box 1, Folder 4, MCH.

136. Marge DuMond, interview with author, February 28, 2005. Very similar terms have been used to describe Ella Baker's significance to young women in SNCC. Barbara Ransby, *Ella Baker and the Black Freedom Movement: A Radical Democratic Vision* (Chapel Hill: University of North Carolina Press, 2003), 256.

137. Claudia Mansbach, interview with author, April 19, 2004.

138. Susan Cohen, interview with author, June 14, 2004.

139. See, among others, Naples, *Grassroots Warriors*, chapter 5.

140. Joe Hyler, interview with author, April 25, 2004; Edwin "Tito" Delgado, interview with author, April 16, 2004; Jane Wood memorial service, June 6, 2004

141. Executive board minutes, June 28, 1971, Box 4, Folder 2, MCH; Press release, October 7, 1966, Box 26, Folder 19, MCH; Assembly minutes, December 18, 1967, Box 1, Folder 3, MCH; Assembly minutes, March 15, 1971, Box 1, Folder 4, MCH; Executive Board minutes, August 6, 1966; September 28, 1970; September 13, 1971; and April 17, 1972, Box 4, Folders 1–5, MCH.

142. Cohen, interview.

143. Goldin, interview.

144. Susan Brownmiller, interview with author, February 14, 2012.

145. Ibid.

146. Executive Board minutes, August 24, 1970, Box 4, Folder 3, MCH.

147. Kate Weigand, *Red Feminism: American Communism and the Making of Women's Liberation* (Baltimore, Md.: Johns Hopkins University Press, 2001), 151. Frances Beal, interview, Voices of Feminism Oral History Collection, Smith College.

148. Nancy Hewitt, "Feminist Frequencies: Regenerating the Wave Metaphor," *Feminist Studies* 38, no. 3 (2012). In this otherwise fine article, Hewitt misstates the relationship between radio-wave frequency and range as a direct rather than inverse one. I have amended the terms in my discussion.

149. Cohen, interview.

150. Kathleen A. Laughlin, Julie Gallagher, Dorothy Sue Cobble, Eileen Boris, Premilla Nadason, Stephanie Gilmore, and Leandra Zarnow, "Is It Time to Jump Ship? Historians Rethink the Waves Metaphor," *Feminist Formations* 22, no. 1 (2010).

151. Tamar Carroll, "Unlikely Allies: Forging a Multiracial, Class-Based Women's Movement in 1970s Brooklyn," in Stephanie Gilmore, ed., *Feminist Coalitions: Historical Perspectives on Second-Wave Feminism in the United States* (Urbana: University of Illinois Press, 2008), 197.

152. Delgado, interview.

153. Norma Aviles, conversation with author, Wood memorial.

154. Major Owens, Jane Benedict memorial service, October 22, 2005.

155. Delgado, interview.

156. Goldin, interview.

157. A 1969 study found more private than public tenant activity nationally, but that aggregate likely reflects a preponderance of data from New York. Thea K. Flaum and Elizabeth C. Salzman, *The Tenants' Rights Movement* (Chicago: The Urban Research Corporation, 1969), 9. Sources below indicate that in other cities, public tenant councils outdid organizations of private tenants.

Private housing tenants in Chicago, Baltimore, Washington, and other cities also organized in the late 1960s and early 1970s but won little palpable change. Peter Marcuse, "The Rise of Tenant Organizations," *TNAT*, July 19, 1971. On Chicagoans' frequent losses and meager gains, see "Bitter Tenants," *CT*, January 14, 1965; "The Battle of the Slums," *CD*, March 16, 1966; "Seize 6," *CT*, September 2, 1966; "More Facing Eviction," *CD*, September 4, 1966; "Tenant Groups," *CD*, August 21, 1967; "Garfield Tenants," *CT*, November 23, 1967; "Rent Strike," *CT*, December 21, 1967; "Westsiders in Court," *CD*, March 16, 1968; "Judge OKs Rent Strike," *CD*, August 25, 1971; Amanda I. Seligman, *Block by Block: Neighborhoods and Public Policy on Chicago's West Side* (Chicago: University of Chicago Press, 2005), 64–65, 206–207. Searches of other major city papers during this period yield similarly sparse results.

158. Flaum and Salzman, *Tenants' Rights Movement*, 33; Joe W. Trotter and Jared N. Day, eds., *Race and Renaissance: African Americans in Pittsburgh since World War II* (Pittsburgh, Pa.: University of Pittsburgh Press, 2010), 121–24; "St. Louis Protest," *CD*, March 4, 1969; "D.C. Tenants," *WP*, May 29, 1966; "Tenant Union," *WP*, November 18, 1966; "HUD Gives Tenants Voice," *WP*, November 18, 1967; "Tenants Help Plan," *WP*, March 3, 1969; "Tenants' Rent Strike," *WP*, March 4, 1969; "Tenants End," *WP*, October 30, 1969; "Tenant Boards," *LAT*, December 16, 1970, show significant public tenant council activity in St. Louis, Washington, and Los Angeles.

159. Rhonda Y. Williams, *The Politics of Public Housing: Black Women' Struggles against Urban Inequality* (New York: Oxford University Press, 2004), 155–228.

160. Sudhir Alladi Ventakesh, *American Project: The Rise and Fall of a Modern Ghetto* (Cambridge, Mass.: Harvard University Press, 2000), 54–60, 65–109.

161. "A Woman's World," *NYAN*, August 13, 1966; Nicholas Dagen Bloom, *Public Housing That Worked: New York in the Twentieth Century* (Philadelphia: University of Pennsylvania Press, 2008); "New Locks," *NYAN*, April 2, 1966.

162. Carroll, "Unlikely Allies."

163. Williams, *Politics of Public Housing*, 242; Andrew J. Diamond, "The Long March toward Neoliberalism: Race and Housing in the Postwar Metropolis," *JOUH* 36, no. 6: (November 2010): 925.

164. John H. Mollenkopf, *The Contested City* (Princeton, N.J.: Princeton University Press, 1983), 184–86, 192–93; Peter Medoff and Holly Sklar, *Streets of Hope: The Fall and Rise of an Urban Neighborhood* (Cambridge, Mass.: South End Press, 1994), 20–21; Mel King, *Chain of Change: Struggles for Black Community Development* (Cambridge, Mass.: South End Press, 1981), 68–72.

165. Rita Lakin et al., *Mod Squad*, Season 2, Episode 12, "In This Corner, Sol Alpert," original air date December 16, 1969.

166. "They Shall Not Be Moved," *WIN*, September 15, 1970.

167. Ibid.

168. Roy Rozenzweig and Elizabeth Blackmar, *The Park and the People: A History of Central Park* (New York: Henry Holt, 1992), 77; Catherine McNeur, "The 'Swinish Multitude': Controversies over Hogs in Antebellum New York City," *JOUH* 37, no. 5 (2011).

169. David Harvey, "The Future of the Commons," *Radical History Review* 109 (Winter 2010): 105–6. See also, in the same issue, Robert Gioielli, "'We Must Destroy You to Save You': Highway Construction and the City as Modern Commons."

170. E. P. Thompson, *Customs in Common* (New York: The New Press, 1993), 253, 271, 337.

171. "St. John's," *NYT*, October 29, 1967.

172. "Morningside House," *MS*, October 4, 1969; "Six Years," *MS*, May 18, 1970.

173. Mary Anne Brotherton, "Conflict of Interests, Law Enforcement, and Social Change: A Case Study of Squatters on Morningside Heights," PhD diss., Fordham University, 1974, 61–64.

174. Ibid., 66–67, 81–83.

175. "Squatters Score," *NYT*, August 1, 1970; Muzio, "Struggle against 'Urban Renewal,'" 124–25.

176. "The Squatters Come to Morningside," *Connection*, November 12, 1970.

177. Runyon, interview; Muzio, "Struggle against 'Urban Renewal,'" 124.

178. Brotherton, "Conflict of Interests," 90.

179. Ibid., 66, 76, 129–30, 135, 164; "12th Day," *MT*, August 8, 1970.

180. "Protesters Rally," *NYT*, July 27, 1970.

181. Brotherton, "Conflict of Interests," 61.

182. Trial flyers, Box 30, Folder 2, MCH.

183. Ibid.

184. Eleanor Magid, conversation with author, February 27, 2001.

185. Housing Crimes Trial transcript, 9, 10, and 14.

186. Reaven, "Citizen Participation," 217–18.

187. Housing Crimes Trial transcript, 5.

188. Ibid., 13–14. The "master plan" was likely the Lindsay Administration's proposed 1969 Plan for New York City.

189. Brotherton, "Conflict of Interests," 155; "Sit-in Delays," *TN*, September–October 1968.

190. Muzio, "Struggle against 'Urban Renewal,'" 125.

191. "Squatters Asked," *NYT*, June 14, 1971.

192. Allen, "A Frontier Challenge," 338–40.

193. "On the Squatter Scene," *TN*, September–November 1970.

194. Testimony of squatters and organizers, Wood memorial; "Squatter Movement Grows," *NYT*, July 22, 1970.

195. "150 Police," *NYT*, August 3, 1970; "4 Held," *NYT*, August 23, 1970; "14 Supporters," *NYT*, September 6, 1970; "Phone Company," *NYT*, October 6, 1970; "Chelsea Tenants," *NYT*, June 13, 1972.

196. Stern, Mellins, and Fishman, *New York 1960*, 80.

197. "Columbia Buys Sites," *NYT*, April 21, 2004.

Chapter 7. *"To Plan Our Own Community"*

1. ARCH, *West Harlem, Morningside: A Community Proposal* (New York: ARCH, 1968), 3, 7.

2. Yolanda Sánchez, interview with author, February 6, 2012.

3. "Nixon Tapes," *NYT*, December 14, 2003.

4. David Goldberg, "From Landless to Landlords: Black Power, Black Capitalism, and the Co-optation of Detroit's Tenants' Rights Movement, 1964–69," in Laura Warren Hill and Julia Rabig, eds., *The Business of Black Power: Community Development, Capitalism, and Corporate Responsibility in Postwar America* (Rochester, N.Y.: University of Rochester Press, 2012), 168.

5. Edward Christie Banfield, "Making a New Federal Program: Model Cities, 1964–68," in Allan Paul Sindler, ed., *Policy and Politics in America: Six Case Studies* (New York: Little, Brown, 1973), 129, 132.

6. Peter Siskind, "'Rockefeller's Vietnam'? Black Politics and Urban Development in Harlem, 1969–1974," http://www.gothamcenter.org/festival/2001/confpapers/siskind .pdf (accessed August 15, 2004).

7. Peter Siskind, "Shades of Black and Green: The Making of Racial and Environmental Liberalism in Nelson Rockefeller's New York," *JOUH* 34, no. 2 (2008): 245.

8. "Slum Plan," *NYT*, February 29, 1968; "Mayor Questions State," *NYT*, March 1, 1968.

9. "Single City Housing Head," *NYT*, January 16, 1966.

10. "Mayor and the Slums," *NYT*, November 17, 1966.

11. Metropolitan Council on Housing, *A Citizens' Survey of Vacant Land* (New York: 1964).

12. Vivian Dee, interview with author, October 16, 2012.

13. Michael N. Danielson and Jameson W. Doig, *New York: The Politics of Urban Regional Development* (Berkeley: University of California Press, 1982), 275–76.

14. Robert A.M. Stern, Thomas Mellins, and David Fishman, *New York 1960: Architecture and Urbanism between the Second World War and the Bicentennial* (New York: Monacelli Press, 1995), 999.

15. Ibid., 998–1,000; Jerald E. Podair, *The Strike That Changed New York: Blacks, Whites, and the Ocean Hill–Brownsville Crisis* (New Haven, Conn.: Yale University Press, 2002), 186–

87; Jewell Bellush, "Housing: The Scattered-Site Controversy," in Jewell Bellush and Stephen David, eds., *Race and Politics in New York City* (New York: Praeger, 1971), 123; "100 Protest," *NYT*, February 4, 1971; "Public Housing Is Fought," *NYT*, February 21, 1971; "Forest Hills Homeowners," *NYT*, May 21, 1971.

16. Danielson and Doig, *New York: The Politics*, 276–77;

17. Stern, Mellins, and Fishman, *New York 1960*, 997–98.

18. Podair, *Strike That Changed New York*, 187.

19. "'Bigot' and 'Liar,'" *NYT*, November 22, 1971; Bellush, "Housing," 124–25.

20. "A Silent Minority," *NYT*, November 23, 1971.

21. "Public Housing," *NYT*, February 21, 1971; Bellush, "Housing," 124–25.

22. "Scatter Sites," *TN*, September–October 1967; "Harambee," *TN*, January–February 1968; "100 Protest," *NYT*, February 4, 1971; Vincent J. Cannato, *The Ungovernable City* (New York: Basic Books, 2002), 511.

23. "The Battle of Forest Hills," *NYT*, February 20, 1972.

24. Stern, Mellins, and Fishman, *New York 1960*, 998–1,000; Danielson and Doig, *New York: The Politics*, 277; Bellush, "Housing," 1, 26; "B'nai B'rith," *NYT*, November 25, 1971.

25. Stern, Mellins, and Fishman, *New York 1960*, 1,000–1,001; Danielson and Doig, *New York: The Politics*, 277.

26. Noel A. Cazenave, *Impossible Democracy: The Unlikely Success of the War on Poverty Community Action Programs* (Albany, N.Y.: State University of New York Press, 2007), 87–95.

27. "What Are HAG's Specific Goals?" Box 8, Folder 14, NSM.

28. Cazenave, *Impossible Democracy*, 86, 93, 101–3, 107–14, 116.

29. "Anti-JD Agency," *NYDN*, August 16, 1964.

30. Frances Fox Piven, interview with author, March 20, 2003.

31. Cazenave, *Impossible Democracy*, 121–22, 129, 131–32.

32. John M. Goering, Maynard Robison, and Knight Hoover, *The Best Eight Blocks in Harlem: The Last Decade of Urban Reform* (Washington, D.C.: University Press of America, 1977), 5–10, 14.

33. Ibid., 19, 21–22.

34. Ibid., 13–18, 27–29, 52, 59.

35. Frances Levenson, interview with author, June 23, 2012.

36. Goering, Robison, and Hoover, *Best Eight Blocks*, 60–63, 70–75, 120–21.

37. Ibid.,15–16, 19–22, 26–27, 31, 34–36, 45–47,

38. Ibid., 5, 65, 96.

39. Ibid., 96–99.

40. Ibid., 105.

41. Ibid., 130–57,170–72, 187–89.

42. Ibid., 175–79, 182.

43. Siskind, "Rockefeller's Vietnam," 13–15.

44. Christopher Klemek, *The Transatlantic Collapse of Urban Renewal Postwar Urbanism from New York* (Chicago: University of Chicato Press, 2011), 200.

45. ARCH, *West Harlem*, unnumbered page.

46. ARCH, *West Harlem*, 19.

47. Ibid., 3, 7.

48. Ibid., 35.

49. Ibid., 19.

50. Author walk-through, July 6, 2004; Friends of Morningside Park, "Park History," www.morningsidepark.org./history.html (accessed July 6, 2004).

51. Walter Thabit, *How East New York Became a Ghetto* (New York: New York University Press, 2003), 7.

52. Ibid., 7, 45–48, 65–67.

53. Walter Thabit, interview with Matthew Lyons, Cornell University Libraries, 1989, 23.

54. Thabit, *East New York*, 21–22, 101–13.

55. Ibid. 103; Leo Lillard, interview with author, August 28, 2012.

56. Lillard, interview.

57. Leo Lillard Jr., "Model Cities, Model Airplanes, Model Trains," *JAIP* 35, no. 2 (1969): 103.

58. Thabit, *East New York*, 101–13,122–23.

59. Ibid., 57, 111.

60. Ibid., 125–27, 130.

61. Michael B. Katz, "Why Don't American Cities Burn Very Often?," *JOUH* 34, no. 2 (2008): 190; Goldberg, "From Landless to Landlords," 173, 175.

62. Thabit, *East New York*, 131–37.

63. Siskind, "Rockefeller's Vietnam," 4–5.

64. Ibid., 8–10.

65. Siskind, "Rockefeller's Vietnam," 7, 9; Abiola Sinclair and Klytus Smith, *The Harlem Political/Cultural Movements, 1960–1970* (New York: Gumbs and Thomas, 1995), 46.

66. "State Progresses," *NYT*, August 11, 1967; "State Project," *NYT*, October 12, 1967.

67. Siskind, "Rockefeller's Vietnam," 6.

68. "State Office Building," *NYT*, May 21, 1974.

69. Siskind, "Rockefeller's Vietnam," 25.

70. Eric Darnton, *Divided We Stand: A Biography of the World Trade Center* (New York: Basic Books, 2007), 90–92.

71. Robert Fitch, *The Assassination of New York* (New York: Verso, 1993), 136–37.

72. "The Changing City," *NYT*, June 5, 1969.

73. Frank Stricker, *Why America Lost the War on Poverty—and How We Can Win It* (Chapel Hill: University of North Carolina Press, 2007).

74. "Signing of Model Cities," *NYT*, November 4, 1966.

75. Bernard J. Frieden and Marshall Kaplan, *The Politics of Neglect: Urban Aid from Model Cities to Revenue Sharing* (Cambridge, Mass.: MIT Press, 1975), 82–85, 97–98, 125, 215–17; George Washnis, *Community Development Strategies: Case Studies of Major Model Cities* (New York, Praeger, 1974), 5.

76. Washnis, *Community Development*, 349–50.

77. Alice O'Connor, "Swimming against the Tide: A Brief History of Federal Policy in Poor Communities," in Ronald F. Ferguson and William T. Dickens, eds., *Urban Problems and Community Development* (Washington, D.C.: Brookings Institution, 1999), 110.

78. Cazenave, *Impossible Democracy*, 173–81; Frieden and Kaplan, *Politics of Neglect*; Bret Weber and Amanda Wallace, "Revealing the Empowerment Revolution: A Literature Review of the Model Cities Program," *JOUH* 38, no. 1 (2012).

79. Washnis, *Community Development*, 5–9; Thabit, *East New York*,138.

80. Washnis, *Community Development*, 68–69, 393.

81. Ibid., 35, 40–41, 43.

82. Thabit, *East New York*, 139.

83. Ibid.,113–14, 138–49, 378. Thabit allows that George Jaffee, a villain in Washnis' account, did a "fairly good job" in East New York, but under the earlier Vest Pocket program, not Model Cities.

84. Washnis, *Community Development*, 348–49; "Friction Slows Harlem," *NYT*, August 22, 1970; "Future Looks Bleak," *NYT*, January 18, 1973.

85. Sánchez, interview; Luis Antonio Cardona, *A History of the Puerto Ricans in the United States of America, Volume 2* (Alpharetta, Georgia: Carreta Press, 1998), 342–44.

86. Sánchez, interview; Jane Vélez, interview with author, February 17, 2012; Stern, Mellins, and Fishman, *New York 1960*, 869; narrative typescript on East Harlem Tenants Council, n.d., Box 1, Folder 20, James Weldon Johnson Community Centers Collection, Schomburg Center.

87. Sánchez, interview.

88. "E. Harlem Leader," *NYAN*, May 2, 1964 ; "Taino: 'Dream' Housing," *CL* 4, no. 2 (February 1979), and January 5, 2009.

89. Goering, Robison, and Hoover, *Best Eight Blocks*, 47.

90. Sánchez, interview.

91. Ibid.

92. Margaret Power, "Puerto Rican Nationalism, the Communist Party, and the U.S. Government during the Cold War: The Challenges of 'Domestic' Decolonization," paper presented at the Tamiment Library, March 28, 2012, 16–18.

93. Sánchez, interview.

94. Ibid.; Thea Martínez, interview with author, May 1, 2012; "Residents Protest," *NYT*, July 16, 1968; Lisa Kaplan, email to author, August 23, 2012; Lower East Side Coalition Housing Development, Inc., "Organization Profile," document in author's possession. The 1,600 figure includes the Campos, Bracetti, Coalition, Del Este, Seward Park Extension, Hernández, and Pueblo Nuevo developments.

95. Martínez, interview; Frances Goldin, interview with author, February 4, 2012.

96. Sánchez, interview.

97. Ibid.

98. Stephen D. Mittenthal and Hans B. C. Spiegel, *Urban Confrontation: City Versus Neighborhood in the Model Cities Planning Process* (New York: Institute of Urban Environment, 1970), 256–57.

99. Bellush, "Housing," 101–2, 107–8, 118; Jonas Vizbaras, *Bronx Plan 1968–72: A Report on the Bronx Model Cities Neighborhood* (New York: Bronx Model Cities, 1972), 21–22.

100. "Project in South Bronx," *NYT*, July 14, 1970; Vizbaras, *Bronx Plan 1968–72*, 17; *Data Development Book*, http://www.nyc.gov/html/nycha/downloads/pdf1/pdb2011 .pdf 4 (accessed March 24, 2012).

101. "The Restoration Corporation," *NYT*, December 16, 1976; David Rusk, *Inside Game/Outside Game: Winning Strategies for Saving Urban America* (Washington, D.C.: Brookings Institution Press, 1999), 25–26.

102. Thomas Angotti, *New York for Sale: Community Planning Confronts Global Real Estate* (Cambridge, Mass.: MIT Press, 2008), 102.

103. Harold DeRienzo, *The Concept of Community; Lessons from the Bronx* (Milano: IPOC, 2008), 46–47.

104. Brian Sahd, "Community Development Corporations and Social Capital: Lessons from the South Bronx," in Robert Mark Silverman, ed., *Community-Based Organizations: The Intersection of Social Capital and Local Context* (Detroit, Mich.: Wayne State University Press, 2004), 95, 104–7, 119.

105. Ibid., 104–6.

106. Joel Schwartz, "The New York City Rent Strikes of 1963–1964," *SSR* 57, no. 4 (1983): 557.

107. Janice Ruth Fine, *Worker Centers: Organizing Communities at the Edge of the Dream* (Ithaca, N.Y.: Cornell University Press, 2006), 25, 55–56.

108. Washnis, *Community Development*, 397. The total figure rose somewhat when Taino Towers and other delayed projects were finally completed.

109. Emanuel Tobier and Barbara Gordon Espejo, "Housing," in Gerald Benjamin and Charles Brecher, eds., *The Two New Yorks: State-City Relations in the Changing Federal System* (New York: Russell Sage, 1988), 469.

110. Lillard, "Model Cities," 103–4.

111. Martínez, interview.

112. Gil Scott-Heron, "Whitey on the Moon," *Small Talk at 125th and Lenox* (New York: RCA Records, 1970).

113. Joshua B. Freeman, *Working-Class New York: Life and Labor since World War II* (New York: The New Press, 2000), 119.

114. Peter R. Eisenstadt, *Rochdale Village: Robert Moses, 6,000 Families and New York's Great Experiment in Integrated Housing* (Ithaca, N.Y.: Cornell University Press, 2010).

115. Tony Schuman, "Labor and Housing in New York City: Architect Herman Jessor and the Cooperative Housing Movement," http://urbanomnibus.net/main/wp-content/uploads/2010/03/LABOR-AND-HOUSING-IN-NEW-YORK-CITY.pdf (accessed November 28, 2011), 4.

116. Suzanne Stephens, "High-Rise in Harlem," *PA* 76, no. 3 (n.d.): 65; "New York, NY: Design for a 1600-unit East Harlem Project," *AF* 134, no. 4, 44.

117. "New York, NY: Design for a 1600-unit," 44.

118. Stephens, "High-Rise in Harlem," 65–67.

119. Shirley Jenkins, interview with author, January 10, 2012.

120. Ibid.

121. Ibid.

122. Jenkins, interview.

123. William Dames, conversation with author, December 2011.

124. "Reminiscences of Abraham Kazan" (1975), Columbia Oral History Research Office, 471–72; Freeman, *Working-Class New York*, 120; Stern, Mellins, and Fishman, *New York 1960*, 969.

125. Stern, Mellins, and Fishman, *New York 1960*, 969–70; Betsy Brown, "Co-opting a Dream," *Empire State Report* (March 1977): 106.

126. Freeman, *Working-Class New York*, 120–21.

127. Schuman, "Labor and Housing," 7.

128. Freeman, *Working-Class New York*, 120–23; Brown, "Co-opting a Dream," 107–9; John Sayles, "At the Anarchists' Convention," in *The Anarchists Convention* (Boston: Little, Brown, 1979).

129. "Albany Pact," *NYT*, January 30, 2004.

130. Schuman, "Labor and Housing," 8.

131. Ibid., 7–8.

132. Ibid., 9.

133. "For Co-op Complexes," *NYT*, February 2, 2002.

134. "Electchester Getting Less Electrical," *NYT*, March 15, 2004.

Chapter 8. "A Piece of Heaven in Hell"

1. Staple Singers, "City in the Sky," *City in the Sky* (Memphis, Tenn.: Stax Records, 1974).

2. Ira S. Lowry calculated 189,000 ownerless units by 1968. Lowry, *Rental Housing in New York City: Confronting the Crisis* (New York: Rand Corporation, 1970). Thirty thousand more were abandoned the next year. "Housing Supply," *NYT*, February 8, 1970.

3. "Landlord Bids," *NYT*, May 24, 1968.

4. Stephen Barton, "The Urban Housing Problem: Marxist Theory and Community Organizing," *Review of Radical Political Economics* 9, no. 4 (1977): 17–21.

5. Peter Marcuse, "The Targeted Crisis: On the Ideology of the Urban Fiscal Crisis and Its Uses," *International Journal of Urban and Regional Research* 5, no. 3 (1981): 337–41.

6. "Rent Rise," *NYT*, April 25, 1969.

7. Ronald Lawson with Reuben B. Johnson III, "Tenant Responses to the Urban Housing Crisis, 1970–1984," in Ronald Lawson and Mark Naison, eds., *The Tenant Movement in New York City, 1904–1984* (New Brunswick, N.J.: Rutgers University Press, 1986), 210–11; "Revising Rent Control," *NYT*, February 10, 1970.

8. "Council Passes," *NYT*, June 28, 1970; Leif Johnson, *Lindsay's Rent Increase Plan* (New York: Met Council Community Improvement Fund, 1970) 2, 5–6, Box 7, no folder, MCH.

9. Acts of June 1, 1971, chs. 371–72, 1971 N.Y. Laws 1159–64.

10. Jane Benedict, interview with author, November 13, 2001.

11. Minutes, June 26, 1967, Box 4, Folder 4, MCH.

12. Minutes, April 30 –May 13, 1968, Box 1, Folder 4, MCH.

13. On dire finances, see minutes, January 8, 1968, Box 4, Folder 4, MCH.

14. Lawson and Johnson, "Tenant Responses," 212.

15. Michael McKee, interview with author, August 7, 2012; building updates and stapled list of buildings and assigned organizers, ca. 1971, Box 31, Folder 20, MCH; clippings and building flyers, Box 31, Folder 21, MCH.

16. Assembly agenda, July 20, 1970, Box 1, Folder 3, MCH.

17. McKee, interview.

18. Ibid.

19. Ibid.; Frances Goldin, interview with author, January 8, 2001, and November 17, 2012. McKee also recalled tension between Goldin and Peter Hawley and Dick Levenson during this period. McKee, interview.

20. Frances Goldin to Executive Board, June 9, 1971, Box 4, Folder 2, MCH; "Tenant Strike Report," September 27, 1971, Box 1, Folder 4, MCH. McKee made the motion under pressure from Benedict. McKee, interview.

21. McKee, interview; minutes, October 9, 1972, Box 4, Folder 1, MCH.

22. Minutes, December, Box 4, Folder 2 MCH; and October 23, 1972, Box 4, Folder 1, MCH.

23. Such a turnabout is suggested although not proven by two articles in *Party Affairs*: "The Struggle for Housing," 6, no. 6 (April 1972): 37–38, and "The Party's Role in the Elections," 6, no. 8, (September 1972): 1–5. The first, written by the Party's New York housing commission, lauds coalition among tenant, welfare, and similar groups. The second denounces cooperation with Democratic politicians.

24. McKee, email to author, August 20, 2012; Minutes, November 13, 20, and 27, and December 27, 1972, Box 4, Folder 1, MCH. See especially backdated motion stapled to November 13 minutes.

25. Kate Weigand, *Red Feminism: American Communism and the Making of Women's Liberation* (Baltimore, Md.: Johns Hopkins University Press, 2001),156–57; Jon Wiener, "The Communist Party Today and Yesterday: An Interview with Dorothy Healey," *Radical America* 11, no. 3 (1977): 38.

26. Lawson and Johnson, "Tenant Responses"; New York State Tenants and Neighbors Coalition, *20/20* (New York: Tenants and Neighbors, 1995), booklet in author's possession, 7–8.

27. Lawson and Johnson, "Tenant Responses," 218–19.

28. New York State Tenants and Neighbors Coalition, *20/20*, 9.

29. Ellen Schrecker, *Many Are the Crimes: McCarthyism in America* (Princeton, N.J.: Princeton University Press, 1999), 8.

30. Mansbach, interview.

31. Hyler, interview.

32. Mansbach, Hyler, and Cohen, interviews.

33. Mansbach, interview.

34. Ibid.

35. McKee, interview.

36. Jenny Laurie, conversation with author.

37. DuMond, interview; Tito Delgado, interview with author, April 16, 2004.

38. Cohen, interview.

39. Ibid.

40. Delgado, interview.

41. Cohen, interview.

42. "Governor Approves," *NYT*, July 20, 1965.

43. Thomas Angotti, *New York for Sale: Community Planning Confronts Global Real Estate* (Cambridge, Mass.: MIT Press, 2008), 97.

44. Lawson and Johnson, "Tenant Responses," 228.

45. Ibid., 221.

46. "Mayor Proposes," *NYT*, May 13, 1970.

47. "Officials Are Cautious," *NYT*, March 21, 1971.

48. "Tenants Buy," *NYT*, June 1, 1972; Yolanda Sánchez, interview with author, February 6, 2012.

49. "Officials Are Cautious," *NYT*, March 21, 1971.

50. "Tenants Buy," *NYT*, June 1, 1972.

51. "Tenants Look," *NYT*, September 17, 1972.

52. Lawson and Johnson, "Tenant Responses," 221–23; Jacqueline Leavitt and Susan Saegert, *From Abandonment to Hope: Community-Households in Harlem* (New York: Columbia University Press, 1990), 42, 46.

53. David Goldberg, "From Landless to Landlords: Black Power, Black Capitalism, and the Co-optation of Detroit's Tenants' Rights Movement, 1964–69," in Laura Warren Hill and Julia Rabig, eds., *The Business of Black Power: Community Development, Capitalism, and Corporate Responsibility in Postwar America* (Rochester, N.Y.: University of Rochester Press, 2012), 159–60.

54. Leavitt and Saegert, *From Abandonment to Hope*, 37, 43, 50–54.

55. Lawson and Johnson, "Tenant Responses," 267.

56. Leavitt and Saegert, *From Abandonment to Hope*, 130.

57. Ibid., 109, 115–18. A later overview confirmed the importance of technical assistance. Rachel G. Bratt, "Community-Based Housing Programs: Overview, Assessment and Agenda for the Future," *Journal of Planning, Education and Research* 5, no. 3 (1986): 171.

58. Sánchez, interview.

59. Bratt, "Community-Based Housing Programs," 167.

60. Miranda J. Martinez, *Power at the Roots: Gentrification, Community Gardens, and the Puerto Ricans of the Lower East Side* (Lanham, Md.: Lexington Books, 2010) 16–17; "Good Fences," *Rat*, June 26–July 10, 1970.

61. Angotti, *New York for Sale*, 21.

Afterword

1. "Tenant Rebel," *NYT*, December 6, 2002.

2. Craig Gurian, "Let Them Rent Cake: George Pataki, Market Ideology and the Attempt to Dismantle Rent Regulation in New York," *Fordham Urban Law Journal* 31 (2004).

3. Sharon Zukin, *Naked City: The Death and Life of Authentic Urban Places* (New York: Oxford University Press, 2011).

4. City of New York Office of the Comptroller, *Affordable No More: New York City's Looming Crisis in Mitchell-Lama and Limited Dividend Housing* (New York: Office of the Comptroller, 2004), 3.

5. Ira Katznelson, *City Trenches: Urban Politics and the Patterning of Class in the United States* (New York: Pantheon Books, 1981), 135–43.

6. Brian Sahd, "Community Development Corporations and Social Capital: Lessons

from the South Bronx," in Robert Mark Silverman, ed., *Community-Based Organizations: The Intersection of Social Capital and Local Context* (Detroit, Mich.: Wayne State University Press, 2004); Thomas Angotti, *New York for Sale: Community Planning Confronts Global Real Estate* (Cambridge, Mass.: MIT Press, 2008), 103.

7. Nicholas Dagen Bloom, "Learning from New York," *Journal of the American Planning Association* 78, no. 4 (2012): 429.

8. "What Is Rent Wars?" http://www.rentwars.com/about.htm (accessed January 2, 2012).

9. Susan Cohen, interview with author, June 14, 2004.

10. "68.7 Million Settlement," *NYT*, November 29, 2012.

11. Bernice Siegal and Ruth Messinger, Jane Benedict memorial service, October 22, 2005.

12. Angotti, *New York for Sale*, 122–27.

13. Frances Goldin, interview with author, February 11, 2001.

Index

ROBERTA S. GOLD teaches history and American studies at Fordham University. She has been an active member of her tenants' association in Harlem for twenty years.